OFFICIAL
Netscape JavaScript 1.2

Programmer's Reference

Windows, Macintosh & UNIX

OFFICIAL

Netscape JavaScript 1.2

PROGRAMMER'S REFERENCE

WINDOWS, MACINTOSH & UNIX

NETSCAPE PRESS

An Imprint of
Ventana Communications Group

PETER KENT
KENT MULTER

VENTANA

Official Netscape JavaScript 1.2 Programmer's Reference
Copyright © 1997 by Peter Kent & Kent Multer

All rights reserved. This book may not be duplicated in any way without the expressed written consent of the publisher, except in the form of brief excerpts or quotations for the purposes of review. The information contained herein is for the personal use of the reader and may not be incorporated in any commercial programs, other books, databases, or any kind of software without written consent of the publisher or author. Making copies of this book or any portion for any purpose other than your own is a violation of United States copyright laws.

Library of Congress Catalog Card Number: 97-61616

First Edition 9 8 7 6 5 4 3 2 1

Printed in the United States of America
Published and distributed to the trade by Ventana Communications Group
P.O. Box 13964, Research Triangle Park, NC 27709-3964
919.544.9404
FAX 919.544.9472
http://www.vmedia.com

Ventana Communications Group is a division of International Thomson Publishing.

Netscape Publishing Relations
Suzanne C. Anthony
Netscape Communications Corporation
501 E. Middlefield Rd.
Mountain View, CA 94043
http://home.netscape.com

Limits of Liability & Disclaimer of Warranty
The authors and publisher of this book have used their best efforts in preparing the book and the programs contained in it. These efforts include the development, research, and testing of the theories and programs to determine their effectiveness. The authors and publisher make no warranty of any kind, expressed or implied, with regard to these programs or the documentation contained in this book.
   The authors and publisher shall not be liable in the event of incidental or consequential damages in connection with, or arising out of, the furnishing, performance or use of the programs, associated instructions and/or claims of productivity gains.

Trademarks
Trademarked names appear throughout this book and on the accompanying compact disk, if applicable. Rather than list the names and entities that own the trademarks or insert a trademark symbol with each mention of the trademarked name, the publisher states that it is using the names only for editorial purposes and to the benefit of the trademark owner with no intention of infringing upon that trademark.
   Netscape and Netscape Navigator are registered trademarks of Netscape Communications Corporation in the United States and other countries. Netscape's logos and Netscape product and service names are also trademarks of Netscape Communications Corporation, which may be registered in other countries.

President
Michael E. Moran

Associate Publisher
Robert Kern

Editorial Operations Manager
Kerry L. B. Foster

Production Manager
Jaimie Livingston

Brand Manager
Jamie Jaeger Fiocco

Art Director
Marcia Webb

Creative Services Manager
Diane Lennox

Project Editors
Amy E. Moyers
Julia Higdon

Development Editor
Michelle Corbin Nichols

Copy Editor
Ellen Strader

CD-ROM Specialist
Shadrack Frazier

Technical Reviewer
Richard F. Jessup

Desktop Publisher
Scott Hosa

Proofreader
Beth Snowberger

Indexer
Rachel Rice

Interior Designer
Patrick Berry

Cover Illustrator
Lisa Gill

About the Authors

Peter Kent has 16 years of experience in technical writing and software-interface design. Among the 33 titles he's written are the *Official Netscape JavaScript Book, PGP Companion for Windows* (both from Ventana), and *The Complete Idiot's Guide to the Internet*. His articles have appeared in *Internet World*, *Dr. Dobb's Journal*, and many others.

Kent Multer of Carrollton, Texas is a freelance writer, programmer, artist, and musician—not necessarily in that order. His previously published works range from *Zen and the Art of Documentation* to the short science fiction story *Wind Warrior 2000*. He can be reached at Magic Metal Productions, P.O. Box 701895, Dallas, TX 75370; by e-mail to **kent@dallas.net**; or on the World Wide Web at **http://www.dallas.net/~kent**.

Acknowledgments

The authors wish to thank the JavaScript gurus at Netscape, especially Brendan Eich and Matthew Fisher, who weathered a storm of e-mail and provided us with lots of invaluable information.

Contents

Jump Table xv

Introduction xxxi

Part I: JavaScript Concepts

Chapter 1 Basic Structure 1
JavaScript vs. Java 2
JavaScript & HTML 2
Anatomy of a Script 4
Supporting Browsers Without JavaScript 6
JavaScript Versions 6

Chapter 2 Data Types & Declarations 9
Numbers 9
Strings 11
Boolean Values 12
null 12

Undefined Values 12
Primitive Values 12
Regular Expression Patterns 13
Variables 13
Arrays 14

Chapter 3 Operators & Expressions 17

Arithmetic 18
Assignment 19
Bitwise 20
Boolean 21
Comparison 21
Conditional 22
String 22
Special Operators 23
Operator Precedence 24
Type Conversion 25
Regular Expressions 25

Chapter 4 Statements & Functions 31

Conditionals 32
Multi-way Branch 32
Loops 34
Functions 37
Special-purpose Statements 40

Chapter 5 Objects, Properties & Methods 43

Objects & Properties 43
Methods 48

| Chapter 6 | **Windows, Documents & Graphics** | 51 |

Windows 51
Documents 52
Frames 53
Layers 54
Style Sheets 54
Graphics 59

| Chapter 7 | **Input / Output** | 61 |

Dialogs 61
Forms 63
Event Handling 67
Cookies 73

| Chapter 8 | **The Navigator Environment** | 75 |

Navigator Objects 75
LiveConnect 76
Security 78
Plug-ins & MIME Types 83

PART II: JavaScript Reference

A	89	N	269
B	108	O	276
C	126	P	315
D	147	R	346
E	158	S	364
F	171	T	407
G	189	U	430
H	196	V	434
I	210	W	440
J	221	X	451
K	223	Y	452
L	225	Z	453
M	249		

PART III: Appendices

Appendix A Reserved Words — 457

Appendix B Symbols — 459

Appendix C Color Codes — 463

Appendix D The ISO ISO 8859-1 Latin 1 Character Set — 469

Appendix E Finding More JavaScript Information — 477

Appendix F About the Companion CD-ROM — 485

Index — 487

Jump Tables

Function A	Category	Flags	Page
$' $& $* $_ $' $+		Version 1.2	89
$1, $2, ... $9		Version 1.2 Read-only	89
ABORT		Version 1.2 Read-only	90
above		Version 1.2 Read-only	90
abs( )		Version 1.0	91
acos( )		Version 1.0	92
action		Version 1.0 External Tainted	92
alert( )		Version 1.0	93
align		Version 1.2	93
alinkColor		Version 1.0	94
ALT_MASK		Version 1.0 Read-only	95
anchor( )		Version 1.0	95
Anchor		Version 1.0 Read-only External	96
anchors		Version 1.0 Read-only External	97
appCodeName		Version 1.0 Read-only	98
Applet		Version 1.0 Read-only External	98
applets		Version 1.0 Read-only	99
appName		Version 1.0 Read-only	100
appVersion		Version 1.0 Read-only	100
Area		Version 1.1 External	101

Function A	Category	Flags	Page
arguments		Version 1.0 Special scope	102
arity		Version 1.2	103
Array		Version 1.1	104
asin( )		Version 1.0	105
atan( )		Version 1.0	105
atan2( )		Version 1.0	106
availHeight		Version 1.2 Read-only	107
availWidth		Version 1.2 Read-only	107
back()		Version 1.0	108
background		Version 1.2	108
backgroundColor		Version 1.2	109
backgroundImage		Version 1.2	109
below		Version 1.2 Read-only	110
bgColor		Version 1.0	111
big()		Version 1.0	112
blink()		Version 1.0	112
blur()		Version 1.0	113
BLUR		Version 1.2 Read-only	114
bold()		Version 1.0	114
Boolean		Version 1.1	115
border		Version 1.1 Read-only	116
borderBottomWidth		Version 1.2	116
borderColor		Version 1.2	117
borderLeftWidth		Version 1.2	118
borderRightWidth		Version 1.2	119
borderStyle		Version 1.2	120
borderTopWidth		Version 1.2	121
borderWidths()		Version 1.2	122
bottom		Version 1.2	123
break		Version 1.0	123
Button		Version 1.0 External	124
caller		Version 1.0 Read-only Special scope	126
captureEvents( )		Version 1.2	126
case		Version 1.2	127
ceil( )		Version 1.0	127
CHANGE		Version 1.2 Read-only	128

Jump Tables

Function A	Category	Flags	Page
charAt( )		Version 1.0	128
charCodeAt( )		Version 1.2	129
Checkbox		Version 1.0 External	129
checked		Version 1.0 External Tainted	131
classes		Version 1.2	131
clear		Version 1.2	134
clearInterval( )		Version 1.2	134
clearTimeout( )		Version 1.1	135
click( )		Version 1.0 External	135
CLICK		Version 1.2 Read-only	136
clip		Version 1.2	136
close( )	DOCUMENT	Version 1.0	137
close( )	WINDOW	Version 1.0	138
closed		Version 1.1 Read-only	138
color		Version 1.2	139
colorDepth		Version 1.2 Read-only	140
compile( )		Version 1.2	140
complete		Version 1.1 Read-only	141
concat( )	ARRAY	Version 1.2	141
concat( )	STRING	Version 1.2	142
confirm( )		Version 1.0	143
constructor		Version 1.1 Read-only	143
continue		Version 1.0	144
CONTROL_MASK		Version 1.0 Read-only	144
cookie		Version 1.0 Tainted	145
cos( )		Version 1.0	145
current		Version 1.1 Read-only Tainted	146
data		Version 1.2 Special scope Signed scripts	147
Date		Version 1.0	148
DBLCLICK		Version 1.2 Read-only	149
defaultChecked		Version 1.0 External Tainted	150
defaultSelected		Version 1.0 External Tainted	150
defaultStatus		Version 1.0 External Tainted	151
defaultValue		Version 1.0 External Tainted	152
delete		Version 1.2	152
description		Version 1.1 Read-only External	153

Function A	Category	Flags	Page
disableExternalCapture()		Version 1.2 Signed scripts	153
display		Version 1.2	154
do		Version 1.2	155
document		Version 1.0 Read-only External	155
domain		Version 1.1 External Tainted	156
DRAGDROP		Version 1.2 Read-only	157
E		Version 1.0 Read-only	158
elements		Version 1.0 Read-only External	158
else		Version 1.0	159
Embed		Version 1.0 External	159
embeds		Version 1.0 Read-only External	160
enabledPlugin		Version 1.1 Read-only External	161
enableExternalCapture()		Version 1.2 Signed scripts	161
encoding		Version 1.0 External	162
ERROR		Version 1.2 Read-only	162
escape()		Version 1.0	163
eval()		Version 1.0	164
event		Version 1.2 Special scope Signed scripts	165
Event		Version 1.2 Read-only	166
exec()		Version 1.2	168
exp()		Version 1.0	170
export		Version 1.2	170
fgColor		Version 1.0 External	171
filename		Version 1.1 Read-only External	171
FileUpload		Version 1.1 Read-only External Signed scripts	172
find()		Version 1.2 External	173
fixed()		Version 1.0	174
floor()		Version 1.0	175
focus()		Version 1.0	175
FOCUS		Version 1.2 Read-only	176
fontcolor()		Version 1.0	176
fontFamily		Version 1.2	177
fontsize()		Version 1.0 Unusual spelling or capitalization	178
fontSize		Version 1.2	179
fontStyle		Version 1.2	180
fontWeight		Version 1.2	181

Jump Tables xix

Function A	Category	Flags	Page
for		Version 1.0	181
Form		Version 1.0 External	182
form		Version 1.0 Read-only External	183
forms		Version 1.0 Read-only External Tainted	184
forward()		Version 1.0	184
Frame		Version 1.0 Read-only External	185
frames		Version 1.0 Read-only External	186
fromCharCode()		Version 1.2	187
function		Version 1.0	187
Function		Version 1.1	188
getDate()		Version 1.0	189
getDay()		Version 1.0	189
getHours()		Version 1.0	190
getMinutes()		Version 1.0	190
getMonth()		Version 1.0	191
getSeconds()		Version 1.0	191
getSelection()		Version 1.2	192
getTime()		Version 1.0	192
getTimezoneOffset()		Version 1.0 Unusual spelling or capitalization	193
getYear()		Version 1.0	193
global		Version 1.2 Read-only	194
go()		Version 1.0	195
handleEvent( )		Version 1.2	196
hash	AREA, LINK	Version 1.0 External Tainted	196
hash	WINDOW	Version 1.0 Tainted	197
height	CLIP	Version 1.2 External	198
height	EVENT	Version 1.2 Read-only	199
height	IMAGE	Version 1.1 Read-only	199
height	SCREEN	Version 1.2 Read-only	200
height	STYLE SHEET OBJECTS	Version 1.2	200
Hidden		Version 1.0 External	201
history		Version 1.0 Signed scripts	202
home( )		Version 1.2	204
host	AREA, LINK	Version 1.0 External Tainted	204
host	WINDOW	Version 1.0 Tainted	205
hostname	AREA, LINK	Version 1.0 External Tainted	206

Function A	Category	Flags	Page
hostname	WINDOW	Version 1.0 Tainted	207
href	AREA, LINK	Version 1.0 External Tainted	208
href	WINDOW	Version 1.0 Tainted	208
hspace		Version 1.1 Read-only	209
ids		Version 1.2 External	210
if		Version 1.0	212
ignoreCase		Version 1.2 Read-only	212
Image		Version 1.1	213
images		Version 1.1 External	214
import		Version 1.2	215
in		Version 1.0	215
index		Version 1.0 Read-only External	215
indexOf( )		Version 1.0	216
innerHeight		Version 1.2 Signed scripts	217
innerWidth		Version 1.2 Signed scripts	218
input, $_		Version 1.2 Read-only	218
isNan( )		Version 1.0	219
italics( )		Version 1.0	220
java		Version 1.0	221
javaEnabled( )		Version 1.1	221
join( )		Version 1.1	222
KEYDOWN		Version 1.2 Read-only	223
KEYPRESS		Version 1.2 Read-only	223
KEYUP		Version 1.2 Read-only	224
language		Version 1.2 Read-only	225
lastIndex		Version 1.2 Read-only	225
lastIndexOf( )		Version 1.0	226
lastMatch, $&		Version 1.2 Read-only	227
lastModified		Version 1.0 Read-only Tainted	228
lastParen, $+		Version 1.2 Read-only	228
Layer		Version 1.2	229
layers		Version 1.2 External	232
layerX		Version 1.2 Special scope	232
layerY		Version 1.2 Special scope	233
left	CLIP	Version 1.2 External	234
left	LAYER		234

Jump Tables

Function A	Category	Flags	Page
leftContext, $'		Version 1.2 Read-only	235
length		Version 1.0 Read-only	236
lineHeight		Version 1.2	237
link( )		Version 1.0	238
Link		Version 1.0 External	238
linkColor		Version 1.0	240
links		Version 1.0 Read-only External Tainted	240
listStyleType		Version 1.2	241
LN10		Version 1.0 Read-only	242
LN2		Version 1.0 Read-only	242
load( )		Version 1.2	243
LOAD		Version 1.2 Read-only	243
location	DOCUMENT	Read-only	244
location	WINDOW	Version 1.0	244
locationbar		Version 1.2 Signed scripts	246
log( )			246
LOG10E		Version 1.0 Read-only	247
LOG2E		Version 1.0 Read-only	247
lowsrc		Version 1.1	248
marginBottom		Version 1.2	249
marginLeft		Version 1.2	249
marginRight		Version 1.2	250
margins( )		Version 1.2	251
marginTop		Version 1.2	251
match( )		Version 1.2	252
Math		Version 1.0	254
max( )		Version 1.0	255
MAX_VALUE		Version 1.1 Read-only	255
menubar		Version 1.2 Signed scripts	256
META_MASK		Version 1.2 Read-only	256
method		Version 1.0 External	257
MimeType		Version 1.1 Read-only External	257
mimeTypes		Version 1.1 Read-only	258
min( )		Version 1.0	259
MIN_VALUE		Version 1.1 Read-only	259
modifiers		Version 1.2 Special scope	260

Function A	Category	Flags	Page
MOUSEDOWN		Version 1.2 Read-only	261
MOUSEMOVE		Version 1.2 Read-only	262
MOUSEOUT		Version 1.2 Read-only	262
MOUSEOVER		Version 1.2 Read-only	263
MOUSEUP		Version 1.2 Read-only	263
MOVE		Version 1.2 Read-only	264
moveAbove( )		Version 1.2	264
moveBelow( )		Version 1.2	265
moveBy( )		Version 1.2 Signed scripts	266
moveTo( )		Version 1.2 Signed scripts	266
moveToAbsolute( )		Version 1.2	267
multiline, $*		Version 1.2	268
name		Version 1.0 Read-only External	269
NaN		Version 1.1 Read-only	270
navigator		Version 1.0 Read-only	271
NEGATIVE_INFINITY		Version 1.1 Read-only	272
netscape		Version 1.0	272
new		Version 1.0	273
next		Version 1.1 Read-only Tainted Signed scripts	273
Number		Version 1.1	274
onabort		Version 1.1	276
onblur		Version 1.0	277
onchange		Version 1.0	278
onclick		Version 1.0	279
ondblclick		Version 1.2	281
ondragdrop		Version 1.2 Signed scripts	282
onerror		Version 1.1	283
onfocus		Version 1.0	285
onkeydown		Version 1.2	286
onkeypress		Version 1.2	288
onkeyup		Version 1.2	289
onload		Version 1.0	291
onmousedown		Version 1.2	292
onmousemove		Version 1.2	294
onmouseout		Version 1.1	295
onmouseover		Version 1.0	296
onmouseup		Version 1.2	298

Jump Tables

Function A	Category	Flags	Page
onmove		Version 1.2	300
onreset		Version 1.1	301
onresize		Version 1.2	302
onselect		Version 1.0	303
onsubmit		Version 1.1	303
onunload		Version 1.0	304
open( )	DOCUMENT	Version 1.0 Version 1.1	305
open( )	WINDOW	Version 1.0 Signed scripts	307
opener		Version 1.1	310
Option		Version 1.1	311
options		Version 1.0 Read-only External	312
outerHeight		Version 1.2 Signed scripts	313
outerWidth		Version 1.2 Signed scripts	314
Packages		Version 1.1 Read-only	315
paddingBottom		Version 1.2	315
paddingLeft		Version 1.2	316
paddingRight		Version 1.2	317
paddings()		Version 1.2	318
paddingTop		Version 1.2	320
pageX	EVENT	Version 1.2 Special scope	321
pageX	LAYER	Version 1.2	322
pageXOffset		Version 1.2 Read-only	323
pageY	EVENT	Version 1.2 Special scope	323
pageY	LAYER	Version 1.2	324
pageYOffset		Version 1.2 Read-only	325
parent		Version 1.0 Read-Only	325
parentLayer		Version 1.2 Read-only	326
parse()		Version 1.0	327
parseFloat()		Version 1.0	328
parseInt()		Version 1.0	329
Password		Version 1.0 External	330
pathname	AREA, LINK	Version 1.0 Read-only External	331
pathname	LOCATION	Version 1.0 Tainted	332
personalbar		Version 1.2 Signed scripts	333
PI		Version 1.0 Read-only	334
pixelDepth		Version 1.2 Read-only	334
platform		Version 1.2 Read-only	335

Function A	Category	Flags	Page
Plugin		Version 1.1 External	335
plugins		Version 1.1 Read-only	336
port	AREA, LINK	Version 1.0 External	337
port	LOCATION	Version 1.0 Tainted	338
POSITIVE_INFINITY		Version 1.1 Read-only	339
pow()		Version 1.0	339
preference()		Version 1.2 Signed scripts	340
previous		Version 1.1 Read-Only Tainted	341
print()		Version 1.2	342
prompt()		Version 1.0	342
protocol	AREA, LINK	Version 1.0 Read-only External	343
protocol	LOCATION	Version 1.0 Tainted	344
prototype		Version 1.1	345
Radio		Version 1.0 External	346
random()		Version 1.0	347
referrer		Version 1.0 Read-only Tainted	348
refresh()		Version 1.1	348
RegExp		Version 1.2	349
releaseEvents()		Version 1.2	352
reload()		Version 1.1	353
replace()	LOCATION	Version 1.1	354
replace()	STRING	Version 1.2	355
reset()		Version 1.1 External	356
Reset		Version 1.0 Read-only External	356
RESET		Version 1.2 Read-only	357
RESIZE		Version 1.2 Read-only	358
resizeBy()		Version 1.2 Signed scripts	358
resizeTo()		Version 1.2 Signed scripts	359
return		Version 1.0	360
reverse()		Version 1.1	360
right		Version 1.2	360
rightContext, $'		Version 1.2 Read-only	361
round()		Version 1.0	362
routeEvent()		Version 1.2 Special scope	363
screen		Version 1.2 Read-only	364
screenX		Version 1.2 Special scope	364
screenY		Version 1.2 Special scope	365

Function A	Category	Flags	Page
scroll( )		Version 1.1	366
scrollbars		Version 1.2 Signed scripts	367
scrollBy( )		Version 1.2	368
scrollTo( )		Version 1.2	368
search	AREA, LINK	Version 1.0 Read-only External	369
search	LOCATION	Version 1.0 Tainted	370
search( )		Version 1.2	371
Select		Version 1.0 External	372
select( )		Version 1.0	373
SELECT		Version 1.2 Read-only	374
selected		Version 1.0 Tainted	374
selectedIndex		Version 1.0 Tainted	375
self		Version 1.0 Read-only	376
setDate( )		Version 1.0	377
setHours( )		Version 1.0	377
setInterval( )		Version 1.2	378
setMinutes( )		Version 1.0	378
setMonth( )		Version 1.0	379
setSeconds( )		Version 1.0	379
setTime( )		Version 1.0	380
setTimeout( )		Version 1.2	380
setYear( )		Version 1.0	381
SHIFT-MASK		Version 1.2 Read-Only	382
siblingAbove		Version 1.2 Read-only	382
siblingBelow		Version 1.2 Read-only	383
sin( )		Version 1.0	384
slice( )	ARRAY	Version 1.2	384
slice( )	STRING	Version 1.2	386
small( )		Version 1.0	387
sort( )		Version 1.1	387
source		Version 1.2	389
split( )		Version 1.1	390
sqrt( )		Version 1.0	391
SQRT1_2		Version 1.0 Read-only	391
SQRT2		Version 1.0 Read-only	392
src	IMAGE	Version 1.1	392
src	LAYER	Version 1.2	393

Function A	Category	Flags	Page
status		Version 1.0 Tainted	394
statusbar		Version 1.2 signed scripts	395
stop( )		Version 1.2	396
strike( )		Version 1.0	396
String		Version 1.0	397
sub( )		Version 1.0	400
submit( )		Version 1.0	400
Submit		Version 1.0 External	401
SUBMIT		Version 1.2 Read-only	402
substr( )		Version 1.2	403
substring( )		Version 1.0 Version 1.2	403
suffixes		Version 1.1 Read-only	404
sun		Version 1.0	405
sup( )		Version 1.0	405
switch		Version 1.2	406
tags		Version 1.2 External	407
taint( )		Version 1.1	409
taintEnabled( )		Version 1.1	410
tan( )			410
target	AREA, LINK	Version 1.0 External	411
target	EVENT	Version 1.2 Special scope	411
target	FORM	Version 1.0 External	412
test( )		Version 1.2	413
Text		Version 1.0 External	414
text		Version 1.0 Tainted	415
textAlign		Version 1.2	416
Textarea		Version 1.0 External	416
textDecoration		Version 1.2 External	418
textTransform		Version 1.2 External	418
this		Version 1.0 Read-only Special scope	419
title		Version 1.0 Read-only Tainted	420
toGMTString( )		Version 1.0	421
toLocaleString( )		Version 1.0	421
toLowerCase( )		Version 1.0	422
toolbar		Version 1.2 Signed scripts	422
top	CLIP	Version 1.2 External	423
top	LAYER	Version 1.2 External	424
top	WINDOW	Version 1.0 External	424

Function A	Category	Flags	Page
toString( )		Version 1.0	425
toUpperCase( )		Version 1.0	426
type	EVENT	Version 1.2 Read-only Special scope	426
type	FORM ELEMENTS	Version 1.1 Read-only External	427
type	MIMETYPE	Version 1.2 Read-only Special scope	429
typeof	Operator		429
unescape( )		Version 1.0	430
UNLOAD		Version 1.2 Read-only	430
untaint( )		Version 1.1	431
URL		Version 1.0 Read-only Tainted	432
userAgent		Version 1.0 Read-only	432
UTC( )		Version 1.0	433
value		Version 1.0 External Tainted	434
valueOf( )		Version 1.1	435
var			435
verticalAlign		Version 1.2 External	436
visible		Version 1.2 Signed scripts	437
visibility		Version 1.2 External	437
vlinkColor		Version 1.0	438
void			439
vspace		Version 1.1 Read-only	439
which		Version 1.2 Read-only	440
while			440
whiteSpace		Version 1.2 External	441
width	CLIP	Version 1.2 External	442
width	EVENT	Version 1.2 Read-only	442
width	IMAGE	Version 1.1 Read-only	443
width	SCREEN	Version 1.2 Read-only	444
width	STYLE SHEET OBJECTS	Version 1.2	444
window		Version 1.0	445
with			449
write( )		Version 1.0	449
writeln( )		Version 1.0	450
x	ANCHOR	Version 1.0 Read-only External	451
x	EVENT	Version 1.2 Read-only	451
y	ANCHOR	Version 1.0 Read-only External	452
y	EVENT	Version 1.2 Read-only	452
zIndex		Version 1.2	453

Category	Function A	Flags	Page
ANCHOR	x	Version 1.0 Read-only External	451
ANCHOR	y	Version 1.0 Read-only External	452
LINK	hash	Version 1.0 External Tainted	196
LINK	host	Version 1.0 External Tainted	204
LINK	hostname	Version 1.0 External Tainted	206
LINK	href	Version 1.0 External Tainted	208
LINK	protocol	Version 1.0 Read-only External	343
LINK	search	Version 1.0 Read-only External	369
LINK	hash	Version 1.0 External Tainted	196
AREA	host	Version 1.0 External Tainted	204
AREA	hostname	Version 1.0 External Tainted	206
AREA	href	Version 1.0 External Tainted	208
AREA	protocol	Version 1.0 Read-only External	343
AREA	search	Version 1.0 Read-only External	369
ARRAY	concat( )	Version 1.2	141
ARRAY	slice( )	Version 1.2	384
CLIP	height	Version 1.2 External	198
CLIP	left	Version 1.2 External	234
CLIP	top	Version 1.2 External	423
DOCUMENT	close( )	Version 1.0	137
DOCUMENT	location	Read-only	244
EVENT	height	Version 1.2 Read-only	199
EVENT	pageX	Version 1.2 Special scope	321
EVENT	target	Version 1.2 Special scope	411
EVENT	type	Version 1.2 Read-only Special scope	426
EVENT	x	Version 1.2 Read-only	451
EVENT	y	Version 1.2 Read-only	452
FORM	target	Version 1.0 External	412
FORM ELEMENTS	type	Version 1.1 Read-only External	427
IMAGE	height	Version 1.1 Read-only	199
IMAGE	src	Version 1.1	392

Category	Function A	Flags	Page
LAYER	left		234
LAYER	pageY	Version 1.2	324
LAYER	src	Version 1.2	393
LAYER	top	Version 1.2 External	424
LOCATION	pathname	Version 1.0 Tainted	332
LOCATION	port	Version 1.0 Tainted	338
LOCATION	replace( )	Version 1.1	354
LOCATION	search	Version 1.0 Tainted	370
MIMETYPE	type	Version 1.2 Read-only Special scope	429
SCREEN	height	Version 1.2 Read-only	200
SCREEN	width	Version 1.2 Read-only	444
STRING	concat( )	Version 1.2	142
STRING	replace( )	Version 1.2	355
STRING	slice( )	Version 1.2	386
STYLE SHEET OBJECTS	height	Version 1.2	200
STYLE SHEET OBJECTS	width	Version 1.2	444
WINDOW	close( )	Version 1.0	138
WINDOW	hash	Version 1.0 Tainted	197
WINDOW	host	Version 1.0 Tainted	205
WINDOW	hostname	Version 1.0 Tainted	207
WINDOW	href	Version 1.0 Tainted	208
WINDOW	location	Version 1.0	244

Introduction

JavaScript is a programming language that is used in conjunction with HTML for access on the World Wide Web, and on private intranets using the same protocols. An interpreter for JavaScript has been built into Netscape Navigator since version 2, and is also found in most other web browsers. It is useful to enhance web pages with interactive features, and to perform computing tasks that would otherwise require a remote server.

This book is a reference manual for the JavaScript language version 1.2, as implemented in Netscape Navigator version 4.0. If you are using a different browser, you should check its documentation for any compatibility issues. Being based on Navigator, this book documents only "client-side" JavaScript. For information on additional features available with servers, see Appendix E.

Part I of this book gives an overview of the language's features, with chapters for the following topics:

- *Basic Structure* describes how scripts are written, and how they are integrated with HTML.
- *Data Types & Declarations* describes the formats of numeric, string, and other data, and the structure of variables and arrays.
- *Operators & Expressions* describes operators that manipulate data, and how they are combined into expressions.
- *Statements & Functions* describes the statement forms and keywords that define program structure and execution.
- *Objects, Properties & Methods* describes JavaScript's object-oriented features.

- *Windows, Documents & Graphics* describes display features such as frames, layers, style sheets, and graphic functions.
- *Input/Output* describes dialogs, forms, event handling, and the use of cookies.
- *The Navigator Environment* describes plug-ins, security, and other aspects of JavaScript's relationship with the browser and web pages.

Part II of this book is a detailed reference on every object, property, and method, listed in alphabetical order for quick lookup.

Part III contains Appendices with specifications and other useful information, as well as information about how to use the CD-ROM that comes with this book.

Who Can Use This Book

JavaScript is a programming language, and this book is intended for programmers. If you are familiar with Java, or with at least one structured programming language such as C or Pascal, this book will provide everything you need to start writing scripts. To insert your scripts into web pages, you should have some familiarity with HTML coding. If you've only created web pages with a high-level editor like Navigator Gold, you will need to learn some HTML in order to use JavaScript.

"Your Mileage May Vary . . ."

Both Navigator and JavaScript are evolving so rapidly that providing accurate documentation is a challenge. The situation is complicated by the fact that, as a web site creator, you need to be aware that people with older versions of many different browsers will try to read your pages.

This manual is based on the latest possible information from Netscape developers as it applies to JavaScript version 1.2. Features that were added after version 1.0 are identified as such. Some of the features described in this manual are not documented in Netscape's published documentation.

Because Navigator is used on many different platforms, and many beta versions are also in circulation, there may be some users who are unable to properly run your scripts. Chapter 1 gives some advice on handling these issues.

JavaScript Concepts

I

Basic Structure 1

JavaScript is an interpreted, object-oriented programming language that is integrated into Netscape Navigator and most other web browsers. It is intended mainly to add power and interactivity to web pages in order to provide better interaction with the user and cut down on network and server traffic. Actually, it has most of the features of a modern general-purpose programming language, and scripts can be quite sophisticated.

JavaScript is in many ways a simple language to use. Features such as the lack of fixed variable types make it easy to write code that gets things done, without a lot of planning and formal declarations. The only tools you need to develop and run scripts are your browser and a text editor, or an HTML editor that can work with scripts.

JavaScript vs. Java

There are some important differences between JavaScript and Java, as summarized in the following table:

JavaScript	Java
Interpreted.	Compiled.
Simple language, intended for web pages.	Complex, general-purpose language.
All you need to develop scripts is a Netscape Navigator and a text editor.	To create software, you need compilers, class libraries, and other development tools.
Source code is embedded directly in web pages, or placed in separate text files.	Source code is compiled into applets, which are referenced by web pages. May also be general-purpose programs not associated with web pages.
Some object-oriented features: properties and methods, but no classes or inheritance.	Fully object-oriented.
"Casual" programming style: no strong typing, variables need not be declared.	"Strict" programming style appropriate to large projects.

JavaScript & HTML

Here's a simple example of a script. This can be inserted into the HTML text of any web page:

```
<SCRIPT language="javascript">
   document.write("This document was last modified on ")
   document.write(document.lastModified)
</SCRIPT>
```

This script will cause the text "This document was last modified on" and the appropriate date to appear at that point on the web page. This example illustrates a few key points:

- JavaScript source code can be placed inline with HTML code, contained within the <SCRIPT> and </SCRIPT> tags.
- JavaScript uses the dot (.) character for object structures.
- An object may have properties (document.lastModified) and methods (document.write).
- JavaScript has many built-in variables and functions for interacting with web page content.

You can place pieces of JavaScript code, enclosed by the <SCRIPT> and </SCRIPT> tags anywhere in an HTML file. When a browser loads the file, it scans it from front to back, invoking the JavaScript interpreter each time it encounters a script. Therefore, functions must be declared before they are used. However, the declaration and the uses do not need to be in the same script (inside the same <SCRIPT> ... </SCRIPT> pair). JavaScript code can be spread around the source file in many small scripts. Variables do not need to be explicitly declared, except some local variables of functions (see Chapter 4), however it is good programming practice to do so.

Besides scripts, JavaScript code can be placed in HTML tags to define *event handlers*. For example:

```
<FORM>
<INPUT type="button" value="Push Me" onclick="alert('Thank you very
   much.')">
</FORM>
```

This HTML creates a button in a form. The mouse click event handler for the button is a single JavaScript statement that displays an alert box with a message. The statement could also be a call to a function you wrote to provide a more useful response.

JavaScript URLs

JavaScript code can also be placed in URLs. A JavaScript URL consists of the label `javascript:` followed by a statement. For instance:

```
<A HREF="JavaScript:JumpTo(dest)"> Go now! </A>
```

This HTML creates a link that looks like a normal hyperlink. But clicking it runs a JavaScript function called `JumpTo`, and passes it an argument `dest` which is presumably a variable that was set by a previous button click or other interaction with the user. The `JavaScript:someStatement` notation can be used anywhere a normal URL can go. You can even type something like:

```
JavaScript:alert("This actually works.")
```

right into Navigator's "Location:" or "Go To:" window, and it will be executed when you press Enter.

The `javascript:` header may use any combination of uppercase and lowercase letters. But remember that within the statement, reserved words and identifiers are case-sensitive.

Anatomy of a Script

Let's look at the content of a script in more detail. As we mentioned, it must start with the `<SCRIPT>` tag, and end with `</SCRIPT>`. `<SCRIPT>` can take an optional `language` attribute. By convention, all browsers should check this attribute, and ignore any script that they cannot interpret. All versions of Netscape Navigator recognize `language=javascript`, and each version recognizes some variations (see "JavaScript Versions" below).

The browser scans the text between `<SCRIPT>` and `</SCRIPT>`, just like the text between other HTML containers such as `<A>` and `</A>`. So it is conceivable that some part of the script could cause a browser error. To prevent this, you should further enclose the contained text by the HTML comment tags, `<!--` and `-->`. So the complete script form is:

```
<SCRIPT>         (May have optional language= attribute.)
<!--             HTML comment start marker.
...
...
...              JavaScript statements.
//-->            JavaScript and HTML comment end marker.
</SCRIPT>
```

Scripts in Separate Files

It may be useful to keep a script in a separate source file, rather than inserting it directly into the HTML source. You could do this if the script is large, or if you want to use different editors for JavaScript and HTML. The way to do it is with the SRC attribute on the SCRIPT tag, as in:

```
<SCRIPT SRC="http://mywebsite.com/myfile.js">
   alert("Error loading script file.")
</SCRIPT>
```

Even if you specify a SRC, you still need to write a matching `</SCRIPT>` tag, as in the preceding example. The JavaScript statements between the tags will be executed only if the specified file can not be loaded.

Comments

The `<!--` and `-->` comment delimiters are standard HTML; they are not part of JavaScript. JavaScript provides two ways to put comments in a script:

- A double slash (`//`) marks the beginning of a comment that continues to the end of the line:

   ```
   var x = 0     // initialize x
   ```

- You can enclose longer comments with the /* and */ delimiters that you may recognize from PL/I or C programs:

  ```
  /* Initialize the x and y coordinates. This is necessary for
     the display manager. */
  var x = 0; var y = 0
  ```

Basic Syntax

The body of a script consists of JavaScript statements. Like most modern languages, the format of the statements is quite flexible. You can spread a statement over several lines (although string literals must be contained on a single line; see Chapter 2). You can place several statements on one line if they are separated by semicolons (;). You can use spaces, tabs, blank lines, and comments freely to improve the appearance of a script.

JavaScript is case-sensitive: uppercase and lowercase letters are *not* equivalent. (In HTML, however, they are; beware of confusing the two.)

HTML Reflection

JavaScript has a number of built-in variables that are initialized as the web page is loaded. Many of these variables are copies, or *reflections*, of the attribute values of various HTML tags. For example, the variable document.bgColor is a reflection of the bgcolor attribute of the <BODY> tag.

These built-in variables reflect much of the content of the web page, allowing scripts to read and, in some cases, modify this information. A script can change the web page background color with a statement like:

```
document.bgColor = "red"
```

A more powerful example is:

```
document.tags.H1.color = "blue"
```

This changes the color of all <H1> headings on the web page.

An important use of HTML reflection is to interact with the user through forms. For example, here is some HTML code that creates a simple form:

```
<FORM>
Enter a number:
<INPUT TYPE="text" NAME="num1" > <P>
Enter another number:
<INPUT TYPE="text" NAME="num2" > <P>
<INPUT type="button" value="Add the numbers"
 onclick="addFields(this.form)"> <P>
The sum is:
<INPUT TYPE="text" NAME="result" > <P>
</FORM>
```

The user types numbers into two text fields in the form, and clicks a button. Then the sum of the two inputs is presented in a third text field. The click event handler for the button uses the expression `this.form` to pass the form to the JavaScript function `addFields`, which looks like this:

```
function addFields(form) {
   var sum = eval(form.num1.value) + eval(form.num2.value)
   form.result.value = sum
}
```

This function references the content of each text field with expressions like `form.num1.value`.

Supporting Browsers Without JavaScript

Although most web browsers now include JavaScript interpreters, you may wish to include alternate web page content for any user whose browser does not support JavaScript. You can do this with the <NOSCRIPT> HTML tag, as in:

```
<NOSCRIPT>
<H1> Sorry ... </H1>
   To see this web page, you need a browser that supports JavaScript.
   You can download the latest version of Navigator from <A
   HREF="http://home.netscape.com/"> Netscape</A>.
</NOSCRIPT>
```

The <NOSCRIPT> text will also be displayed by versions of Navigator that have interpreters, if the user has disabled JavaScript in the Preferences dialog.

JavaScript Versions

JavaScript version 1.0 was released in Netscape Navigator version 2.0. JavaScript was upgraded to version 1.1 in Navigator 3.0, and to 1.2 in Navigator 4.0. This book documents JavaScript through version 1.2. Features that were added after version 1.0 are identified as such.

The <SCRIPT> tag's language attribute allows you to specify a version. If you write <SCRIPT language="javascript1.1"> or <SCRIPT language="javascript1.2">, the script will only be loaded by a browser that can support that version. This allows you to write a web page that contains several scripts, and each browser will load the one(s) with which it is compatible.

If your script is structured carefully, you may be able to isolate the version-specific part to a few functions or sections. Another way to handle version dependencies is by writing something like:

```
<SCRIPT language="javascript1.2">
location.replace("ver12page.html")
</SCRIPT>
<SCRIPT language="javascript1.1">
location.replace("ver11page.html")
</SCRIPT>
<SCRIPT language="javascript>
...
...          // version 1.0 scripts
...
</SCRIPT>
```

The `location.replace` method causes the browser to load a new web page, which can contain HTML and scripts that are designed for a specific version of JavaScript.

In practice, you will probably find that it is difficult to maintain web pages that support several versions of JavaScript. The simplest approaches are either to avoid using advanced features that require newer versions, or to provide links to Netscape's web site and encourage your users to obtain the latest version of Navigator.

Moving On

In this chapter, we have shown the basic structure of a script and how it relates to the browser and the web environment. In the next few chapters, we will look at various aspects of the language in more detail.

Data Types & Declarations 2

JavaScript supports the numeric, string, and logical data types common to most programming languages. It also supports several other special-purpose values and local and global variables. Data structuring is provided with array and object variables.

Numbers

JavaScript supports integer and floating-point numeric values. It also provides a number of standard and special-purpose values, such as π, *e*, and even infinity.

Integers

JavaScript supports three types of integers:
- **Decimal integers** use the digits 0 to 9. They must not include any leading zeroes.
- **Octal integers** use the digits 0 to 7, and must start with a leading zero.
- **Hexadecimal integers** use the digits 0 – 9 and A – F or a – f, and must start with a leading zero and the letter X or x.

Negative values are indicated by a leading minus sign.
Examples:

    127   decimal 127
    0127   octal 127 (decimal 87)
    0x127   hexadecimal 127 (decimal 295)

Floating-Point Numbers

Floating-point numbers may contain a leading sign, decimal digits, a decimal point, and an exponent. The exponent consists of the letter E or e, followed by an optional leading plus or minus sign, and a decimal integer value.

Examples:

0.1	one-tenth
1.0E-1	equivalent to the above
3.1416	an approximation of π (see `Math.PI` below)
52e6	fifty-two million

Built-in Values

JavaScript's built-in `Math` object provides convenient access to a number of numeric values:

Expression	Value
`Math.E`	Base of natural logarithms (2.71828...)
`Math.LN2`	Natural log of 2 (0.693...)
`Math.LN10`	Natural log of 10 (2.302...)
`Math.LOG2E`	Base 2 log of e (1.442...)
`Math.LOG10E`	Base 10 log of e (0.434...)
`Math.PI`	Value of π (3.14159...)
`Math.SQRT1_2`	One-half the square root of 2 (0.707...)
`Math.SQRT2`	Square root of 2 (1.414...)

Special Values

The built-in `Number` object provides properties that represent special values for numeric operations:

Expression	Value
`Number.MAX_VALUE`	The largest value that a number can have: approximately 1.79E+308. Any operations that attempt to exceed this value will return one of the "infinite" values described below.
`Number.MIN_VALUE`	The smallest value that a number can have ("smallest" meaning closest to zero, not most negative): approximately 2.22E-308. Any operations that attempt to produce a result lower than this will return zero.
`Number.NEGATIVE_INFINITY`	A special value that acts like negative infinity in numeric operations. Dividing by it always returns 0; adding to it always returns negative infinity; comparing to it always returns "greater," and so forth.

Expression	Value
Number.POSITIVE_INFINITY	A special value that acts like infinity in numeric operations. Dividing by it always returns 0; adding to it always returns infinity; comparing to it always returns "less," and so forth.
Number.NaN	A special value representing a non-numeric result, such as the square root of a negative number. NaN stands for "not a number." Arithmetic operations with this value always return zero. Comparisons to it always return "not equal," so to test for this value, scripts must use the built-in isNaN( ) function.

Strings

A string literal is represented by a series of characters enclosed in single or double quotes. When entering a string, you must not type Newline; that is, the opening and closing quotes must both be on the same line of the script. Some early versions of Navigator have a bug that affects string literals over 255 characters, so this is a good limit to observe.

Some examples of string literals are:

```
"This is a string in double quotes."
'This one uses single quotes.'
"This string has 'nested' quotes."
"This string has \"escaped\" quotes."
```

You can also create an empty string by writing "".

As the fourth example shows, you can insert some special characters into strings by preceding them with a backslash (\), as shown in the following list:

Symbol	Meaning
\"	Double quote
\'	Single quote
\\	Backslash
\b	Backspace
\f	Form feed
\n	Newline
\r	Carriage return
\t	Tab

The String object provides a large number of methods for searching, rearranging, converting, and reformatting strings. For more details, see the listing for String in Part II of this manual.

Boolean Values

JavaScript uses the keywords `true` and `false` for Boolean, or logical, values. These values are used for branching (`if`) and looping (`while`) structures, as well as in Boolean expressions. When converting other types to Boolean, zero, the empty string `""`, `null`, and undefined values become `false`; any other value becomes `true`.

null

`null` is a special value that is used to represent an empty or non-existent condition; for instance, the `above` property of a document layer is `null` for the highest layer in a stack.

In arithmetic and logical operations, `null` is equivalent to zero. In string operations, `null` is equivalent to the string `"null"`. In Boolean operations, `null` is equivalent to `false`.

Undefined Values

JavaScript returns a special value when it cannot determine a value, such as for an array element that has not been initialized.

In arithmetic and logical operations, this value is equivalent to `Number.NaN` (not-a-number; see above). In string operations, it is equivalent to the string `"undefined"`. In Boolean operations, it is equivalent to `false`; this allows a script to test whether an object exists without risking an undefined-symbol error.

Primitive Values

Numbers, strings, `true`, `false`, `null`, and undefined values are known as *primitive values*. Anything else in JavaScript is an *object*, which may have a collection of values instead of a single one. Objects are handled differently in some operations. In particular, assigning a primitive value to a variable makes a copy; but assigning an object to a variable makes a reference (see "Assignment" in Chapter 3).

Some objects are able to return primitive values when the syntax of a statement requires it. For instance, the built-in `Date` object can return a string containing a time and date in a standard format. Other objects, that do not have a way to return a primitive value, will return a string containing `"[object]"`. For more details about objects, see Chapter 5.

Regular Expression Patterns

JavaScript supports patterns for matching regular expressions. This is one of JavaScript's more powerful features, and is described in detail in Chapter 3.

Some simple examples of patterns are:

```
/[a-z]/        any lowercase letter
/\d+/          one or more digits
/\d{3}\-\d{4}/ a telephone number: 3 digits, a dash, and four
               digits
```

Variables

A JavaScript variable is a named entity that contains some data. The first character of a variable name must be a letter or the underscore (_) character. The remaining characters can be letters, underscores, or digits. JavaScript is case-sensitive, so upper- and lowercase characters are *not* equivalent.

Examples of variable names are:

```
x
x1
ABC
firstName
area_code
```

A JavaScript variable can be created in one of three ways:

- You can declare it with the `var` keyword, as in:
    ```
    var x
    ```
- You can declare it and also assign an initial value:
    ```
    var firstName = "Fred"
    ```
- If you are assigning an initial value, you can omit the `var` (except for local variables; see the following):
    ```
    firstName = "Fred"
    ```

Variable Scope

A variable that is declared inside a function definition (see Chapter 4), using the `var` keyword, is *local* to that function: it cannot be referenced anywhere except inside the function. It is created dynamically each time the function runs, and it is destroyed when the function terminates. The same variable name may be declared in several functions, but each one is a separate variable.

Variables that are not declared inside a function, or that are declared without the `var` keyword, are *global*: they can be referenced by any JavaScript code in the document. A helpful practice is to place all global variable declarations in the `<HEAD>` section of the HTML.

Variables in other windows or frames can be referenced as `win.var`, where `win` is a `window` object, and `var` is a variable declared by a script in that window. (For more on windows and frames, see Chapter 6.)

Besides global and local, there are some built-in objects that have limited or specialized scopes:

- The `event` object, which is used to call event handlers, can only be referenced from within the event handler strings attached to HTML objects such as buttons (see Chapter 7).
- The `this` object is used in constructor functions (see Chapter 5) and event handlers for HTML tags (see Chapter 7).
- The `arguments` and `caller` properties can only be used inside functions (see Chapter 4).

Variable Types

Unlike many other languages, JavaScript does not assign a fixed type to variables. A variable may be used to contain numeric data one moment, and a string or logical value the next.

To determine the type of a variable's value, you can use the `typeof` operator. The expression `typeof x`, or `typeof(x)`, always returns a string identifying x's type. The string's value may be `"number"`, `"string"`, `"boolean"`, `"function"`, `"object"`, or `"undefined"`.

Arrays

Starting in version 1.1, JavaScript provides an `Array` type for ordered sets of data. Array indexes are represented by expressions in square brackets, such as `item[50]`. The `Array` object provides a number of methods for rearranging and converting arrays. For more details, see the listing for `Array` in Part II of this manual.

You can create an array using the `new` operator, with a statement like:

```
a = new Array(10)
```

To create an array and also initialize its elements, you can write:

```
regionName = new Array("North", "Central", "South")
```

These two forms create a conflict over the meaning of:

```
a = new Array(1)
```

Is 1 a value or a length? Older versions of JavaScript treated it as a length; so the statement would create an array with one element, whose value is undefined. But JavaScript 1.2 can take the other approach, producing an array whose element is initialized to 1. This only occurs if the statement is in a `<SCRIPT>` that has the `LANGUAGE="javascript1.2"` attribute.

Starting with JavaScript 1.2, you can use an even shorter syntax for creating arrays:

```
regionName = ["North", "Central", "South"]
```

(You do *not* need to specify `LANGUAGE="javascript1.2"` to use this.)

Array indexing is zero-based: in the preceding example, `regionName[0]` is `"North"`, and `regionName[2]` is `"South"`. There is no `regionName[3]`. Element values are undefined until they are assigned some value by a statement.

The current length of an array can be obtained with the `length` property. Continuing the preceding example, `regionName.length` returns 3.

You can extend arrays simply by assigning values to additional elements. Continuing the preceding example, the statement:

```
regionName[8] = "Japan"
```

assigns the value and changes the array's length to 9. Elements 3 through 7 are still undefined.

You can truncate arrays by assigning a new, smaller value to the `length` property. Continuing the preceding example, the statement:

```
regionName.length = 3
```

returns the array to its original length. Single array elements can be deleted with the `delete` operator.

To create a multi-dimensional array, you can nest arrays:

```
row1 = new Array(3)
row2 = new Array(3)
row3 = new Array(3)
grid = new Array(row1, row2, row3)
```

To reference a single element, write two indexes, such as `grid[row][column]`. An expression such as `grid[0]` returns a copy of the `row1` array.

Arrays With String Indexes

Arrays can be indexed with string values, instead of numbers, as in:

```
var person = new Array()
person["firstName"] = "Mary"
person["lastName"] = "Jones"
person["zipCode"] = 12345
```

The handling of this type of element varies with the version of JavaScript in use. In version 1.0, numeric and string indexes are two different ways of referring to the same elements; so, in the preceding example, `person[0]` and `person["firstName"]` would be equivalent.

In JavaScript version 1.1 and later, elements with string indexes are stored separately from those with numeric indexes; so, in the preceding example, `person[0]` would be undefined, and `person.length` would return zero even though three elements were created. However, there are exceptions to this for the built-in arrays that reflect HTML content, such as `forms`, `links`, `layers`, etc. For those arrays, numeric and string indexes reference the same elements, although string indexes are not available in some cases.

Arrays as Objects

In all versions of JavaScript, `person["firstName"]` is equivalent to `person.firstName`. The latter format, using the dot (.) character, is the standard notation for an object property. Objects are discussed in more detail in Chapter 5.

Moving On

We have now described the basic types and features of JavaScript data. In the next chapter, we will look at ways to combine data and operators to form expressions.

Operators & Expressions 3

A JavaScript expression is a sequence of operators and operands that returns, or is evaluated to, a value. An operand may be a literal value, variable, array element, property, or function that returns a value. Operators may be unary or binary. Expressions are evaluated from left to right, subject to the precedence of various operators, except assignment operators, which are evaluated from right to left. Parentheses may be used to enclose expressions and subexpressions, to add clarity, and to affect the order of evaluation.

Expressions may have side effects if they contain function or method calls that modify data. Also, the ++ and — operators modify their operand; and, of course, an assignment operator modifies its left operand.

Arithmetic

JavaScript provides the following operators for numeric values:

Operator	Meaning
+	Addition
-	Subtraction
*	Multiplication
/	Division
%	Modulus. a % b returns the modulus, or remainder, of a divided by b. The result may be floating-point; for example, 12.3 % 5 returns 2.3.
++	Increment. Unary operator, may be prefix or postfix. Either form returns a value, and adds one to the operand as a side effect. ++a returns the incremented value; a++ returns the original value.
--	Decrement. Unary operator, may be prefix or postfix. Either form returns a value, and subtracts one from the operand as a side effect. --a returns the decremented value; a-- returns the original value.
-	Unary negation (prefix)

Mathematical Functions

The built-in `Math` object provides methods for mathematical functions, listed as follows. They are described in detail in Part II of this manual.

Method	Function
Math.abs(x)	Absolute value
Math.acos(a)	Arc cosine
Math.asin(a)	Arc sine
Math.atan(a)	Arc tangent (1 argument)
Math.atan2(x, y)	Arc tangent (2 arguments)
Math.ceil(x)	Ceiling (lowest greater integer)
Math.cos(a)	Cosine
Math.exp(x)	Natural exponent (*e* to the power of...)
Math.floor(x)	Floor (greatest lower integer)
Math.log(x)	Natural (base *e*) logarithm
Math.max(a, b)	Return greater value
Math.min(a, b)	Return lesser value
Math.pow(a, b)	Exponentiation (a to the power of b)
Math.random()	Return a pseudo-random number between 0 and 1
Math.round(x)	Round to the nearest integer: down if the fractional part is less than .5, or up if the fractional part is .5 or greater
Math.sin(a)	Sine
Math.sqrt(x)	Square root
Math.tan(a)	Tangent

Assignment

JavaScript uses the single equal sign (=) character for assignment. For example, the statement:

v = expr

sets the variable v to the value of expr, which may be a literal, variable, function that returns a value, or an expression combining any of those.

Unlike other operators, multiple assignments are evaluated from right to left. The statement:

a = b = c = 0

sets all three variables to zero.

When used as expressions, assignments return the value of the right operand. The statement:

a = (b = (5 + 3))

sets both a and b to 8.

JavaScript allows combining assignment with arithmetic and logical operators, listed as follows:

Operator	Equivalent
a += b	a = a + b
Note that this performs either addition (for numbers) or concatenation (for strings).	
a -= b	a = a - b
a *= b	a = a * b
a /= b	a = a / b
a %= b	a = a % b
a <<= b	a = a << b
a >>= b	a = a >> b
a >>>= b	a = a >>> b
a &= b	a = a & b
a |= b	a = a	b
a ^= b	a = a ^ b

Assignment expressions return the value of their right operand. The statement

a = (b = 5) * 2

sets b to 5, and a to 10.

Assignment statements make a copy of the right operand. So, for instance, after executing the statements:

```
a = 1
b = a
b = 2
```

a contains 1, and b contains 2. The statement b = a does *not* link the variables together in a way that would allow a change in one to affect the other. This is true for all assignments of primitive values (numbers, strings, Booleans, null, and undefined). For objects, however, the assignment operator copies a *reference* rather than an actual value. So, for instance, after executing the statements:

```
a = new Date()   // create an object
b = a
```

a and b both contain references to the same object. So, for instance, calling a.setTime() will affect the value returned by b.getTime(). To create new objects, you must use the new operator. For more details on objects, see Chapter 5.

Bitwise

JavaScript provides bit-shifting and logical operators. Operand values are converted to 32-bit integers before the operator is applied. The result is converted to the type of the left operand. Note that the bitwise operators do *not* return true or false.

Operator	Meaning
&	Bitwise logical AND
|	Bitwise logical OR
^	Bitwise logical XOR
~	Bitwise logical NOT (unary prefix)
<<	Logical left shift. Zeros are shifted in from the right. a << 4 returns the value of a shifted left by 4 bits.
>>	Arithmetic right shift. The leftmost bit value is propagated right. a >> 4 returns the value of a shifted right by 4 bits.
>>>	Logical right shift. Zeros are shifted in from the right. a >>> 4 returns the value of a shifted right by 4 bits.

Boolean

JavaScript provides three Boolean operators:

Operator	Meaning
!	Logical NOT (unary prefix)
&&	Logical AND
||	Logical OR

Note that for these operators, an operand is considered "true" if it is anything other than false, zero, the empty string "", null, or undefined.

! always returns the Boolean opposite of its operand, either true or false. && and || are a bit more complicated. Although they evaluate their operands as Booleans, they do not always return true or false. Instead, the && operator returns the value of its left operand if it is not "true" in the sense described above. If the left operand is "true," && returns the right operand. Similarly, the || operator returns the value of left operand if it is "true," otherwise it returns the right operand. This behavior allows the actual values, rather than the Boolean conversions, to be passed though the script as long as possible.

In evaluating AND and OR operators, JavaScript may take "shortcuts" by stopping evaluation of the expression. For example, in evaluating a && b, if a is false, then the result must be false, so there is no need to evaluate b. In that case, if b is an expression that was intended to cause side effects or perform other functions, they will not occur. The same thing can occur for a || b if a is true.

Comparison

JavaScript comparison operators return true or false based on the operand values; for instance, a == b returns true if a and b have equal values.

Operator	Meaning
==	Equal
!=	Not equal
>	Greater
<	Less
>=	Greater or equal
<=	Less or equal

Equality in JavaScript 1.2

Starting with JavaScript 1.2, the behavior of the == and != operators was changed somewhat. To prevent this from affecting older scripts, the new behavior is only used in scripts that specify the LANGUAGE=Javascript1.2 attribute on the <SCRIPT> tag. For these scripts, when evaluating a comparison, automatic type conversion is never performed. If two operands are not the same type, they are considered unequal. (You can write explicit type conversions, as explained later in this chapter.)

For earlier versions of JavaScript, and for scripts in JavaScript 1.2 that do not explicitly specify LANGUAGE=Javascript1.2, a comparison for equality has the following behavior:

- If both operands are object references, they must both refer to the same object. (Even if two objects are the same type, and have the same values in all their properties, they are not considered "equal.")
- null and undefined are considered equal (but neither of these is considered equal to zero, the empty string, or false).
- If one operand is an object, and the other is a string, convert the object to a string and compare the strings.
- Otherwise, convert both operands to numbers and compare them numerically.

Conditional

JavaScript supports conditional expressions with the ? and : operators, as used in C and C++. The expression c ? a : b returns the value of a if c is true, and the value of b otherwise.

String

JavaScript provides the + operator for concatenating strings. For instance, "Java" + "Script" returns "JavaScript". The assignment notation += also works in this way for strings.

Special Operators

JavaScript provides several operators for functions such as manipulating objects and controlling script execution.

Comma

Commas are used in function argument lists, such as `scrollTo(x, y)`. They can also be used in other types of expressions. A list of items used as an expression returns the value of the last item. For example, the statement

```
x = a, b, c
```

sets `x` to `c`. Note that all the items are evaluated, and if any of them are function calls or other expressions that have side effects, those actions will occur.

Commas can also be used to separate statements (see Chapter 4).

delete

This unary operator is used to delete a property of an object or an element of an array, as in:

```
delete a[4]
delete person1.zipCode
```

The operator returns `true` if the deletion is successful, and `false` otherwise. If the deletion succeeds, the property or element's value will be undefined.

(There is no explicit way to delete an entire JavaScript object. Storage management and "garbage collection" are handled automatically.)

new

The unary prefix operator `new` is used to create objects using constructor functions, as in:

```
var weekDays = new Array("Su", "Mo", "Tu", "We", "Th", "Fr", "Sa")
```

`new` can be used with built-in objects as just shown, or with user-written constructors.

typeof

The unary prefix operator `typeof` returns a string identifying the data type of its operand. The returned value may be `"number"`, `"string"`, `"boolean"`, `"object"`, `"function"`, or `"undefined"`.

> **TIP**
>
> *Note that the keyword typeof is all lowercase.*

void

The unary prefix operator `void` is used to prevent an expression from returning any value, while still allowing it to be evaluated. For example, in links, the URL expression `javascript:void(stmt)` can be used to execute the statement `stmt` when the user clicks on the link. Since `void` returns no value, the link will execute the statement, but will not jump to a new location.

Operator Precedence

In evaluating an expression, JavaScript applies operators, and other symbols such as parentheses, in the precedence order listed in the following table. You can alter the order by using parentheses.

Precedence	Operator	
Highest		
·	Function call:	a(b)
·	Array member:	a[b]
·	Object property:	a.b
·	Unary operators:	! ~ - ++ -- typeof void
·	Multiply/divide:	* / %
·	Add/subtract:	+ -
·	Bitwise shift:	<< >> >>>
·	Inequality:	< > <= >=
·	Equality:	== !=
·	Bitwise AND:	&
·	Bitwise OR:	|
·	Boolean AND:	&&
·	Boolean OR:	||
·	Conditional:	c ? a : b
Lowest	Assignment:	= += -= *= /= %= <<= >>= >>>= &= |= ^=

Type Conversion

Since JavaScript is a loosely typed language, many operations perform implicit type conversions. Techniques are available to force a value to a specific type. In JavaScript version 1.2, you can use the functions `String(x)`, `Number(x)`, or `Boolean(x)` to return x's value converted to one of these types. Note that this notation does not create a new object, since the `new` operator is not used.

For compatibility with older versions of JavaScript, you can use these familiar tricks:

- To convert a value to a string, concatenate it to the empty string using the + operator:
  ```
  str = "" + x
  ```
- To convert a value to a number, subtract zero (note that addition may not always work, since for strings the + operator performs concatenation):
  ```
  num = x - 0
  ```
- To convert a value to a Boolean, use either:
  ```
  boo = x ? true : false
  boo = !!x
  ```

Regular Expressions

Starting with version 1.2, JavaScript supports regular expression objects for manipulating text, and a number of methods that use them for searching and replacing strings. (For an explanation of objects, properties, and methods, see Chapter 5.)

The syntax for regular expressions, also called *patterns*, is based on that used in the Perl language. Like numbers and strings, they can be declared implicitly in statements such as:

```
var pat = /s\d+/
```

which matches a lowercase s followed by one or more digits, or:

```
var pat = /s\d+/i
```

which is the same thing except that the i modifier specifies a case-insensitive match, so either an upper- or lowercase s will match. There is also a g modifier which specifies a "global" match; the actual use of this modifier depends on the method being called (see the following).

Besides \d, JavaScript accepts a number of special symbols in patterns:

Symbol	Matches:
\t	Tab character
\n	Newline character
\r	Carriage return character
\f	Form-feed character
\v	Vertical tab character
\\	Back slash character
\w	Any "word" character: letters, digits, or underscore (_).
\W	Any "non-word" character
\s	Any white-space character: space, tab, newline, etc.
\S	Any non-white-space character
\d	Any digit
\D	Any non-digit
\b	Any word boundary: a point in the string between a word and non-word character.
\B	Any non-word boundary: a point in the string between two characters that are both word characters, or are both non-word.
.	Any single character except Newline
^	The beginning of the string
$	The end of the string
\n	(where *n* is any number) If *n* is less than or equal to the number of memorized values (the number of left parentheses encountered so far in the pattern), this expression matches the *n*th memorized value. If *n* is greater than the number of memorized values, it is interpreted as an octal number, and the expression matches the character whose code is the specified value.

Note: the back slash character may be used before special pattern characters in order to override their meanings. For example, a circumflex (^) is a special character in patterns. To actually match a circumflex, use the pattern /\^/.

There are some other symbols that can be used in patterns to create more complex structures:

Pattern example	Matches:
p | q	Either *p* or *q*, where *p* and *q* are patterns
p+	One or more consecutive occurrences of pattern *p*
p*	Zero or more consecutive occurrences of pattern *p*
p?	Zero or one occurrence of pattern *p*
p{n}	Exactly *n* consecutive occurrences of pattern *p*

Pattern example	Matches:
p{n,}	At least *n* consecutive occurrences of pattern *p*
p{n,m}	At least *n*, and at most *m*, consecutive occurrences of pattern *p*
[aeiou]	Any one of the characters in the specified set. This example matches any vowel (lowercase only unless the i modifier is used).
[^aeiou]	Any character not in the specified set. This example matches any character except a vowel (lowercase only unless the i modifier is used).
[0-9]	Any one character in the specified range. This example matches any decimal digit.
[^0-9]	Any character not in the specified range. This example matches anything except a decimal digit.

You can also use parentheses in a pattern. They have the expected effect of grouping several pattern components into one unit; for example, /(ab){3}/ matches the string ababab. Parentheses have another effect: a substring that matches the parenthesized portion of the pattern will be "memorized." After the operation, it may be available in the array of results returned by the method. It will also be stored in one of the $1 through $9 properties of the RegExp constructor (see below). For example, the pattern /(\w+) Smith/ will match any word followed by Smith, and place the word (presumably a first name) in the property RegExp.$1.

The RegExp Object

Patterns are supported as a type of object, called RegExp. Besides the literal declarations shown above, patterns can also be declared by using the RegExp() constructor function. For instance:

var pat = new RegExp("s\\d+", "i")

is another way of writing /s\d+/i. Note the different syntax: the beginning and ending slashes are not present in this case, and the modifiers are placed in a second argument. Also, the usual rules for string literals apply, so the \ character must be doubled.

Using new RegExp() has the advantage that the pattern and its modifiers can be variables whose value is created or changed while the script is running. There is also a disadvantage which arises because patterns created this way are stored as strings. Patterns declared in statements are compiled into an internal format that results in faster execution. However, a pattern created with RegExp() can be converted to the faster format by calling the compile() method.

RegExp objects have a number of properties that provide information about the pattern, and in one case (lastIndex) also controls operation of a match:

global
: Returns true if the pattern is global (g modifier was specified). This is a read-only property.

ignoreCase
: Returns true if the pattern is case-insensitive (i modifier was specified). This is a read-only property.

lastIndex
: This is only used by the exec() and test() methods. If global is true, lastIndex specifies where to start the next match, and also returns the index of the first character after the last match.

source
: The text of the pattern. This is a read-only property.

The RegExp constructor also has some properties; these are only available for RegExp itself, not for patterns:

$1, $2, ... $9
: Strings representing memorized substrings specified by parentheses in the pattern.

input or $_
: A copy of the last string matched. This can also be used as input to the exec() and test() methods.

lastMatch or $&
: The last substring matched. This property is read-only.

lastParen or $+
: The last substring memorized. This property is read-only.

leftContext or $`
: The substring from the start of the source string to just before the last match. This property is read-only. (Note the use of the accent character, not the apostrophe.)

multiline or $*
: A Boolean property that controls how matches are performed in a string that contains newline characters. If multiline is true, the symbol ^ in patterns will match the point after a newline, as well as its usual function of matching the beginning of the string. Similarly, the symbol $ will match the point just before a newline, as well as the end of the string.

rightContext or $'
: The substring from just after the last match to the end of the source string. This property is read-only.

Note that because these are properties of a constructor, they are shared by all scripts running in any window. So if you have several scripts in a window that use regular expressions, they may affect each others' results.

Using Regular Expressions

There are six methods that apply regular expressions to strings: the `match()`, `replace()`, `search()`, and `split()` methods for strings, and the `exec()` and `test()` methods for `RegExp` objects. All of them are described in detail in Part II. In the following brief descriptions, `rex` is a regular expression and `str` is a string:

`str.match(rex)`	Searches `str` for one or more substrings that match `rex`. Returns an array containing several types of results.
`str.replace (rex, str2)`	Returns a copy of `str` in which one or more substrings that match `rex` have been replaced by `str2`.
`str.search(rex)`	Searches `str` for a substring that matches `rex`. Returns a number indicating the position of the match.
`str.split(rex, max)`	Returns an array of strings formed by dividing `str` at each point where a substring that matches `rex` is found, up to a specified maximum number. (This method can also be used with a string as the separator, instead of a regular expression.)
`rex.exec(str)`	Searches `str` for a substring that matches `rex`. Returns an array containing several types of results.
`rex.test(str)`	Searches `str` for a substring that matches `rex`. Returns true if a match is found, false otherwise.
`rex(str)`	This "null method" is equivalent to `rex.exec(str)`.

Besides their returned values, these methods all provide additional result information in properties of `rex` and of `RegExp` itself, the constructor (previously described).

As mentioned earlier, the g modifier, which specifies a "global" operation, is used in two different ways. For the `match()` and `replace()` methods, g causes the operation to find or replace all substrings that match `rex`. For `exec()` and `text()`, the g modifier causes the method to find the "next" matching substring, rather than the first. This is done by having the operation start at the position in `str` specified by the `rex.lastIndex` property; and if a match is found, `lastIndex` is updated to indicate the next character after the matching substring. Thus several successive calls to `exec()` or `test()` can step through a string looking for a series of matches.

Moving On

We have now discussed all the ways that JavaScript represents data. In the next chapter, we will look at the statements and functions that determine what a script does with the data.

Statements & Functions 4

As mentioned in Chapter 1, JavaScript provides flexible statement syntax and formatting similar to C and Java. You can spread a statement over several lines (although string literals must be contained on a single line; see "Strings" in Chapter 2). You can use spaces, tabs, blank lines, and comments freely to improve the appearance of a script.

You can place several statements on one line if they are separated by semicolons (;), as in:

```
a = 1; b = 2; c = 3
```

You can also use commas (,) to separate statements. Commas, which have a lower precedence than semicolons, are commonly used in `for` statements, such as:

```
for (a = 0, b = 1; result != 0; a++, b += 10)
    result = someFunction(a, b)
```

This example uses two loop variables, a and b, which are initialized to different values, and incremented by different amounts. Commas may also be used to create multi-statement loops and conditionals without using braces. However, these are unconventional programming techniques, and should be used with care.

JavaScript is case-sensitive: uppercase and lowercase letters are *not* equivalent. (In HTML, however, they are; beware of confusing the two.)

A script consists of a series of statements enclosed by the <SCRIPT> and </SCRIPT> tags. These statements are read and executed by Navigator in a single pass as it loads the web page. So in many cases, variables must be declared before they are referenced. Also, statements that refer to any part of the web page must be located at a point in the file after the referenced part of the page has been loaded.

Block structuring is provided by the "curly brackets" or brace characters, { and }. A series of statements enclosed in braces is syntactically equivalent to a single statement for conditionals and loops.

Conditionals

JavaScript's syntax for conditional execution is:

```
if (expr) stmt1
```
or:
```
if (expr) stmt1
else stmt2
```

where *expr* is an expression, and *stmt1* and *stmt2* are statements (or groups of statements enclosed in braces). *expr* is evaluated as a Boolean: it is considered "true," allowing *stmt1* to be executed if it evaluates to anything other than 0, `false`, `null`, or the empty string `""`. If *expr* returns one of those four "non-true" values, or if it is undefined, then *stmt1* will not be executed; but *stmt2*, if present, will be.

Note that `else` is a separate statement, not an extension of `if`. So if you want to put both cases on one line, you must use a semicolon:

```
if (expr) stmt1; else stmt2
```

> **TIP**
>
> *When using "if" to test whether two values are equal, remember to use the double equal sign, ==, not the assignment operator, =.*

JavaScript also provides conditional expressions using the : and ? operators (see Chapter 3).

Multi-way Branch

JavaScript's `switch` statement has the form:

```
switch(expr) {

case label1:
    stmts
    break

case label2:
    stmts
    break
```

...

```
case labelN:
   stmts

default:
   stmts
}
```

JavaScript evaluates *expr*, and if the value matches the label of one of the `case` statements, execution continues at the statement after the label. If the value of *expr* does not match any of the labels, then execution continues after the `default` label. The labels may be numeric or string values.

The body of each case is one or more statements; they do not need to be enclosed in braces. The `break` statement at the end of the case causes execution to continue after the closing brace at the end of the `switch` statement. The `break` is optional, but if it is not present, execution will "fall through" to the next case. This is useful in some situations to create a sort of multiple-entry structure.

Multiple labels may be assigned to a single case, as in:

```
switch (whatTheUserTyped.substring(0,1)) {

case "A":
case "B":
case "C":
   location = "Volume1.html"
   break

case "D":
case "E":
   location = "Volume2.html"
   break

...

case "W":
case "X":
case "Y":
case "Z":
   location = "Volume9.html"
   break

default:
   alert("Your entry must start with a letter.")
}
```

This example uses the `location` property to open one of several web pages, based on the first letter of some value entered by the user.

Loops

JavaScript provides loop structures with `while`, `do...while`, `for`, and `for...in` statements.

while

The `while` loop has the form:

```
while (expr)
    stmt
```

where *stmt* is a single statement, or a series of statements enclosed in braces. JavaScript evaluates *expr*, and if it is "true" (anything other than 0, `false`, `null`, the empty string `""`, or undefined), *stmt* is executed. Then *expr* is evaluated again. Repeated execution and testing continue until *expr* evaluates to a "non-true" value. Thus *stmt* may execute as few as zero times, or as many as inifinity.

Execution of `while` loops can be modified by `break` and `continue` statements (described below).

do...while

The `do...while` loop has the form:

```
do
    stmt
while (expr)
```

where *stmt* is a single statement, or a series of statements enclosed in braces. JavaScript executes *stmt*, and then evaluates *expr*. If *expr* returns a "true" value (anything other than 0, `false`, `null`, the empty string `""`, or undefined), control loops back to *stmt*.

This structure is equivalent to the `while` loop, except that the test of *expr* is done after executing *stmt*, rather than before. Thus *stmt* is always guaranteed to run at least once.

Execution of `do...while` loops can be modified by `break` and `continue` statements (described below).

for

The `for` loop has the form:

```
for (init; test; adv)
    body
```

where:
- *init* is an initialization statement.
- *test* is an expression that controls looping.
- *adv* is a statement that advances the loop.
- *body* is the body of the loop, which may be either a single statement or a series of statements enclosed in braces.

To process the loop, JavaScript uses the following procedure:
1. Execute the *init* statement.
2. Evaluate the *test* expression. If it is "non-true" (0, false, null, the empty string "", or undefined), exit from the loop.
3. Execute the *body* of the loop, followed by the advancing statement, *adv*.
4. Go back to step 2.

Both *init* and *adv* may be omitted if those functions are handled by other parts of your script; but both semicolons must be present in the for statement. If you need to write more than one statement in *init* or *adv*, you can do so by separating them with commas, as in:

```
for (a = 0, b = 1; result != 0; a++, b += 10)
    result = someFunction(a, b)
```

This example uses two loop variables, a and b, which are initialized to different values, and incremented by different amounts.

Execution of for loops can be modified by break and continue statements (described below).

for...in

This special-purpose loop allows you to access the properties of an object with a loop of the form:

```
for v in obj
    stmt
```

where:
- *v* is a variable that is set to property names.
- *obj* is the object being examined.
- *stmt* is the body of the loop, which may be either a single statement or a series of statements enclosed in braces.

stmt will be executed once for each property of *obj*. Each time it executes, *v* is set to a string value containing the name of one of the properties of *obj*.

In JavaScript, the object property reference a.b is equivalent to the array reference a["b"]. So the string value of *prop* can be used to access the property.

The following function will display all the properties of any object:

```
function writeProps(obj) {
var prop
for (prop in obj)
   document.write(prop, " is ", obj[prop], ".<BR>")
}
```

Execution of `for...in` loops can be modified by `break` and `continue` statements (described below).

break

The `break` statement can be used to exit from a loop, as in:

```
while (expr) {
   stmt1
   if (someCondition) break
   stmt2
}
stmt3
```

If the `break` is executed, the loop will be immediately terminated, and execution will proceed at *stmt3*. The `break` statement works in the same manner for `do...while`, `for`, and `for...in` loops.

The `break` statement can include a label to allow flexible exiting from nested loops, as in:

```
Outer:
   while (exp1) {
      Inner:
         while (exp2) {
            ...
            if (cond1) break Inner
            ...
            if (cond2) break Outer
            ...
         }
         ...              // continue here after inner break
   }
   ...                    // continue here after outer break
```

Note that the label must come *before* the loop. The label does not specify where to go; it specifies which statement, or block of statements, is being exited.

`break` is also used with the `switch` statement, as described previously. To exit from nested `switch` statements, you can use a labeled `break` structure like that shown for nested loops.

continue

The `continue` statement causes a loop to immediately advance to the next iteration, as in:

```
for (k = 0; k < 10; k++) {
   stmt1
   if (someCondition) continue
   stmt2
}
```

If the `continue` is executed, k will be incremented, and execution will continue at *stmt1*; *stmt2* will not be executed for this iteration. The `continue` statement works in the same manner for `while`, `do...while`, and `for...in` loops.

The `continue` statement can include a label to allow flexible control of nested loops, as in:

```
Outer:
   for (row = 0; row < 3; row++) {
      Inner:
         for (column = 0; column < 4; column++){
            ...
            if (nextColumn) continue Inner
            ...
            if (nextRow) continue Outer
            ...
         }
   }
```

Note that the label must come *before* the loop. The label does not specify where to go; it specifies which loop is being advanced.

Functions

A JavaScript function declaration has the form:

```
function name (arg1, arg2, ... argN) {
   body
}
```

where:

- *name* is the function name.
- *arg1 ... argN* are the names of arguments for the function. Arguments are optional, but the parentheses are required.
- *body* is a statement or series of statements. Note that the *body* must be enclosed by braces, even if it only a single statement.

To call a function, use a statement of the form:

name (*expr1, expr2, ... exprN*)

Starting with JavaScript 1.2, a function declaration can be nested inside another. The resulting function, like a local variable, can only be used by the function in which it is declared.

The Function object (described below) provides several properties that help you work with functions:

- arity allows scripts to determine how many arguments a function "expects," based on the number of arguments in its declaration.
- arguments is an array that allows a function to determine how many arguments were actually passed to it, and to read any arguments that are beyond those in the function's declaration.
- caller allows a function to determine what function called it.

Each of these objects is described in detail in Part II of this manual.

Call by Value

In JavaScript, function arguments are passed by value: the values of *expr1* through *exprN* are evaluated, and copied to local variables in the function. This is demonstrated by the following example:

```
function tryToChange (x, v) {
   x = v
   document.write("Changed it to ", v)
}

myVar = 1
tryToChange(myVar, 0)
document.write ("... but its value is still ", myVar, ".<BR>")
```

The function can change the value of its argument x, but that change does not apply to the actual variable myVar that was specified in the function call. When executed, these statements cause the following to appear on the screen:

Changed it to 0... but its value is still 1.

Figure 4-1: The result of modifying the function argument.

This behavior applies to all arguments with primitive values (see Chapter 2), but objects are handled somewhat differently. If a function argument is an object, a function can modify the object's properties. For more details on objects, see Chapter 5.

Returning Values

The return statement can be used to have the function return a value, as in:

```
function factorial (n) {
   var f = 1
   if (n == 0) return 0
   while (n > 1) {
      f = f * n
      n--
   }
   return f
}
```

To use the returned value, write the function call as an operand or expression, such as:

```
result = factorial(someNumber)
```

The Function Object

You can use the Function object constructor to create new functions at run time with a statement of the form:

```
var funcName = new Function(arg1, arg2, ... argN, body)
```

All the arguments must be string values. *arg1, arg2, ... argN* are strings containing names for the function's arguments, if any; these are optional. body is a string containing JavaScript source code for the body of a function, without the header or enclosing braces. For example:

```
calc = new Function ("x", "y", "z",
   "return ((x * y) + 2) / z)")
```

Function objects are handy when assigning event handlers to object properties, as in:

```
document.images[0].onabort
   = new Function ("alert('Error on image 0.')")
```

which is easier and quicker to write than:

```
function img0error() {
   alert('Error on image 0.')
}
document.images[0].onabort = img0error
```

Special-purpose Statements

There are two statements that have special functions related to object names. The `var` statement is used to declare variables, while the `with` statement is used to simplify references to complex object structures.

var

The `var` statement is used to declare variables, as in:

```
var amount
var x, y, z
```

`var` can also assign initial values, as in:

```
var amount = 0
var x = 0, y = 1, z = 2
```

In most cases, the use of `var` is optional, because JavaScript automatically declares a variable the first time it encounters the name. However, you must use `var` when declaring local variables inside a function. For example:

```
function something() {
   a = 0      // this should define a local variable
   ...
}
```

The variable `a` is actually global. If there is a global variable called `a` elsewhere in your script, then the function will modify that `a` every time it is called.

with

The `with` statement provides a useful shortcut when dealing with a complex structure of objects and properties, by allowing you to specify a default object or "starting point" for all references. For example, these statements:

```
obj.prop.subprop.itemA = 1
obj.prop.subprop.itemB = "ABC"
obj.prop.subprop.doSomething(obj.prop.subprop.itemA, "X")
```

can be replaced by:

```
with (obj.prop.subprop) {
   itemA = 1
   itemB = "ABC"
   doSomething(itemA, "X")
}
```

Moving On

We have now covered the standard data and control structures that are found in most programming languages. In the next chapter, we will move on to the more advanced area of object-oriented features.

Objects, Properties & Methods   5

This chapter describes JavaScript's implementation of objects, which allows easy and flexible structuring of data. It is similar to the system used in Java and in other object-oriented languages such as C++. However, JavaScript's implementation is simpler, trading power for ease of use.

Objects & Properties

In JavaScript, an *object* is a structured set of data items, called *properties*, and code (functions), called *methods*. For example:

```
var person = new Array()
person.firstName = "Mary"
person.lastName = "Jones"
person.age = 34
```

This creates an object named `person` with three properties. Note that `person` is declared as an `Array`. In our description of arrays, we pointed out that using string indexes, such as `person["firstName"]`, is equivalent to writing `person.firstName`, which represents an object and its property. Internally, JavaScript uses the same handler for objects with properties that it uses for arrays with string indexes.

However, it seems inelegant to declare something as an array when we want to use it as an object. A clearer approach is to write a *constructor* function for the object, and use the constructor with the new operator. For example, a constructor for person objects might look like this:

```
function person(first, last, yrs) {
   this.firstName = first
   this.lastName = last
   this.age = yrs
}
```

Note the use of the this keyword to create properties for the new object. To use the constructor to create some objects, you call it with the new operator, as in:

```
var Mary = new person("Mary", "Jones", 34)
var Bob = new person("Bob", "Lee", 27)
```

After the object is constructed, its properties can be referenced by using the variable name and property name separated by the dot (.) character, as in Mary.firstName, Bob.age, etc.

The name of the constructor is effectively the name for the class or type of object that the constructor creates. This is about as close as JavaScript gets to the concept of object classes, as found in Java and other fully object-oriented languages.

Starting with JavaScript 1.2, you can also construct objects "on the fly" with expressions enclosed in braces of the form:

```
{prop1:val1, prop2:val2, ... propN:valN}
```

where each *prop* is a property name, and each *val* is an expression denoting a property's value. For example, a person object could be created by a statement such as:

```
var carroll = {firstName:"Sally", lastName:"Forth", age:42}
```

These expressions can be nested, as in:

```
var family = {dad:{firstName:"George",
               lastName:"Jones", age:58},
            mom: {firstName:"Martha",
               lastName:"Forth", age:42},
            numKids: 2.7
               }
```

Built-in Objects

The following object types (constructors) are built into JavaScript:
- `Array`: creates an ordered array of values (see below).
- `Boolean`, `String`, and `Number`: these constructors are not normally written in scripts. They are used internally by JavaScript, and they are available to you for special operations, such as using `prototype` to add new properties.
- `Date`: used for managing dates and times. Methods are provided for conversion to and from many formats.
- `Function`: creates a JavaScript function from a string.
- `Image`: manages graphic data, allows you to change displays at run time, load images from various files, etc.
- `Layer`: creates a document layer.
- `Math`: provides mathematical values and functions such as π, logarithms, sines and cosines, etc.
- `Option`: creates an option for a select box in a form.

Each of these object types is described in detail in Part II of this manual.

External Objects

JavaScript provides a number of *external* object types. These are objects that have no constructors; you cannot create new objects of these types with the `new` operator. Instead, the browser provides these objects as needed. The external object types are listed below:
- `Anchor`: reflects a named anchor in a document.
- `Applet`: reflects a Java applet in a web page.
- `Area`: reflects one region of an image map.
- `Button`: reflects a button in a form.
- `Checkbox`: reflects a check box in a form.
- `FileUpload`: reflects a file browser box in a form.
- `Form`: reflects a form in a document, and all its elements.
- `Frame`: reflects a frame defined by a frameset in a document.
- `Hidden`: reflects a hidden form input element.
- `Link`: reflects a hypertext link in a document.
- `MimeType`: provides information about a MIME data type that the browser supports.
- `Password`: reflects a password box in a form.

- **Plugin**: provides information about a plug-in application installed in the browser, and possibly methods and properties of the plug-in.
- **Radio**: reflects a radio button in a form.
- **Reset**: reflects a reset button in a form.
- **Select**: reflects a select box in a form.
- **Submit**: reflects a submit button in a form.
- **Text**: reflects a text box in a form.
- **Textarea**: reflects a text area in a form.

Each of these object types is described in detail in Part II of this manual.

Values & References

An important point about JavaScript objects is that, unlike primitive values, they are manipulated by *references*. A reference is a pointer or label that specifies where some actual values are stored. For instance, continuing to work with the person object from the earlier examples, after executing the statements:

```
var p1 = new person("George", "Smith", 42)
p2 = p1
p2.firstName = "Martha"
p2.age = 30
```

you might think that p2 would contain information on Martha Smith, while p1 is still about George Smith. But p1 is a reference, and the statement p2 = p1 copies the reference; so p1 and p2 now refer to the same object. p1, as well as p2, now refer to the information about Martha. To create an actual new object, you must use the new operator with a constructor function.

Objects also behave differently from primitive values when used as function arguments. As mentioned in Chapter 4, arguments are passed by value, so a function cannot modify its arguments. However, if an argument is an object, a function can modify its properties, as in:

```
function nextYear(p) {
   p.age++
}
```

which increments a person's age.

Deleting Objects

An object can be deleted by setting any variables that reference it to null in JavaScript versions 1.1 and later. (Objects cannot be deleted in version 1.0.) To delete specific properties of an object or elements of an array, you can use the delete operator (see Chapter 3).

Properties as Objects

A property of an object can itself be an object. For instance, the built-in document object contains a large number of properties pertaining to the contents of a web page. Many of these properties are arrays or objects. If your web page contains a form named info, you could refer to it in a script as document.forms.info. As a more extreme example, if you create a web page with several layers, and one of those layers contained some sublayers, you might write a statement to set a sublayer's property such as:

```
document.layers.lyr5.layers.sublyr2.width = 200
```

You can create nested objects like this by writing constructors that use new to create objects that contain objects. For example, suppose you want to create a job object to describe a task that some person is handling. You could write a constructor like:

```
function job(what, who, yr, mo, dy) {
   this.title = what
   this.person = who
   this.startDate = new Date(yr, mo, dy)
}
```

Then a job object can be created like this:

```
var Joe = new person("Joe", "Zeelane", 46)
   .
   .
   .
project1 = new job("Report", Joe, 97, 06, 13)
```

This creates a job object named project1. The property project1.person is a person object: a copy of the variable Joe. The property project1.startDate is also an object, of the built-in Date type.

Adding Properties to Objects

You can add properties to existing objects by using the special prototype property, which is available for all objects that are created with the new operator. This includes the built-in object types as well as any constructors that you write. For instance, to identify each person as male or female, you could add a gender field to the person object by writing:

```
person.prototype.gender = ""
```

This statement adds a new property called gender to the person object. All instances of this new property will be set to the specified value, which in this case is the empty string. The gender property will be added to person objects that have already been constructed, as well as to any that are created later.

Methods

JavaScript *methods* are functions that are associated with an object. Many useful built-in methods are available. For instance, to reverse the order of the elements of an array a, you can use the `Array` object's built-in `reverse` method:

```
a.reverse()
```

Or to form a string by combining an array's elements, separated by spaces, you can use the `join` method by writing:

```
string s = a.join(" ")
```

JavaScript's built-in methods are all described in Part II of this manual.

You can also create your own methods. Continuing our `person` example, we might want to have a function that formats a person's data as a string for output.

```
function personText() {
   var s = this.firstName + " " + this.lastName + "(" + this.age + ")"
   return s
}
```

This function returns a string containing the person's first and last name, separated by a space, and followed by the age enclosed in parentheses. Once again we have used the `this` keyword to allow the function to access the object by which it is called.

To make this function a method of `person`, add a line to your constructor function to assign it:

```
function person(first, last, yrs) {
   this.firstName = first
   this.lastName = last
   this.age = yrs
   this.formatted = personText
}
```

The last line of the constructor gives the `person` object a method called `formatted`, which is actually the `personText` function. Note that there are *no* parentheses after the name of the function; this indicates that we are making a reference to the function, not calling it.

So, to display an object `Joe` created with this constructor, you can write a statement such as:

```
document.write(Joe.formatted())
```

The call to `Joe.formatted` is passed to `personText`, which returns a string containing Joe's name and age.

Universal Methods

There are three methods that are available for all objects:
- `eval` evaluates a string as JavaScript code in the context of the calling object, and returns its value.
- `toString` returns a string representing a numeric value in a specified radix.
- valueOf returns the primitive value of an object.

Two other methods are available for large numbers of objects:
- `constructor()` is available for all objects created by constructor functions. It returns the function that created an object.
- `handleEvent()` is available for all objects that have event handlers. It calls an event handler for a specific event.

Moving On

We have now introduced all the basic features of JavaScript as an "abstract" language that manipulates data. Starting with the next chapter, we will cover "real world" features that allow scripts to interact with the user and the browser environment.

Windows, Documents & Graphics

6

Much of your scripts' activities revolve around managing documents in windows. This chapter describes the basic operations of the `window` and `document` objects. It also covers related topics such as frames, layers, style sheets, and graphics.

Windows

Every script runs in a window, and the `window` object is the global or "outermost" object in the JavaScript hierarchy. All variables and functions declared in scripts are actually properties and methods of the `window`; so, for example, a variable `x` is actually `window.x`.

In most cases, properties and methods of `window` can be referred to by their name, e.g. `document` instead of `window.document`, because `window` is the default owner for all identifiers in a script.

The symbol `self` is equivalent to `window`, in case you prefer it.

Each `window` object corresponds to one browser window on the host computer's screen. To open additional windows, use the `window.open()` method, which returns a new `window` object as in:

```
var win2 = open("someFile.htm", "newWin", features)
```

This opens a new browser window, and returns a new `window` object in the variable `win2`. The new window can now be accessed with statements such as:

```
win2.document.write(someText)
win2.toolbar.visible = false
```

Conversely, a script in the newly opened window can reference the window from which it was opened by using the `opener` property in statements such as:

```
opener.win2status = "ready"
```

Two other properties that sometimes refer to `window` objects are `parent` and `top`. They are used with frames (see "Frames" below).

Scripts can control most window features such as size, position on the screen, presence of scroll bars and toolbars, etc. They can create web page content by writing to the window's `document`. They can also load an HTML document into the window by setting the `location` property or accessing the `history` list.

Documents

Every `window` has a `document` property which manages all text, graphics, and other data displayed in the window. A script can reference its own document simply as `document`, since `window` is the default context. It can reference other documents as properties of `window` objects, such as `win2.document`.

A `document` object has properties that reflect the HTML elements in the window. Many of these properties are arrays:

- Links are created in a web page by the `<A>` tag. They are reflected by Link objects in the `document.links` array. Links that have a `<NAME>` attribute are also reflected by Anchor objects in the `anchors` array.

- Images are included in a web page by the `<IMG>` tag. They are reflected by Image objects in the `document.images` array.

- Image map regions are created in a web page by the `<AREA>` tag. They are reflected by Area objects which, being a type of link, are stored in the `document.links` array.

- Java applets are included in a web page by the `<APPLET>` tag. They are reflected by Applet objects in the `document.applets` array.

- Video, audio, and other types of files are included in a web page by the `<EMBED>` tag. They are reflected by Embed objects in the `document.embeds` array. (The list of supported data types is available in the `navigator.mimeTypes` array, described in Chapter 8.)

- Forms are created in a web page by the `<FORM>` tag. They are reflected by Form objects in the `document.forms` array. The buttons, text boxes, and other elements of a form are reflected by various types of objects in the form's `elements` array, a property of the Form object (see Chapter 7).

- Document layers are created by the `<LAYER>` tag. They are reflected by Layer objects in the `document.layers` array.

As mentioned previously, a `document` can be loaded with content from an HTML file. This is what happens whenever the user visits a web page; also, scripts have several ways to load new documents.

Writing to a Document

Instead of loading a file, scripts can create document content dynamically by using methods that provide the familiar "open, write, close" process used by most programming languages.

To write to a document, you must first initialize it by calling `document.open()`. Then you execute one or more calls to `document.write()` or `document.writeln()` to send text to the document.

When writing to a document, note that you are writing HTML, so you can place tags such as `<H1>` or `<P>` in the output stream and they will have the usual effect on the display. There are a number of `String` methods such as `bold()`, `italics()`, and `color()`, that can generate tagged text, making your scripts simpler and clearer. Note that the contents of a document correspond to the `<BODY>` portion of an HTML file, so you do not need to write `<HTML>`, `<HEAD>`, etc.

Text that you write may be stored in a buffer and not actually appear on the screen until a line break is generated by writing a `<BR>` or `<P>` element. After you have written all text, you should execute `document.close()` to ensure that the text buffer is flushed and the document is left in a stable condition. (The Netscape "meteor shower" animated logo on the Navigator toolbar will continue to move until the window's document is closed.)

Frames

Frames are sections of a window created by the HTML `<FRAMESET>` and `<FRAME>` tags. Their use is somewhat restricted, compared to using multiple windows, since they must be defined with fixed sizes and locations.

When Navigator loads a document, it creates Frame objects corresponding to each `<FRAME>` tag, and stores them as elements of the `window.frames` array. Frames have many of the same features as windows, so Frame objects have most of the same properties and methods as `window` objects.

Each Frame object has a `document` property, which is equivalent to a `document` object in a window. You can load a file into a frame's document by assigning a URL to the layer's `location` property. You can also create content dynamically by writing to the document as explained previously.

A frame can be divided into more frames, called child frames. Child frames may also have children, and so on for many levels of nesting. If a frame contains children, its Frame object will have corresponding Frame objects in its `frames` array.

To help scripts navigate through the frame hierarchy, JavaScript provides properties called `parent` and `top`. `parent` returns the `window` or Frame object that contains the current frame; expressions such as `parent.parent` can be used to access different levels. `top` is a shortcut to the highest or outermost level: it always returns a `window` object. It is helpful for accessing features such as the status bar and toolbar, which are available for windows but not for frames.

Layers

Starting with version 1.2, JavaScript supports document layers to provide more versatility in web page layout. A layer is somewhat similar to a frame: it is a rectangular region contained in a window, and possibly having child layers, which may have additional children in a nested fashion. However, layers have more flexibility than frames. They can be of any size, and can overlap each other or extend past the boundaries of the window. The browser maintains a sequence called the z-order that determines which layer is "above" another when they overlap. Layers have a `zIndex` property that returns their position in the z-order, and there are several methods for moving a layer to a different position in the z-order.

Layers can be freely created, moved around, and removed from display while the script is running. You can create simple animation by moving a layer in small, rapid steps. Also, you can hide a layer while it is loading a large text or graphic file, so that the user does not see the content until it is completely loaded.

When Navigator loads a web page, it creates `Layer` objects corresponding to all `<LAYER>` tags in the document. These objects are stored in the `document.layers` array. You can also create `Layer` objects dynamically by using the `new Layer()` constructor.

Every layer has a `document` property, which is equivalent to a `document` object in a window or frame. You can load a file into the document by assigning a URL to the layer's `src` property. You can also create content dynamically by writing to the document as explained previously. If a layer has child layers, they are reflected by `Layer` objects that are stored in the layer's `document.layers` array.

Style Sheets

Starting with version 1.2, JavaScript supports style sheets that provide powerful features to control the appearance of text on a web page. Every `document` object has properties named `tags`, `classes`, and `ids`. These serve as "holders" for additional properties that create the actual styles. Each of these objects has a specific usage:

- The appearance of HTML tags can be modified by assigning properties to the `tags` object.
- Variations on the styles of HTML tags, and groups of related styles, can be created by assigning properties to the `classes` object.
- New styles can be created by assigning properties to the `ids` object.

JavaScript style sheets are largely identical to scripts, except that they are enclosed by <STYLE> and </STYLE> tags; for example:

```
<STYLE TYPE="text/javascript">
   tags.H1.color = "red"
</STYLE>
```

This simple style sheet causes all <H1> elements in the document to be displayed in red instead of the usual black (or whatever color is assigned in the browser's Preferences dialog). To apply a style to all HTML tags, assign it to `tags.body`, since all tags inherit their properties from <BODY>.

Large style sheets can be placed in separate files that are linked to a document by a tag of the form:

```
<LINK REL=stylesheet TYPE="text/javascript" HREF="fileName">
```

Using Style Sheets

Although `tags` is a property of the `document` object, style sheets can refer to `tags` rather than `document.tags` because style sheets are evaluated in the `document` context. You can reference `tags` in regular scripts, but in that case you must write `document.tags`. These rules also apply to `classes` and `ids`.

Note that style sheet assignments only affect text that comes after them in the document. A further restriction is that, for a style sheet to assign properties to `tags.body`, it must be placed in the <HEAD> portion of the document.

Each property of the `tags` object specifies styles for a single tag. Sometimes, though, more flexibility is needed. For example, suppose you want to define a style called `bright` for highlighting important text. Normally, it will display text in bold, orange characters. But you have already specified (in the previous example) that <H1> headings are displayed in red, which looks nearly the same as orange on some users' computers. So you want the `bright` style to make an exception for <H1> headings, and display them in gold. This can be implemented with style sheet statements such as:

```
classes.bright.all.color = "orange"
classes.bright.all.fontWeight = "bold"
classes.bright.H1.color = "gold"
```

These statements create a style class called `bright`. The assignments to `bright.all` define the default behavior for the class as orange, bold characters. The assignment to `bright.H1` makes a special case for <H1>. Additional exceptions can be created for other tags, so a single class can have many different appearances, depending on which tags it is applied to.

The styles assigned to `classes` are applied to HTML by the CLASS attribute in tags; for example:

```
<P CLASS="bright"> This text will be orange bold. </P>

<H1 CLASS="bright"> A Gold Bold Heading. </H1>
```

Assignments to `tags` and `classes` create variations on existing HTML tags, but there may be times when you want to create your own styles; you can do this with the `ids` object. For instance, to create a style called `gu` that displays text in green underlined characters, write statements such as:

```
ids.gu.color = "green"
ids.gu.textDecoration = "underline"
```

The style can be applied to any HTML tag by the ID attribute as in:

```
<P ID="gu"> This paragraph is green and underlined. </P>
```

Styles can also be applied to arbitrary regions of text with the `<SPAN>` tag as in:

```
Here is some text with <SPAN ID="gu"> a few green underlined words
</SPAN> in the middle.
```

Measurement Units in Style Sheets

Many style properties define sizes of text, margins, borders, etc. These measurements can be defined in several different ways:

- Absolute units define measurements that are constant, regardless of how the text is displayed or what other properties it has inherited from the enclosing HTML element. Absolute measurements are represented as strings containing a number and a suffix. Available units are:
    - Picas (1/12 inch), for example: `"2pi"`.
    - Points (1/72 inch), for example: `"12pt"`.
- Relative units are based on the value inherited from the enclosing HTML element. Relative measurements are represented as strings containing a number and a suffix. Available units are:
    - Em units: one em equals the current font size. For example, for a style with a font size of `"10pt"`, a measurement of `"2.5em"` would indicate 25 points.
    - Ex units: one ex equals the height of a lowercase "x" in the inherited font. (This "x-height" is a common unit of measure in the printing and typesetting trades.) For example, a measurement of `"3ex"` indicates a distance equal to three times the current x-height.
    - Percentages: for example, `"75%"` indicates a measurement relative to some other value. The specific function depends on the property, and is described in Part II of this manual.

Chapter 6: Windows, Documents & Graphics

- Pixel units express a distance as a number of pixels on the screen. The actual size of the result depends on the host computer. Netscape suggests a "reference pixel" size corresponding to one dot on a 90dpi screen, viewed at arm's length from the user. Pixel measurements are represented as strings containing a number and the suffix "px"; for example, "45px" to specify approximately $1/2$ inch.

Style Properties

Following is a complete list of all the properties that are available for style sheet objects. Remember that these properties are used in three different ways:

- For the `tags` object, assign them to `tags.`*`tagName`*, where *`tagName`* is the name of an existing HTML tag such as <H1>, <P>, etc. Assignments to `tags.body` apply to all tags. For example:

    ```
    tags.H1.color = "red"
    ```

- For the `classes` object, assign them to `classes.`*`className`*`.`*`tagName`*, where *`className`* is a user-defined class name, and tagName is the name of an existing HTML tag or `all`. For example:

    ```
    classes.ImportantItem.H1.color = "red"
    ```

- For the ids object, assign them to `ids.`*`styleID`*, where *`styleID`* is a user-defined name for the style. For example:

    ```
    ids.BigRedText.color = "red"
    ```

Font Properties

`fontFamily`	Font name: actual or generic.
`fontSize`	Number or keyword specifying text size.
`fontStyle`	Keyword specifying italics and/or small capitals.
`fontWeight`	Number or keyword specifying text "boldness."

Text Properties

`lineHeight`	Number or expression specifying line spacing.
`textAlign`	Keyword specifying horizontal position of text.
`textDecoration`	Keyword specifying underline, overline, overstrike, or blink.
`textIndent`	Number or expression specifying indentation for the first line of a paragraph.
`textTransform`	Keyword specifying capitalization.
`verticalAlign`	Keyword specifying vertical position of text.

Block-level Properties

In HTML, *block-level* elements are those that define a rectangular region on the screen, such as `<P>` for text or `<IMG>` for images. (Elements such as `<B>`, that can start and end in the middle of a line of text, are not block-level.) The properties listed below only apply to block-level elements:

`align`	Keyword specifying horizontal position (floating) of HTML object.
`borderBottomWidth,` `borderLeftWidth,` `borderRightWidth,` `borderTopWidth`	Number specifying the width of the border.
`borderColor`	Keyword specifying color of border.
`borderStyle`	Keyword specifying style of border.
`clear`	Keyword specifying whether floating objects may be positioned alongside this object.
`height`	Number or keyword specifying the height of the HTML object.
`marginBottom,` `marginLeft,` `marginRight,` `marginTop`	Number or expression specifying the spacing between HTML objects.
`paddingBottom,` `paddingLeft,` `paddingRight,` `paddingTop`	Number or expression specifying the spacing between HTML object content and border.
`width`	Number, expression, or keyword specifying the width of the HTML object.

Color & Background Properties

`color`	String specifying text color.
`backgroundImage`	String specifying URL of image file.
`backgroundColor`	String specifying background color.

Classification Properties

`display`	Keyword specifying how object is displayed.
`listStyleType`	Keyword specifying how objects are marked or numbered.
`whiteSpace`	Keyword specifying handling of white space characters.

Graphics

At this time, JavaScript does not have many built-in graphics operations. However, the use of a windowed, "graphical" user interface requires some awareness of graphics operations. Properties such as the size and position of windows, or the location where a mouse click occurred, are measured in horizontal and vertical coordinates from the top left corner of the screen. Increasing horizontal or X coordinates represent movement to the right; increasing vertical or Y coordinates represent movement downward. Measurements are specified in pixels, which means that the actual distance depends on the host computer's hardware and configuration. The built-in screen object allows scripts to find out the screen's height and width, and the maximum number of colors that can be displayed.

Color is an important part of web page design. JavaScript allows you to specify the color of several types of text and backgrounds. Colors are specified in two ways:

- By a string containing six hexadecimal digits, with an optional leading pound sign (#) character, in the form *rrggbb*, where *rr* specifies red, *gg* specifies green, and *bb* specifies blue.
- By a string containing one of the color name keywords listed in Appendix C.

For example:

"00ff00"	No red, maximum green, no blue
"#8000ff"	50% red, no green, maximum blue
"cornsilk"	Netscape keyword

More advanced graphic functions can be included in web pages with the help of embedded applets, and with graphic or video data that is viewed with the help of plug-ins. For more information on these, see Chapter 8.

The Image Object

The JavaScript Image object allows scripts to perform some basic operations on images stored in files. As mentioned above, Image objects are created automatically when Navigator encounters <IMG> tags in a document; these objects become properties of the document.images array. Also, scripts can create Image objects and assign them to variables with the new Image() constructor. These objects are not displayed on the screen. They can be loaded with images from files and later copied to other images that are in the document. This allows you to change an image quickly in response to user actions, without waiting for a file to be downloaded from a server. Also, you can create simple animation by rapidly sequencing through a series of images.

Image Maps

Images are also used to create image maps. Maps can be used to send queries to a server, if the `<IMG>` tag has the `ISMAP` attribute. With JavaScript, it is easy to create *client-side* maps that are processed entirely by the browser. For example, an image can be defined by HTML such as:

```
<IMG SRC="Eye-open.gif" WIDTH=100 HEIGHT=100 USEMAP="#myMap">
```

The `USEMAP` attribute makes this a client-side image map. It also specifies that the `<MAP>` element named `myMap` defines the map's format with one or more `<AREA>` tags such as:

```
<MAP NAME="myMap">
   <AREA NAME="topArea" COORDS="0,0,99,49"
   HREF="javascript:alert('top')">
   <AREA NAME="bottomArea" COORDS="0,50,99,99"
   HREF="javascript:alert('bottom')">
</MAP>
```

The JavaScript URLs in the `<AREA>` tags can perform any action that is useful to your application. In this simple example, they merely notify the user where the mouse click occurred.

Moving On

This chapter has described how JavaScript displays text and graphics to the user. The next chapter will cover features that allow the user to talk back to your scripts, as well as some other input/output operations.

Input / Output 7

This is one area where JavaScript is not rich in features—but that is appropriate for its intended use in web browsers. Too much freedom to read and write the host computer's files and devices could be a security hazard; indeed, it has been so several times recently, in well-publicized cases. As Internet security improves, more power will no doubt be added. Features such as digital signatures and embedded applets (see Chapter 8) already allow programmers to extend JavaScript's built-in functions.

One I/O technique that is not discussed in this chapter is writing to document objects. This is described in Chapter 6.

Dialogs

For simple communication with users, JavaScript provides several types of dialog boxes that can be used with a single statement. These dialogs are all available through methods of the `window` object, except `print()`, which is available for windows and frames.

alert(*message*) Creates an alert box that displays the specified string. The user must click the OK button to proceed.

`confirm(message)` — Creates a confirm box that displays the specified string and two buttons. Returns `true` if the user clicks OK, or `false` if the user clicks Cancel.

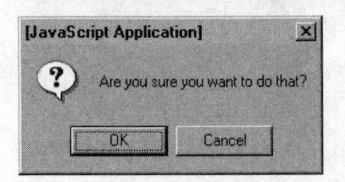

`prompt(message, default)` — Creates a dialog box that displays the specified string *message*, as well as a text box and two buttons. The *default* string is initially displayed and highlighted in the text box; the user may enter other text. If the user clicks OK, `prompt` returns a string containing the contents of the text box. If the user clicks Cancel, `prompt` returns `null`.

`find()` — This method is used to search for text in a window's document. If it is called with no arguments, it displays the same dialog box that Navigator presents when a user selects the Find menu option. The user can then specify the search parameters. `find()` returns `true` if it finds the specified text, `false` otherwise.

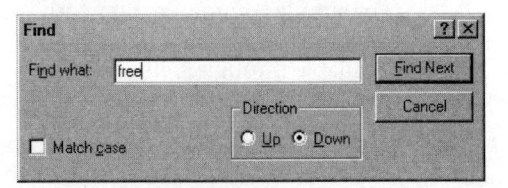

print()   This method allows a user to print text from a window or frame. It displays the same dialog box that Navigator presents when a user clicks the Print button on the toolbar.

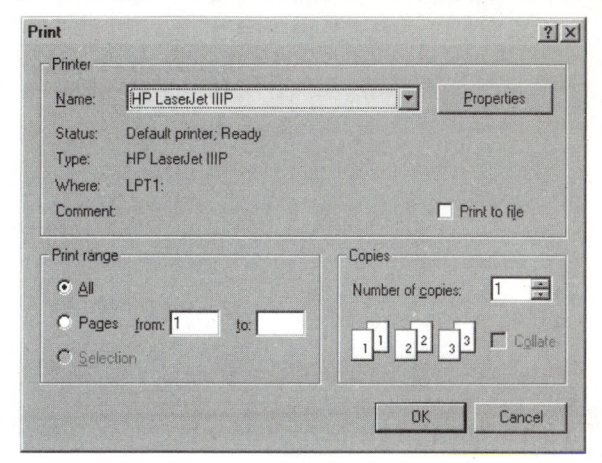

Forms

HTML forms are a very powerful way to interact with the user of a web page. Although they were originally intended for sending information to servers, the use of JavaScript allows the browser to manipulate forms without help from another computer.

When Navigator loads a web page, it creates Form objects corresponding to all HTML <FORM> tags. These objects are stored as elements of the document.forms array; so, for instance, the first form in a document would create forms[0]. If the <FORM> tag has a NAME attribute, the Form object can be referenced by its name as a property of document. For example, a form created by the tag:

<FORM NAME="userData">

can be referenced as document.userData.

A form contains interactive elements such as buttons and text boxes, which are created by HTML tags. Navigator creates objects for each type of form element. These objects are stored in the elements array, which is a property of the Form object, so they can be referenced as elements[0], elements[1], and so forth. If the elements' HTML tags have NAME attributes, the objects can be referenced by their names as properties of the form. For example, after loading this form:

```
<FORM NAME="userData">
   First name:  <INPUT TYPE="text" NAME="first"> <BR>
   Last name: <INPUT TYPE="text" NAME="last"> <BR>
   Address:
   <TEXTAREA NAME="addr" ROWS="4" COLS="32"></TEXTAREA> <P>
   <INPUT TYPE="button" NAME="btn" VALUE="Accept data"
      ONCLICK="processData(this.form)">
   <INPUT TYPE="reset" NAME="rst" VALUE="Start over">
</FORM>
```

which looks something like:

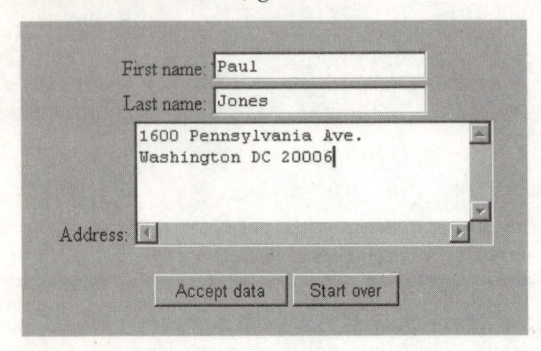

the first text box could be referenced by any one of the following expressions:

```
document.userData.first
document.userData.elements[0]
document.forms[0].first
document.forms[0].elements[0]
```

(The use of forms[0] assumes that this is the first form in the document.)

JavaScript in Forms

Form objects and all their properties and elements can be referenced by any statements in a script. Some properties of these objects are read-only, but many can be modified by a script. For instance, text boxes can be both read and written by scripts. Options can be added to or removed from a select box; additional `Option` objects can be created with the `new Option()` constructor.

The usual way to bring forms to life is with event handler attributes on HTML tags, which are strings containing JavaScript statements. In the preceding example, the first button has an `ONCLICK` event handler that calls a user-defined function. Note the use of the `this` object in the event handler. `this` returns a reference to the object being created: a Button in this case. Button objects, like all form elements, have a property called `form` that references the Form object that contains the element. So the expression `this.form` has the effect of passing the entire form as an argument to the function `processData()`.

`processData()` can manipulate the Form object and its elements. For example, it could contain statements such as:

```
function processData (fo) {
   ...
   fullName = fo.first.value + " " + fo.last.value
   ...
}
```

In this example, the function retrieves the first and last name typed by the user from the `value` properties of the two text boxes, and concatenates them with an intervening space to form a single string containing the user's full name. The properties could also be referenced explicitly, with expressions such as `document.userData.first.value`. The use of a Form object (passed by using `this` as explained previously) is more portable, allowing `processData()` to be called from several different forms.

Form Elements

The following table lists the types of objects that JavaScript creates to reflect form elements. Each object is described in detail in its listing in Part II of this manual.

Object type	HTML	Function	Appearance
Button	`<INPUT TYPE="button">`	Creates a button that the user can click.	Do something
Checkbox	`<INPUT TYPE="checkbox">`	Creates a check box that can be checked or unchecked.	☑ Check this out
FileUpload	`<INPUT TYPE="file">`	Creates a button and text window that allows the user to choose a file from the host computer's file system.	D:\DOWNLOAD\RT.HTM Browse...
Hidden	`<INPUT TYPE="hidden">`	Creates an element that is not visible on the screen, but whose value is passed to a server when the form is submitted.	None
Password	`<INPUT TYPE="password">`	Creates a text box that displays asterisks instead of the actual characters that the user types.	Password: ******
Radio	`<INPUT TYPE="radio">` (one for each button in a set)	Creates a set of check box–like "radio" buttons; when one is checked, all others in the set are unchecked.	⦿ A ○ B ○ C
Reset	`<INPUT TYPE="reset">`	Creates a button that resets all form elements to their initial states.	Reset
Select and Option	`<SELECT>` `<OPTION>` ... `<OPTION>` `</SELECT>`	Create a box containing a list of items; the user can select one, or more than one if the MULTIPLE attribute is specified.	Windows 3.1 / Windows 95/NT / Macintosh / Unix
Submit	`<INPUT TYPE="submit">`	Creates a button that submits the form to a server.	Send the form
Text	`<INPUT TYPE="text">`	Creates a box to hold a single line of text.	Last name: Jones
Textarea	`<TEXTAREA>` (initial text) `</TEXTAREA>`	Creates a multiline box to hold a large amount of text.	Address: 1600 Pennsylvania Ave. Washington, DC 20006

Event Handling

Event handling allows scripts to have very flexible responses to user interactions such as mouse clicks and key presses, as well as browser conditions such as errors. Event handlers can be assigned to objects by HTML attributes, as shown for the button in the previous example:

```
<INPUT TYPE="button" NAME="btn" VALUE="Accept data"
   ONCLICK="processData(this.form)">
```

Starting with JavaScript 1.1, event handlers can also be assigned by scripts. For instance, if you want a script to disable the above button, use statements such as:

```
function buttonOff() {
   alert("Sorry, button disabled.")
}
document.userData.btn.onclick = buttonOff
```

This defines a function buttonOff, and makes the function serve as an event handler by assigning it to the button's onclick property. Note that there are no parentheses after the name of the function, indicating that this is a reference to the function, not a call to it.

A more compact way to write this is by using the Function() constructor:

```
document.userData.btn.onclick
   = new Function("alert('Sorry, button disabled.')")
```

This syntax is useful for small functions that only have one caller.

Some event handlers can return a value that specifies what other actions the browser will take. For example, suppose the user clicks on a link which would normally cause the browser to load a new document, but the link's onclick handler is called first. If the handler returns false, the link will not be followed, and the new document will not be loaded. If the handler returns true, or does not return any value, the link will be followed. The descriptions of event handlers in Part II describe what function a returned value has for each type of event.

In some cases, one user action can produce several events. For instance, a single key press can result in calling onkeydown, onkeypress, and onkeyup event handlers, but the onkeypress handler is skipped if the onkeydown handler returns false.

Types of Events

The following table lists all the properties that are available to handle various types of events. Note that some events are not available in all versions of JavaScript. All the events are described in more detail in Part II of this manual, listed under the names of the handler properties (on---). Note that these properties' names are always lowercase in JavaScript, unlike HTML attributes which can use upper- or lowercase.

Event handler	Called when	Property of
onabort	The user stops loading of the image by clicking on a link or the browser's Stop button.	Image
onblur	The user moves focus away from an object.	Button, Checkbox, FileUpload, Frame, Layer, Password, Radio, Reset, Select, Submit, Text, Textarea, window
onchange	The user changes the contents of the form element.	FileUpload, Select, Text, Textarea
onclick	The user clicks a mouse button.	Button, Checkbox, document, Link, Radio, Reset, Submit
ondblclick	The user double-clicks a mouse button.	Button, Checkbox, document, FileUpload, Hidden, Link, Password, Radio, Reset, Select, Submit
ondragdrop	The user drags and drops objects onto a window.	window
onerror	An error occurs while loading a document or image.	Image, window
onfocus	The user moves focus onto an object.	Button, Checkbox, FileUpload, Frame, Layer, Password, Radio, Reset, Select, Submit, Text, Textarea, window
onkeydown	The user presses a key.	document, Image, Link, Text, Textarea
onkeypress	The user presses a key. Multiple events occur if the user holds the key down.	document, Image, Link, Text, Textarea
onkeydown	The user releases a key.	document, Image, Link, Text, Textarea
onload	The document body is completely loaded into the browser.	Frame, Image, Layer, window
onmousedown	The user presses a mouse button.	Button, document, Link
onmousemove	The user moves the mouse cursor.	none; enabled by event capturing (see below).
onmouseout	The user moves the mouse cursor out of an object's region on the screen.	Area, Layer, Link
onmouseover	The user moves the mouse cursor into an object's region of the screen.	Area, Layer, Link
onmouseup	The user releases a mouse button.	Button, document, Link
onmove	The user moves a window.	Frame, window
onreset	The user clicks a Reset button.	Form

Event handler	Called when	Property of
onresize	The user resizes a window.	Frame, window
onselect	The user selects (highlights) text in the form element.	Text, Textarea
onsubmit	The user clicks a Submit button.	Form
unload	The user exits a page (loads a new document).	Frame, window

The event Object

JavaScript can pass an event object (all lowercase) to event handlers, which contain a number of properties that provide detailed information about the event. This object is available in two ways. Event handler attributes of HTML tags can reference it by name, for example, ONCLICK="myHandler(event)".

Event handlers assigned to object properties can receive an event object as an argument. For example, this simple function, which could be useful for debugging, is written to accept an event object:

```
function reportEvent(ev) {
   alert("Event of type " + ev.type
   + " occurred at X=" + ev.pageX
   + ", Y=" + ev.pageY)
}
```

This function can be assigned to an object with a statement such as:

```
document.links[2].onclick = reportEvent
```

(Again, note that there are no parentheses after the name of reportEvent.)

When the user clicks the link, reportEvent( ) will be called and passed an event object that includes the X and Y coordinates where the click occurred.

Event handlers created by new Function( ) can also accept an event object. For example, this function simply saves the object for later use:

```
document.links[2].onclick = new Function("e",
   "saveEvent = e; return false")
```

The properties of the event object are listed as follows. Note that not all properties are used for all types of events.

type	A string specifying the type of event, such as "click".
target	The object to which the event was originally sent, in case of capturing.
layerX, layerY	Horizontal and vertical cursor position within the document layer where the event occurred.
which	Number specifying the mouse button or key that was pressed.

`modifiers`	A bit mask specifying modifier keys that were pressed when a mouse or keyboard event occurred. Bits may be tested with the built-in values `ALT_MASK`, `CONTROL_MASK`, `SHIFT_MASK`, and `META_MASK`, which are properties of the `Event` object.
`data`	An array of strings containing URLs of objects that were dragged and dropped.
`pageX, pageY`	Horizontal and vertical cursor position within the web page where the event occurred.
`screenX, screenY`	Horizontal and vertical cursor position within the computer screen where the event occurred.
`width, height`	Width and height of the window after resizing.

Event Capturing

Event capturing allows a script to handle events that would otherwise be handled by a different object's handler. To capture this event takes two steps:

- Call `captureEvents( )` to enable capturing.
- Assign a function as a handler for the event.

For example, clicks on the right mouse button are normally handled by Navigator, which pops up a menu of options. You can capture this event with the statement:

```
window.captureEvents(Event.MOUSEDOWN)
```

This call uses `Event.MOUSEDOWN` (see below) to specify the type of event that is being captured. Next, assign a function with a statement such as:

```
window.onmousedown = myClick
```

The function `myClick` will now be called for all mouse clicks that occur in this window. But we only wanted to capture right-button clicks; we want left clicks to be processed in the normal manner. This can be managed inside the handler:

```
function mymouse(ev) {
   if (ev.which == 1) {
      return (routeEvent(ev))
   }
   else
// If we get here, it's a right click
   ...
}
```

The function receives an `event` object in the argument `ev`. It checks `ev.which`, which will contain 1 for the left button, or 3 for the right.

After an event has been captured, the handler has several options. It can call routeEvent( ), as shown previously, and pass the event object on to its intended target or to any other handlers that may be capturing this type of event. A handler can also call handleEvent( ), to explicitly pass the event to any object that has a handler for it.

As mentioned earlier, the value returned by an event handler has an effect on what happens next. A handler that calls routeEvent( ) or handleEvent( ) may need to save the value that these functions return, and return that value when it exits.

The Event Object

The Event object (do not confuse this with the all-lowercase event) serves as a holder for some read-only properties. These properties return values that are used as bit masks in event handling. Some of these properties are used to specify event types in calls to captureEvents( ) and releaseEvents( ), as shown above. To capture several types of events, combine the bit masks with the logical OR operator, as in:

captureEvents(Event.CLICK | Event.DBLCLICK
 | Event.DRAGDROP)

The values that may be used for this purpose are listed below:

Name	Used by	Meaning
ABORT	images	Transfer interrupted by the user.
BLUR	windows, frames, and all form elements	Focus removed from an object.
CHANGE	FileUpload, text, text area, and select box form elements	User changed the contents or settings of the element.
CLICK	all button form elements, documents, links	Single mouse click.
DBLCLICK	documents, links	Double mouse click.
DRAGDROP	windows	Object(s) dragged and dropped.
ERROR	windows, images	Error occurred during loading of image or document.
FOCUS	windows, frames, and all form elements	Focus applied to an object.
KEYDOWN	documents, images, links, text area form elements	Key pressed by user.
KEYPRESS	documents, images, links, text area form elements	Key pressed or held by user.
KEYUP	documents, images, links, text area form elements	Key released by user.

Name	Used by	Meaning
LOAD	document	Page loaded by Navigator.
MOUSEDOWN	all button form elements, documents, links	Mouse button pressed by user.
MOUSEMOVE	normally none; can be captured	Mouse cursor moved by user.
MOUSEOUT	links, document layers	Mouse cursor moved away from object.
MOUSEOVER	links, document layers	Mouse cursor moved onto an object.
MOUSEUP	all button form elements, documents, links	Mouse button released.
MOVE	windows and frames	Window or frame moved on the screen.
RESET	forms	Reset button clicked.
RESIZE	windows and frames	Window or frame resized.
SELECT	text, text area, and select box form elements	Element selected by user.
SUBMIT	forms	Submit button clicked.
UNLOAD	documents	Window closed, or a new document loaded.

Event also has properties that are used as bit masks to test the `event.modifiers` property, in order to determine what modifier keys were pressed when an event occurred. These masks are used with logical AND operations, such as:

```
if (event.modifiers & Event.ALT_MASK) {
   ...            // Alt key was pressed
}
```

The available properties for this use are listed as follows.

Name	Meaning
ALT_MASK	Alt key was pressed.
CONTROL_MASK	Ctrl key was pressed.
META_MASK	Meta key was pressed.
SHIFT_MASK	Shift key was pressed.

Cookies

A browser *cookie* is a small amount of information stored in a file on the host computer. Cookies allow a web page to store some information that will persist on the user's computer after it exits from the page. Since the amount of data is small, and it can only be used in certain restricted ways, it does not pose a security hazard.

A cookie is a string whose most basic form is:

`"name = value"`

It may have additional components separated by semicolons:

`"name =value;EXPIRES = date;DOMAIN = host;PATH = pathname;SECURE"`

The `name` and `value` fields may be any user-defined strings. They must not contain reserved characters such as semicolon (;). If necessary, use the `escape( )` and `unescape( )` functions to make sure these characters are not present. The `date` string should be in the standard format returned by JavaScript `Date` objects, such as "12-31-1999 23:59:59".

The `DOMAIN` field is optional. If present, it specifies the server and/or domain of the web page that uses the cookie. The `PATH` field is also optional. If present, it specifies the pathname (on the server from which the document was loaded) of the web page that uses the cookie.

Both `DOMAIN` and `PATH` may be partially specified. For instance, if the `DOMAIN` field's value is `myCompany.com`, the cookie can be used by web pages from `www.myCompany.com`, `retail.myCompany.com`, and so forth. Similarly, if `PATH` contains `/user`, the cookie can be used by web pages from `/user/tom`, `/user/sarah`, and so forth.

The `SECURE` field is optional. If it is present, the cookie may only be sent if the connection is secure (HTTPS protocol).

Navigator will allow up to 20 cookies to be defined for each server or domain, and up to 300 cookies for all URLs. The maximum length of a cookie is 4000 bytes. If a script or server attempts to create a cookie longer than that, it will be truncated, but the name will remain intact if it is less than 4000 bytes long.

The `cookie` Property

JavaScript provides a `cookie` property for `document` objects. (For a `document` in a layer, this property is equivalent to the enclosing window or frame's `document.cookie`.) It returns a string containing the *name* and *value* portions of all cookies associated with the URL from which a document was loaded.

Scripts can create cookies by appending them to `cookie` with statements such as:

```
document.cookie +=
   "newCookie=something;expires 01-01-2001"
```

Actually, the `+=` operator is optional, because `cookie` does not behave like a normal string. You can write:

```
document.cookie = "anotherCookie=somethingElse"
```

and the effect will be to append the string to `cookie`, even though the `=` operator was used. Continuing the above example, the statement:

```
document.cookie = "anotherCookie=aThirdValue"
```

changes the *value* of `anotherCookie` without affecting any other cookies in the document. To delete a cookie, set its value to empty, and its expiration date to something earlier than the current time, as in:

```
document.cookie = "oldCookie=;expires=01-Jan-90"
```

Moving On

We have now discussed all of JavaScript's functions for manipulating data and communicating with the user. In the last chapter of Part I, we will look at some features that are specifically related to web browsers.

The Navigator Environment 8

This chapter discusses some features of JavaScript that are specifically related to Netscape Navigator.

Navigator Objects

There are several types of built-in objects that allow scripts to get information about the browser. Navigator creates numerous types of objects to reflect the contents of web pages. Many of these are *external* objects; that is, they cannot be constructed with the new operator. External objects are discussed in Chapter 5, and described in detail in Part II of this manual.

The built-in navigator object has a number of properties that provide information about the browser, as follows:

appCodeName	Returns the internal or "code name" of the browser.
appName	Returns the "official" name of the browser.
appVersion	Returns version, platform, and language/country information about the browser.
language	Returns a string identifying the browser's language.
mimeTypes	An array of MimeType objects that identify all the Multipurpose Internet Mail Extensions (MIME) data types that the browser supports.
platform	Returns a string identifying the browser's platform.
plugins	An array of Plugin objects that identify all plug-ins installed in the browser.
userAgent	Returns a string identifying the browser, which is sent to servers as part of HyperText Transfer Protocol (HTTP) data requests.

The `navigator` object also has several methods:

`javaEnabled()`	Returns `true` if the browser is able to run Java applets.
`preference()`	Reads and sets various preferences, equivalent to settings in Navigator's Preferences dialog.
`taintEnabled()`	Returns `true` if data tainting is enabled.

The built-in `screen` object has properties that provide information about the display screen of the user's computer, as follows:

`availHeight`	The height of the screen, in pixels, not counting any permanent or semi-permanent features, such as a taskbar.
`availWidth`	The width of the screen, in pixels, not counting any permanent or semi-permanent features, such as a scroll bar.
`height`	The height of the complete screen, in pixels.
`width`	The width of the complete screen, in pixels.
`pixelDepth`	The number of bits per pixel in the display device.
`colorDepth`	The maximum number of colors that can be displayed, based on hardware and/or operating system limits.

LiveConnect

LiveConnect is Netscape's name for a set of features that allow scripts to interact with Java applets and plug-ins. To use LiveConnect, the browser must have both Java and JavaScript enabled in the Preferences dialog. A complete understanding of LiveConnect requires expertise with the Java language. This section will describe some of the basic features, requiring some use of Java terminology.

Accessing Java Applets From JavaScript

LiveConnect allows scripts to read and write objects in applets and call their functions and methods by using the appropriate syntax. Specifically, scripts can access all `public` variables declared in an applet, and its ancestor classes and packages. Also, scripts can access static methods and properties declared in an applet as properties and methods of the Applet object.

For example, an applet that displays graphs can be embedded in a web page by HTML such as:

```
<APPLET NAME="showGraph" CODE="graph.class" WIDTH=400 HEIGHT=200>
```

This creates an Applet object that scripts can reference by its name, `document.showGraph`, or as an element of the `document.applets` array. If the applet contains a method called `draw()`, a script can call it with a statement such as:

```
document.showGraph.draw(myData)
```

where `myData` is some JavaScript variable, perhaps an array, containing data to be displayed.

Navigator contains a built-in object called `Packages`, which serves as a holder for Java packages; you can reference them as properties of `Packages`. There are built-in packages named `java` and `netscape`; since these are commonly used, you can reference them without using `Package`. For instance, `java.lang.System` is equivalent to `Packages.java.lang.System`. Scripts can write to the Java console (see below) by referencing `java.lang.System.out`.

When passing JavaScript data to applets, the following type conversion rules apply:

- Strings, numbers, and Boolean values are converted to the corresponding Java type.
- Objects that are wrappers around Java objects are unwrapped.
- Other objects are wrapped with `JSObject`.

Accessing JavaScript From Java Applets

From the Java side, similar capabilities exist, but the syntax is different. The `netscape` package includes a class, `netscape.javascript.JSObject`, that is used as a wrapper when Java applets reference JavaScript objects. Applets can use the static method `JSObject.getWindow()` to get access to a JavaScript window. Other `JSObject` methods, such as `getMember()`, `setMember()`, and `call()`, allow an applet to read and write JavaScript objects and call JavaScript functions and methods. There is also a class, `netscape.plugin.Plugin`, with methods that allow an applet to access plug-in applications.

When passing Java data to scripts, the following type conversion rules apply:

- Java `byte`, `char`, `short`, `int`, `long`, `float`, and `double` values are converted to numbers.
- Java Boolean values are converted to JavaScript Boolean values.
- Java arrays are converted to a "pseudo-array" object that behaves like the JavaScript `Array`.
- An object of class `JSObject` is converted to the original JavaScript object.
- An object of any other class is converted to a wrapper, which scripts can use to access methods and properties of the original object. If a script converts the object to a string, number, or Boolean, the original object's `toString()`, `floatValue()`, or `booleanValue()` method will be called.

The Java Console

The Java Console is a window that Java applets use to send simple text messages to the user. It is a descendant of the teletype-style consoles that were widely used on computers before graphic displays became commonplace. Java applets reference it as `System.out`, so scripts can reference it as `java.lang.System.out`. A script can write a message to the console with a statement such as:

`java.lang.System.out.println("Hello from JavaScript.")`

To see the Java Console, select it by pulling down the appropriate menu option. (In Navigator version 4, the Show Java Console option is on the Communicator menu.)

Security

As use of the Internet becomes more widespread, data security has become an increasingly important issue. JavaScript has taken two different approaches to this.

Data Tainting

Data tainting is a feature that was introduced in JavaScript 1.1, but removed in version 1.2, when object signing provided a more powerful security system. It allows the user to prevent JavaScript data from being passed to a server other than the one from which a web page was originally loaded.

When data tainting is not enabled, scripts cannot access data from a different server. When tainting is enabled, an object's value can be marked or *tainted* by the built-in `taint()` function. If a script tries to pass a tainted object to a different server, Navigator will display a dialog box asking the user's permission for the transfer.

If a tainted value is used in a calculation, the result will also be tainted. If a tainted value is used as an argument to a function or method, the returned value will be tainted. If a script uses a tainted value in an `if`, `for`, or `while` statement, the script itself becomes tainted.

Some object properties are initially tainted by default, as follows:

Object	Properties
document	cookie, domain, forms, lastModified, links, referrer, title, URL
Form	action
Checkbox, Radio	checked, defaultChecked, name, value
Password, Text, Textarea	defaultValue, name, value
Select	name, options.selectedIndex, value
Option	defaultSelected, selected, text, value
All form elements	name, value
location, Link	hash, host, hostname, href, pathname, port, protocol, search
window	defaultStatus, status

Tainting is enabled or disabled by a host computer environment variable named `NSENABLE_TAINT`. The way to set this variable depends on the platform:
- On UNIX platforms, use the `setenv` shell command.
- On Windows platforms, use a `set` statement in the `AUTOEXEC.BAT` file, or Windows NT user settings.
- On Macintosh platforms, edit the application resource with type `Envi` and number 128 by removing the `//` comment marker before the `NS_ENABLE_TAINT` text.

The variable can be set to any value; Netscape suggests "1."

Scripts can use the `navigator.taintEnabled()` method to determine whether tainting is enabled. When tainting is enabled, scripts can use the `taint()` and `untaint()` functions to control tainting.

Object Signing

Object signing is a powerful security tool that was introduced in JavaScript 1.2. It allows a script to obtain privileges to perform restricted operations if a *digital signature* has been attached to the script.

A digital signature allows the user to be certain that the identity of a script's author is known and that the script has not been tampered with since it was signed. A signature is packaged in a file called a *certificate*, which guarantees the identity of the person or organization that owns the signature. Certificates are issued by *certificate authorities* (CAs), which are trusted third-party organizations, including a number of telephone companies and government postal services, as well as private businesses around the world.

If you display Navigator's Security Information window, you can see lists of certificates that may already be installed in your browser. There is a Get a Certificate option that can direct you to the web sites of some CAs, in order to obtain a certificate of your own.

You can attach signatures to scripts in web pages, as well as to those stored in separate files, and to any other type of downloadable file. To create signed scripts, you will need a certificate of your own, as well as a copy of the certificate of the CA that issued your certificate. You will also need a software tool to sign scripts, and one for managing Java archive (JAR) files. Netscape provides a JAR Packager, a Page Signer, and several other utilities to help you create and manage signed scripts. You can download these tools, and additional documentation, from Netscape's web site.

Writing Signed Scripts

Signatures must be stored in a JAR file before they can be used to sign objects. To create a signed script in a web page, add `ARCHIVE` and `ID` attributes to the `<SCRIPT>` tag, as in:

```
<SCRIPT ARCHIVE="myJar.jar" ID="sigName">
   ...
</SCRIPT>
```

The `ARCHIVE` attribute specifies the name of the JAR file in which the signature is stored. The `ID` attribute specifies a string which is the name assigned to the signature. If there is more than one signed script in the web page, and all the signatures come from the same JAR file, you only need to specify the `ARCHIVE` for the first script.

Signatures may also be attached to scripts that are stored in separate files, as in:

```
<SCRIPT SRC="aScript.js" ARCHIVE="myJar.jar">
```

In this case, the `ID` attribute is not needed.

Your web page may contain short scripts in the event handler attributes of various HTML tags, for which you cannot specify an `ARCHIVE` and `ID`. These scripts use the signature that was specified in the previous `<SCRIPT>`. For example, if a script is followed by a form, as in:

```
<SCRIPT ARCHIVE="myJar.jar" ID="someSig">
   ...
</SCRIPT>

...

<FORM>
   ...
   <INPUT TYPE="button" VALUE="Secure operation"
      ONCLICK="doSecure()">
</FORM>
```

then the button's `ONCLICK` handler has the same signature as the `<SCRIPT>` tag.

Privileges

Signed scripts have abilities to read and write several types of data that are normally restricted. These operations are divided into categories called *targets*. A script requests a privilege with the statement:

```
netscape.security.PrivilegeManager.enablePrivilege(target)
```

where `target` is one of the strings described below. If there is more than one script in a web page, privileges must be enabled by each script that needs them.

"UniversalBrowserRead"
This privilege allows reading restricted browser data. The actions allowed by this privilege are:
- Reading properties of the `history` object.
- Reading the `event.data` property after a drag-and-drop event.
- Using an `"about:"` URL.

"UniversalBrowserWrite"
This privilege allows writing restricted browser data. The actions allowed by this privilege are:
- Writing properties of the `event` object.
- Hiding or displaying a `window`'s scroll bars, toolbar, location bar, menu bar, personal toolbar (directory bar), or status bar.
- Calling the `window.enableExternalCapture()` method.
- Calling `window.close()` without asking the user for confirmation.
- Using `window.moveBy()` or `moveTo()` to move a window off the screen.
- Using `window.open()` to create a window that is:
    - off the screen.
    - larger than the screen.
    - smaller than 100 x 100 pixels.
    - has no title bar.
    - has the `AlwaysRaised`, `AlwaysLowered`, or `z-lock` features.
- Using the `window.resizeBy()` or `resizeTo()` methods, or the `innerHeight` or `innerWidth` properties, to make a window larger than the screen, off the screen, or smaller than 100 x 100 pixels.

"UniversalFileRead"
This privilege allows writing the `value` property of a FileUpload object, so that scripts can select files without the user's help.

"UniversalPreferencesRead"
This privilege allows reading user preferences with the `navigator.preference()` method.

"UniversalPreferencesWrite"
This privilege allows writing user preferences with the `navigator.preference()` method.

"UniversalSendMail"
This privilege allows the script to send mail from the user's e-mail address. This can be done by submitting a form to a `mailto:` or `news:` URL.

Using Privileges Without a Signature

There are times, such as during debugging, when it is useful to test the privileged features of signed scripts without generating signatures for them. You can allow this by modifying the Navigator preference file. The exact location of this file depends on the platform and version of Navigator. Common locations for the file are listed below:

- On Windows, the file is: \Program Files\Netscape\Users\default\prefs.js.
- On Windows NT, the file is: \Netscape\Users\username\prefs.js.
- On UNIX, the file is: ~/.netscape/preferences.js.
- On the Macintosh, the file is: System Folder:Preferences:Netscape f: (where the last f is a special script f character).

Make sure that Navigator is not running, and add the following line to the preference file:

user_pref("signed.applets.codebase_principal_support", true);

Once this is done, scripts without signatures can request privileges. The scripts do not need to have the ARCHIVE or ID attributes. When a script requests a privilege, the browser will display a dialog box allowing the user to decide whether or not to grant the privilege.

You should use this feature with caution. It is recommended for debugging or private usage only; when you publish a script that uses privileges, it should be signed.

export & import

Although scripts can read and write other scripts' data, signed scripts are normally prohibited from sharing data with scripts that are not protected by the same signature. To overcome this restriction, a script can use the export statement to make objects, properties, and functions available to other scripts. For example, the statement:

export a, b.p1, b.p2, myFunc

will make available one object, two properties, and one function. Note that there are no parentheses after the function name, since this is a reference, not a call. You can also write export * to make all objects, properties, and functions available.

In order to use the exported items, a script must request them with a corresponding import statement such as:

import a, b.*, myFunc

Note the use of b.*, a shortcut that requests all properties and methods of b.

Plug-ins & MIME Types

Plug-ins are "helper" applications that allow a browser to display or work with types of data that are not explicitly supported by HTML. The HTML <EMBED> tag is used to include files in a web page, and to specify the type of data that they contain. If the browser has an installed plug-in that supports the data type, the plug-in is assigned the job of handling the file. If a plug-in is not available, the browser displays a dialog box asking the user what to do with the file.

There is some confusion among users about the meaning of the term plug-in. Many people use the term to mean the embedded files. Strictly speaking, though, it refers to the applications, not the files; and that is how the term is used throughout this manual.

When Navigator loads a web page, it creates Embed objects corresponding to all <EMBED> tags in the document. These objects may have additional properties and methods for interfacing with the plug-in. For instance, if a Musical Instrument Digital Interface (MIDI) file is embedded in a web page by HTML such as:

```
<EMBED SRC="test.mid" HEIGHT=80 WIDTH=160>
```

then playback of the file can be started by a statement such as:

```
document.embeds[0].play( )
```

The reference to `embeds[0]` assumes that the MIDI file is the first, or only, embedded file in the document.

All of the MIME data types that the browser supports are reflected as properties of the `navigator.mimeTypes` object. Each property is a MimeType object, which has properties that return information such as a description of the data, and the filename suffixes (extensions) that indicate data of this type.

All installed plug-ins are reflected as elements of the `navigator.plugins` array. Each element is a Plugin object, which has properties that return information such as a description of the plug-in and a list of MIME types that it supports.

For more details on MimeType and Plugin objects, see Part II of this manual.

Moving On

These chapters have presented an overview of JavaScript's syntax and features. Part II of this manual is a "dictionary" of every built-in object, property, method, and function in the language. In Part II, you will find detailed descriptions, more examples, and cross-references to help you find related items.

JavaScript Reference

11

JavaScript Reference

This section of the book gives a description of every built-in object, method, property, function, and variable in Netscape Navigator's implementation of JavaScript. The entries in this section are in alphabetical order for quick reference. Each item includes some or all of the following information:

- Item name.
- Icons to denote JavaScript versions that support the item, as well as special attributes such as read-only, limited scope, etc.
- What it is (object, method, etc.) and, for a property or method, its owner.
- What it does: the value it returns, action it performs, HTML object it reflects, etc.
- Syntax notation that describes how it is used in scripts.
- Descriptions of properties, methods, and other attributes or features.
- List of event handlers, if any.
- Discussion or notes on any additional points.
- Example of usage in a script.

Syntax Notation

In the Syntax descriptions, the following conventions are used:

- Text in `this font` must be typed exactly as it appears. For example:

    `navigator.appName`

    is the name of a property.

- Text in `*this font*` represents items for which you will substitute your own names or expressions. For example, the notation:

    `Math.Abs(*number*)`

    means that `Math.Abs` and the parentheses must be typed as shown, but `*number*` can be any numeric value, variable, expression, function that returns a value, etc.

$', $&, $*, $_, $`, $+

Version 1.2

Properties of the RegExp constructor

These names are abbreviations for properties of RegExp:

RegExp.$'   is equivalent to RegExp.rightContext.
RegExp.$&   is equivalent to RegExp.lastMatch.
RegExp.$*   is equivalent to RegExp.multiline.
RegExp.$_   is equivalent to RegExp.input.
RegExp.$`   is equivalent to RegExp.leftContext. Note the accent grave character, not apostrophe.
RegExp.$+   is equivalent to RegExp.lastParen.

Each of these properties is listed elsewhere in this manual by its full name. For more about regular expressions, see Chapter 3.

Note that these are properties of the constructor, that is, of RegExp itself, not of objects created by new RegExp(). That means that they are shared by all scripts running in a window. If there are several scripts in one window that use regular expressions, they may affect each other's results.

See Also   RegExp

$1, $2, ... $9

Version 1.2   **Read-only**

Properties of the RegExp constructor

Return the values memorized when a pattern from a RegExp object is matched.

Syntax   RegExp.$1
RegExp.$2
.
.
.
RegExp.$9

Discussion   Memorized values are selected by enclosing parts of a pattern in parentheses. (For details on regular expressions, see Chapter 3.)

Example   The following code will extract a telephone number from a string by memorizing groups of 3, 3, and 4 digits, while ignoring any spaces or punctuation:

```
var s = someStringValue
var p = /(\d{3})\D*(\d{3})\D*(\d{4})/

s.match(p)
areaCode = RegExp.$1
exchange = RegExp.$2
last4Digits = RegExp.$3
```

See Also   RegExp

ABORT

Version 1.2   Read-only

Property of the Event object

Returns a mask for capturing abort events.

Syntax   `Event.ABORT`

Discussion   This property is used to capture and release abort events, which occur when the user interrupts the loading of an image or document. For more details on event handling, see Chapter 7.

Example   To enable capturing of abort events:

`myWindow.captureEvents (Event.ABORT)`

See Also   `captureEvents(), event, Event, onabort, releaseEvents()`

above

Version 1.2   Read-only

Property of the Layer object

Returns the layer immediately above the specified layer.

Syntax	`layerObject.above`
	`layerObject` `document.layerName`, or an expression denoting a `Layer` object.
Properties	Since `above` returns a reference to a `Layerobject`, it has all the properties, methods, and event handlers of the referenced layer.
Discussion	This property returns the layer that is immediately above the specified one in the z-index order. The z-index order is used to position layers, and is initially set by the `Z-INDEX` attribute of the `<LAYER>` tag. A low number indicates a low position in the order; in an area where two layers overlap, the one with the higher z-index is displayed.
	If the `Layer` object has no layer above it in the z-index order, the property returns a reference to the enclosing `window` or Frame object. Note that this property may return a parent or child layer; the `siblingAbove` property can be used to access only sibling layers.
	This is a read-only property. To modify the z-index ordering of layers, use the `zIndex` property, or the `moveAbove()` or `moveBelow()` methods.
Examples	This statement causes the layer above `layer1` to become invisible:
	`layer1.above.visibility = "hide"`
	This statement obtains a reference to the layer two layers above `myLayer`:
	`twoUpLayer = MyLayer.above.above`
See Also	`below`, `Layer`, `siblingAbove`, `siblingBelow`, `zIndex`

abs( )

Version 1.0

Method of the Math object

Returns the absolute value of a number.

Syntax	`Math.abs(number)`
	`number` The number whose absolute value is to be returned.
Example	`a = Math.abs(x)`
See Also	`Math`

acos( )

Version 1.0

Method of the Math object

Returns the arc cosine of a number.

Syntax   `Math.acos(number)`
`number`   The value whose arc cosine is to be returned.

Discussion   `acos` returns a value between zero and π if the `number` argument is in the range of –1 to 1. If `number` is outside this range, `acos` returns zero.

Example   `theta = Math.acos(x)`

See Also   `asin()`, `atan()`, `atan2()`, `cos()`, `Math`, `sin()`, `tan()`

action

Version 1.0   External   Tainted

Property of the Form external object

Specifies the destination URL for submitting a form.

Syntax   `formObject.action`
`formObject`   A form name, or an expression denoting a Form object.

Discussion   Initially, this property reflects the `ACTION` attribute of an HTML `<FORM>` tag. However, your scripts can modify the value.

Example   `document.form1.action = "http://www.mySite.com/myCGI.pl"`

See Also   Form

alert( )

Version 1.0

Method of the `window` object

Displays a JavaScript alert box on the screen.

Syntax
: `alert(message)`

  message   String value representing a message to be displayed.

Discussion
: `alert` causes the specified message to be displayed in an alert dialog box on the screen. The box includes an OK button. Execution of the script is suspended until the user presses the button. `alert` only accepts one argument, so to display a long message made of several strings, you must concatenate them using the + operator, as follows.

Example
: `alert("There are " + itemCount + " items.")`

![JavaScript Application dialog: There are 42 items. OK]

See Also
: `window`, Frame

align

Version 1.2

Property of style sheet objects

Specifies the alignment of floating HTML elements.

Syntax
: `styleObj.align`

  styleObj   Style sheet object: a property of a `classes`, `ids`, or `tags` object.

Discussion
: This property specifies which way the element moves when it is allowed to float, that is, when other elements are allowed to wrap around it. This property is most often used for images.

The value of align may be "left", "right", or "none". If it is "left" or "right", the element floats to the specified margin, and is handled as a block-level element.

This property applies to all elements, and is not inherited. Its initial value is "none".

Note that for align assignments to take effect, they must occur before the browser writes the styled text to the document. An assignment to tags.body.align must be done within the <HEAD> ... </HEAD> section of the HTML.

Example
document.ids.pictureFrame.align = "right"

See Also
classes, clear, ids, tags

alinkColor

Version 1.0

Property of the document object

Specifies the color in which an active link is displayed.

Syntax
docObject.alinkColor

docObject   document for the current window's document, or an expression denoting a document object.

Discussion
This property may be set to a string of six hexadecimal digits, with an optional leading pound sign (#) character, in the form rrggbb, where rr specifies red, gg specifies green, and bb specifies blue. alinkColor may also be set to one of the color names listed in Appendix C. The returned value is always in hexadecimal with a leading #.

This property is initially set to the color specified by the ALINK attribute, if any, of the HTML <BODY> tag.

Examples
```
document.alinkColor = "00ff00"    // no red
                                  // max. green
                                  // no blue

parent.document.alinkColor = "#8000ff"    // 50% red
                                          // no green
                                          // max. blue

otherWindow.document.alinkColor
    = "cornsilk"                          // Netscape keyword
```

See Also
linkColor, vlinkColor, document

ALT_MASK

Version 1.0 Read-only

Property of the Event object

Returns a mask for checking if the Alt key was pressed during an event.

Syntax   `Event.ALT_MASK`

Discussion   This property is a bit mask for testing the `event.modifiers` property to find out if the Alt key was pressed when the event occurred.

Example   The following statements could be used in an event handler:

```
if (myEvent.modifiers & Event.ALT_MASK) {
    ...     // the Alt key was pressed
}
else
    ...     // Alt was not pressed
```

See Also   `event`, `Event`

anchor( )

Version 1.0

Method of the String object

Returns a string containing HTML code for a named anchor.

Syntax   `stringObj.anchor(name)`

     `stringObj`   String object or expression to be formatted as an anchor.
     `name`   String value representing a name for the anchor.

Discussion   This method returns a string consisting of HTML code. The code includes the HTML `<A>` and `</A>` tags so that, if the returned string is written to a document, it will appear as an anchor with a name that can be referenced by links.

Example The following statements:

```
var s = "Welcome to My Page"
var a = s.anchor("TopOfPage")
```

will set the value of a to:

`<A NAME="TopOfPage">Welcome to My Page</A>`

See Also anchors, Anchor, String

Anchor

Version 1.0   Read-only   External

External object

Reflects one named anchor in the HTML document. Anchors are named if the HTML `<A>` tag includes a NAME attribute.

Syntax
```
docObject.anchors.name
docObject.anchors[index]
```

docObject	document for the current window's document, or an expression denoting a document object in any window.
index	A numeric or string value specifying one of the elements of the anchors array.
name	An anchor's name.

Properties

name	String specifying the anchor name.
x	Number specifying the horizontal position of the anchor on the screen relative to the left side of the document.
y	Number specifying the vertical position of the anchor on the screen relative to the top of the document.

Discussion When Navigator loads a web page, it creates Anchor objects corresponding to all named anchors, that is, HTML `<A>` tags that have a NAME attribute. You can reference these objects as elements or properties of a document object's anchors array.

HTML anchors are also reflected by Link objects, which are stored in the links array. These objects have additional properties not available with the Anchor object.

Example An Anchor object defined by HTML such as:

```
<A NAME="link1" HREF="somewhere.html">
   Click to go somewhere
</A>
```

can be referenced with statements such as:

```
document.write("The first anchor in this document
   is named \"", document.anchors[0].name, "\". <BR>")
```

See Also anchor( ), anchors, links, Link

anchors

Version 1.0 Read-only External

Property of the document object

Reflects all named anchors in the HTML document.

Syntax `docObject.anchors`

    `docObject` document for the current window's document, or an expression denoting a document object in any window.

Properties `length` Number of elements in the array; also the number of named anchors in the reflected HTML.

Discussion Each element of the array is an Anchor external object (described above). One of these objects is created for each `<A>` tag that has a `NAME` attribute.

Example
```
document.write("There are ", document.anchors.length, " named anchors
   in this document. <BR>")
```

See Also anchor( ), Anchor, document

appCodeName

Version 1.0   Read-only

Property of the `navigator` object

A string value that reflects the code name of the browser.

Syntax
: `navigator.appCodeName`

Discussion
: This property gives the internal or "code name" of the browser program that is running the script. Its value is `"Mozilla"` for Navigator versions 2, 3, and 4.

Example
: `document.write("Your browser's code name is \"", navigator.appCodeName, "\".<P>")`

See Also
: `appName`, `appVersion`, `navigator`

Applet

Version 1.0   Read-only   External

External object

Reflects a Java applet embedded in the web page by the HTML `<APPLET>` tag.

Syntax
: `docObject.applets.name`
  `docObject.applets[index]`

`docObject`	document for the current window's document, or an expression denoting a `document` object in any window.
`name`	An applet's name.
`index`	A numeric or string expression specifying one of the elements of the `applets` array.

Properties
: All public properties of the applet can be referenced by scripts.

Discussion	When Navigator loads a web page, it creates Applet objects corresponding to all HTML <APPLET> tags. You can reference these objects as elements or properties of a document object's applets array. For more information on interacting with applets, see Chapter 8.

Example	An applet that draws graphs could be included in a web page with HTML such as:
	
	`<APPLET NAME="drawGraph" CODE="draw.class" WIDTH=400 HEIGHT=200`
	`   MAYSCRIPT>`
	`</APPLET>`
	
	An array of data could be passed to a method in the applet called display by a statement such as:
	
	`document.drawGraph.display(myArray)`

See Also	applets, MimeType, Plugin

applets

Version 1.0   Read-only

Property of the document object

Reflects all applets in the HTML document.

Syntax	docObject.applets	
	docObject	document for the current window's document, or an expression denoting a document object in any window.
Properties	length	Number of elements in the array (also the number of anchors in the reflected HTML).
Discussion	Each element of the array is an Applet external object (described earlier).	
Example	`document.write("This web page contains ", document.applets.length, "` `   applets.  ")`	
See Also	Applet, document	

appName

Version 1.0   Read-only

Property of the navigator object

A string value that reflects the name of the browser.

Syntax
: `navigator.appName`

Discussion
: This property gives the "official" name of the browser program that is running the script. Its value is `"Netscape"` for Navigator versions 2, 3, and 4.

Example
: `document.write("You are using the ", navigator.appName, " browser.<P>")`

See Also
: `appCodeName, appVersion, navigator`

appVersion

Version 1.0   Read-only

Property of the navigator object

A string value that reflects the version of the browser.

Syntax
: `navigator.appVersion`

Discussion
: This property gives version information for the browser program that is running the script. Its value is a string of the form:

    `releaseNumber (platform; country)`

    where:
    - `releaseNumber` is the browser version number.
    - `platform` is the platform on which the browser is running.
    - `country` is either I for international release, or U for domestic U.S. release. The U.S. version has a more advanced encryption feature.

Example
: If the statement:

    `vs = navigator.appVersion`

sets vs to:

"4.0b4 (Win95; I)"

it indicates Navigator version 4.0, beta release 4 for Windows 95, international version.

See Also   `appCodeName`, `appName`, `navigator`

Area

Version 1.1   External

External object

Reflects an HTML `<AREA>` tag.

Syntax
: `document.links[index]`
: `index`   A number specifying the Area object.

Properties
: `hash`   Specifies an anchor name in the link's URL, starting with a # character.
: `host`   Specifies the host domain and server names, or IP address, and port number of the link's URL.
: `hostname`   Specifies the server and domain name, or IP address, of the link's URL.
: `href`   Specifies the link's entire URL.
: `pathname`   Specifies the file pathname of the link's URL, starting with a / character.
: `port`   Specifies the port number of the link's URL.
: `protocol`   Specifies the protocol part of the link's URL, including the trailing : character.
: `search`   Specifies the query portion of the link's URL, starting with a ? character.
: `target`   Reflects the `TARGET` attribute of the HTML tag.

Event Handlers
: `onmouseout`, `onmouseover`.

Discussion
: Area objects are reflected in the `document.links` array. They have the same properties as Link objects. Not all attributes of the `<AREA>` tag are reflected. In particular, the `NAME` attribute is not reflected, so you must use a numeric index, such as `document.links[0]`, to reference one of these objects.

Example In a script containing the following image map:

```
<MAP NAME="myMap">
   <AREA NAME="upper" COORDS="0,0,100,50"
   HREF="javascript:upperClick()">
   <AREA NAME="lower" COORDS="0,50,100,100"
   HREF="javascript:lowerClick()">
</MAP>
<IMG SRC="something.gif" HEIGHT="100" WIDTH="100" USEMAP="#myMap">
```

the Area objects could be referenced as elements of document.links, with statements such as:

```
upperURL = document.links[0].href
```

(The reference to links[0] assumes that this map is placed before any other anchors or maps in the document.)

See Also Link, links

arguments

Version 1.0   Special scope

Property of the Function object

An array that contains arguments passed to a function.

Syntax funcName.arguments[n]

funcName   Name of this function, that is, the one within which this reference is written.

Properties This object, being an array, has all the properties and methods of Array objects.

Discussion This array contains all the arguments passed to a function by the caller. This can be used to write functions that accept a variable number of arguments. The length property gives the number of arguments.

This array has a limited scope. Its elements only have values when the function is called, so they may not be referenced outside the function.

Example This function accepts a variable number of arguments, and writes them to the current document, placing each one on a separate line.

```
function writeLines() {
   for (var i = 0; i < writeLines.arguments.length; i++)
      document.write(writeLines.arguments[i], "<BR>")
}
```

See Also Function, Array, arity

arity

Version 1.2

Property of the Function object

Returns the number of arguments expected by the function.

Syntax funcName.arity

funcName   Name of a JavaScript function.

Discussion arity returns the number of arguments that were specified in the function header. Regardless of how the function was defined, it may accept varying numbers of arguments at run time, and use the arguments array to access them.

Example
```
if (myHandler.arity == 4)
   myHandler(x, y, label, flags)
else
   myHandler(x, y)
```

See Also arguments, Function

Array

Version 1.1

Object type (constructor)

Creates a new `Array` object.

Syntax   `name = new Array(initial)`

`name`   The name for the array.
`initial`   Either a single numeric value representing the number of elements to allocate, or a series of initial values separated by commas.

Properties   `length`   The number of elements in the array.

Methods
`concat(array)`   Returns a new array containing two arrays' elements concatenated.
`join(sep)`   Used to join the elements of an array together, creating a single string. The value of `sep` is used as a separator between elements.
`reverse()`   Switches the elements in an array; the first becomes the last, and the last becomes the first.
`slice(begin, end)`   Returns a new array containing a subset of a larger array.
`sort(func)`   Sorts the elements held by the array, using the ordering determined by a specified function.

Discussion   For detailed information, see "Arrays" in Chapter 2.

Version 1.2   The `concat()` and `slice()` methods were added in JavaScript 1.2.

Example
```
cards = new Array(52)
suits = new Array("clubs", "diamonds", "hearts", "spades")
```

See Also   `concat()`, `join()`, `length` (property of Array), `reverse()`, `slice()`, `sort()`

asin( )

Version 1.0

Method of the Math object

Returns a number representing the arc sine (in radians) of a number.

Syntax   Math.asin(number)
number   The value whose arc sine is to be returned.

Discussion   asin returns a value between $-\pi/2$ and $\pi/2$ if the number argument is in the range of –1 to 1. If number is outside this range, asin returns zero.

Example   theta = Math.asin(y)

See Also   acos( ), atan( ), atan2( ), cos( ), sin( ), tan( ), Math

atan( )

Version 1.0

Method of the Math object

Returns a number representing the arc tangent (in radians) of a number.

Syntax   Math.atan(number)
number   The value whose arc tangent is to be returned.

Discussion   atan returns a value between $-\pi/2$ and $\pi/2$.

Example   theta = Math.atan(y/x)

See Also   acos( ), asin( ), atan2( ), cos( ), sin( ), tan( ), Math

atan2( )

Version 1.0

Method of the Math object

Returns a number representing the arc tangent (in radians) of the quotient of two numbers.

Syntax `Math.atan2(yPart, xPart)`

yPart   The Y-coordinate (sine) of the value whose arc tangent is to be returned.

xPart   The X-coordinate (cosine) of the value whose arc tangent is to be returned.

Discussion Frequently, programmers use arc tangents to find the angle of a line specified by X and Y coordinates, by writing a statement like:

`angle = atan (y / x)`

The problem with this approach is that if the line is vertical, x will be zero, and the division by zero will produce an error even though the correct answer is clearly 90 (or 270) degrees. For this reason, JavaScript, like many other languages, provides a special arc tangent function that accepts X and Y as separate values.

    `atan2` returns a value between zero and 2π. This value is the angle (in radians) between the X axis and a line drawn from (0, 0) to the specified point.

    Note that the Y argument comes first when calling `atan2`.

Example
```
startX = 123
startY = 456
endX = 789
endy = 1011

XTravel = endX - startX
YTravel = endY - startY

// Note multiplication to convert radians to degrees

angle = Math.atan2 (YTravel, XTravel) * 57.2958

document.write ("You traveled at a heading of ",
   angle, " degrees.")
```

See Also `acos( )`, `asin( )`, `atan( )`, `cos( )`, `Math`, `sin( )`, `tan( )`

availHeight

Version 1.2   Read-only

Property of the screen object

Returns the height of the available region of the display screen.

Syntax   `screen.availHeight`

Discussion   This property returns the height of the screen, in pixels, not counting any permanent or semi-permanent features such as a taskbar.

Example   `Ymax = screen.availHeight - 1`

See Also   `availWidth`, `height` and `width` (properties of various objects), `screen`

availWidth

Version 1.2   Read-only

Property of the screen object

Returns the width of the available region of the display screen.

Syntax   `screen.availWidth`

Discussion   This property returns the width of the screen, in pixels, not counting any permanent or semi-permanent features such as a scroll bar.

Example   `Xmax = screen.availWidth - 1`

See Also   `availHeight`, `height` and `width` (properties of various objects), `screen`

back( )

Version 1.0

Method of the `history` object

Loads the window's previous URL, equivalent to the user pressing Navigator's Back button.

Syntax `history.back()`

Example You can create a link that functions like the Back button in the Navigator toolbar, by writing HTML code with a JavaScript URL, such as:

`<A HREF="javascript:history.back()"> Go back </A>`

See Also `forward()`, `go()`, `history`

background

Version 1.2

Property of the `Layer` object

Specifies the background image for the layer.

Syntax `layerObject.background`

`layerObject`   A layer name, or an expression denoting a `Layer` object.

Discussion This is a string object that may contain a filename or URL. Setting it to `null` will remove any image, allowing the background color (set by the `bgColor` property) to display.

Example `layer1.background = "mylogo.gif"`

See Also `Layer`

backgroundColor

Version 1.2

Property of style sheet objects

Specifies the color of an HTML element's background.

Syntax
: `styleObj.backgroundColor`

  `styleObj`   Style sheet object: a property of a `classes`, `ids`, or `tags` object.

Discussion
: This property sets the color of an element's background. It may be set to:
  - A string of six hexadecimal digits, with an optional leading pound sign (#) character, in the form *rrggbb*, where *rr* specifies red, *gg* specifies green, and *bb* specifies blue.
  - One of the color names listed in Appendix C.
  - The keyword `"transparent"`.

  This property applies to all elements, and is inherited. Its initial value is `"transparent"`.

  Note that for `backgroundColor` assignments to take effect, they must occur before the browser writes the styled text to the document. An assignment to `tags.body.backgroundColor` must be done within the `<HEAD>` ... `</HEAD>` section of the HTML.

Example
: `document.ids.box.backgroundColor = "aquamarine"`

See Also
: `backgroundImage`, `borderColor`, `classes`, `color`, `ids`, `tags`

backgroundImage

Version 1.2

Property of style sheet objects

Specifies an image file to be used as an HTML element's background.

Syntax
: `styleObj.backgroundImage`

  `styleObj`   Style sheet object: a property of a `classes`, `ids`, or `tags` object.

Discussion	This property specifies the image used as an element's background. It may be set to a string containing the URL of an image file, or to the empty string to specify no image.
This property applies to all elements, and is inherited. Its initial value is the empty string.
Note that for `backgroundImage` assignments to take effect, they must occur before the browser writes the styled text to the document. An assignment to `tags.body.backgroundImage` must be done within the `<HEAD> ... </HEAD>` section of the HTML.
Example	`document.ids.box.backgroundImage = "myLogo.gif"`
See Also	`backgroundColor, classes, color, ids, tags`

below

Version 1.2   Read-only

Property of the Layer object

Returns the layer immediately below the specified layer.

Syntax	`layerObject.below`
`layerObject`   A layer name, or an expression denoting a `Layer` object.
Properties	Since `below` returns a reference to a `Layer` object, it has all the properties, methods, and event handlers of the referenced layer.
Discussion	This property returns the layer that is immediately below the specified one in the z-index order. The z-index order is used to position layers, and is initially set by the `Z-INDEX` attribute of the `<LAYER>` tag. A low number indicates a low position in the order; in an area where two layers overlap, the one with the higher z-index is displayed.
If the `Layer` object has no layer below it in the z-index order, the property returns `null`. Note that this property may return a parent or child layer; the `siblingBelow` property can be used to access only sibling layers.
This is a read-only property. To modify the z-index ordering of layers, use the `zIndex` property, or the `moveAbove( )` or `moveBelow( )` methods.

Example	This statement causes the layer below `layer1` to become visible. `layer1.below.visibility = "show"`
See Also	`above`, `siblingAbove`, `siblingBelow`, `Layer`

bgColor

Version 1.0

Property of the document and Layer objects

Specifies the document or layer background color.

Syntax	*docObject*.bgColor
	docObject `document` for the current window's document, or an expression denoting a `document` or `Layer` object.
Discussion	This property may be set to a string of six hexadecimal digits, with an optional leading pound sign (#) character, in the form *rrggbb*, where *rr* specifies red, *gg* specifies green, and *bb* specifies blue. `bgColor` may also be set to one of the color names listed in Appendix C. The returned value is always in hexadecimal with a leading #. This property is initially set to the color specified by the `BGCOLOR` attribute, if any, of the HTML `<BODY>` or `<LAYER>` tag.

Examples	`document.bgColor = "ff0000"` `// max. red`
	                                                  `// no green`
	                                                  `// no blue`
	
	`parent.document.bgColor = "#8000ff"` `// 50% red`
	                                                           `// no green`
	                                                           `// max. blue`
	
	`otherWindow.document.bgColor = "limegreen"` `// Netscape`
	                                                                                 `// keyword`

See Also	`fgColor`, `document`, `Layer`

big( )

Version 1.0

Method of the String object

Returns a string containing HTML code to format a string in large characters.

Syntax   `stringObj.big()`

         `stringObj`   String object or expression to be formatted in large characters.

Discussion   This method returns a string consisting of HTML code. The code includes the HTML `<BIG>` and `</BIG>` tags so that, if the returned string is written to a document, it will appear in a larger size.

Example   The statement:

`document.write("An ", "important".big(), " announcement!")`

will write to the web page:

An **important** announcement!

See Also   `blink()`, `bold()`, `fixed()`, `fontcolor()`, `fontsize()`, `italics()`, `small()`, `split()`, `strike()`, `String`, `sub()`, `sup()`

blink( )

Version 1.0

Method of the String object

Returns a string containing HTML code to format a string in blinking characters.

Syntax   `stringObj.blink()`

         `stringObj`   String object or expression to be formatted in blinking characters.

Discussion   This method returns a string consisting of HTML code. The code includes the HTML <BLINK> and </BLINK> tags so that, if the returned string is written to a document, the characters will blink.

Example   The statement:

```
document.write("A news ", "flash".blink(), "!")
```

will write to the web page:

A news flash!

with the word "flash" appearing in blinking characters.

See Also   `big()`, `bold()`, `fixed()`, `fontcolor()`, `fontsize()`, `italics()`, `small()`, `split()`, `strike()`, String, `sub()`, `sup()`

blur( )

Version 1.0

Method of the `window` object, and of Button, Checkbox, FileUpload, Frame, Password, Radio, Reset, Select, Submit, Text, and Textarea external objects

Removes focus from an object on the screen.

Syntax   *obj*.blur( )

obj   Object that may have focus.

Discussion   This method removes screen focus from the specified object.
   In JavaScript version 1.0, this method is only available for the Password, Select, Text, and Textarea external objects.

Version 1.1   This property was added to the Button, Checkbox, FileUpload, Frame, Radio, Reset, Submit, and `window` objects in JavaScript 1.1.

Example   `document.forms.myForm.textBox1.blur()`

See Also   `focus()`, `window`, Button, Checkbox, FileUpload, Frame, Password, Radio, Reset, Select, Submit, Text, Textarea

BLUR

Version 1.2   Read-only

Property of the Event object

Returns a mask for capturing blur events.

Syntax   `Event.BLUR`

Discussion   This property is used to capture and release blur events, which occur when the focus moves off of an object on the screen. For more details on event handling, see Chapter 7.

Example   To enable capturing of blur events (as well as focus):

`myWindow.captureEvents (Event.BLUR | Event.FOCUS)`

See Also   `captureEvents(), event, Event, onblur, releaseEvents()`

bold( )

Version 1.0

Method of the String object

Returns a string containing HTML code to format a string in bold characters.

Syntax   *stringObj*`.bold( )`

stringObj   String object or expression to be formatted in bold characters.

Discussion   This method returns a string consisting of HTML code. The code includes the HTML `<B>` and `</B>` tags so that, if the returned string is written to a document, it will appear in bold characters.

Example The statement:

document.write("A ", "daring".bold(), " achievement!")

will write to the web page:

A **daring** achievement!

See Also big(), blink(), fixed(), fontcolor(), fontsize(), italics(), small(), split(), strike(), sub(), sup(), String

Boolean

Version 1.1

Object type (constructor)

Creates a new `Boolean` object or converts a value to Boolean.

Syntax Boolean(*value*)

value   Any object or expression.

Discussion This constructor is not usually used in scripts, since `Boolean` objects can be created by simply declaring variables and assigning Boolean values to them. For example,

mode = new Boolean(true)

is equivalent to

mode = true

In fact, `Boolean()` was not available in JavaScript 1.0, so all Booleans had to be created by assignments.

Used without `new`, `Boolean()` is a type-conversion function that returns the Boolean equivalent of its argument.

If the *value* argument is zero, `false`, the empty string, `null`, or undefined, `Boolean()` returns `false`. For any other *value*, it returns `true`.

For more information on Boolean values and operations, see Chapters 2 and 3.

Example same = new Boolean(a == b)

border

Version 1.1   Read-only

Property of the Image object

Reflects the width, in pixels, of an image border.

Syntax
: `imgObject.border`
: *imgObject*   An expression denoting an `Image` object.

Discussion
: This property is available for all images that are declared by the HTML `<IMG>` tag. `border` reflects the `BORDER` attribute of the tag. For objects created by calling `new Image()`, this property is zero.

Example
: `borderWidth = document.images[0].border`

See Also
: `Image`

borderBottomWidth

Version 1.2

Property of style sheet objects

Specifies the thickness of an HTML element's bottom border.

Syntax
: *styleObj*`.borderBottomWidth`
: *styleObj*   Style sheet object: a property of a `classes`, `ids`, or `tags` object.

Discussion
: JavaScript style sheets can be used to create boxes around text or images. This property sets the width of an element's bottom border. It may be set to:
  - An absolute measurement, such as `"2pt"`.
  - A measurement relative to the current font, size such as `"0.5em"`.
  - A pixel measurement, such as `"3px"`.
  - The keyword `"thin"`, `"medium"`, or `"thick"`.

  This property applies to all elements, and is not inherited. Its initial value is `"medium"`.

Note that for `borderBottomWidth` assignments to take effect, they must occur before the browser writes the styled text to the document. An assignment to `tags.body.borderBottomWidth` must be done within the `<HEAD>` ... `</HEAD>` section of the HTML.

The `paddingBottom` property can be used to define how close the bottom border is to the enclosed text or image.

Example This style sheet creates a class that puts borders around text or an image, and an ID that uses `paddingBottom` to define the distance between the text or image and the bottom border:

```
<STYLE TYPE="text/javascript">
    classes.box.all.borderTopWidth = "1em"
    classes.box.all.borderRightWidth = "6pt"
    classes.box.all.borderBottomWidth = "12px"
    classes.box.all.borderLeftWidth = "thin"
    classes.box.all.borderStyle = "3D"

    ids.padded.paddingBottom = "12pt"
</STYLE>
```

See Also borderColor, borderLeftWidth, borderRightWidth, borderStyle, borderTopWidth, borderWidths(), classes, ids, paddingBottom, paddingLeft, paddingRight, paddings(), paddingTop, tags

borderColor

Version 1.2

Property of style sheet objects

Specifies the color of an HTML element's borders.

Syntax *styleObj*.borderColor

styleObj   Style sheet object: a property of a `classes`, `ids`, or `tags` object.

Discussion JavaScript style sheets can be used to create boxes around text or images. This property sets the color of an element's borders. It may be set to:

- A string of six hexadecimal digits, with an optional leading pound sign (#) character, in the form *rrggbb*, where *rr* specifies red, *gg* specifies green, and *bb* specifies blue.
- One of the color names listed in Appendix C.
- The keyword `"none"`.

This property applies to all elements, and is not inherited. Its initial value is "none".

Note that for `borderColor` assignments to take effect, they must occur before the browser writes the styled text to the document. An assignment to `tags.body.borderColor` must be done within the `<HEAD>` ... `</HEAD>` section of the HTML.

Example
: `document.ids.box.borderColor = "limegreen"`

See Also
: `borderBottomWidth, borderLeftWidth, borderRightWidth, borderStyle, borderTopWidth, borderWidths(), classes, ids, tags`

borderLeftWidth

Version 1.2

Property of style sheet objects

Specifies the thickness of an HTML element's left border.

Syntax
: *styleObj*`.borderLeftWidth`
: *styleObj* — Style sheet object: a property of a `classes`, `ids`, or `tags` object.

Discussion
: JavaScript style sheets can be used to create boxes around text or images. This property sets the width of an element's left border. It may be set to:
  - An absolute measurement, such as `"2pt"`.
  - A measurement relative to the current font size, such as `"0.5em"`.
  - A pixel measurement, such as `"3px"`.
  - The keyword `"thin"`, `"medium"`, or `"thick"`.

  This property applies to all elements, and is not inherited. Its initial value is `"medium"`.

  Note that for `borderLeftWidth` assignments to take effect, they must occur before the browser writes the styled text to the document. An assignment to `tags.body.borderLeftWidth` must be done within the `<HEAD>` ... `</HEAD>` section of the HTML.

  The `paddingLeft` property can be used to define how close the border is to the enclosed text or image.

Example
: This style sheet creates a class that puts borders around text or an image, and an ID that uses `paddingLeft` to define the distance between the text or image and the left border:

```
<STYLE TYPE="text/javascript">
  classes.box.all.borderTopWidth = "1em"
  classes.box.all.borderRightWidth = "6pt"
  classes.box.all.borderBottomWidth = "12px"
  classes.box.all.borderLeftWidth = "thin"
  classes.box.all.borderStyle = "3D"

  ids.padded.paddingLeft = "12pt"
</STYLE>
```

See Also borderBottomWidth, borderColor, borderRightWidth, borderStyle, borderTopWidth, borderWidths(), classes, ids, paddingBottom, paddingLeft, paddingRight, paddings(), paddingTop, tags

borderRightWidth

Version 1.2

Property of style sheet objects

Specifies the thickness of an HTML element's right border.

Syntax *styleObj*.borderRightWidth

styleObj   Style sheet object: a property of a `classes`, `ids`, or `tags` object.

Discussion JavaScript style sheets can be used to create boxes around text or images. This property sets the width of an element's right border. It may be set to:

- An absolute measurement, such as `"2pt"`.
- A measurement relative to the current font size, such as `"0.5em"`.
- A pixel measurement, such as `"3px"`.
- The keyword `"thin"`, `"medium"`, or `"thick"`.

This property applies to all elements, and is not inherited. Its initial value is `"medium"`.

Note that for `borderRightWidth` assignments to take effect, they must occur before the browser writes the styled text to the document. An assignment to `tags.body.borderRightWidth` must be done within the `<HEAD>` ... `</HEAD>` section of the HTML.

The `paddingRight` property can be used to define how close the border is to the enclosed text or image.

Example This style sheet creates a class that puts borders around text or an image, and an ID that uses `paddingRight` to define the distance between the text or image and the left border:

```
<STYLE TYPE="text/javascript">
   classes.box.all.borderTopWidth = "1em"
   classes.box.all.borderRightWidth = "6pt"
   classes.box.all.borderBottomWidth = "12px"
   classes.box.all.borderLeftWidth = "thin"
   classes.box.all.borderStyle = "3D"

   ids.padded.paddingRight = "12pt"
</STYLE>
```

See Also borderBottomWidth, borderColor, borderLeftWidth, borderStyle, borderTopWidth, borderWidths(), classes, ids, paddingBottom, paddingLeft, paddingRight, paddings(), paddingTop, tags

borderStyle

Version 1.2

Property of style sheet objects

Specifies the style of an HTML element's borders.

Syntax *styleObj*.borderStyle

styleObj   Style sheet object: a property of a `classes`, `ids`, or `tags` object.

Discussion JavaScript style sheets can be used to create boxes around text or images. This property sets the style of an element's borders. It may be set to `"none"`, `"solid"`, or `"3D"`.

This property applies to all elements, and is not inherited. Its initial value is `"none"`.

Note that for `borderStyle` assignments to take effect, they must occur before the browser writes the styled text to the document. An assignment to `tags.body.borderStyle` must be done within the `<HEAD>` ... `</HEAD>` section of the HTML.

Example `document.ids.box.borderStyle = "solid"`

See Also borderBottomWidth, borderLeftWidth, borderRightWidth, borderColor, borderTopWidth, borderWidths(), classes, ids, tags

borderTopWidth

Version 1.2

Property of style sheet objects

Specifies the thickness of an HTML element's top border.

Syntax `styleObj.borderTopWidth`

`styleObj` Style sheet object: a property of a `classes`, `ids`, or `tags` object.

Discussion JavaScript style sheets can be used to create boxes around text or images. This property sets the width of an element's top border. It may be set to:

- An absolute measurement, such as `"2pt"`.
- A measurement relative to the current font size, such as `"0.5em"`.
- A pixel measurement, such as `"3px"`.
- The keyword `"thin"`, `"medium"`, or `"thick"`.

This property applies to all elements, and is not inherited. Its initial value is `"medium"`.

Note that for `borderTopWidth` assignments to take effect, they must occur before the browser writes the styled text to the document. An assignment to `tags.body.borderTopWidth` must be done within the `<HEAD>` ... `</HEAD>` section of the HTML.

The `paddingTop` property can be used to define how close the border is to the enclosed text or image.

Example This style sheet creates a class that puts borders around text or an image, and an ID that uses `paddingTop` to define the distance between the text or image and the left border:

```
<STYLE TYPE="text/javascript">
  classes.box.all.borderTopWidth = "1em"
  classes.box.all.borderRightWidth = "6pt"
  classes.box.all.borderBottomWidth = "12px"
  classes.box.all.borderLeftWidth = "thin"
  classes.box.all.borderStyle = "3D"

  ids.padded.paddingTop = "12pt"
</STYLE>
```

See Also `borderBottomWidth`, `borderColor`, `borderLeftWidth`, `borderRightWidth`, `borderStyle`, `borderWidths()`, `classes`, `ids`, `paddingBottom`, `paddingLeft`, `paddingRight`, `paddings()`, `paddingTop`, `tags`

borderWidths( )

Version 1.2

Method of style sheet objects

Specifies the thicknesses of borders around an HTML element.

Syntax   *styleObj*.borderWidths(*topValue*, *rightValue*, *bottomValue*, *leftValue*)

    styleObj   Style sheet object: a property of a `classes`, `ids`, or `tags` object.

    topValue, *rightValue*, *bottomValue*, *leftValue*,   String values specifying the border widths.

Discussion   JavaScript style sheets can be used to create boxes around text or images. This method can be used to specify all four border widths at once. This method applies to all elements, and is not inherited.

Each argument value may be:

- An absolute measurement, such as `"2pt"`.
- A measurement relative to the current font size, such as `"0.5em"`.
- A pixel measurement, such as `"3px"`.
- The keyword `"thin"`, `"medium"`, or `"thick"`.

Note that for calls to `borderWidths()` to take effect, they must occur before the browser writes the styled text to the document. A call to `tags.body.borderWidths()` must be done within the `<HEAD>` ... `</HEAD>` section of the HTML.

The `paddingBottom`, `paddingLeft`, `paddingRight`, and `paddingTop` properties, or the `paddings()` method, can be used to define how close the border is to the enclosed text or image.

Example   `document.ids.box.borderWidths`
        `("2em", "4em", "2em", "4em")`

See Also   `borderBottomWidth`, `borderColor`, `borderLeftWidth`, `borderRightWidth`, `borderTopWidth`, `borderStyle`, `classes`, `ids`, `tags`

bottom

Version 1.2

Property of the `clip` object

Specifies the lower clipping limit of a layer.

Syntax
: `layerObj.clip.bottom`
: `layerObj`   `document.layerName`, or other expression denoting a Layer object.

Discussion
: This property specifies the lower clipping limit for a layer, in pixels. It is initially equal to the height of the layer. Decreasing its value causes rows of pixels at the bottom of the layer to become invisible, allowing the lower layers or the enclosing document to be seen.

Example
: To cause the bottom 64 rows of pixels in a layer to be clipped, use a statement such as:

    `document.layers.myLayer.clip.bottom -= 64`

See Also
: `height`, `left`, `right`, `top`, `width` (properties of `clip`), `Layer`

break

Version 1.0

Keyword used in statements

This keyword is used to exit from a loop or `switch` statement. For more details, see Chapter 4.

Button

Version 1.0　External

Property of the Form external object

Reflects a button in a form.

Syntax	*formObject.buttonName* *formObject*.elements[*index*]

	formObject	Name of a form, or expression denoting a Form object.
	buttonName	Name specified in the NAME attribute of the HTML <INPUT> tag.
	index	Number or string specifying the position of the button in the form.
Properties	form	Returns the Form object that contains the button.
	name	Reflects the name specified in the NAME attribute of the HTML <INPUT> tag.
	type	Reflects the value specified in the TYPE attribute of the HTML <INPUT> tag. This is always "button" for Button objects.
	value	Reflects the value specified in the VALUE attribute of the HTML <INPUT> tag. This is the button's label that appears on the screen.
Methods	blur()	Removes focus from the button.
	click()	Simulates a mouse click, that is, calls the button's onclick handler.
	focus()	Sets focus on the button.
Event Handlers	onblur, onclick, ondblclick, onfocus, onmouseup, onmousedown	
Discussion	When Navigator loads a web page, it creates Button objects corresponding to all buttons in forms in the document. You can reference these objects as properties of the Form object, or as elements of the form's elements array.	

Version 1.1
　　The type property, onblur and onfocus event handlers, and blur and focus methods were added in Version 1.1.

Version 1.2
　　The ondblclick, onmouseup, and onmousedown event handlers were added in Version 1.2.

Example A button can be defined by HTML such as:

```
<FORM NAME="myForm">
  <INPUT TYPE="button" NAME="myButton"
   VALUE="Continue"
   ONCLICK="pushed(this)">
...
</FORM>
```

Note the use of the `this` object to pass the button. The button can then be referenced by JavaScript statements such as:

```
function pushed(b) {
   alert("The " + b.value + " button was pressed.")
}
```

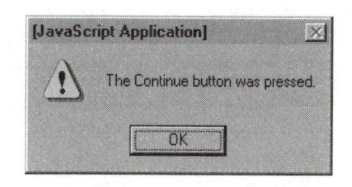

[JavaScript Application dialog: "The Continue button was pressed." OK]

See Also Form

caller

Version 1.0 Read-only Special scope

Property of the Function object

Returns the function that called the currently executing function.

Syntax   `functionName.caller`

functionName   Name of this function, that is, the one in which the reference to `caller` is written.

Discussion   `caller` allows a function to determine what function called it. The returned value is a reference to the caller's `Function` object. If the function was called from the top level, that is, not from within any function, the returned value is `null`.

This property can only be used within a function, and must refer to the function itself, not any other function that may be executing.

Example
```
function lookBack() {
    document.write("lookBack was called by " + lookBack.caller)
}
```

See Also   `Function`

captureEvents( )

Version 1.2

Method of the document, Layer, and window objects

Specifies events that the object will capture.

Syntax   `obj.captureEvents(mask)`

obj   Reference to a `window`, `document`, `Frame`, or `Layer` object.
mask   Bit mask that specifies events.

Discussion   This method allows an object to intercept and process events that would otherwise be ignored or passed to other handlers. The mask value must be a bitwise OR of some of the values which are available as properties of the `Event` object:

```
Event.ABORT        Event.KEYDOWN      Event.MOUSEUP
Event.BLUR         Event.KEYPRESS     Event.MOVE
Event.CHANGE       Event.KEYUP        Event.RESET
Event.CLICK        Event.LOAD         Event.RESIZE
Event.DBLCLICK     Event.MOUSEDOWN    Event.SELECT
Event.DRAGDROP     Event.MOUSEMOVE    Event.SUBMIT
Event.ERROR        Event.MOUSEOUT     Event.UNLOAD
Event.FOCUS        Event.MOUSEOVER
```

Besides calling this method, your script must also assign the functions that handle the events as properties of the object (see Chapter 7).

Example myWindow.captureEvents(Event.CLICK | Event.DBLCLICK | Event.DRAGDROP)

See Also enableExternalCapture( ), handleEvent( ), releaseEvents( ), routeEvent( )

case

Version 1.2

Keyword used in statements

This keyword is used inside `switch` statements to create multi-way branches. For details, see "Multi-way Branch" in Chapter 4.

ceil( )

Version 1.0

Method of the Math object

Returns the "ceiling" (lowest greater integer) of a number.

Syntax Math.ceil(*number*)

number   The number whose ceiling is to be returned.

Discussion Note that "greater" means more positive. For example, Math.ceil(12.3) returns 13; but Math.ceil(-12.3) returns -12, not -13.

Example c = Math.ceil(x)

See Also floor( ), Math

CHANGE

Version 1.2   Read-only

Property of the Event object

Returns a mask for capturing change events.

Syntax   `Event.CHANGE`

Discussion   This property is used to capture and release change events, which occur when the focus moves off of a form element after the user has changed its contents. For more details on event handling, see Chapter 7.

Example   To enable capturing of change events:

`myWindow.captureEvents (Event.CHANGE)`

See Also   `captureEvents()`, `event`, `Event`, `onchange`, `releaseEvents()`

charAt( )

Version 1.0

Method of the String object

Returns a single character from a string.

Syntax   *stringObj*.charAt(*index*)

stringObj	String variable, literal, or expression.
index	Number specifying the character position.

Discussion   charAt returns a string of length 1 containing the specified character. To obtain the character set code, use `charCodeAt`.
   Note that strings, like arrays, start with element 0.

Example
```
var str = "Hello!"
document.write("The 3rd character is ", str.charAt(2), ".<BR>")
document.write("The last character is ", str.charAt(str.length - 1),
   ".<BR>")
```

See Also   `charCodeAt()`, `String`

charCodeAt( )

Version 1.2

Method of the String object

Returns the character set code number of one character from a string.

Syntax
stringObj.charCodeAt(*index*)

stringObj   String variable, literal, or expression.
index   Number specifying the character position.

Discussion
charCodeAt returns a number containing the specified character's value in the ISO-Latin-1 code set. To obtain the character itself, use charAt.
    Note that strings, like arrays, start with element 0.

Examples
```
var str = "Hello!"
document.write("The 3rd character's code is ", str.charCodeAt(2),
   ".<BR>")
document.write("The last character's code is ",
   str.charCodeAt(str.length - 1), ".<BR>")
```

See Also   charAt( ), String

Checkbox

Version 1.0   External

Property of the Form external object

Reflects a check box in a form.

Syntax
formObj.*boxName*
formObj.elements[*index*]

formObj   document.*formName* or other expression denoting a Form object.
boxName   String value representing a name assigned by the NAME attribute of the HTML <INPUT> tag.
index   Number or string specifying an element of the form's elements array.

Properties	checked	Boolean value that specifies whether the box is checked.
	defaultChecked	Boolean value that reflects the CHECKED attribute of the HTML <INPUT> tag. This determines whether the box is initially checked when the web page is loaded.
	form	The form object that contains the check box.
	name	Reflects the name specified in the NAME attribute of the HTML <INPUT> tag.
	type	Reflects the value specified in the TYPE attribute of the HTML <INPUT> tag. This is always "checkbox" for Checkbox objects.
	value	Reflects the value specified in the VALUE attribute of the HTML <INPUT> tag. This is the string that is passed to the server when the form is submitted.
Methods	blur()	Removes focus from the check box.
	click()	Simulates a mouse click, and calls the check box's onclick handler.
	focus()	Sets focus on the check box.
Event Handlers	onblur, onclick, onfocus	

Discussion

When Navigator loads a web page, it creates Checkbox objects corresponding to all HTML <INPUT> tags with the TYPE="checkbox" attribute. You can reference these objects by name, or as elements of a form's elements array.

Version 1.1

The type property, onblur and onfocus event handlers, and blur and focus methods were added in Version 1.1.

Example

The following HTML creates a form with a check box and a button. The button's onclick handler toggles the check box on and off:

```
<FORM>
  <INPUT TYPE="checkbox" NAME="cbox" VALUE="enabled"> Check this
  out<BR>

<INPUT type="BUTTON" name="button2" value="Toggle"
 onclick="this.form.cbox.checked = !this.form.cbox.checked"> <P>
</FORM>
```

Note the use of the this object to pass the check box.

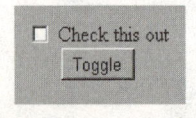

See Also Form

checked

Version 1.0 External Tainted

Property of the Checkbox and Radio external objects

Specifies whether a button in an HTML form is checked.

Syntax *buttonObj*.checked

buttonObj document.*formName.buttonName* or some other expression denoting a Checkbox or Radio object.

Discussion This is a Boolean property; when it is true, the check box or button is checked.

Example For a form such as:

```
<FORM name="myForm">
   <INPUT TYPE="radio" NAME="btns" VALUE="A"> A <BR>
   <INPUT TYPE="radio" NAME="btns" VALUE="B"> B <BR>
   <INPUT TYPE="radio" NAME="btns" VALUE="C"> C <BR>
</FORM>
```

You can cause option A to be selected with a statement such as:

```
document.myForm.btns[0].checked = true
```

See Also Checkbox, Form, Radio

classes

Version 1.2

Property of the document object

Specifies classes of styles for HTML tags.

Syntax *docObject*.classes.*className*.*tag*.*prop*

docObject document for the current window's document, or an expression denoting a document or Layer object.
className Name of the style class.
tag Name of an HTML tag, such as H1, or all.
prop Style property such as color or fontWeight.

Properties classes may have a property corresponding to each user-defined style class. The property name is the same as the name of the class. Note that, unlike most JavaScript identifiers, upper- and lowercase are equivalent for these names, e.g, document.classes.editorial is equivalent to document.classes.EDITORIAL.

Each property of classes will itself have properties corresponding to HTML tags, such as H1, P, etc. Each of these properties will in turn have properties, which specify the actual appearance of text to which the style is applied. (All of these names may also be upper- or lowercase.) The available properties are summarized below:

classes may also have a property named all. Style properties assigned to all will apply to all HTML tags in the class.

Font Properties	fontFamily	Font name: actual or generic.
	fontSize	Number or keyword specifying text size.
	fontStyle	Keyword specifying italics and/or small capitals.
	fontWeight	Number or keyword specifying text "boldness."
Text Properties	lineHeight	Number or expression specifying line spacing.
	textAlign	Keyword specifying horizontal position of text.
	TextDecoration	Keyword specifying underline, overline, overstrike, or blink.
	textIndent	Number or expression specifying indentation for the first line of a paragraph.
	TextTransform	Keyword specifying capitalization.
	verticalAlign	Keyword specifying vertical position of text.
Block-level Properties	align	Keyword specifying horizontal position (floating) of HTML object.
	borderBottomWidth, borderLeftWidth, borderRightWidth, borderTopWidth	Number specifying the width of the border.
	borderColor	Keyword specifying color of border.
	borderStyle	Keyword specifying style of border.
	clear	Keyword specifying whether floating objects may be positioned alongside this object.

	`height`	Number or keyword specifying the height of the HTML object.
	`marginBottom,` `marginLeft,` `marginRight,` `marginTop`	Number or expression specifying the spacing between HTML objects.
	`paddingBottom,` `paddingLeft,` `paddingRight,` `paddingTop`	Number or expression specifying the spacing between HTML object content and border.
	`width`	Number, expression, or keyword specifying the width of the HTML object.
Color and Background Properties	`color`	String specifying text color.
	`BackgroundImage`	String specifying URL of image file.
	`BackgroundColor`	String specifying background color.
Classification Properties	`display`	Keyword specifying how object is displayed.
	`listStyleType`	Keyword specifying how objects are marked or numbered.
	`whiteSpace`	Keyword specifying handling of white space characters.

Methods   Note that `classes` itself has no methods. These methods are actually used on the properties of properties of `classes`, that is, the specific styles associated with a class and tag.

`borderWidths()`	Sets the four border width properties for the style.
`margins()`	Sets the four margin properties for the style.
`paddings()`	Sets the four padding width properties for the style.

Discussion   `classes` reflects all style classes defined by style sheets in the document. You can also create new style classes at runtime by assigning new properties to `classes`. Note that assignments to `classes` do not affect text that has already been written to the document.

Example   The following statement creates a new style class called `giant`, and sets its font size for level 1 headings (HTML <H1> tag) to twice their normal size:
`document.classes.giant.H1.fontSize = document.tags.H1.fontSize * 2`

See Also   `ids, tags`

clear

Version 1.2

Property of style sheet objects

Specifies where floating elements may not be placed.

Syntax   *styleObj*.clear

           styleObj   Style sheet object: a property of a `classes`, `ids`, or `tags` object.

Discussion   This property specifies what region near an HTML element must be kept clear of images and other floating elements. The value may be `"left"`, `"right"`, `"both"`, or `"none"`. This is equivalent to the `CLEAR` attribute of HTML tags.
          This property applies to all HTML elements. Its initial value is `"none"`.
          Note that for `clear` assignments to take effect, they must occur before the browser writes the styled text to the document. An assignment to `tags.body.clear` must be done within the `<HEAD>` ... `</HEAD>` section of the HTML.

Example   To cause all `<H2>` headings to be kept clear on both sides:

```
document.tags.H2.clear = "both"
```

See Also   `classes`, `ids`, `tags`

clearInterval( )

Version 1.2

Method of the Frame and `window` objects

Stops repeated execution of a function that was started by `setInterval()`.

Syntax   `clearInterval(`*ID*`)`

           ID   The ID value returned by `setInterval()`.

Example   If a function `blink()` is scheduled for repeated execution by a statement such as:

```
blink2 = setInterval("blink()", 5000)
```

It can be stopped by a statement such as:

```
clearInterval(blink2)
```

See Also   `clearTimeout()`, `setInterval()`

clearTimeout( )

Version 1.1

Method of the Frame and window objects

Stops delayed execution that was started by setTimeout.

Syntax clearTimeout(*ID*)

ID The ID value returned by setTimeout( ).

Example If a function is scheduled for execution after a 30-second delay by a statement such as:

blink2 = setTimeout("doSomething()", 30000)

it can be stopped before the 30 seconds has elapsed by a statement such as:

clearTimeout(blink2)

See Also clearInterval( ), setTimeout( )

click( )

Version 1.0   External

Method of the Button, Checkbox, Radio, Reset, and Submit external objects

Simulates a mouse click on an object.

Syntax For radio buttons:

formObj.*radioName*[*num*].click( )

For other objects:

formObj.*objName*.click( )
formObj.elements[*index*].click( )

formObj	document.*formName*, or other expression denoting a Form object.
radioName	Name of a Radio object.
num	Number specifying one button in a radio button set.
objName	Name of a Button, Checkbox, Reset, or Submit object.
index	Number identifying the object in the form.elements array.

Discussion	This method forces execution of an object's onclick handler, if any. It also updates the appearance of the screen, and performs other actions associated with the object. For instance, using click() on a Submit object submits the form.
Example	`document.myForm.button1.click()`
See Also	Button, Checkbox, Radio, Reset, Submit

CLICK

Version 1.2   Read-only

Property of the Event object

Returns a mask for capturing mouse click events.

Syntax	`Event.CLICK`
Discussion	This property is used to control event capturing (see Chapter 7).
Example	To enable capturing of mouse click events (as well as double click): `myWindow.captureEvents(Event.CLICK | Event.DBLCLICK)`
See Also	`captureEvents()`, `Event`, `releaseEvents()`

clip

Version 1.2

Property of the Layer object

Specifies clipping boundaries for the displayed portion of the layer.

Syntax	`layerObj.clip`	
	layerObj	Description
Properties	`bottom`	Vertical position of the bottom edge of the visible area.
	`height`	Height of the visible area.
	`left`	Horizontal position of the left side of the visible area.

right	Horizontal position of the right side of the visible area.	
top	Vertical position of the top edge of the visible area.	
width	Width of the visible area.	

Discussion The visibility of a layer may be reduced or "clipped" to a rectangular zone of a specified size. You can explicitly set the location of this zone by assigning values to the `top`, `bottom`, `left`, and `right` properties. Or you can simplify your code by setting the `height` or `width` properties, which cause JavaScript to adjust the `top` or `right` values, respectively, to produce the desired measurement.

Example This statement clips (makes invisible) a section along the left side of a layer, 100 pixels wide:

```
document.layers.layer1.clip.left = 100
```

See Also `bottom`, `height`, `Layer`, `left`, `right`, `top`, `width`

close( )

DOCUMENT

Version 1.0

Method of the document object

Closes a document stream and forces all data to be displayed.

Syntax *docObject*.close( )

docObject   `document` for the current document, or an expression denoting a `document` object in any window

Discussion Closing a stream means that no more text may be written to the document until it is opened again. Use of `close( )` is recommended, since `write( )` does not always work immediately. Calling `close( )` also displays "Document: Done" in the window status bar, and stops the movement of the animated Netscape "meteor shower" logo.

Example These statements open a window, open its document, write some text, and then close the window to ensure that the text is completely written:

```
var msgWindow = window.open()
msgWindow.document.open()
msgWindow.document.write("Message: ", msgText, "<P>")
msgWindow.document.close()
```

See Also `close( )` (method of `window`), `document`, `open( )` (method of `document`)

close( )

WINDOW

Version 1.0

Method of `window` object

Closes a window, causing it to be removed from the screen.

Syntax   `close( )`
`windowObj.close( )`

windowObj   `window` for the current window, or an expression denoting a `window` object.

Discussion   As a security feature, if a script attempts to close a window that was not opened by a JavaScript `open` statement, Navigator will ask the user to confirm. However, there will be no confirmation if the window has no entries in its history list except the current location; this is useful for temporary windows that dispatch the user to some other location and then close.
   Writing `close( )` without an owner is equivalent to writing `window.close( )`, since `window` is the default owner for JavaScript expressions. However, in HTML object event handlers, you must write `window.close( )`.

Example   `otherWindow.close( )`

See Also   `close( )` (method of `document`), `open( )` (method of `window`), `window`

closed

Version 1.1   Read-only

Property of the `window` object

Returns `true` if a window is closed, or `false` if it is open.

Syntax   *windowObj*`.closed`
windowObj   `window` object name, or an expression denoting a `window` object.

Discussion   When a window is closed, the window object still exists, but most operations on it will not function correctly. Use this property to determine if it is open or closed, and take appropriate action.

Example	`if (replyWindow.closed)` `    alert("Can't show the reply until you open the window.")`
See Also	`close( )` (method of `window`), `open( )` (method of `window`), `window`

color

Version 1.2

Property of style sheet objects

Specifies the color of text.

Syntax	*styleObj*`.color`
	styleObj — Style sheet object: a property of a `classes`, `ids`, or `tags` object.
Discussion	This property specifies the text color for a style. It may be set to a string of six hexadecimal digits, with an optional leading pound sign (#) character, in the form *rrggbb*, where *rr* specifies red, *gg* specifies green, and *bb* specifies blue. `Color` may also be set to one of the color names listed in Appendix C. The returned value is always in hexadecimal with a leading #. Note that for `color` assignments to take effect, they must occur before the browser writes the styled text to the document. An assignment to `tags.body.color` must be done within the `<HEAD>` ... `</HEAD>` section of the HTML.

Examples	`document.tags.H1.color`
	`    = "ff0000"   // max. red, no green, no blue`
	
	`document.ids.myStyle.color`
	`    = "#8000ff"  // 50% red, no green, max. blue`
	
	`document.classes.myClass.H2.color`
	`    = "limegreen"// Netscape keyword`

See Also	`backgroundColor`, `bgColor`, `classes`, `ids`, `fgColor`, `tags`

colorDepth

Version 1.2   Read-only

Property of the screen object

Returns the number of different colors that the computer screen can display.

Syntax `screen.colorDepth`

Example `document.write("Your computer can display ", screen.colorDepth,`
`" colors. <BR>")`

See Also `screen`.

compile( )

Version 1.2

Method of the RegExp object

Converts a pattern to a compiled form for faster execution.

Syntax `obj.compile(pattern, modifiers)`

`obj`   A variable or expression denoting a `RegExp` object.
`pattern`   String defining a pattern.
`modifiers`   String containing modifier characters `i` and/or `g`.

Discussion Operations on regular expressions execute more quickly if the pattern is compiled into an internal format. A statement such as:

`p = /D+/`

compiles the pattern when the script is loaded. But if the pattern `p` may change at run time, you may write a statement such as:

`p = new RegExp(s)`

where `s` is a string that was typed by the user or modified by some other part of your script. One disadvantage of these string-based patterns is that execution of matches with them is not as fast as with compiled patterns. `compile( )` converts a pattern to the compiled form, resulting in faster execution.

Example   To read pattern components from variables, and then compile the result, use statements such as:

```
p = new RegExp()
p.compile(patn, mods)
```

See Also   RegExp

complete

Version 1.1   Read-only

Property of the Image object

Returns `true` if the image is completely loaded, `false` otherwise.

Syntax   *imageObj*.complete

imageObj   document.*imageName*, or other expression denoting an Image object.

Example
```
if (!myLogo.complete)
    alert("Please wait until the picture is fully visible.")
```

See Also   Image

concat( )

ARRAY

Version 1.2

Method of the Array object

Returns a new array formed by concatenating (joining) two existing arrays.

Syntax   *result* = *array1*.concat(*array2*)

result   Variable that is assigned the new array.
array1   First array to be concatenated.
array2   Second array to be concatenated.

Discussion Since `concat` creates a new array, neither of the two source arrays is modified; all their elements are copied to the *result* array. But remember that in JavaScript, objects are copied by reference. So after calling `concat`, if any objects from *array1* or *array2* are modified, the change will apply to *result* as well.

Example The following statements will display the text "ABCXYZ" on the screen:

```
var a1 = new Array ("A", "B", "C")
var a2 = new Array ("X", "Y", "Z")
var a3 = a1.concat(a2)
for (i = 0; i < a3.length; i++)
   document.write (a3[i])
```

See Also Array, concat( ) (of String)

concat( )

STRING

Version 1.2

Method of the String object

Returns a new string formed by concatenating (joining) two existing strings.

Syntax `result = string1.concat(string2)`

result	Variable that is assigned the new array.
string1	First string to be concatenated.
string2	Second string to be concatenated.

Discussion Since `concat` creates a new string, neither of the two source strings is modified; all their characters are copied to the *result* string.

Example The following statements will display the text "something" on the screen:

```
var s1 = "some"
var s2 = "thing")
var s3 = s1.concat(s2)
document.write (s3)
```

See Also concat( ) (of Array), String

confirm( )

Version 1.0

Method of the window object

Displays a dialog box asking the user to confirm or cancel some action.

Syntax confirm(*message*)

message   A string variable, literal, or expression.

Discussion confirm displays a dialog box with two buttons, labeled "OK" and "Cancel." If the user presses "OK," confirm returns true. If the user presses "Cancel," confirm returns false.

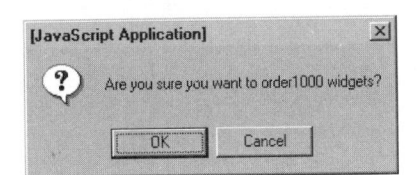

Example
```
answer = confirm("Are you sure you want to order + " orderQty +
    " widgets?")
if (answer)
    submitOrder()
```

See Also alert( ), prompt( ), window

constructor

Version 1.1   Read-only

Property of Array, Boolean, Date, Function, Image, Layer, Math, Number, Option, and String objects, and of all user-defined object types

Returns the constructor function that created an object.

Syntax *obj*.constructor

obj   Object that was created by a constructor function.

Discussion	Since the `typeof` operator always returns `"object"` when applied to an object, you may need a way to find out more about an object's structure. The `constructor` property allows you to find out what function was used to create an object.
Example	This statement creates a new object using the same constructor as an existing object: `var newObj = new existingObj.constructor()`
See Also	`Array`, `Boolean`, `Date`, `Function`, `Image`, `Math`, `Number`, `Option`, `String`

continue

Version 1.0

Keyword used in statements

This keyword is used inside a loop, and causes execution to proceed immediately to the next iteration. For details, see "`continue`" in Chapter 4.

CONTROL_MASK

Version 1.0   Read-only

Property of the Event object

Returns a mask for checking if the Ctrl key was pressed during an event.

Syntax	`Event.CONTROL_MASK`
Discussion	This property is a bit mask for testing the `event.modifiers` property to find out if the Ctrl key was pressed when the event occurred.

Example	The following statements could be used in an event handler:
	``if (myEvent.modifiers & Event.CONTROL_MASK) {
	   ... // the Ctrl key was pressed
	}
	else
	   ... // Ctrl was not pressed```

See Also	`event`, `Event`

cookie

Version 1.0 Tainted

Property of the document object

Specifies the values of the document's cookies.

Syntax `docObject.cookie`

docObject `document` for the current document, or an expression denoting a `document` object.

Discussion A cookie is a small amount of data that is stored in a file, providing scripts a way to store information on the user's computer. Cookies have a name, a value, and several optional fields including an expiration date.

`document.cookie` returns a string containing the name and value fields of all cookies associated with a document, separated by semicolons (;). You can add cookies to this object, and you can search it for a particular name. Note that, although `cookie` returns a string value, it behaves differently from normal strings. For instance, to delete a cookie, you must change its expiration to some date that has already passed. For more information on cookies, see Chapter 7.

The comma, semicolon, and space characters have special meanings in cookies. You may need to use the `escape()` and `unescape()` functions to process your cookie text, in order to prevent these characters from interfering with Navigator's handling of the cookie.

Example
```
document.cookie = "myCookie=" +
    escape(cookieText) + ";expires=31-Dec-99;"
```

See Also `document`, `escape()`, `unescape()`

cos( )

Version 1.0

Method of the Math object

Returns the cosine of a number.

Syntax `Math.cos(number)`

number The value whose cosine is to be returned.

Discussion cos returns a value between -1 and 1. Note that the argument is assumed to be in radians, not degrees.

Example This statement computes a cosine after converting theta from degrees to radians:

```
x = Math.cos(theta / 57.2958)
```

See Also acos(), asin(), atan(), atan2(), Math, sin(), tan()

current

Version 1.1   Read-only   Tainted

Property of the history object

Returns the URL that specifies the current document's location.

Syntax history.current

Discussion The history object is an array that keeps a record of URLs that the browser visits. current returns a string containing the URL of the currently loaded document.

Version 1.1 In JavaScript 1.1, current can only be used when data tainting is enabled.

Version 1.2 In JavaScript 1.2, current can only be used in a signed script with the "UniversalBrowserRead" privilege enabled.

Example
```
document.write("You are now viewing ",
    history.current, ".<BR>")
```

See Also back(), forward(), go(), history, next, previous

data

| Version 1.2 | Special scope | Signed scripts |

Property of the event object

Returns an array of strings representing objects passed by a drag-and-drop mouse operation.

Syntax *eventObj*.data

eventObj   event, or an expression denoting a copy of event, such as a function argument passed to an event handler.

Discussion This property contains one or more strings, each of which contains the URL of a file or other object that was dropped on the window. This property can be used by a signed script with the *"The Universal Browser Read"* privilege. (See Chapter 8.)

Example To obtain the dropped data, you can write a function to read the passed event object such as:

```
function catchDrop (e) {
  var i
  var d = e.data
  numberOfDroppedThings = d.length
  for (i = 0; i < d.length; i++)
    doSomethingWith(d[i]) // handle one dropped object
}
```

Your script must also enable capturing for the event with statements such as:

```
captureEvents(Event.DRAGDROP)
window.onDragDrop = catchDrop
```

Note that there are no parentheses after the name of the handler function in the assignment.

See Also captureEvents( ), event

Date

Version 1.0

Object type (constructor)

Creates a new `Date` object.

Syntax
```
v = new Date()
v = new Date(stringObj)
v = new Date(yr, mo, dy)
v = new Date(yr, mo, dy, hr, min, sec)
```

v	Variable or object to which the new `Date` is assigned.
stringObj	String specifying a date and time (see the following).
yr, mo, dy, hr, min, sec	Number representing the year, month, day, hour, minute, and second.

Methods

`getDate()`	Returns the day of the month.
`getDay()`	Returns a number representing the day of the week (0 for Sunday, 1 for Monday, etc.).
`getHours()`	Returns the hour.
`getMinutes()`	Returns the minute.
`getMonth()`	Returns a number representing the month (0 for January, 1 for February, and so forth).
`getSeconds()`	Returns the second.
`getTime()`	Returns the date and time in internal format.
`getTimezoneOffset()`	Returns the difference in minutes between local time and GMT.
`getYear()`	Returns the year. Note that this is a method of the `Date` constructor itself, not of objects created with *new Date()*.
`Date.parse(string)`	Returns the specified date and time as a single number representing the number of milliseconds since 00:00:00 on January 1, 1970.
`setDate(number)`	Sets the day of the month.
`setHours(number)`	Sets the hour.
`setMinutes(number)`	Sets the minute.
`setMonth(number)`	Sets the month (0 for January, 1 for February, and so forth).

setSeconds(*number*)	Set the second.
setTime(*number*)	Sets the date and time from a single number representing the number of milliseconds since 00:00:00 on January 1, 1970.
setYear()	Sets the year.
toGMTString()	Returns a string representing the date and universal (GMT) time.
toLocaleString()	Returns a string representing the date and local time.
Date.UTC (*yr, mo, dy, hr, min, sec*)	Returns the specified date and time as a single number representing the number of milliseconds since 00:00:00 on January 1, 1970.

Discussion Calling `Date()` with no arguments creates an object containing the current date and time.

Example
```
todayNow = new Date()
myBirthday = new Date(8, 13, 55)
newCenturyParty = new Date("Jan 1, 2001 20:00:00")
```

DBLCLICK

Version 1.2 Read-only

Property of the Event object

Returns a mask for capturing double-click mouse events.

Syntax `Event.DBLCLICK`

Discussion This property is used to capture and release double-click events. For more details on event handling, see Chapter 7.

Example To enable capturing of double-click events (as well as click):

`myWindow.captureEvents (Event.DBLCLICK | Event.CLICK)`

See Also `captureEvents()`, `event`, `Event`, `ondblclick`, `releaseEvents()`

defaultChecked

Version 1.0   **External**   **Tainted**

Property of the Checkbox and Radio external objects

Specifies the default state of a check box or radio button.

Syntax   `screenObj.defaultChecked`

          `screenObj`   Checkbox or Radio object in a form.

Discussion   This is a Boolean property that is initially `true` if the `CHECKED` attribute is specified in the HTML for the check box or button. Scripts can modify the value, but this has no effect on the object's appearance on the screen (use `checked` for that).

Example   This loop locates the default button in a set of radio buttons:

```
for (b in document.myForm.myRadio)
   if (document.myForm.myRadio[b].defaultChecked)
      alert("The default setting is "
        + document.myForm.myRadio[b].value)
```

See Also   Checkbox, checked, Radio

defaultSelected

Version 1.0   **External**   **Tainted**

Property of the `Option` object

Specifies the default selection(s) in a select box.

Syntax   `optionObj.defaultSelected`

          `optionObj`   Option object in a form.

Discussion   This is a Boolean property that is initially `true` if the `SELECTED` attribute is specified in the HTML for the option. Scripts can modify the value, but this has no effect on the object's appearance on the screen (use `selected` for that).

If the Select object is allowed to have multiple selections, more than one of its `Option` objects may have this property set to `true`. Otherwise, setting any `Option` object's `defaultSelected` to `true` will cause all the others to be set to `false`.

Example This loop locates the default options in a select box:

```
for (i = 0; i < document.myForm.mySelect.length; i++)
   if (document.myForm.mySelect.options[i].defaultSelected)
      alert(document.myForm.mySelect.options[i].text
         + " is a default setting.")
```

See Also Option, Select, `selected`

defaultStatus

Version 1.0   External   Tainted

Property of the `window` object

Specifies the default message for the window status bar.

Syntax For the current window:

```
defaultstatus
self.defaultStatus
window.defaultStatus
```

For other windows:

windowObj`.defaultStatus`

windowObj   An expression denoting a `window` object.

Discussion The default message is displayed when no higher priority message has been specified by the `status` property. If `defaultStatus` is modified inside an `onMouseOver` or `onMouseOut` event handler, the handler must return `true` in order to update the display.

Example `window.defaultStatus = "Welcome to my home page!"`

See Also `onMouseOut`, `onMouseOver`, `status`, `window`

defaultValue

Version 1.0 External Tainted

Property of the Password, Text, and Textarea external objects

Specifies the default text for an object when it is displayed on the screen.

Syntax *screenObj*.defaultValue

screenObj   Password, Text, or Textarea object in a form.

Discussion This property is initially set to the value specified by the object's HTML:
- For Text objects, it reflects the VALUE attribute.
- For Textarea objects, it reflects the text specified between the <TEXTAREA> and </TEXTAREA> tags.
- For Password objects, it is always null for security; the VALUE attribute, if present, is *not* reflected.

Scripts can modify defaultValue, but this has no effect on the object's appearance on the screen (use value for that).

Example This statement reads the default value of a text box and stores it in a variable:

defaultCountry = document.myForm.Country.defaultValue

See Also Password, Text, Textarea, value

delete

Version 1.2

Operator used in expressions

This operator is used to delete elements of an array or properties of an object. For details, see Chapter 3.

description

Version 1.1 Read-only External

Property of the MimeType and Plugin external objects

Describes a MIME type or plug-in.

Syntax
: ```
navigator.mimeTypes[index].description
navigator.plugins[index].description
```
  *index*          Number or string specifying one MIME type or plug-in.

Discussion
: For MimeType objects, this property provides a description of the data associated with the MIME type. For Plugin objects, this property provides a description of the plug-in; its value is set by the plug-in.

Example
: The following loop displays the names and descriptions of all installed plug-ins:

    ```
    document.write("<P> Installed plug-ins:<BR>".bold())
    for (i in navigator.plugins) {
       document.write(i, " is \"", navigator.plugins[i].description,
       "\".<BR>")
    }
    ```

See Also
: MimeType, Plugin

disableExternalCapture( )

Version 1.2 Signed scripts

Method of the window object

Disables scripts from capturing events in pages loaded from different servers.

Syntax
: ```
disableExternalCapture()
self.disableExternalCapture()
window.disableExternalCapture()
```

Discussion	This method disables external event capturing, which may have been enabled by the `enableExternalCapture()` method. Due to security concerns, this method may only be used in signed scripts (see Chapter 8).
Example	`window.disableExternalCapture()`
See Also	`captureEvents()`, `enableExternalCapture()`

display

Version 1.2

Property of style sheet objects

Specifies how HTML elements are displayed.

Syntax	*styleObj*.display
	styleObj Style sheet object: a property of a `classes`, `ids`, or `tags` object.
Discussion	This property specifies how HTML elements are displayed. The value may be one of:

`"block"`	Displays the element as a block-level element, with margins, borders, and so forth.
`"inline"`	Displays the element as text that may span part of a line or several lines.
`"list-item"`	Displays the element as a list item with marking or numbering and indentation.
`"none"`	Causes the element to not appear on the screen.

    This property applies to all elements, and is not inherited. Its initial value depends on the element.

    Note that for `display` assignments to take effect, they must occur before the browser writes the styled text to the document. An assignment to `tags.body.display` must be done within the `<HEAD>` ... `</HEAD>` section of the HTML.

Example	`document.ids.pictureFrame.display = "block"`
See Also	`classes`, `ids`, `listStyleType`, `tags`

do

Version 1.2

Keyword used in statements

This keyword is used to create do...while loops. For details, see Chapter 4.

document

Version 1.0   Read-only   External

Property of the Layer and window objects and Frame external object

Reflects a document in a window.

Syntax
: For the current window:

    document
    self.document
    window.document

    For other windows:

    windowObj.document

windowObj	An expression denoting a window object.

Properties
: | | |
  |---|---|
  | alinkColor | Color for displaying active links. |
  | anchors | Array reflecting named anchors in the document. |
  | applets | Array reflecting applets in the document. |
  | bgColor | Background color. |
  | cookie | Specifies all cookies associated with the document. |
  | classes | Provides style sheet properties for style classes. |
  | domain | Specifies the domain name of the server from which the document was loaded. |
  | embeds | Array reflecting embedded files in the document. |
  | fgColor | Normal text color. |
  | forms | Array reflecting forms in a document. |
  | ids | Provides style sheet objects for individual styles. |
  | images | Array reflecting images in a document. |
  | lastModified | Returns the date when the document was last modified. |
  | layers | Array reflecting layers in a document. |

	linkColor	Specifies the color for displaying links that have not been visited.
	links	Array reflecting Area and Link objects in a document.
	location	Equivalent to the URL property, but not recommended for use, as it will be removed in a future release of Navigator.
	referrer	Reflects the URL of the document from which a link was followed to the current document.
	tags	provides style sheet properties for HTML tags.
	title	Reflects the contents of the HTML <TITLE> ... </TITLE> tags.
	URL	Reflects the complete URL of a document.
	vlinkColor	Specifies the color for displaying links that have already been visited.
Methods	captureEvents()	Allows a document to receive captured events.
	close()	Closes a document and forces all text to be displayed.
	getSelection()	Returns a string containing text selected by the cursor.
	open()	Opens a document for writing.
	releaseEvents()	Releases previously captured events.
	routeEvent()	Passes a captured event to other objects that can receive it.
	write(*arg*, ... *arg*)	Writes one or more objects to the document.
	writeln (*arg*, ... *arg*)	Writes one or more objects and a newline character to the document.

Event Handlers onclick, ondblclick, onkeydown, onkeypress, onkeyup, onmousedown, onmouseup

You may also use event handlers of the window object that contains the document.

Discussion The document object reflects all HTML text between the <BODY> and </BODY> tags, including forms, images, links, and other objects and their properties.

Version 1.2   The event handlers, the classes, ids, layers, and tags properties, and the captureEvents(), getSelection(), releaseEvents(), and routeEvent() methods, were added in JavaScript 1.2.

Example The following statements open a new window, open its document, write some text to the document, and close the document:

```
var win2 = window.open("", "Window2")
win2.document.open()
win2.document.write("Hello!")
win2.document.close()
```

See Also Frame, window

domain

Version 1.1   External   Tainted

Property of the document object

Specifies the domain name of the server from which the document was loaded.

Syntax   `docObject.domain`

          `docObject`   document for the current document, or an expression denoting a document object in any window.

Discussion   This property can be modified, but only in a limited way: it can only be changed to a suffix of itself. For example, if it is initially `"server.company.com"`, it can be changed to `"company.com."` The reason for this is security-related. When data tainting is not in effect, scripts cannot read properties of windows loaded from different servers. But a large company might have several servers that need to read each other's scripts. If one window is loaded from `server1.xyz.com`, and another from `server2.xyz.com`, scripts in both windows can change their domain property to `xyz.com`.

Example   `document.domain = "ourplace.com"`

See Also   `taint()`, `untaint()`

DRAGDROP

Version 1.2   Read-only

Property of the Event object

Returns a mask for capturing drag-and-drop mouse events.

Syntax   `Event.DRAGDROP`

Discussion   This property is used to control event capturing (see Chapter 7). The URLs of the dropped objects are available as array elements of the `data` property of the `event` object.

Example   To enable capturing of drag-and-drop events (as well as click):

          `myWindow.captureEvents (Event.DRAGDROP | Event.CLICK)`

See Also   `captureEvents()`, `event`, `Event`, `releaseEvents()`

E

Version 1.0   Read-only

Property of the Math object

Returns the value of Euler's constant *e*, the base of natural logarithms (approximately 2.718281828459045).

Syntax   `Math.E`

See Also   `LN2`, `LN10`, `LOG2E`, `LOG10E`, `Math`, `PI`, `SQRT1_2`, `SQRT2`

elements

Version 1.0   Read-only   External

Property of the Form external object

Reflects the elements of an HTML form.

Syntax   *formObj*.`elements`

formObj   `document.`*formName* or other expression denoting a Form object.

Properties   `length`   Number of elements in the array (and in the form).

Discussion   Each Form object (which itself is an element of the document.forms array) has an elements array that reflects the text boxes, buttons, and other elements in an HTML form. Many of these elements may have names assigned with the HTML `NAME` attribute, in which case they can be referenced as `document.`*formname*.*elementname*. However, they may also be referenced as array elements; an element's position in the array is based on the order in which the elements are defined in the HTML.

Although `elements` is a read-only array, some of the properties of its elements can be modified. For instance, Checkbox objects have a checked property that scripts can modify.

Example   This loop displays the names of all a form's elements:

```
for (i = 0; i < document.myForm.elements.length; i++)
   document.write(i, ": ", document.myForm.elements[i].name, "<BR>")
```

See Also   `Button`, `Checkbox`, `FileUpload`, `Form`, `Hidden`, `Option`, `Password`, `Radio`, `Reset`, `Select`, `Submit`, `Text`, `Textarea`

else

Version 1.0

Keyword used in statements

This keyword is used to create conditional statements. For details, see Chapter 4.

Embed

Version 1.0   External

External object

Reflects an audio, video, or other file embedded in a document.

Syntax
: *docObject*.embeds.*name*
  docObject.embeds[*index*]

  docObject   document for the current document, or an expression denoting a document in any window.
  name   String value representing a name assigned by the NAME attribute of the HTML <EMBED> tag.
  index   Number or string specifying an element of the embeds array.

Properties
: An Embed object may have various properties and methods, depending on the file type and the plug-in application that handles it. For more information, see the documentation for the plug-in.

Discussion
: When Navigator loads a web page, it creates Embed objects corresponding to all embedded files. You can reference these objects as elements of a document's embeds array.

Example
: If a MIDI music file is embedded in a document with HTML such as:

  `<EMBED SRC="test.mid" HEIGHT=80 WIDTH=160>`

  then playback of the file can be started by a statement such as:

  `document.embeds[0].play()`

  (The reference to embeds[0] assumes that the MIDI file is the first, or only, embedded file in the document.)

See Also
: embeds, MimeType, Plugin

embeds

Version 1.0 Read-only External

Property of the document object

Contains Embed objects that reflect files embedded in a document.

Syntax
: `docObject.embeds.name`
  `docObject.embeds[index]`

`docObject`	document for the current document, or an expression denoting a document in any window.
`name`	Name assigned by the `NAME` attribute of the HTML `<EMBED>` tag.
`index`	Number or string specifying an element of the `embeds` array.

Properties
: `length` — Length of the array, that is, number of embedded files in the document.

Discussion
: This array is read-only, in that its elements cannot be modified. However, some of the elements may have properties that can be modified, depending on the file type and the plug-in application that handles the file. For more information, see the documentation for the plug-in.

Example
: If a MIDI music file is embedded in a document with HTML such as:

  `<EMBED SRC="test.mid" HEIGHT=80 WIDTH=160>`

  then playback of the file can be started by a statement such as:

  `document.embeds[0].play()`

  (The reference to `embeds[0]` assumes that the MIDI file is the first, or only, embedded file in the document.)

See Also
: Embed, MimeType, Plugin

enabledPlugin

Version 1.1   Read-only   External

Property of the MimeType external object

Reflects the plug-in that is configured for a type of file.

Syntax
: `navigator.mimeTypes[index].enabledPlugin`
  index   String or number specifying the MIME type.

Discussion
: If Navigator has been configured to use a plug-in for a MIME type, this property returns a reference to the Plugin object. If no plug-in is configured for the MIME type, `enabledPlugin` returns `null`.

Example
: This nested `if` statement checks if the browser recognizes AVI video, and if so, whether a plug-in has been configured:

    ```
    if(navigator.mimeTypes['video/avi'])
       if(! navigator.mimeTypes['video/avi'].enabledPlugin)
          alert("Sorry, you are not set up to view the video.")
    ```

    (The nested `if` is needed because, if the second `if` was executed in a browser that did not recognize the AVI type, an undefined-symbol error would occur.)

See Also
: MimeType, `mimeTypes`

enableExternalCapture( )

Version 1.2   Signed scripts

Method of the `window` object

Enables scripts to capture events in pages loaded from different servers.

Syntax
: `enableExternalCapture()`
  `self.enableExternalCapture()`
  `window.enableExternalCapture()`

Discussion
: This method enables external event capturing. Due to security concerns, this method can only be used in signed scripts that have acquired the `"UniversalBrowserWrite"` privilege (see Chapter 8).

A script can disable external event capturing with the (disableExternalCapture) method. Also, Navigator may disable external capturing if it detects a downgrading of security for the page.

Example `window.enableExternalCapture()`

See Also `captureEvents(), disableExternalCapture()`

encoding

Version 1.0   External

Property of the Form external object

Specifies the MIME encoding type for a form.

Syntax *formObj*.encoding

formObj   document.*formname* or other expression denoting a Form object.

Discussion Initially this property reflects the ENCTYPE attribute of the HTML <FORM> tag. Scripts can modify the property at any time.

Example `formType = document.myForm.encoding`

See Also Form

ERROR

Version 1.2   Read-only

Property of the Event object

Returns a mask for capturing error events.

Syntax `Event.ERROR`

Discussion   This property is used to capture and release error events, which occur when the browser encounters an error condition while loading an image or document. For more details on event handling, see Chapter 7.

Example   To enable capturing of error events:

    myWindow.captureEvents (Event.ERROR)

See Also   captureEvents(), event, Event, onerror, releaseEvents()

escape( )

Version 1.0

Built-in function

Returns a string in which special characters are converted to numeric equivalents.

Syntax   escape(*string*)

    string   Any String object or expression.

Discussion   This function returns a string in which all non-alphanumeric characters of its argument are converted to the form %*xx*, where *xx* is a hexadecimal code representing the character. This may be useful to prevent special characters such as quotation marks or white space from interfering with normal handling of the string.
    You can convert an escaped string back to normal by using unescape( ).

Example   The statement:

    s = escape("You & me")

    returns the string "You%20%26%20me."

See Also   unescape( )

eval( )

Version 1.0

Built-in function/method of all objects

Evaluates a string as JavaScript source code.

Syntax As a built-in function:

eval(*str*)

As a method:

obj.eval(*str*)

str   A string value to be evaluated.
obj   Any object.

Discussion This function accepts a string containing JavaScript statements or expressions, and executes it as if it were part of a script. If the string contains an expression that returns a value, eval( ) returns that value.

In some versions of JavaScript (see below), eval( ) may be called as a method of an object, in which case it evaluates its argument in the context of that object. In other words, the statement:

```
result = myObject.eval(someString)
```

is equivalent to:

```
with myObject {
   result = eval(someString)
}
```

Version 1.1
Version 1.2

The history of eval( ) in JavaScript is somewhat complex. In JavaScript 1.0, eval( ) was a built-in function, not a method.

In JavaScript 1.1, it was made a method as well.

Later, some other software companies, and the international standards organization ECMA, defined eval( ) as a built-in function only. So when JavaScript 1.2 was first released in Navigator version 4.0, eval( ) was again provided only as a built-in function. However, due to changing standards and the need to support scripts written for older versions, eval( ) was again provided as both a method and a built-in function, starting with Navigator version 4.02.

Example
: You can use `eval()` to add a "mini-debugger" to any web page with HTML such as:

```
<FORM NAME="debugger">
<INPUT TYPE="text" NAME="stmt" SIZE=64>
<INPUT TYPE="button" VALUE="Do it"
 ONCLICK="eval(this.form.stmt.value)">
</FORM>
```

You can type a JavaScript statement into the text box, and execute it by clicking the button.

See Also
: `valueOf()`

event

Version 1.2   Special scope   Signed scripts

Built-in object

Passes a set of properties to an event handler.

Syntax
: `event`

Properties
: `data` — An array of strings containing URLs of objects that were dragged and dropped. Only available for signed scripts (see below).
: `height, width` — Width and height of the window after resizing.
: `layerX, layerY` — Horizontal and vertical cursor position within the document layer where the event occurred.
: `modifiers` — A bit mask specifying modifier keys that were pressed when a mouse or keyboard event occurred. Bits may be tested with the built-in values `ALT_MASK`, `CONTROL_MASK`, `SHIFT_MASK`, and `META_MASK`, which are properties of the Event object.
: `pageX, pageY` — Horizontal and vertical cursor position within the web page where the event occurred.
: `screenX, screenY` — Horizontal and vertical cursor position within the computer screen where the event occurred.
: `target` — For captured events, this property returns the object for which the event was originally intended.
: `type` — A string specifying the type of event, such as `"click"`.
: `which` — Number specifying the mouse button or key that was pressed.

Discussion event has limited scope. It may only be used in two specific cases:
- It may be referenced by name in the event handler strings attached to HTML objects (see the following example). Usually it is immediately passed as an argument to a function.
- It is passed as an argument to functions that are used for event capturing.

Not all properties will have values in all cases. For instance, `event.data` is undefined for anything but drag-and-drop events.

Properties of `event` are read-only, except for a signed script with the `"UniversalBrowserWrite"` privilege. Also, in order to read dropped filenames from the `data` property, a script must have the `"UniversalBrowserRead"` privilege.

Example An HTML object can pass `event` in a handler such as:

```
<A HREF="somewhere.html" ONCLICK="goHandle(event)">
```

See Also `captureEvents(), Event`

Event

Version 1.2   Read-only

Built-in object

Provides properties that are used as bit masks to manage event handlers.

Syntax Event

Properties The following properties are used with the `captureEvents()` and `releaseEvents()` methods to control event capturing:

Name	Used by	Meaning
ABORT	images	Transfer interrupted by the user.
BLUR	windows, frames, and all form elements	Focus removed from an object.
CHANGE	text, text area, and select box form elements	User changed the contents or settings of the element.
CLICK	All button form elements, documents, links	Single mouse click.
DBLCLICK	documents, links	Double mouse click.

Name	Used by	Meaning
DRAGDROP	windows	Object(s) dragged and dropped.
ERROR	windows, images	Error occurred during loading of image or document.
FOCUS	windows, frames, and all form elements	Focus applied to an object.
KEYDOWN	documents, images, links, text area form elements	Key pressed by user.
KEYPRESS	documents, images, links, text area form elements	Key pressed or held by user.
KEYUP	documents, images, links, text area form elements	Key released by user.
LOAD	document	Page loaded by Navigator.
MOUSEDOWN	All button form elements, documents, links	Mouse button pressed by user.
MOUSEMOVE	normally none; can be captured	Mouse cursor moved by user.
MOUSEOUT	links, document layers	Mouse cursor moved away from object.
MOUSEOVER	links, document layers	Mouse cursor moved onto an object.
MOUSEUP	All button form elements, documents, links	Mouse button released.
MOVE	windows and frames	Window or frame moved on the screen.
RESET	forms	Reset button clicked.
RESIZE	windows and frames	Window or frame resized.
SELECT	text, text area, and select box form elements	Element selected by user.
SUBMIT	forms	Submit button clicked.
UNLOAD	documents	window closed, or a new document loaded.

The following properties are used to test the `modifiers` property of the `event` object:

Name	Meaning
ALT_MASK	Alt key was pressed.
CONTROL_MASK	Ctrl key was pressed.
META_MASK	Meta key was pressed.
SHIFT_MASK	Shift key was pressed.

Discussion For more details on event handlers, see Chapter 7.

Example `myWindow.captureEvents(Event.CLICK | Event.DBLCLICK | Event.DRAGDROP)`

See Also `captureEvents()`, `event`

exec( )

Version 1.2

Method of the RegExp object

Executes a search for matches in a string.

Syntax

```
results = patternObj.exec(stringObj)
results = patternObj(stringObj)
```

`results`	Variable to contain the search results.
`patternObj`	Name or expression denoting a `RegExp` object.
`stringObj`	Optional name or expression denoting a string to be searched. If omitted, `exec()` will search `RegExp.input`.

Discussion

This method scans the specified string looking for a substring that matches the regular expression. If no match is found, `exec()` returns `null`. If a match is found, `exec()` returns an array of results, and also modifies properties of the pattern object and the global `RegExp` object.

In the results array, element 0 will contain the matched substring. Elements 1 and beyond will contain memorized substrings specified by parentheses in the pattern. In addition to these numbered elements, the array will have two properties that are referenced by their name, that is `myArray.name` or `myArray["name"]`.

`index`	A number indicating where the match occurred: the position of the match in the source string.
`input`	A copy of the string to be searched.

In the pattern object, `exec` stores additional results in the following properties:

`global`	Returns `true` if the match is global (g modifier).
`ignoreCase`	Returns `true` if the match is case-insensitive (i modifier).
`lastIndex`	If `global` is `true`, this property allows a script to step through a string, returning one match at a time. Specifically, `exec()` starts searching at the position in the string specified by this property; and if a match is found, `exec()` updates this property to specify the position immediately after the matched substring.
`source`	The text of the pattern.

Note that strings are indexed starting from 0.

In the `RegExp` object, `exec` stores additional results in the following properties:

`$1, $2, ... $9`	Strings representing memorized substrings specified by parentheses in the pattern.
`lastMatch` or `$&`	The last substring matched.
`lastParen` or `$+`	The last substring memorized.
`leftContext` or `` $` ``	The substring from the start of the source string to just before the last match. (Note the use of the accent character, not the apostrophe.)
`rightContext` or `$'`	The substring from just after the last match to the end of the source string.

Note that these are properties of `RegExp` itself, not of objects constructed by `new RegExp()`. These properties are shared by all scripts running in a window. If you have several scripts in one window that use regular expressions, they may affect each other's results.

`exec()` can also be called as a "null method" of `RegExp` objects; for instance, if `pat` is a pattern and `str` is a string, then `pat(str)` is equivalent to `pat.exec(str)`.

Example The following statements demonstrate a pattern that could be used to find e-mail addresses, consisting of a username and domain with the usual punctuation:

```
userText = "Contact me at cast@fish.net."
pattern = /(\w+)@(\w+)\.(\w{3})/i
results = pattern.exec(userText)
```

(For this simple example, the `\w` symbol is used, which accepts letters, digits, and the underscore (_) character. Some actual user and domain names may use other characters.)

After executing these statements, `results` will have four elements and two properties:

`results[0]` will contain `cast@fish.net`.
`results[1]` will contain `cast`.
`results[2]` will contain `fish`.
`results[3]` will contain `net`.
`results.index` will contain 14.
`results.input` will contain `Contact me at cast@fish.net`.

Properties of `pattern` will have the following values:

`pattern.source` will contain `(\w+)@(\w+)\.(\w{3})`.
`pattern.global` will contain `false`.
`pattern.ignoreCase` will contain `true`.
`pattern.lastIndex` will contain 0.

Properties of `RegExp` will have the following values:
`RegExp.lastMatch` will contain `cast@fish.net`.
`RegExp.lastParen` will contain `net`.
`RegExp.leftContext` will contain `Contact me at `.
`RegExp.rightContext` will contain `.(period)`.
`RegExp.$1` will contain `cast`.
`RegExp.$2` will contain `fish`.
`RegExp.$3` will contain `net`.

See Also `compile( )`, `exec( )`, `RegExp`, `test( )`

exp( )

Version 1.0

Method of the `Math` object

Returns *e* (Euler's constant, the base of natural logarithms, 2.71828459045...) to the power of a number.

Syntax `Math.exp(number)`

number Numeric value to be exponentiated.

Example `y = Math.exp(x)`

See Also `E`, `log( )`, `Math`

export

Version 1.2

Keyword used in statements

This keyword is used by signed scripts to make objects, properties, and methods available to other scripts. For more details, see Chapter 8.

fgColor

Version 1.0　External

Property of the document object

Specifies the document's foreground (text) color.

Syntax
: *docObject*.fgColor
  docObject　　document for the current window's document, or an expression denoting a document object.

Discussion
: This property specifies the color that is used for normal text, that is, text that is not in a link, and whose color has not been changed by style sheets or other operations. fgColor may be set to a string of six hexadecimal digits, with an optional leading pound sign (#) character, in the form *rrggbb*, where *rr* specifies red, *gg* specifies green, and *bb* specifies blue. fgColor may also be set to one of the color names listed in Appendix C. The returned value is always in hexadecimal with a leading #.

  This property is initially set to the color specified by the TEXT attribute, if any, of the HTML <BODY> tag.

Examples
: ```
  document.fgColor = "ff0000"   // max. red
                                 // no green
                                 // no blue

  parent.document.fgColor = "#8000ff"   // 50% red
                                         // no green
                                         // max. blue

  otherWindow.document.fgColor = "limegreen"// Netscape
                                            // keyword
  ```

See Also
: bgColor, document

# filename

**Version 1.1　Read-only　External**

### Property of the Plugin external object

Reflects the filename of a plug-in application.
  ```

Syntax
: `navigator.plugins[index].filename`

index   Number specifying one element of the `plugins` array, or a string specifying the name of a Plugin object, as defined by the object's `name` property (see the following).

Discussion
: This property is a string containing the complete pathname of the program file from which the plug-in was loaded. The exact format of the pathname is platform-dependent.

Example
: On a typical installation of Navigator, the statement:

`document.write(navigator.plugins[0])`

can result in a display such as:

> E:\APPS\NETSCAPE 4.01 FOR WIN95\PROGRAM\plugins\nplau32.dll

See Also
: Plugin, `plugins`

FileUpload

Version 1.1   Read-only   External   Signed scripts

Property of the Form external object

Reflects a file upload box in an HTML form.

Syntax
: `formObject.uploadName`
`formObject["uploadName"]`
`formObject.elements[index]`

formObject   Name of a form, or expression denoting a Form object.
uploadName   Name specified in the NAME attribute of the HTML `<INPUT>` tag.
index   Number specifying the position of the upload box in the form.

Properties
: *form*   Reference to the Form object that contains this upload box.
name   Reflects the NAME attribute of the HTML `<INPUT>` tag.
type   Reflects the TYPE attribute of the HTML `<INPUT>` tag (this is always `"file"` for FileUpload objects).
value   A string specifying the pathname of the file selected by the user. This property is read-only, except for signed scripts with the `"UniversalBrowserWrite"` privilege.

Methods	`blur()`	Removes focus from the upload box.
	`focus()`	Sets focus on the upload box.
Event Handlers	`onblur, onchange, onfocus`	
Discussion	When Navigator loads a web page, it creates FileUpload objects corresponding to all file upload boxes. You can reference these objects as elements of a form's `elements` array.	
Example	An upload box created by HTML such as:	

```
<INPUT TYPE="file" NAME="browze">
```

can be used to select a file, whose pathname can then be obtained by a statement such as:

```
chosenFile = document.myForm.browze.value
```

See Also   Form

find( )

Version 1.2 External

Method of the `window` object

Returns `true` if the specified string is found in a window's document.

Syntax   For the current window:

`find(string, matchCase, backward)`
`self.find(string, matchCase, backward)`
`window.find(string, matchCase, backward)`

   For any window:

`windowObj.find(string, matchCase, backward)`

`string`	Optional argument. String to be searched for.
`matchCase`	Optional argument. If present and `true`, selects a case-sensitive search.
`backward`	Optional argument. If present and `true`, selects a backward search (toward the top of the document).
`windowObj`	An expression denoting a `window` object.

Discussion find may be called with zero, one, or three arguments (but not two):
- If no arguments are specified, a Find dialog box is displayed, and the user can enter the search parameters interactively.
- If either of the *matchCase* or *backward* arguments is used, both must be present. If both are omitted, the search is case-insensitive and forward.

find returns true if the specified text is found, or false if it is not found, except when it is called with no arguments. In that case, find immediately returns an undefined result, so that the script can continue to execute without waiting for the user.

If any text in the window is selected when find is called, it starts searching immediately after (for a forward search) or before (for a backward search) the selection. Otherwise, the search starts at the beginning (forward) or end (backward) of the window.

Example To provide a Find dialog box for text in a secondary window, use statements such as:

```
var otherWindow = window.open("fileToSearch.txt")
otherWindow.find()
```

See Also Frame, window

fixed( )

Version 1.0

Method of the String object

Returns a string containing HTML code to format a string in fixed-width characters.

Syntax *stringObj*.fixed( )

stringObj   String object or expression to be formatted in fixed-width characters.

Discussion This method returns a string consisting of HTML code. The code includes the HTML <TT> and </TT> tags so that, if the returned string is written to a document, it will appear in a fixed-width ("teletype") font.

Example The statement

document.write("An ", "immovable".fixed(), " object")

will write to the web page:

> Meeting an `immovable` object

See Also big( ), blink( ), bold( ), fontcolor( ), fontsize( ), italics( ), small( ), split( ), strike( ), String, sub( ), sup( )

floor( )

Version 1.0

Method of the Math object

Returns the "floor" (greatest lower integer) of a number.

Syntax Math.floor(*number*)

number   The number whose floor is to be returned.

Discussion Note that "lower" means more negative. For example, Math.floor(12.3) returns 12; but Math.floor(-12.3) returns -13, not -12.

Example f = Math.floor(x)

See Also ceil( ), Math

focus( )

Version 1.0

Method of the window object, and of Button, Checkbox, FileUpload, Frame, Password, Radio, Reset, Select, Submit, Text, and Textarea external objects

Sets focus to an object on the screen.

Syntax   `obj.blur()`

           `obj`   Object that may have focus.

Discussion   This method sets the screen focus to the specified object.
           In JavaScript version 1.0, this method is only available for the Password, Select, Text, and Textarea external objects.

Version 1.1   This property was added to the Button, Checkbox, FileUpload, Frame, Radio, Reset, Submit, and `window` objects in JavaScript 1.1.

Example   `document.forms.myForm.textBox1.focus()`

See Also   `blur()`, Button, Checkbox, FileUpload, Frame, Password, Radio, Reset, Select, Submit, Text, Textarea, `window`

FOCUS

Version 1.2   Read-only

Property of the Event object

Returns a mask for capturing focus events.

Syntax   `Event.FOCUS`

Discussion   This property is used to capture and release focus events, which occur when an object on the screen receives focus. For more details on event handling, see Chapter 7.

Example   To enable capturing of focus events (as well as blur):

`myWindow.captureEvents (Event.BLUR | Event.FOCUS)`

See Also   `captureEvents()`, event, Event, onfocus, releaseEvents()`

fontcolor( )

Version 1.0

Method of the String object

Returns a string containing HTML code to format a string in colored characters.

Syntax   *stringObj*.fontcolor(*color*)

stringObj   String object or expression to be formatted in fixed-width characters.

color   String that specifies the color (see the following).

Discussion   This method returns a string consisting of HTML code. The code includes the HTML <FONT COLOR=...> and </FONT> tags so that, if the returned string is written to a document, it will appear in the specified color.

color may be set to a string of six hexadecimal digits, with an optional leading pound sign (#) character, in the form *rrggbb*, where *rr* specifies red, *gg* specifies green, and *bb* specifies blue. *color* may also be set to one of the color names listed in Appendix C.

Example   The statement

document.write("It's a ", "gray".fontcolor("#808080"), " area.")

will write to the web page:

It's a gray area.

See Also   big( ), blink( ), bold( ), fixed( ), fontsize( ), italics( ), small( ), split( ), strike( ), String, sub( ), sup( )

fontFamily

Version 1.2

Property of style sheet objects

Specifies the font for text in HTML elements.

Syntax   *styleObj*.fontFamily

styleObj   Style sheet object: a property of a `classes`, `ids`, or `tags` object.

Discussion   This property specifies the name of the font used for displaying text. The value is a string that may contain a specific font name such as `"Helvetica"`, or one of the generic font names `"serif"`, `"sans-serif"`, `"cursive"`, `"monospace"`, or `"fantasy"`. The specific font used for a generic name depends on the browser and the user's computer.

The value may also be a series of font names separated by commas. If the first font is not available, the browser continues along the list attempting to find a substitute. If none of the specified fonts is available, text will be displayed in the browser's default font.

This property applies to all elements, and is inherited. Its initial value is the browser's default font.

Note that for `fontFamily` assignments to take effect, they must occur before the browser writes the styled text to the document. An assignment to `tags.body.fontFamily` must be done within the <HEAD> ... </HEAD> section of the HTML.

Example
```
document.classes.textbook.all.fontFamily =
    "New Century Schoolbook, Century New, Century, serif"
```

See Also `classes, color, fontSize, fontStyle, fontWeight, ids, tags`

fontsize( )

Version 1.0   Unusual spelling or capitalization

Method of the `String` object

Returns a string containing HTML code to format a string in a specified size.

Syntax `stringObj.fontsize(size)`

stringObj   String object or expression to be formatted in fixed-width characters.

size   Numeric or string value that specifies the size (see the following).

Discussion   This method returns a string consisting of HTML code. The code includes the HTML <FONT SIZE=...> and </FONT> tags so that, if the returned string is written to a document, it will appear in the specified size.

size may be set to a number between 1 and 7, to select one of Navigator's standard sizes. It may also be a string containing a relative value such as "+2" to change the size in relation to the surrounding text.

Note that the name of this method is all lowercase. Starting in JavaScript 1.2, the name `fontSize` is used as a property of style sheet objects; beware of confusing the two.

Example   The statement:

```
document.write("A really ", "big".fontsize("+3"),
" show.")
```

will write to the web page:

A really **big** show.

See Also   big(), blink(), bold(), fixed(), fontcolor(), italics(), small(), split(), strike(), String, sub(), sup()

fontSize

Version 1.2

Property of style sheet objects

Specifies the font for text in HTML elements.

Syntax   *styleObj*.fontSize

styleObj   Style sheet object: a property of a `classes`, `ids`, or `tags` object.

Discussion   This property specifies the size of text. The value may be one of the following:
- An absolute measurement, such as `"12pt"`.
- A measurement relative to the parent element's font size, such as `"1.5em"`.
- A percentage of the parent element's font size, such as `"150%"`.

Also, the browser has a built-in table of font sizes, which may be used by specifying one of the following:
- One of the keywords `"x-small"`, `"small"`, `"medium"`, `"large"`, `"x-large"`, or `"xx-large"`.
- The keyword `"larger"` or `"smaller"`, to select a size relative to the parent element's size.
- A positive or negative numeric value to select a size relative to the parent element's size. For instance, 1 is equivalent to `"larger"`, and -1 is equivalent to `"smaller"`.

This property applies to all elements, and is inherited. Its initial value is `"medium"`.

Note that for `fontSize` assignments to take effect, they must occur before the browser writes the styled text to the document. An assignment to `tags.body.fontSize` must be done within the `<HEAD>` ... `</HEAD>` section of the HTML.

Example   `document.ids.triple.fontSize = "3em"`

See Also   `classes, color, fontFamily, fontStyle, fontWeight, ids, tags`

fontStyle

Version 1.2

Property of style sheet objects

Specifies the style of text in HTML elements.

Syntax   *styleObj*.fontStyle

styleObj   Style sheet object: a property of a `classes`, `ids`, or `tags` object.

Discussion   This property specifies the style of characters. The value may be `"normal"`, `"italic"`, `"italic small-caps"`, `"oblique"`, `"oblique small-caps"`, or `"small-caps"`.

This property applies to all elements, and is inherited. Its initial value is `"normal"`.

Note that for `fontStyle` assignments to take effect, they must occur before the browser writes the styled text to the document. An assignment to `tags.body.fontStyle` must be done within the `<HEAD>` ... `</HEAD>` section of the HTML.

Example   `document.ids.header.fontStyle = "small-caps"`

See Also   `classes, color, fontFamily, fontSize, fontWeight, ids, tags`

fontWeight

Version 1.2

Property of style sheet objects

Specifies the weight or "boldness" of text in HTML elements.

Syntax `styleObj.fontWeight`

`styleObj`   Style sheet object: a property of a `classes`, `ids`, or `tags` object.

Discussion This property specifies the style of characters. The value may be `"normal"`, `"bold"`, `"bolder"`, or `"lighter"`. It may also be a number from 100 to 900, with 900 being the most bold.

This property applies to all elements, and is inherited. Its initial value is `"normal"`.

Note that for `fontWeight` assignments to take effect, they must occur before the browser writes the styled text to the document. An assignment to `tags.body.fontWeight` must be done within the `<HEAD>` ... `</HEAD>` section of the HTML.

Example `document.ids.header.fontWeight = "bold"`

See Also `classes, color, fontFamily, fontSize, fontStyle, ids, tags`

for

Version 1.0

Keyword used in statements

This keyword is used to create for and for...in loops. For more details, see Chapter 4.

Form

Version 1.0 External

External object

Reflects an HTML form in a document.

Syntax	*docObject.formName* *docObject.forms[index]*	
	docObject	document for the current document, or an expression denoting a document object.
	formName	Name of a form, as specified by the NAME attribute of the HTML <FORM> tag.
	index	Number specifying an array element, or string specifying a form name.
Properties	action	Reflects the destination URL for submitting the form, as specified by the ACTION attribute of the <FORM> tag.
	elements	An array reflecting all buttons, text boxes, and other form elements. Each element of the array is a Button, Checkbox, FileUpload, Hidden, Password, Radio, Reset, Select, Submit, Text, or Textarea external object.
	encoding	Reflects the MIME encoding for form submissions, as specified by the ENCTYPE attribute of the <FORM> tag.
	length	Reflects the number of elements in the form (length of the elements array).
	name	Reflects the name of the form, as specified by the NAME attribute of the <FORM> tag.
	method	Reflects the submission type "get" or "post", as specified by the METHOD attribute of the <FORM> tag.
	target	Reflects the target window for form results, as specified by the TARGET attribute of the <FORM> tag.
Methods	reset()	Resets the form's elements, equivalent to a user pressing a Reset button.
	submit()	Submits the form data, equivalent to a user pressing a Submit button.
Event Handlers	onreset, onsubmit	
Discussion	Form objects are constructed by Navigator when it encounters the HTML <FORM>...</FORM> tags. You can reference them as elements of the document's forms array.	

Example   The HTML shown below creates a simple form with a text box and a button. The button's `ONCLICK` handler is a JavaScript statement that reads the contents of the text box and passes it to a function.

```
<FORM NAME="form1">
  <INPUT TYPE="text" NAME="myText">
  <INPUT TYPE="button" VALUE="Click me"
    ONCLICK="alert(document.form1.myText.value)">
</FORM>
```

See Also   document, form, forms

form

Version 1.0   Read-only   External

Property of form element external objects: Button, Checkbox, FileUpload, Hidden, Password, Radio, Reset, Select, Submit, Text, Textarea

Returns the form that contains a form element.

Syntax   *elementObj*.form

elementObj   document.*formName*.*elementName*, or other expression denoting a form element.

Properties   Since `form` returns a Form object, it has all the properties, methods, and event handlers of the referenced object.

Discussion   The form property provides each element with a pointer to its "parent," that is, the form that contains it. This may be useful when a form element is passed as an argument to a function (see Example).

Example   The following function accepts a text box as an argument `txt`. It reads the text, and places a modified copy in a text box called `result`, which must be present in the same form as `txt`.

```
function showResult(txt) {
  var s = "You typed " + txt.value
  txt.form.result.value = s
}
```

See Also   Form, forms

forms

Version 1.0 Read-only External Tainted

Property of the document object

Reflects the HTML forms in a document.

Syntax *docObject*.forms

docObject   document for the current document, or an expression denoting a document object.

Properties length   Length of the array (number of forms in the document).

Discussion Each element of the forms array is a Form object reflecting one form. Although some of the Form objects may have properties that can be modified, the forms array itself is read-only.

Example
```
document.write("Form 1 has ",
    document.forms.form1.length, " elements.<BR>")
document.write("The text box contains \"",
    document.forms.form1.myText.value, "\".")
```

See Also Form, form, document

forward( )

Version 1.0

Method of the history object

Advances the browser to the next URL in the history list, equivalent to the user pressing the browser's Forward button.

Syntax history.forward()

Example You can create a link that functions like the Forward button in the Navigator toolbar, by writing HTML code with a JavaScript URL such as:
`<A HREF="javascript:history.forward()"> Go ahead </A>`

See Also back(), go(), history

Frame

Version 1.0   Read-only   External

External object

Reflects an HTML frame.

Syntax	`windowObj.frameName`
	`windowObj.frames["frameName"]`
	`windowObj.frames[index]`	

	`windowObj`	Optional property. Omitted, `self`, or `window` for the current window or frame; or an expression denoting another window or frame.
	`frameName`	Name defined by the NAME attribute of the HTML <FRAME> tag.
	`index`	A string or number specifying an element of the `frames` array.
Properties	`document`	The currently displayed document.
	`frames`	An array reflecting any child frames.
	`name`	A string reflecting the frame name, as defined by the NAME attribute of the HTML <FRAME> tag.
	`length`	Length of the `frames` array (number of child frames).
	`parent`	Window or frame containing this frame.
	`self, window`	"Synonym" reference to the current frame.
	`top`	The actual browser window, not a frame or subframe, in which the script is executing.
Methods	`blur()`	Removes focus from the frame.
	`clearInterval(ID)`	Cancels a repeated execution.
	`clearTimeout(ID)`	Cancels a delayed execution.
	`focus()`	Sets focus on the frame.
	`print()`	Activates the Print dialog box, equivalent to the user pressing Navigator's Print button.
	`setInterval(function, time, arg1, arg2, ... argN)`	Schedules a function for repeated execution.
	`setTimeout(function, time, arg1, arg2, ... argN)`	Schedules a function for delayed execution.
Event Handlers	`onblur, onfocus, onmove, onresize`	

Discussion	When Navigator loads a web page, it creates Frame objects corresponding to all frames in the document. You can reference these objects as elements of the `frames` array.
Version 1.1	The `blur` and `focus` methods, as well as the `onBlur` and `onFocus` event handlers, were added in JavaScript version 1.1
Version 1.2	The `clearInterval` and `setInterval` methods, and the `onmove` and `onresize` event handlers, were added in JavaScript version 1.2.
Example	A button in a frame can write data to a text box in another frame by a reference to `parent`, such as:

```
<FORM>
<INPUT TYPE="text" NAME="txt">
<INPUT TYPE="button" VALUE="Write"
 ONCLICK="parent.frame2.document.siblingForm.txt.value =
   this.form.txt.value">
</FORM>
```

See Also	frames, window

frames

Version 1.0   Read-only   External

Property of the window object and Frame external object

Reflects the HTML frames in a document.

Syntax	`windowObj.frames["frameName"]` `windowObj.frames[index]`	
	windowObj	Optional property. Omitted, `self`, or `window` for the current window or frame; or an expression denoting another window or frame.
	frameName	Name defined by the `NAME` attribute of the HTML `<FRAME>` tag.
	index	A string or number specifying an element of the `frames` array.
Properties	`length`	Number of elements in the array (frames in the window or frame).
Discussion	Each element of the `frames` array is a Frame object reflecting one frame.	

Example   document.write("The document containing this frame also contains ",
          parent.frames.length - 1, " other frames.")

See Also Frame, window

fromCharCode( )

Version 1.2

Method of the String constructor

Returns a string constructed from numeric values representing characters.

Syntax   String.fromCharCode(*char1*, *char2*, ... *charN*)
          char1, *char2*, ... *charN*   Numeric values representing characters in the ISO Latin-1 character set.

Discussion   Character code values can be extracted from a string by the charCodeAt( ) method. Also, they are passed to scripts when event handlers are used to handle keyboard input.
          Note that this is a method of the constructor, that is, of String itself, not of objects created with new String( ).

Example   This form allows you to enter a number and display the corresponding character:

```
<FORM>
    <INPUT TYPE="text" NAME="code">
    <INPUT TYPE="button" VALUE="Convert"
     ONCLICK="alert('The character is ' +
    String.fromCharCode(this.form.code.value))">
</FORM>
```

See Also charCodeAt( ), String

function

Version 1.0

Keyword used in statements

This keyword is used to declare functions. For more details, see Chapter 4.

Function

Version 1.1

Object type (constructor)

Creates a new `Function` object.

Syntax

```
v = new Function(body)
v = new Function
(arg1, arg2, ... argN, body)
```

`v`	Variable or object to which the new `Function` is assigned.
`arg1, arg2, ... argN`	Optional arguments. Strings containing JavaScript object names, used as arguments to the function.
`body`	String containing JavaScript statements for the new function body.

Properties

`arguments`	Array containing the arguments passed to the function.
`arity`	Returns the number of arguments that the function "expects" (the number in its declaration).
`caller`	Returns a reference to the function, if any, that called the current function.

Discussion

The usual way to define `Function` objects is by writing function declarations in a script. However, the `Function` constructor provides some additional flexibility. It allows a script to create special-purpose functions at run time. Also, it provides a convenient way to declare small functions and assign them to event handlers with a single statement (see Example).

Note that `Function` objects are not compiled; the strings are re-evaluated each time the function is called. This means they do not execute as quickly as declared functions, which are compiled. Also, the meaning of object names in the function body may vary, depending on the context in which the function is evaluated.

Example

To make a window change color when it has focus, two functions must be declared, and they must be assigned as the `onBlur` and `onFocus` event handlers. Each function can be declared and assigned to an event handler with one statement as in:

```
window.onfocus = new Function("document.bgColor = 'yellow'")
window.onblur = new Function("document.bgColor = 'brown'")
```

getDate( )

Version 1.0

Method of the Date object

Returns the day of the month stored in the object.

- **Syntax**   *dateObj*.getDate( )

  dateObj   Date object or expression.

- **Discussion**   This method returns an integer from 1 to 31.

- **Example**   These statements will write the number 14 to the web page:

  ```
  valentine = new Date("Feb 14 1998")
  document.write(valentine.getDate())
  ```

- **See Also**   Date, getDay( ), getHours( ), getMinutes( ), getMonth( ), getSeconds( ), getTime( ), getTimeZoneOffset( ), getYear( ), setDate( )

getDay( )

Version 1.0

Method of the Date object

Returns the day of the week stored in the object.

- **Syntax**   *dateObj*.getDay( )

  dateObj   Date object or expression.

- **Discussion**   This property returns an integer value: 0 for Sunday, 1 for Monday, and so forth.

- **Example**   These statements will write the number 6, representing Saturday, to the web page:

  ```
  valentine = new Date("Feb 14 1998")
  document.write(valentine.getDay())
  ```

- **See Also**   Date, getDate( ), getHours( ), getMinutes( ), getMonth( ), getSeconds( ), getTime( ), getTimeZoneOffset( ), getYear( ), setDay( )

getHours( )

Version 1.0

Method of the Date object

Returns the hour stored in the object.

Syntax   *dateObj*.getHours( )
          dateObj   Date object or expression.

Discussion   This property returns an integer between 0 and 23.

Example   These statements will write the number 20, representing the hour, to the web page:

```
party1999 = new Date("Dec 31, 1999 20:30:00")
document.write(party1999.getHours())
```

See Also   Date, getDate( ), getDay( ), getMinutes( ), getMonth( ), getSeconds( ), getTime( ), getTimeZoneOffset( ), getYear( ), setHours( )

getMinutes( )

Version 1.0

Method of the Date object

Returns the minute stored in the object.

Syntax   *dateObj*.getMinutes( )
          dateObj   Date object or expression.

Discussion   This property returns an integer between 0 and 59.

Example   These statements will write the number 30, representing the minute, to the web page:

```
party1999 = new Date("Dec 31, 1999 20:30:00")
document.write(party1999.getMinutes())
```

See Also   Date, getDate( ), getDay( ), getHours( ), getMonth( ), getSeconds( ), getTime( ), getTimeZoneOffset( ), getYear( ), setMinutes( )

getMonth( )

Version 1.0

Method of the Date object

Returns the month stored in the object.

Syntax *dateObj*.getMonth( )

dateObj   Date object or expression.

Discussion This property returns an integer from 0 to 11: 0 for January, 1 for February, and so forth.

Example These statements will write the number 11, representing December, to the web page:

```
party1999 = new Date("Dec 31, 1999 20:30:00")
document.write(party1999.getMonth())
```

See Also Date, getDate( ), getDay( ), getHours( ), getMinutes( ), getSeconds( ), getTime( ), getTimeZoneOffset( ), getYear( ), setMonth( )

getSeconds( )

Version 1.0

Method of the Date object

Returns the second stored in the object.

Syntax *dateObj*.getSeconds( )

dateObj   Date object or expression.

Discussion This property returns an integer from 0 to 59.

Example These statements will write the number 0, representing the second, to the web page:

```
party1999 = new Date("Dec 31, 1999 20:30:00")
document.write(party1999.getSeconds())
```

See Also Date, getDate( ), getDay( ), getHours( ), getMinutes( ), getMonth( ), getTime( ), getTimeZoneOffset( ), getYear( ), setSeconds( )

getSelection( )

Version 1.2

Method of the document object

Returns a string containing text selected by the cursor.

Syntax   *docObject*.getSelection( )

docObject   document for the current document, or an expression denoting any document object.

Discussion   This method returns a string containing a copy of any text in the web page that had been selected by the user dragging the mouse cursor.

Example   `saveSelection = document.getSelection( )`

See Also   document

getTime( )

Version 1.0

Method of the Date object

Returns a single number representing the date and time stored in the object.

Syntax   *dateObj*.getTime( )

dateObj   Date object or expression.

Discussion   This property returns a value representing the date and time as the number of milliseconds since January 1, 1970, 00:00:00 GMT. This is a convenient and efficient form to use when copying a Date value from one object to another, or storing it for later use.

Example   A script that needs to keep a log by storing the times at which various operations occur could use a statement such as:

`timeLog[next++].time = transaction.getTime( )`

See Also   Date, getDate( ), getDay( ), getHours( ), getMinutes( ), getMonth( ), getSeconds( ), getTimeZoneOffset( ), getYear( ), setTime( )

getTimezoneOffset( )

Version 1.0 — Unusual spelling or capitalization

Method of the `Date` object

Returns the time zone offset, measured in minutes from GMT, for the current locale.

Syntax
: `dateObj.getTimezoneOffset()`
: `dateObj`   `Date` object or expression.

Discussion
: The time zone offset is the number of minutes' difference between the current local time and GMT.
: Note that the z in `getTimezoneOffset` is not capitalized.

Example
: A script running in U.S. Central Daylight Time (CDT) will write the number 360, representing six hours behind GMT, to the web page:
: `document.write(someDateObject.getTimezoneOffset())`

See Also
: `Date`, `getDate()`, `getDay()`, `getHours()`, `getMinutes()`, `getMonth()`, `getSeconds()`, `getTime()`, `getYear()`

getYear( )

Version 1.0

Method of the `Date` object

Returns the year stored in the object.

Syntax
: `dateObj.getYear()`
: `dateObj`   `Date` object or expression.

Discussion
: For years from 1900 to 1999, the returned value is a two-digit number representing the actual year minus 1900. For other years, the returned value is the full four-digit value.

Example
: The following statements write the numbers 99 and 2001 to the web page:

```
now = new Date("Jul 18, 1999 20:30:40")
later = new Date("Jul 18, 2001 20:30:40")
document.writeln(now.getYear())
document.writeln(later.getYear())
```

See Also
: Date, getDate( ), getDay( ), getHours( ), getMinutes( ), getMonth( ), getSeconds( ), getTime( ), getTimeZoneOffset( ), setYear( )

global

Version 1.2   Read-only

Property of the RegExp object

Returns true if the regular expression specifies a global match.

Syntax
: *reObj*.global
: *reObj*   A regular expression object.

Discussion
: This Boolean property tells whether or not a regular expression is constructed to perform global matches. The exact function of this depends on the method. Global matching is specified by the g modifier when the object is constructed (see Examples). For more details on regular expressions, see Chapter 3.

Examples
: Global expressions are created with the g modifier by statements such as:

```
re1 = /^\d+/g
pattern = new RegExp("(\w+)\.(\w{3})", "g")
```

See Also
: exec( ), match( ), RegExp, replace( ) and search( ) (methods of String), split( ), test( )

go( )

Version 1.0

Method of the history object

Reloads a previously visited web page from a URL in the history list.

Syntax history.go(*str*)
history.go(*n*)

str   A string specifying a URL or partial URL of a previously visited web page.
n   A number specifying the amount to move forward or back in the history list.

Discussion If the argument is a string, Navigator will reload the history entry whose URL contains the string, and which is nearest to the current position in the list. Note that the specified string may be only a portion of the complete URL.

If the argument is a number, Navigator moves forward or back the specified number of positions in the history list. history.go(-1) is equivalent to pressing the Back button on the Navigator toolbar; history.go(1) is equivalent to pressing the Forward button.

Example To create a link that functions like two consecutive presses of the Back button, write HTML such as:

```
<A HREF="javascript:history.go(-2)"> Go back 2 </A>
```

See Also back( ), forward( ), history, reload( ), replace( )

handleEvent( )

Version 1.2

Method of all objects with event handlers

Calls the event handler assigned to a specified object.

Syntax `obj.handleEvent(ev)`

    `obj`   Any object that may have event handlers.
    `ev`   An **event** object, or a copy of one.

Discussion A script can use this method to explicitly call an object's event handler, even though no event occurred that would normally pass to the object. This allows a handler for one object to pass events to another, and it allows scripts to simulate events by calling event handlers when no event occurred.

Note that although this method may be called at any time, the **event** object has limited scope, and is only passed to scripts in specific ways.

Example To pass an event from the handler that received it to another object's handler, use a statement such as:

`otherWindow.document.links[0].handleEvent(ev)`

(This example assumes that the variable **ev** is an event object, or a copy of one.)

See Also event

hash

AREA, LINK

Version 1.0 External Tainted

Property of the Area and Link external objects
(see also `hash` as a property of `window.location`)

Reflects the name of an anchor, as specified by the portion of a URL that follows the # character.

Syntax `document.links[index].hash`

    `index`   Number specifying the position of the link in the document's `links` array.

Discussion	This property reflects the part of a URL that specifies a specific location within a document, which is marked by the # character. (The name `hash` comes from the # character which is sometimes called a "hash mark.") The value of `hash` is a # followed by a string which is presumably the name assigned to a link in the document by the NAME attribute of an HTML <A> or <AREA> tag.
Version 1.1	This property was added to Area objects in JavaScript 1.1.
Example	If a file contains a link such as: `<A HREF="story.htm#chapter2"> Go to Part 2 </A>` then the expression `document.links[n].hash` will return `"#chapter2"` (where n specifies the link's position in the document).
See Also	Anchor, Area, Link

hash

WINDOW

Version 1.0 Tainted

Property of the `window.location` object
(see also `hash` as a property of Area and Link objects)

Specifies a location within a document by identifying a named link.

Syntax	For the current window:
	
	`location.hash`
	`self.location.hash`
	`window.location.hash`
	
	For other windows:
	
	`windowObj.location.hash`
	
	`windowObj` An expression denoting a `window` object.

Discussion	When Navigator loads a document into a window, its URL is placed in the `window.location` object, and various portions of it may be referenced by properties of `location`. The `hash` property will reflect the portion of the URL after the # character (sometimes called a "hash mark," hence the name of the property). This represents a specific location within the document, which is marked by a link that has a name assigned by the NAME attribute of an HTML <A> or <AREA> tag.

Modifying this property will cause the browser to scroll the document to the position of the specified link. The first character must always be the # character.

Note that there is also a `document.location`, but it does not have the above behavior. (Also, it is planned to be removed in a future release of Navigator, so you should avoid using it.)

Example The statement:

```
window.location.hash = "#start"
```

will cause the browser to scroll the document until text at the link named `start` displays at the top of the screen.

See Also Anchor, Area, Link, `location`

height

CLIP

Version 1.2   External

Property of the `clip` object
(see also `height` as a property of the event, Image, screen, and style sheet objects)

Specifies the clipping height of a layer.

Syntax *layerObj*.clip.height

layerObj   `document.`*layerName*, or other expression denoting a Layer object.

Discussion This property returns the clipping height for a layer, in pixels: the difference between the current values of `clip.top` and `clip.bottom`. Modifying this property actually changes the value of `clip.bottom` to produce the desired new height.

Example To reduce the currently visible part of a layer by removing 40 pixels at the bottom, use a statement such as:

```
document.layers.myLayer.clip.height -= 40
```

See Also `bottom`, `left`, `right`, `top`, `width` (properties of `clip`); Layer

height

EVENT

Version 1.2 Read-only

Property of the event object
(see also height as a property of the clip, Image, screen, and style sheet objects)

Returns the height, in pixels, of a window or frame after it is resized by the user.

eventObj.height

eventObj event, or an expression denoting a copy of event, such as a function argument passed to an event handler.

Discussion Note that the event object has limited scope: it can only be referenced in event handlers (see Chapter 7).

Example
```
if (ev.type == "resize") {
    newWidth = ev.width
    newHeight = ev.height
}
```

This example assumes that the variable ev is an event object, or a copy of one.

See Also event, width

height

IMAGE

Version 1.1 Read-only

Property of the Image object
(see also height as a property of the clip, event, screen, and style sheet objects)

Returns the height of an image (in pixels).

Syntax *imageObj*.height

imageObj document.*imageName*, or other expression denoting an Image object.

Discussion For images in web pages, this property reflects the HEIGHT attribute of the <IMG> tag. For Image objects created using the new Image() constructor, this property returns the actual height of the image stored in the object.

Example The following example writes an image's height to the page:

```
document.write("This image is " + document.Image1.height
  " pixels wide.")
```

See Also border, hspace, Image, vspace, width

height
SCREEN
Version 1.2   Read-only

Property of the screen object
(see also height as a property of the clip, event, Image, and style sheet objects)

The height of the screen on which the browser is displayed, measured in pixels.

Syntax screen.height

Example The following example places the pixel width value into a numeric variable named nScreenHeight. For instance, if the screen is using the 800 x 600 video resolution, nScreenHeight will contain 600.

```
nScreenHeight = screen.height
```

See Also availHeight, availWidth, screen, width

height
STYLE SHEET OBJECTS
Version 1.2

Property of style sheet objects
(see also height as a property of the clip, event, Image, and screen)

Specifies the height of HTML elements.

Preliminary   *Note that this property is announced by Netscape, but not yet implemented in*

Navigator as of version 4.01. The information presented here is preliminary.

Syntax *styleObj*.height

    styleObj   Style sheet object: a property of a classes, ids, or tags object.

Discussion This property controls the height of HTML elements. The value may be one of the following:

- An absolute measurement, such as "12pt".
- A measurement relative to the current font size, such as "1.5em".
- A pixel measurement, such as "18px".
- The keyword "auto".

This property applies to all block-level elements, and is not inherited. Its initial value is "auto".

Note that for height assignments to take effect, they must occur before the browser writes the styled text to the document. An assignment to tags.body.height must be done within the <HEAD> ... </HEAD> section of the HTML.

See Also classes, ids, tags

Hidden

Version 1.0 External

External object

Reflects a hidden input field in an HTML form.

Syntax *formObj*.*hiddenName*
formObj["*hiddenName*"]
formObj.elements[*index*]

    formObj   document.*formName,* or an expression denoting a Form object in any document.
    hiddenName   Name specified in the NAME attribute of the HTML <INPUT> tag.
    index   Number specifying the position of the object in the form.

Properties form   The Form object that contains this object.

	name	Reflects the NAME attribute of the HTML <INPUT> tag.
	type	Reflects the TYPE attribute of the HTML <INPUT> tag (this is always "hidden" for Hidden objects).
	value	A string specifying the text that is sent when the form is submitted.

Discussion   When Navigator loads a web page, it creates Hidden objects corresponding to all hidden input fields in the document. These objects contain data that can not be seen or modified by the user, but will be sent to the server with the rest of the form's contents when the form is submitted. You can reference these objects as properties of the form, or as elements in the form's elements array. The object's value property is initially set to the VALUE attribute of the HTML <INPUT> tag, but scripts can modify it at any time.

Version 1.1   The type property was added in JavaScript 1.1.

Example   For a hidden input created by HTML such as:

```
<INPUT TYPE="hidden" NAME="secret1" VALUE="hello">
```

The value can be modified by a statement such as:

```
document.myForm.secret1.value = "goodbye"
```

See Also   Form

history

Version 1.0   Signed scripts

Property of the window object

Maintains the history list of URLs that the browser has visited in this session.

Syntax   For the current window:

```
history
self.history
window.history
```

For other windows:

```
windowObj.history
```

	windowObj	An expression denoting a window object.

Properties
	current	Specifies the URL of the current history entry.

	`length`	Returns the number of URLs in the history list (length of the array).
	`next`	Specifies the URL of the next history entry, i.e., the one whose index is greater by one than the current entry.
	`previous`	Specifies the URL of the previous history entry, that is, the one whose index is greater by one than the current entry.
Methods	`back()`	Go to the previous entry in the history list, equivalent to pressing the browser's Back button.
	`forward()`	Go to the next entry in the history list, equivalent to pressing the browser's Forward button.
	`go(dest)`	Go to the specified location, which may be a string specifying a URL or a number specifying a position in the history list.

Discussion The history list maintains a record of all locations visited by the browser during the session. The `history` object is organized as an array. The URL of the first location visited is stored in `history[0]`; as other locations are visited, their URLs are stored in `history[1]`, `history[2]`, and so forth.

The browser maintains a current position in the array. Although this is usually the last element, it can be changed to another value by the user clicking the browser's Back button, or by statements such as `history.back()` or `history.go(-1)`. The `current` property always returns the URL of the current position. The `previous` and `next` properties return the adjacent elements of the array.

Version 1.1   The `current`, `next`, and `previous` properties, and the ability to reference array elements, were added in JavaScript 1.1.

Version 1.2   Starting in JavaScript 1.2, much of `history`'s functionality is available only to signed scripts. The values of the `current`, `next`, and `previous` properties, as well as array elements, can only be read when the `"UniversalBrowserRead"` privilege is enabled.

Example To display the last location visited by the browser, use a statement such as:
`document.write("You came here from ", history.previous)`
Note that only a signed script can use this property.

See Also `window`

home( )

Version 1.2

Method of the `window` object

Causes a window to display the user's home page.

Syntax For the current window:

```
home( )
self.home( )
window.home( )
```

For other windows:

```
windowObj.home( )
```

windowObj   An expression denoting a `window` object.

Discussion This method causes a window to display the location specified as the user's home page in Navigator's Preferences dialog. `home( )` has the same function as the Home button on Navigator's toolbar.

Example `otherWindow.home( )`

See Also `back( )`, `forward( )` (methods of `window`), `history`

host

AREA, LINK

Version 1.0 External Tainted

Property of the Area and Link external objects
(see also `host` as a property of `window.location`)

Reflects a server name, domain name, and port number, as specified by the portion of a URL that follows the // characters.

Syntax `document.links[index].host`

index   Number specifying the position of the link in the document's `links` array.

Discussion	This property reflects the part of a URL that specifies the server and domain name, such as `www.companyName.com`, or an IP address such as `207.124.103.85`. A port number may follow the domain name, separated by a colon, such as `:80`. The value of `host` is a part of the URL assigned to a link in the document by the HREF attribute of an HTML `<A>` or `<AREA>` tag.
Version 1.1	This property was added to Area objects in JavaScript 1.1.
Example	If a file contains a link such as: `<A HREF="http://www.myCompany.com/welcome.htm"> Go to my company's home page </A>` then the expression `document.links[n].host` will return `"www.myCompany.com"` (where n specifies the link's position in the document).
See Also	Anchor, Area, `hostname`, Link

host

WINDOW

Version 1.0   Tainted

Property of the `window.location` object
(see also `host` as a property of Area and Link objects)

Specifies the host name and port number of the currently displayed document.

Syntax	For the current window:
	`location.host`
	`self.location.host`
	`window.location.host`
	
	For other windows:
	windowObj`.location.host`
	
	windowObj An expression denoting a `window` object.

Discussion	When Navigator loads a document into a window, its URL is placed in the `window.location` object, and various portions of it may be referenced by properties of `location`. The `host` property reflects the portion of the URL after the `//` characters. This contains the server and domain name such as `www.companyName.com`, or an IP address such as `207.124.103.85`. A port number may follow the domain name, separated by a colon, such as `:80`. Modifying this property causes the browser to load a document from the newly specified host.

Note that there is also a `document.location`, but it does not have the above behavior. (Also, it is planned to be removed in a future release of Navigator, so you should avoid using it.)

Example To display the host from which a document was loaded, use a statement such as:

```
document.write("Welcome to the ", window.location.host,
   " domain.")
```

See Also Anchor, Area, Link, `hostname`, `location`

hostname

AREA, LINK

Version 1.0   External   Tainted

Property of the Area and Link external objects
(see also `hostname` as a property of `window.location`)

Reflects a server and domain name, as specified by the portion of a URL that follows the // characters.

Syntax `document.links[index].hostname`

index Number specifying the position of the link in the document's `links` array.

Discussion This property reflects the part of a URL that specifies the server and domain name. The server and domain name is a string such as `www.companyName.com`, or an IP address such as `207.124.103.85`. The value of `hostname` is a is part of the URL assigned to a link in the document by the HREF attribute of an HTML <A> or <AREA> tag.

Version 1.1 This property was added to Area objects in JavaScript 1.1.

Example If a file contains a link such as:

```
<A HREF="http://www.myCompany.com:80/welcome.htm"> Go to my company's
   home page </A>
```

then the expression `document.links[n].hostname` will return `"www.myCompany.com"`.

See Also Anchor, Area, `host`, Link

hostname

WINDOW

Version 1.0 Tainted

Property of the `window.location` object
(see also `hostname` as a property of Area and Link objects)

Specifies the host name of the currently displayed document.

Syntax   For the current window:

```
location.hostname
self.location.hostname
window.location.hostname
```

For other windows:

```
windowObj.location.hostname
```

windowObj   An expression denoting a `window` object.

Discussion   When Navigator loads a document into a window, its URL is placed in the `window.location` object, and various portions of it may be referenced by properties of `location`. The `hostname` property will reflect the server and domain name. The server and domain name is a string such as `www.companyName.com`, or an IP address such as `207.124.103.85`.

Modifying this property will cause the browser to load a document from the newly specified host.

Note that there is also a `document.location`, but it does not have the above behavior. (Also, it is planned to be removed in a future release of Navigator, so you should avoid using it.)

Example   To display the host name from which a document was loaded, use a statement such as:

```
document.write("Welcome to the ", window.location.hostname, " domain.")
```

See Also   Anchor, Area, `host`, Link, `location`

href

AREA, LINK

Version 1.0   External   Tainted

Property of the Area and Link external objects
(see also href as a property of window.location)

Reflects the URL of a link in a document.

Syntax   document.links[*index*].href

index   Number specifying the position of the link in the document's links array.

Discussion   This property reflects the URL assigned to a link in the document by the HREF attribute of an HTML <A> or <AREA> tag.

Version 1.1   This property was added to Area objects in JavaScript 1.1.

Example   If a file contains a link such as:

<A HREF="http://www.myCompany.com/welcome.htm"> Go to my company's home page </A>

then the expression document.links[n].href will return the string:

"http://www.myCompany.com/welcome.htm"

(where n specifies the link's position in the document).

See Also   Anchor, Area, Link

href

WINDOW

Version 1.0   Tainted

Property of the window.location object
(see also host as a property of Area and Link objects)

Specifies the complete URL of the currently displayed document.

Syntax   For the current window:

location.href
self.location.href
window.location.href

For other windows:

`windowObj.location.href`

windowObj　　An expression denoting a `window` object.

Discussion When Navigator loads a document into a window, its URL is placed in the `window.location` object, and various portions of it may be referenced by properties of `location`. The `href` property will reflect complete URL.

Modifying this property will cause the browser to load a document from the newly specified location.

Note that there is also a `document.location`, but it does not have the above behavior. (Also, it is planned to be removed in a future release of Navigator, so you should avoid using it.)

Example To display the URL from which a document was loaded, use a statement such as:

`document.write("Welcome to ", window.location.href)`

See Also Anchor, Area, Link, `location`

hspace

Version 1.1   Read-only

Property of the Image object

Returns the distance, in pixels, between the left and right edges of an image and the surrounding text.

Syntax *imageObj*.hspace

imageObj　　`document.`*imageName*, or other expression denoting an Image object.

Discussion If the image object was created using the `Image()` constructor, then `hspace` is 0. Otherwise, `hspace` reflects the value set by the `HSPACE` attribute of the `<IMG>` tag.

Example To write the `hspace` value to the page, use a statement such as:

`document.write("The first image is ", document.images[0].hspace "`
`    pixels from the text.")`

See Also `border`, `height`, Image, `vspace`, `width`

ids

Version 1.2   External

Property of the document object

Specifies style sheet properties for user-defined styles.

Syntax	*docObject*.ids
	docObject document for the current document, or an expression denoting a document in any window.
Properties	`ids` may have a property corresponding to each user-defined style. The name of each property is the same as the identifier. Note that unlike most JavaScript identifiers, uppercase and lowercase are equivalent for these property names; for example, `document.ids.boldblue` is equivalent to `document.ids.BoldBlue`.

Each property of `ids` will itself have properties which specify the actual appearance of text to which the style is applied. The available properties are summarized as follows:

Font Properties	`fontFamily`	Font name: actual or generic.
	`fontSize`	Number or keyword specifying text size.
	`fontStyle`	Keyword specifying italics and/or small capitals.
	`fontWeight`	Number or keyword specifying text "boldness."
Text Properties	`lineHeight`	Number or expression specifying line spacing.
	`textAlign`	Keyword specifying horizontal position of text.
	`TextDecoration`	Keyword specifying underline, overline, overstrike, or blink.
	`textIndent`	Number or expression specifying indentation for the first line of a paragraph.
	`TextTransform`	Keyword specifying capitalization.
	`verticalAlign`	Keyword specifying vertical position of text.
Block-level Properties	`align`	Keyword specifying horizontal position (floating) of HTML object.
	`borderBottomWidth,` `borderLeftWidth,` `borderRightWidth,` `borderTopWidth`	Number specifying the width of the border.

	borderColor	Keyword specifying color of border.
	borderStyle	Keyword specifying style of border.
	clear	Keyword specifying whether floating objects may be positioned alongside this object.
	height	Number or keyword specifying the height of the HTML object.
	marginBottom, marginLeft, marginRight, marginTop	Number or expression specifying the spacing between HTML objects.
	paddingBottom, paddingLeft, paddingRight, paddingTop	Number or expression specifying the spacing between HTML object content and border.
	width	Number, expression, or keyword specifying the width of the HTML object.
Color and Background Properties	color	String specifying text color.
	BackgroundImage	String specifying URL of image file.
	BackgroundColor	String specifying background color.
Classification Properties	display	Keyword specifying how object is displayed.
	listStyleType	Keyword specifying how objects are marked or numbered.
	whiteSpace	Keyword specifying handling of white space characters.

Methods Note that `ids` itself has no methods. These methods are actually used on the properties of `ids`, that is, the specific styles associated with an HTML tag.

`borderWidths()`	Sets the four border width properties for the style.
`margins()`	Sets the four margin properties for the style.
`paddings()`	Sets the four padding width properties for the style.

Discussion This property serves as a "holder" for any user-defined styles in the document. It may be used in scripts or in style sheets. When it is used in style sheets, you can write `ids` instead of `document.ids`, since all style sheet statements are evaluated in the context of `document`.

Note that for `ids` property assignments to take effect, they must occur before the browser writes the styled text to the web page.

For more details on style sheets, see Chapter 6.

Examples To create a new style called `redcap` that displays text in red uppercase letters, write statements such as:

```
document.ids.redcap.color = "red"
document.ids.redcap.textTransform = "uppercase"
```

This style can be applied by HTML such as:

```
<P ID="redcap"> This is really important! </P>
```

See Also   `classes, tags`

if

Version 1.0

Keyword used in statements

This keyword is used to create conditional statements. For details, see Chapter 4.

ignoreCase

Version 1.2   Read-only

Property of the RegExp object

Returns `true` if the regular expression specifies a case-insensitive match.

Syntax
: `reObj.ignoreCase`

  `reObj`   A regular expression object created by the `RegExp` constructor.

Discussion
: This property tells whether or not a regular expression is constructed to perform case-insensitive matches, that is, to treat uppercase and lowercase letters as equivalent. Case insensitivity is specified by the `i` modifier when the object is constructed (see Examples).

Examples
: Regular expressions created with the `i` modifier by statements such as:

  ```
  re1 = /^\d+/i
  pattern = new RegExp("(\w+)\.(\w{3})", "i")
  ```

  are case-insensitive, so the expressions `re1.ignoreCase` or `pattern.ignoreCase` would return `true`.

See Also   `RegExp, String`

Image

Version 1.1

Object type (constructor)

Creates an object containing an image that can be displayed in a web page, or reflects an image placed in a document by the HTML <IMAGE> tag.

Syntax	For constructed objects:	
	`v = new Image(width, height)`	
	v	Variable or object to which the new Image is assigned.
	width, height	Optional arguments. Numeric values specifying the width and height of the image in pixels.
	For external objects:	
	`docObject.imageName`	
	`docObject.images[index]`	
	docObject	document for the current document, or an expression denoting a document in any window.
	imageName	String value representing a name assigned by the NAME attribute of the HTML <IMAGE> tag.
	index	Number or string specifying an element of the form's images array.
Properties	border	Reflects the BORDER attribute of the HTML <IMAGE> tag, which specifies the width of the image border. Always zero for constructed objects.
	complete	Returns true if an image file is completely loaded into the object.
	height	Specifies the height of the image in pixels.
	hspace	Reflects the HSPACE attribute of the HTML <IMAGE> tag, which specifies the space at the left and right sides of the image. Always zero for constructed objects.
	lowsrc	Specifies the URL of a low-resolution file to be displayed while the file specified by src is loading. Not used for constructed objects.
	name	Reflects the NAME attribute of the HTML <IMAGE> tag, which specifies the image name. Always null for constructed objects.
	src	Specifies the URL of the image file currently loaded in the object.
	vspace	Reflects the VSPACE attribute of the HTML <IMAGE> tag, which specifies the space at the top and bottom of the image. Always zero for constructed objects.
	width	Specifies the width of the image in pixels.

Event Handlers	`onabort, onerror, onkeydown, onkeypress, onkeyup, onload, onmouseout, onmouseover`
Discussion	When Navigator loads a web page, it creates `Image` objects corresponding to all `<IMG>` tags in the document. You can reference these objects by their name, or as elements of the `images` array. Also, scripts can create Image objects with the `new Image()` constructor. This allows you to have a number of images preloaded and stored in memory, so that they can be displayed quickly for animation effects, or be changed in response to user interaction. **Version 1.2** The `onkeydown, onkeypress, onkeyup, onmouseout,` and `onmouseover` event handlers were added in JavaScript 1.2.

Examples	If a document contains an image specified by HTML such as:
	
	`<IMG NAME="screenEye" SRC="Eye-open.gif">`
	
	and a script creates a new object with statements such as:
	
	`eye2 = new Image()`
	`eye2.src = "Eye-clos.gif"`
	
	then the image in the document can be made to display the constructed object by a statement such as:
	
	`screenEye.src = eye2.src`

See Also	`document, images`

images

Version 1.1 External

property of the document object

Reflects the images in a document.

Syntax	*docObject*.images	
	docObject	`document` for the current document, or an expression denoting a `document` object in any window.
Properties	`length`	Length of the array (number of images in the document).
Discussion	Each element of the `images` array is an `Image` object reflecting one image that was declared by an HTML `<IMG>` tag. Although some of the `Image` objects' properties can be modified, the `images` array itself is read-only.	

Example	To load a new file into the first image in the document, use a statement such as:

`document.images[0].src = "newFile.jpg"` |
| See Also | document, Image |

import

Version 1.2

Keyword used in statements

This keyword is used to allow a script to access the variables of a signed script which have been made available by the `export` statement. For more details, see Chapter 8.

in

Version 1.0

Keyword used in statements

This keyword is used in `for...in` loops to read the properties of an object. For details, see Chapter 4.

index

Version 1.0   Read-only   External

Property of the Option object

Returns the position of the object in the Select object's `options` array.

Syntax	`selectObj.options[index].index` `name.index`
	selectObj `document.`*formName*`.`*objName*, or other expression denoting a Select object in a form in any window.
	index Number specifying the position in the `options` array.
	name Name of a variable denoting an Option object.

Discussion   This property returns the position of the object in the `options` array. Since `Option` objects can be manipulated as variables, this property enables a script to determine an option's position in a select box. JavaScript automatically updates `index` when a select box is modified. When an `Option` object is not an element of any select box, its `index` is 0.

Example   If an option is created with a statement such as:

```
newOp = new Option("my choice")
```

and later placed in a select box, a script can find out where it was placed with a statement such as:

```
myChoicePosition = newOp.index
```

See Also   `Option`, `options`, `Select`

indexOf( )

Version 1.0

Method of the `String` object

Returns a number indicating the position in a string where the first occurrence of a specified substring is found.

Syntax   *str*.indexOf(*sval*, *start*)

str	String object or expression.
sval	The substring to search for.
start	Optional numeric value specifying the position at which to start the search. If omitted, the search starts at the beginning of the string (position 0).

Discussion   `indexOf( )` searches the string from beginning to end; to search in reverse order, use `lastIndexOf( )`. Note that positions in strings start at 0, so the returned value and the *start* argument may have values from 0 to *str*.length − 1.

Example
: For a string declared by a statement such as:

```
myString = "This is a string."
```

the statement:

```
position = myString.indexOf("is")
```

will set `position` to 2, since the first occurrence of the characters "is" starts at the third character.

See Also
: `lastIndexOf()`, `String`

innerHeight

Version 1.2   Signed scripts

Property of the window object

Specifies the height, in pixels, of the document display portion of a window.

Syntax
: For the current window:
```
innerHeight
self.innerHeight
window.innerHeight
```
For other windows:
```
windowObj.innerHeight
```

windowObj   An expression denoting a `window` object.

Discussion
: This property specifies the height of the portion of a window in which a document is displayed, i.e., it does not include space for toolbars, borders, and so forth.
  To set a value less than 100 pixels, this property must be used within a signed script.

Example
: `window.innerHeight = 480`

See Also
: `innerWidth`, `window`

innerWidth

Version 1.2   Signed scripts

Property of the window object

Specifies the width, in pixels, of the document display portion of a window.

Syntax
: For the current window:
```
innerWidth
self.innerWidth
window.innerWidth
```
For other windows:
```
windowObj.innerWidth
```

windowObj   An expression denoting a `window` object.

Discussion
: This property specifies the width of the portion of a window in which a document is displayed, that is, it does not include space for scroll bars, borders, and so forth.

  To set a value less than 100 pixels, this property must be used within a signed script.

Example
: `window.innerWidth = 800`

See Also
: `innerHeight, window`

input, $_

Version 1.2   Read-only

Property of the RegExp constructor

Provides an input string for the `exec( )` and `test( )` methods.

Syntax
: ```
  RegExp.input
  RegExp.$_
  ```

Discussion
: This property provides some flexibility and convenience when using the `RegExp` methods `exec( )` and `test( )`. If either of these methods is called with no argument, it uses the value of `input` as its argument. Scripts may set the value of this property at any time. JavaScript automatically places values in `input` in the following cases:
  ```

- When an event handler is called for a text box form element (Text object), input is set to the text in the box.
- When an event handler is called for a text area form element (Textarea object), input is set to the text in the box. Also, RegExp.multiline is set to true, since a text area may contain several lines of text.
- When an event handler is called for a select box (Select object), input is set to the displayed text of the selected option. If several options are selected, input is set to the text of the first one.
- When an event handler is called for a hypertext link (Link object), input is set to the text between the HTML <A> and </A> tags.

After executing exec( ) or test( ), the value of input is reset to the empty string.

Note that this is a property of the RegExp constructor, not of objects created by new RegExp( ). That means that it is shared by all scripts running in the same window or frame. If you have several scripts in one window that use this property, they may affect each other's results.

Examples For a text box in a form defined by HTML such as:

```
<INPUT TYPE="text" NAME="age"
   ONCHANGE="checkAge(this.form)">
```

the event handler can check to see if the user entered a number with statements such as:

```
pat = /^\d+$/
if (! pat.test())
   alert("Invalid number.")
```

Since test( ) has no argument, it searches input, which was automatcally loaded with the text from the box when the event handler was called.

See Also exec( ), Link, RegExp, Select, test( ), Text, Textarea

isNan( )

Version 1.0

Built-in function

Returns true if the object's value is NaN (not a number).

Syntax isNan(*obj*)

obj   Any object or expression.

Discussion: NaN is a special value that JavaScript uses when an arithmetic expression attempts to compute a nonexistent value, such as the square root of a negative number. NaN always returns "not equal" when compared to any numeric value, so this function is needed to test whether a value is in fact NaN.

JavaScript provides several other types of special results, which are available as properties of the Number object, such as POSITIVE_INFINITY, MAX_VALUE, and so forth.

Example:
```
if (isNaN(someResult)) {
    alert("Non-numeric result; can not proceed")
```

See Also: Math

italics( )

Version 1.0

Method of the String object

Returns a string containing HTML code to format a string in italics.

Syntax: *stringObj*.italics( )

stringObj   String object or expression to be formatted in italic characters.

Discussion: This method returns a string consisting of HTML code. The code includes the HTML <I> and </I> tags so that, if the returned string is written to a document, it will appear in italics.

Example: The statement:

```
document.write("a ", "Roman".italics(), " arch")
```

will write to the web page:

a *Roman* arch

See Also: big( ), blink( ), bold( ), fixed( ), fontcolor( ), fontsize( ), small( ), split( ), strike( ), sub( ), sup( ), String

java

Version 1.0

Property of the Packages object

Provides a number of methods, objects, and properties for use by scripts.

Syntax
: `Packages.netscape`
  `netscape`

Discussion
: This Java package provides objects such as `java.lang`, which is used by scripts to communicate with Java applets. For more information, see Chapter 8.

See Also
: `netscape`, `Packages`, `sun`

javaEnabled( )

Version 1.1

Method of the `navigator` object

Returns `true` if Java is enabled.

Syntax
: `navigator.javaEnabled()`

Discussion
: Some users may wish to prevent Navigator from running Java applets, due to security concerns or limited resources in the computer; they can do this with a setting in Navigator's Preferences dialog. The `javaEnabled( )` method allows a script to find out whether Java is enabled.

Example
: ```
if (! navigator.javaEnabled()) {
    alert("You must enable Java to see the cool applet on this page.")
```
```

join( )

Version 1.1

Method of the Array object

Returns a string formed by combining the elements of an array.

Syntax   *arrayObj*.join(*sep*)

arrayObj   Name of an array variable, or other expression denoting an Array object.

sep   Optional string specifying characters to place between array elements. If omitted, a comma (,) is used.

Discussion   This method converts each element of an array to a string, and then it returns a string consisting of all these individual strings joined together. The specified separator string (or a comma, if no separator is specified) is placed between elements.

Example   For an array defined by statements such as:

```
a = new Array ("North", "East", "South", "West")
```

the statement:

```
s = a.join("...")
```

will set s to "North...East...South...West".

See Also   Array, split( ), String

KEYDOWN

Version 1.2   Read-only

Property of the Event object

Returns a mask for capturing keyboard events.

Syntax Event.KEYDOWN

Discussion This property is used to control event capturing (see Chapter 7). When the event is captured, the value of the pressed key is available in the which property of the event object, and the state of the Shift, Ctrl, Alt, and Meta keys is available in the modifiers property.

Example To enable capturing of key-down events (as well as click):

myWindow.captureEvents (Event.KEYDOWN | Event.CLICK)

See Also captureEvents(), releaseEvents(), event, Event

KEYPRESS

Version 1.2   Read-only

Property of the Event object

Returns a mask for capturing keyboard events.

Syntax Event.KEYPRESS

Discussion This property is used to control event capturing (see Chapter 7). When the event is captured, the value of the pressed key is available in the which property of the event object, and the state of the Shift, Ctrl, Alt, and Meta keys is available in the modifiers property.

Example To enable capturing of key-press events (as well as click):

myWindow.captureEvents (Event.KEYPRESS | Event.CLICK)

See Also captureEvents(), releaseEvents(), event, Event

KEYUP

Version 1.2   Read-only

Property of the Event object

Returns a mask for capturing keyboard events.

Syntax
: `Event.KEYUP`

Discussion
: This property is used to control event capturing (see Chapter 7). When the event is captured, the value of the released key is available in the `which` property of the `event` object, and the state of the Shift, Ctrl, Alt, and Meta keys is available in the `modifiers` property.

Example
: To enable capturing of key-up events (as well as click):

    `myWindow.captureEvents (Event.KEYUP | Event.CLICK)`

See Also
: `captureEvents()`, `event`, `Event`, `releaseEvents()`

language

Version 1.2   Read-only

Property of the `navigator` object

Returns a code indicating the language of the browser.

Syntax
: `navigator.language`

Discussion
: This property allows a script to determine the language of the browser on which it is running, for example, `"en"` for English. This can be used to determine what type of text to display. Some other common values are:

`"de"`	German
`"es"`	Spanish
`"fr"`	French
`"ja"`	Japanese
`"zh"`	Chinese

Example
: ```
  if (navigator.language != "en")
      loadInternationalInfo()
  ```

# lastIndex

**Version 1.2   Read-only**

### A property of the `RegExp` object

Specifies the position in a string just after the most recent match, which is also the location at which to start the next match for global matches with the `exec()` and `test()` methods.

Syntax
: `RegExp.lastIndex`

Discussion
: This property is only used by the regular expression methods, `exec()` and `test()`. It only applies when they are used to do a global match: one for which the pattern's `global` property is true (`g` modifier specified in the pattern). Unlike some other methods, `exec()` and `test()` do *not* search for multiple matches when doing a global match. Instead, they operate in a way that allows you to step through a series of matches by using consecutive calls to the method.
  ```

If `global` is true, `exec()` and `test()` will start at the position in the input string specified by `lastIndex`, instead of at the beginning. Also, they will update `lastIndex` to indicate the position of the next character in the string after the match.

For more information on regular expressions, see Chapter 3.

Example   The statements:

```
str = "This is a test."
pat = /s../g
result = pat.exec(str)
```

will return a match of "s i" in `result[0]`, and will set `pat.lastIndex` to 6. Executing another:

```
result = pat.exec(str)
```

will return a match of "s a" in `result[0]`, and will set `pat.lastIndex` to 9.

See Also   `lastMatch`, `leftContext`, `multiline`, `RegExp`, `rightContext`

lastIndexOf( )

Version 1.0

Method of the `String` object

Returns a number indicating the position in a string where the last occurrence of a specified substring is found.

Syntax   *str*.lastIndexOf(*sval*, *start*)

str   String object or expression.
sval   The substring to search for.
start   Optional numeric value specifying the position at which to start the search. If omitted, the search starts at the end of the string (position *str*.length − 1).

Discussion   `lastIndexOf()` searches the string from end to beginning; to search in forward order, use `indexOf()`. Note that positions in strings start at zero, so the returned value and the *start* argument may have values from 0 to *str*.length − 1.

Example   For a string declared by a statement, such as:

```
myString = "This is a string."
```

the statement:

```
position = myString.indexOf("is")
```

will set `position` to 5, since the last occurrence of the characters "is" starts at the fifth character.

See Also indexOf( ), String

lastMatch, $&

Version 1.2   Read-only

A property of the RegExp constructor

Returns the last string that matched a regular expression.

Syntax RegExp.lastMatch

Discussion This property's value is set when a regular expression match is performed by the exec( ), match( ), replace( ) (of String), or test( ) methods. lastMatch returns a string containing a copy of the last substring that was matched.

The symbol $& is an abbreviation for lastMatch.

Note that this is a property of the RegExp constructor, not of objects created by new RegExp( ). That means that it is shared by all scripts running in the same window or frame. If you have several scripts in one window that use regular expressions, they may affect each other's results.

Example After executing statements such as:

```
str = "Smith,John"
pat = /h./
pat.exec(str)
```

RegExp.lastMatch will return "h,". (The pattern /h./ matches a lowercase h followed by any character.)

See Also $1, $2 ... $9, leftContext, lastParen, RegExp, rightContext

lastModified

Version 1.0 Read-only Tainted

Property of the document object

Returns the most recent time and date when a web page's contents were changed.

Syntax   *docObject*.lastModified

docObject   document for the current document, or an expression denoting a document in any window.

Discussion   This property returns a string containing the time and date values provided by the server when the web page was loaded. If the server did not provide this information, lastModified returns a string containing the local time that corresponds to 00:00:00 GMT on January 1, 1970.

Example   Many web pages contain a statement like this, usually near the end:

```
document.write("This page was last modified on ",
   document.lastModified, ".")
```

See Also   document

lastParen, $+

Version 1.2 Read-only

A property of the RegExp constructor

Returns the last substring that was memorized while matching a regular expression.

Syntax   RegExp.lastParen

Discussion   This property's value is set when a regular expression match is performed by the exec(), match(), replace() (of String), or test() methods. lastMatch returns a string containing a copy of the last substring that was memorized, as specified by parentheses in a regular expression.

The symbol $+ is an abbreviation for lastMatch.

Note that this is a property of the RegExp constructor, not of objects created by new RegExp(). That means that it is shared by all scripts running in the same window or frame. If you have several scripts in one window that use regular expressions, they may affect each other's results.

Example   After matching an e-mail address with statements such as:

```
str = "You can contact me at guy1@someguys.com."
pat = /(\S+)@(\S+)\.([A-Z]{3})/i
pat.exec(str)
```

RegExp.lastParen will return "com". ($1, $2, and $3 will return "guy1", "someguys", and "com", respectively.)

See Also $1, $2 ... $9, leftContext, lastMatch, RegExp, rightContext

Layer

Version 1.2

Object type (constructor)

Creates an object containing a document layer that can be displayed in a web page, or reflects a layer created in a document by the HTML <LAYER> tag.

Syntax   For constructed objects:

v = new Layer(width, parent)

v	Variable or object to which the new Layer is assigned.
width	Numeric value specifying the width of the layer, in pixels.
parent	Optional argument. A Layer object to become the parent of the new layer. If omitted, the new layer becomes a child of the document.

For external objects:

docObject.layerID
docObject.layers.layerID
docObject.layers[index]

docObject	document for the current document, or an expression denoting a document in any window.
layerID	String value representing a name assigned by the ID attribute of the HTML <LAYER> tag.
index	Number or string specifying an element of the form's images array.

Properties   above   A reference to the Layer object that is immediately "above" this one in the z-order, or null if there is none.
below   A reference to the Layer object that is immediately "below" this one in the z-order, or null if there is none.

	background	A reference to an `Image` object that is displayed as the layer's background.
	bgColor	A string specifying the background color for the layer if there is no `background` image.
	clip	An object with four properties named `bottom`, `left`, `right`, and `top`, that specify how much of a layer is displayed.
	document	A `document` object that contains the layer's content.
	left	The horizontal position of the layer's left side, in pixels, relative to the position of its parent layer.
	name	Reflects the name assigned by the `ID` attribute of the HTML `<LAYER>` tag.
	pageX	The horizontal position of the layer's left side, in pixels, relative to the document.
	pageY	The vertical position of the layer's left side, in pixels, relative to the document.
	parentLayer	A reference to the `Layer` object that contains this one, or the enclosing `window` object if there is no parent layer.
	siblingAbove	A reference to the sibling `Layer` object (one with the same parent as this one) that is immediately "above" this one in the z-order, or `null` if there is none.
	siblingBelow	A reference to the sibling `Layer` object (one with the same parent as this one) that is immediately "below" this one in the z-order, or `null` if there is none.
	src	String specifying a URL that contains the document displayed in the layer.
	top	The vertical position of the layer's top edge, in pixels, relative to the position of its parent layer.
	visibility	A string specifying whether the layer is displayed. The value may be `"show"`, `"hide"`, or `"inherit"`.
	zIndex	The layer's position in the z-order that determines which layers are "on top of" others.
Methods	load(*url, width*)	Loads the specified file into the layer, and changes the layer width to the specified value.
	moveAbove(*layer*)	Changes the z-order so that this layer is placed "above" the specified layer.
	moveBelow(*layer*)	Changes the z-order so that this layer is placed "below" the specified layer.
	moveBy(*horiz, vert*)	Moves the layer by the specified amounts.
	moveTo(*horiz, vert*)	Moves the layer to the specified position relative to the parent layer or window.
	moveToAbsolute (*horiz, vert*)	Moves the layer to the specified position relative to the web page.
	resizeBy(*horiz, vert*)	Resizes the layer by changing the `clip.right` and `clip.bottom` properties by the specified amounts.
	resizeTo(*horiz, vert*)	Resizes the layer by changing the `clip.right` and `clip.bottom` properties to produce the specified size.

Event Handlers onblur, onfocus, onmouseout, onmouseover, onload

Discussion When Navigator loads a web page, it creates `Layer` objects corresponding to all `<LAYER>` tags in the document. You can reference these objects by their names, or as elements of the `layers` array.

Also, scripts can create `Layer` objects with the `new Layer()` constructor. After creating a layer in this manner, you can write content into its `document` object, or you can load a file into it by assigning a URL to the `src` property.

Note that when a layer is created, its `visibility` is initially set to `"hide"`; you must change this to `"show"` or `"inherit"` in order to see the layer on the screen. This is helpful if you want to completely initialize a layer (perhaps loading a large image file) before making it visible to the user.

Writing to a layer is much like writing to any `document`. Remember that you must write line breaks or close the document in order to make sure that all text is displayed.

There are a few restrictions on creating and writing to layers:

- Scripts cannot call `new Layer()` until after a web page is completely loaded. So scripts that are written in-line with the HTML, to execute while the page is being loaded, cannot call `new Layer()`.

- Scripts cannot write to a layer's `document` until the web page is completely loaded.

- Scripts can only open one layer's document at a time. After writing to a layer, you must call `document.close()` on it before writing to another layer.

Examples To create a new layer and write some text to it, use statements, such as:

```
var n1
function makeLayer(text) {
   lyr = new Layer (400)
   lyr.pageX = 100
   lyr.pageY = 200
   lyr.bgColor="turquoise"
   lyr.document.write("Here's a message: ", text, "<BR>")
   lyr.visibility = "show"
   lyr.document.close()
   return lyr
}
...
n1 = makeLayer("Testing, 1, 2, 3 ... ")
```

(Note that `makeLayer` cannot be called until the web page is completely loaded.)

See Also document, layers

layers

Version 1.2 External

Property of the document object

Reflects all layers defined in a document.

Syntax *docObject*.layers

docObject   document for the current document, or an expression denoting a document object in any window.

Properties length   Length of the array (number of layers in the document).

Discussion Each element of the layers array is an Layer object reflecting one image that was declared by an HTML <LAYER> tag. Although some of the Layer objects' properties can be modified, the layers array itself is read-only.

Example To load a new file into the first layer in the document, use a statement, such as:

document.layers[0].src = "newlayer.htm"

See Also document, Layer

layerX

Version 1.2 Special scope

Property of the event object

Returns the horizontal position, in pixels, measured from the left side of the layer, where an event occurred.

Syntax *eventObj*.layerX

eventObj   event, or an expression denoting a copy of event such as a function argument passed to an event handler.

Discussion This property returns a position relative to the layer in which the event occurred. If there is no layer present, the value will be equal to the pageX property.

The event object has limited scope: it can only be referenced in event handlers.

Example   To determine the position within a layer where an event occurred, use an event handler with statements such as:

```
function mouseClick(ev) {
    ...
    horiz = ev.layerX
    vert = ev.layerY
    ...
}
```

(This example assumes that the function is called with an **event** object passed to the ev argument.)

See Also   event, layerY, pageX, screenX

layerY

Version 1.2   Special scope

Property of the event object

Returns the vertical position, in pixels, measured from the top edge of the layer, where an event occurred.

Syntax   *eventObj*.layerY

eventObj   event, or an expression denoting a copy of **event**, such as a function argument passed to an event handler.

Discussion   This property returns a position relative to the layer in which the event occurred. If there is no layer present, the value will be equal to the pageY property.

The **event** object has limited scope: it can only be referenced in event handlers.

Example   To determine the position within a layer where an event occurred, use an event handler with statements such as:

```
function mouseClick(ev) {
    ...
    horiz = ev.layerX
    vert = ev.layerY
    ...
}
```

(This example assumes that the function is called with an `event` object passed to the `ev` argument.)

See Also   `event`, `layerX`, `pageY`, `screenY`

left

CLIP

Version 1.2   **External**

Property of the `clip` object
(see also `left` as a property of the Layer object)

Specifies the left clipping limit of a layer.

Syntax   `layerObj.clip.left`

`layerObj`   `document.layerName`, or other expression denoting a Layer object.

Discussion   This property specifies the left clipping limit for a layer, in pixels. It is initially zero. Increasing its value causes columns of pixels at the left side of the layer to become invisible, allowing the lower layers or the enclosing document to be seen.

Example   To cause the left 64 columns of pixels in a layer to be clipped, use a statement such as:

`document.layers.myLayer.clip.left = 64`

See Also   `bottom`, `height`, `right`, `top`, `width` (properties of `clip`); Layer

left

LAYER

Property of the Layer object
(see also `left` as a property of the `clip` object)

Specifies the horizontal position of the left side of the layer.

Syntax   `layerObj.left`

`layerObj`   `document.layerName`, or other expression denoting a Layer object.

Discussion This property controls the horizontal position of the layer. It specifies the distance in pixels, from the left side of the layer to the left side of the parent layer (if any) or the window. Scripts can modify this value at any time, and the position of the layer on the screen will be immediately updated.

Example To place a layer 100 pixels down and 200 pixels right from the top left corner of a window, use statements such as:

```
document.layers.layer1.top = 100
document.layers.layer1.left = 200
```

See Also Layer, top

leftContext, $`

Version 1.2   Read-only

A property of the RegExp constructor

Returns the portion of a string before the most recent match.

Syntax `RegExp.leftContext`

Discussion This property's value is set when a regular expression match is performed by the `exec( )`, `match( )`, `replace( )` (of `String`), or `test( )` methods. `leftContext` returns a string containing characters from the string that was searched, from the beginning of the string to the character just before the most recent match.

The symbol $` is an abbreviation for `leftContext`.

Note that this is a property of the `RegExp` constructor, not of objects created by `new RegExp( )`. That means that it is shared by all scripts running in the same window or frame. If you have several scripts that use regular expressions in one window, they may affect each other's results.

Example After executing statements such as:

```
str = "Smith,John"
pat = /,/
pat.exec(str)
```

`RegExp.leftContext` will return `"Smith"`.

See Also `$1, $2 ... $9, lastMatch, lastParen, RegExp, rightContext`

length

Version 1.0   Read-only

Property of Array, Frame, Select, String, and window objects

Returns the number of elements in an array, or the number of characters in a string.

Syntax

arrayObj.length
stringObj.length

arrayObj	Variable or expression denoting an `Array` object.
stringObj	Variable or expression denoting a `String` object.

Discussion

For `Array` objects, this property returns the number of elements. Note that, since array indexes start at zero, the last element is numbered (length − 1). If a script sets an array's `length` to a lower value, the array is truncated. The reverse is not true; an array cannot be extended by setting its `length` to a higher value. However, if a script assigns a value to an array element beyond the current length, the array is filled with additional elements to the new length.

This property is available for all arrays created by scripts. It is also present for all arrays that are properties of other objects, such as `window.frames` and `document.images`. Also, since Radio objects with the same name are collected into an array, the `length` property of any Radio object returns the number of radio buttons in that set.

For `String` objects, this property returns the number of characters. Note that, since string indexes start at zero, the last character is numbered (length − 1). The length property of `String` objects is read-only.

As a convenience to programmers, additional `length` properties are available for some objects, as in the following list:

Frame object	Returns the length of the object's `frames` array (number of child frames within the frame). This is equivalent to the length property of the `frames` array itself.
Select object	Returns the length of the object's `options` array (number of options in the select box). This is equivalent to the length property of the `options` array itself.
window object	Returns the length of the object's `frames` array (number of frames within the window). This is equivalent to the length property of the `frames` array itself.

Version 1.1	The `Array` object was added in JavaScript 1.1.
Examples	`document.write("This web page contains ", document.images.length, " images.")`
See Also	`Array`, `Frame`, `Select`, `String`, `window`

lineHeight

Version 1.2

Property of style sheet objects

Specifies the spacing between lines of text.

Syntax	*styleObj*.lineHeight
	styleObj Style sheet object: a property of a `classes`, `ids`, or `tags` object.
Discussion	This property sets the line height; that is, the distance between the baselines of two adjacent lines of text. It applies to block-level HTML elements, and is inherited.

This property may be set to:

- An absolute measurement, such as `"12pt"`.
- A measurement relative to the current font size, such as `"1.5em"`.
- A pixel measurement, such as `"18px"`.
- A percentage of the current font size, such as "150%".

Note that for `lineHeight` assignments to take effect, they must occur before the browser writes the styled text to the document. An assignment to `tags.body.lineHeight` must be done within the `<HEAD>` ... `</HEAD>` section of the HTML.

Example	To achieve line spacing in paragraph text (`<P>` tag) that is double the normal amount, use a statement, such as:

`document.tags.p.lineHeight = "200%"`

See Also	`fontSize`, `height` (property of style sheet objects)

link( )

Version 1.0

Method of the `String` object

Returns a string containing HTML code for a hypertext link.

Syntax
: `stringObj.link(url)`

  `stringObj`   String object or expression to be formatted as a link.
  `url`   String value representing a URL that the link will access.

Discussion
: This method returns a string consisting of HTML code. The code includes the HTML `<A>` and `</A>` tags so that, if the returned string is written to a document, it will appear as a hypertext link. The `HREF` attribute of the `<A>` tag will be set to the value of the `url` argument.

Example
: The following statements:

```
var s = "my home page"
var a = s.link("http://www.mySite.com/home.html")
```

set the value of a to the string:

`<A HREF="http://www.mySite.com/home.html">my home page</A>`

See Also
: `Link`, `links`, `String`

Link

Version 1.0   External

External object

Reflects a hypertext link in a document.

Syntax
: `docObject.links[index]`

  `docObject`   document for the current document, or an expression denoting a document in any window.
  `index`   Number or string specifying an element of the document's `links` array.

Properties	hash	Specifies an anchor name in the link's URL, starting with a # character.
	host	Specifies the host domain and server names, or IP address, and port number of the link's URL.
	hostname	Specifies the server and domain name, or IP address, of the link's URL.
	href	Specifies the link's entire URL.
	pathname	Specifies the file pathname of the link's URL, starting with a / character.
	port	Specifies the port number of the link's URL.
	protocol	Specifies the protocol part of the link's URL, including the trailing : character.
	search	Specifies the query portion of the link's URL, starting with a ? character.
	target	Reflects the TARGET attribute of the HTML tag.

Event Handlers onclick, ondblclick, onkeydown, onkeypress, onkeyup, onmousedown, onmouseout, onmouseover, onmouseup

Whenever one of these event handlers is called, the text between the link's <A> and </A> tags is placed in RegExp.input.

Discussion When Navigator loads a web page, it creates Link objects corresponding to all hypertext links in the document, as defined by HTML <A> tags. You can reference these objects as elements of the links array.

Note that if the link is created by an <A> tag with a NAME attribute, it also has an entry in the anchors array.

The links array also contains Area objects corresponding to all HTML <AREA> tags in the document.

Version 1.1 The onmouseout event handler was added in JavaScript 1.1.

Version 1.2 The ondblclick, onkeydown, onkeypress, onkeyup, onmousedown, and onmouseup event handlers were added in JavaScript 1.2.

Example To change the URL associated with a link, use a statement such as:

document.links[0].href = "http://www.myco.com/otherfile.htm"

See Also Anchor, Area, document, links

linkColor

Version 1.0

Property of the document object

Specifies the color in which links are normally displayed.

Syntax `docObject.linkColor`

docObject **document** for the current window's document, or an expression denoting a document in any window.

Discussion This property specifies the color in which links are displayed if they are not active (see `alinkColor`) and have not been recently visited (see `vlinkColor`). This property may be set to a string of six hexadecimal digits, with an optional leading pound sign (#) character, in the form *rrggbb*, where *rr* specifies red, *gg* specifies green, and *bb* specifies blue. `linkColor` may also be set to one of the color names listed in Appendix C. The returned value is always in hexadecimal with a leading #.

This property is initially set to the color specified by the `LINK` attribute, if any, of the HTML `<BODY>` tag.

Examples
```
document.linkColor = "00ff00"          // no red
                                       // max. green
                                       // no blue

parent.document.linkColor = "#8000ff"  // 50% red
                                       // no green
                                       // max. blue

otherWindow.document.linkColor
    = "cornsilk"                       // Netscape keyword
```

See Also `alinkColor`, `bgColor`, `document`, `fgColor`, `vlinkColor`

links

Version 1.0 Read-only External Tainted

Property of the document object

Reflects all hypertext links defined in a document; contains both Link and Area objects.

Syntax `docObject.links`

	docObject	**document** for the current document, or an expression denoting a **document** object in any window.
Properties	`length`	Length of the array (number of links in the document).

Discussion
Each element of the `links` array is a Link or Area object reflecting one link that was declared by an HTML `<LINK>` or `<AREA>` tag. Although some of the objects' properties can be modified, the `links` array itself is read-only.

Note that the NAME attributes of `<LINK>` and `<AREA>` tags are not reflected, so you can only reference these objects by their position in the array.

Example
To place a new URL into the first link in the document, use a statement such as:

`document.links[0].href = "http://www.myco.com/newfile.htm"`

See Also
Area, document, Link

listStyleType

Version 1.2

Property of style sheet objects

Specifies how list elements are displayed.

Preliminary *Note that this property is announced by Netscape, but not yet implemented in Navigator as of version 4.01. The information presented here is preliminary.*

Syntax
`styleObj.listStyleType`

styleObj Style sheet object: a property of a `classes`, `ids`, or `tags` object.

Discussion
This property controls how list items are displayed: it specifies what type of numbering or marking is used. The value may be one of the following:

`"disc"`   `"lower-roman"`
`"circle"`   `"upper-roman"`
`"square"`   `"lower-alpha"`
`"decimal"`   `"upper-alpha"`
`"none"`

This property applies to all elements whose `display` property is set to `"list-item"`. Its initial value is `"disc"`.

Note that for `listStyleType` assignments to take effect, they must occur before the browser writes the styled text to the document. An assignment to `tags.body.listStyleType` must be done within the `<HEAD>` ... `</HEAD>` section of the HTML.

See Also classes, display, ids, tags

LN10

Version 1.0   Read-only

Property of the Math object

Returns the natural logarithm of 10, approximately 2.3025850.

Syntax Math.LN10

Example a = Math.LN10

See Also E, LN2, LOG2E, LOG10E, Math, PI, SQRT1_2, SQRT2

LN2

Version 1.0   Read-only

Property of the Math object

Returns the natural logarithm of 2, approximately 0.6931471.

Syntax Math.LN2

Example a = Math.LN2

See Also E, LN10, LOG2E, LOG10E, Math, PI, SQRT1_2, SQRT2

load( )

Version 1.2

Method of the Layer object

Loads a new document into a layer.

Syntax   `layerObj.load(url, width)`

`layerObj`	document.layerName, or an expression denoting a Layer object in any document.
`url`	String specifying the URL of the file to load.
`width`	Numeric value specifying the width of the layer in pixels.

Discussion   This method resizes the layer to the specified width, and loads the specified file into the layer's `document` object. The layer's `src` property will be changed to reflect the new file.

Example   `document.myLayer.load("http://www.mysite.com/newfile.htm", 320)`

See Also   Layer

LOAD

Version 1.2   Read-only

Property of the Event object

Returns a mask for capturing load events.

Syntax   `Event.LOAD`

Discussion   This property is used to capture and release load events, which occur when the browser finishes loading an image or document. For more details on event handling, see Chapter 7.

Example   To enable capturing of load events (as well as error):

`myWindow.captureEvents (Event.LOAD | Event.ERROR)`

See Also   `captureEvents()`, `event`, `Event`, `onload`, `releaseEvents()`

location

DOCUMENT

Read-only

Property of the document object
(see also `location` as a property of the `window` object)

A synonym for the URL property; not recommended.

Syntax *docObject*.location

docObject document for the current document, or an expression denoting a document in any window.

Discussion This property was included by Netscape for compatibility with some other browsers. It is planned to be removed in a future release of Navigator, so scripts should use `document.URL` instead.

Note that there is also a `window.location`, which behaves quite differently from this property (it is not read-only).

See Also document, location (property of `window`), URL

location

WINDOW

Version 1.0

Property of the `window` object
(see also `location` as a property of the `document` object)

Specifies the URL of the document currently loaded in a window.

Syntax For the current window:

location
self.location
window.location

For other windows:

windowObj.location

	windowObj	An expression denoting a `window` object.
Properties	hash	Specifies an anchor name in the URL, starting with a # character.
	host	Specifies the host domain and server names, or IP address, and port number of the URL.
	hostname	Specifies the server and domain name, or IP address, of the URL.
	href	Specifies the entire URL.
	pathname	Specifies the file pathname of the URL, starting with a / character.
	port	Specifies the port number of the URL.
	protocol	Specifies the protocol part of the URL, including the trailing : character.
	search	Specifies the query portion of the URL, starting with a ? character.
Methods	reload(*force*)	Reloads the current web page, optionally forcing a new download from the server.
	replace(*URL*)	Loads a new web page at the current point in the history list, that is, without creating a new history list entry.

Discussion

This property specifies the URL of the web page currently loaded in the window. Each property of `location` specifies some portion of the URL, except `href`, which specifies the entire URL.

Modifying `location` or any of its properties causes Navigator to load the web page specified by the new URL.

Version 1.1

In JavaScript 1.0, modifying `location` causes a conditional HTTP GET operation, which does not actually download the web page from a server if the browser's cache contains an up-to-date copy of it. Starting with JavaScript 1.1, the effect of modifying `location` depends on the user's settings in the Network Preferences dialog.

Example

To cause a window to scroll to a specified anchor, use a statement such as:

```
otherWindow.location.hash = "chapter2"
```

See Also history, URL, window

locationbar

Version 1.2   Signed scripts

Property of the window object

Specifies the state of the browser window's location bar.

Syntax   For the current window:

```
locationbar
self.locationbar
window.locationbar
```

For other windows:

```
windowObj.locationbar
```

windowObj   An expression denoting a `window` object.

Properties   `visible`   Specifies whether the location bar is visible.

Discussion   The location bar is the bar at the top of a window that contains the text box where users type URLs that they wish to display. Currently, `locationbar` has a single Boolean property, `visible`, that specifies whether the bar is displayed. If the value is `true`, the toolbar is displayed.

Note that you can only modify this property in a signed script.

Example   This statement hides the location bar in a window named `windowOne`:

```
windowOne.locationbar.visible = 0
```

See Also   `menubar, personalbar, scrollbars, statusbar, toolbar, window`

log( )

Method of the Math object

Returns the natural logarithm (base *e*) of a number.

Syntax   `Math.tan(number)`

number   A numeric value greater than zero.

Discussion   If the argument is zero or negative, the returned value will be the negative of
              Number.MAX_VALUE.

Example   y = Math.log(x)

See Also   exp( ), Math, Number

LOG10E

Version 1.0   Read-only

Property of the Math object

Returns the base 10 logarithm of *e*, approximately 0.4342944.

Syntax   Math.LOG10E

Example   a = Math.LOG10E

See Also   E, LN10, LN2, LOG2E, Math, PI, SQRT1_2, SQRT2

LOG2E

Version 1.0   Read-only

Property of the Math object

Returns the base 2 logarithm of *e*, approximately 1.4426950.

Syntax   Math.LOG2E

Example   a = Math.LOG2E

See Also   E, LN10, LN2, LOG10E, Math, PI, SQRT1_2, SQRT2

lowsrc

Version 1.1

Property of the Image object

Specifies a low-resolution image to be displayed while a higher-resolution one is being loaded.

Syntax   *imageObj*.lowsrc

            imageObj   document.*imageName*, or other expression denoting an Image object.

Discussion   High-resolution images are sometimes slow to download if the user's modem is slow or if network traffic is heavy. In order to have something on display while an image is downloading, this property specifies a smaller file to be displayed temporarily, until the large image is ready.

Example

```
myImage.src = "bigfile.jpg"
myImage.lowsrc = "smallfile.gif"
```

See Also   complete, Image, src

marginBottom

Version 1.2

Property of style sheet objects

Specifies the distance between an HTML element's bottom and the adjacent element.

Syntax *styleObj*.marginBottom

styleObj   Style sheet object: a property of a `classes`, `ids`, or `tags` object.

Discussion The `marginBottom` property specifies the space below an HTML element. If the element has a border, the margin is the space below the border (the `paddingBottom` property specifies the space above the border). This property applies to block-level elements and is not inherited.
This property may be set to:
- An absolute measurement, such as "12pt".
- A measurement relative to the current font size, such as "1.5em".
- A pixel measurement, such as "18px".
- A percentage of the parent element's width, such as "15%".

Example `document.ids.wide.marginBottom = "24pt"`

See Also `marginLeft, marginRight, margins(), marginTop, classes, ids, paddingLeft, paddingRight, paddings(), paddingTop, tags`

marginLeft

Version 1.2

Property of style sheet objects

Specifies the distance between an HTML element's left side and the adjacent element.

Syntax *styleObj*.marginLeft

styleObj   Style sheet object: a property of a `classes`, `ids`, or `tags` object.

Discussion   The `marginLeft` property specifies the space to the left of an HTML element. If the element has a border, the margin is the space outside the border (the `paddingLeft` property specifies the space inside the border). This property applies to block-level elements and is not inherited.

This property may be set to:

- An absolute measurement, such as "12pt".
- A measurement relative to the current font size, such as "1.5em".
- A pixel measurement, such as "18px".
- A percentage of the parent element's width, such as "15%".

Example   `document.ids.wide.marginLeft = "24pt"`

See Also   `marginBottom, marginRight, margins(), marginTop, classes, ids, paddingLeft, paddingRight, paddings(), paddingTop, tags`

marginRight

Version 1.2

Property of style sheet objects

Specifies the distance between an HTML element's right side and the adjacent element.

Syntax   *styleObj*.marginRight

styleObj   Style sheet object: a property of a `classes`, `ids`, or `tags` object.

Discussion   The `marginRight` property specifies the space to the left of an HTML element. If the element has a border, the margin is the space outside the border (the `paddingRight` property specifies the space inside the border). This property applies to block-level elements and is not inherited.

This property may be set to:

- An absolute measurement, such as "12pt".
- A measurement relative to the current font size, such as "1.5em".
- A pixel measurement, such as "18px".
- A percentage of the parent element's width, such as "15%".

Example   `document.ids.wide.marginRight = "24pt"`

See Also   `marginBottom, marginLeft, margins(), marginTop, classes, ids, paddingLeft, paddingRight, paddings(), paddingTop, tags`

margins( )

Version 1.2

Method of style sheet objects

Specifies the distances between an HTML element and adjacent elements.

Syntax `styleObj.margins(topValue, rightValue, bottomValue, leftValue)`

`styleObj` Style sheet object: a property of a `classes`, `ids`, or `tags` object.

`topValue, rightValue, bottomValue, leftValue,` String or numeric the parent element's value values specifying the margin spacings.

Discussion The margin properties specify the space between an HTML element and adjacent elements. If the element has borders, the margins are the space outside the borders (the `paddings( )` method specifies the spacing inside the borders). This method applies to block-level elements. Margin values are not inherited.

This property may be set to:

- An absolute measurement, such as `"12pt"`.
- A measurement relative to the current font size, such as `"1.5em"`.
- A pixel measurement, such as `"18px"`.
- A percentage of the parent element's width, such as "15%".

Example `ids.myStyle.margins("4pt", "12pt", "6pt", "8pt")`

See Also `marginBottom, marginLeft, marginRight, marginTop, classes, ids, paddingLeft, paddingRight, paddings( ), paddingTop, tags`

marginTop

Version 1.2

Property of style sheet objects

Specifies the distance between an HTML element's top and the adjacent element.

Syntax `styleObj.marginTop`

`styleObj` Style sheet object: a property of a `classes`, `ids`, or `tags` object.

Discussion The `marginTop` property specifies the space above an HTML element. If the element has a border, the margin is the space outside the border (the `paddingTop` property specifies the space inside the border). This property applies to block-level elements and is not inherited.
This property may be set to:
- An absolute measurement, such as `"12pt"`.
- A measurement relative to the current font size, such as `"1.5em"`.
- A pixel measurement, such as `"18px"`.
- A percentage of the parent element's width, such as "15%".

Examples `document.ids.wide.marginTop = "24pt"`

See Also `marginBottom`, `marginLeft`, `marginRight`, `margins()`, `classes`, `ids`, `paddingLeft`, `paddingRight`, `paddings()`, `paddingTop`, `tags`

match( )

Version 1.2

Method of the `String` object

Matches a regular expression against a string and returns various results.

Syntax `stringObj.match(regexp)`

`stringObj` String object or expression.
`regexp` Regular expression.

Discussion This method is used to search a string for a substring that matches a regular expression (pattern). If the pattern has the `g` (global) modifier, `match( )` searches for all matching substrings. If the pattern has the `i` (case-insensitive) modifier, `match( )` regards upper- and lowercase letters as equivalent.
If no match is found, `match( )` returns `null`. If a match is found, the returned value is an object whose structure depends on whether the `g` modifier is specified:

- If the g modifier is not specified, match( ) returns an array with one element (index 0) containing the matched substring. If the pattern contains any parentheses, the corresponding substrings are returned as additional elements of the array. The array also has a property named input that returns a copy of the input string, and a property named index that returns the position in the input string where the matching substring begins.
- If the g modifier is specified, match( ) returns an array with elements containing each matching substring. (The array's length property returns the number of matches.)

In addition to these results, match( ) also updates properties of the RegExp constructor; that is, properties of RegExp itself, not of the pattern. The properties and their values are in the following list:

$1, $2, ... $9	Strings representing memorized substrings specified by parentheses in the pattern. If the match is global (g modifier), each property will contain the last matching value.
lastMatch or $&	The last substring matched.
lastParen or $+	The last substring memorized.
leftContext or $`	The substring from the start of the source string to just before the last match. (Note the use of the accent character, not the apostrophe.)
rightContext or $'	The substring from just after the last match to the end of the source string.

Note that since RegExp is a constructor, these properties are shared by all scripts running in any window or frame. If you have several scripts that use regular expressions running in one window, they could affect each others' results.

Examples These statements:

```
s = "ababbbcBx"
result = s.match(/B./)
```

set result[0] to "Bx", result.index to 7, and result.input to "ababbbcBx". Changing to a case-insensitive match:

```
result = s.match(/B./i)
```

sets result[0] to "ba", result.index to 1, and result.input to "ababbbcBx". Making the match global as well:

```
result = s.match(/B./ig)
```

sets result[0] to "ba", result[1] to "bb", result[2] to "bc", and result[3] to "Bx".

See Also exec( ), RegExp, replace( ), search( ), test( )

Math

Version 1.0

Built-in object

Provides mathematical functions and values.

Syntax	`Math`	
Properties	`E`	Base of natural logarithms (2.71828...)
	`LN2`	Natural log of 2 (0.693...)
	`LN10`	Natural log of 10 (2.302...)
	`LOG2E`	Base 2 log of *e* (1.442...)
	`LOG10E`	Base 10 log of *e* (0.434...)
	`PI`	Value of π (3.14159...)
	`SQRT1_2`	One-half the square root of 2 (0.707...)
	`SQRT2`	Square root of 2 (1.414...)
Methods	`abs(x)`	Absolute value.
	`acos(a)`	Arc cosine.
	`asin(a)`	Arc sine.
	`atan(a)`	Arc tangent (1 argument).
	`atan2(y, x)`	Arc tangent (2 arguments).
	`ceil(x)`	Ceiling (lowest greater integer).
	`cos(a)`	Cosine.
	`exp(x)`	Natural exponent (*e* to the power of...).
	`floor(x)`	Floor (greatest lower integer).
	`log(x)`	Natural (base *e*) logarithm.
	`max(a, b)`	Return greater value.
	`min(a, b)`	Return lesser value.
	`pow(a, b)`	Exponentiation (a to the power of b).
	`random()`	Returns a pseudo-random number between 0 and 1.
	`round(x)`	Round to the nearest integer: down if the fractional part is less than .5, or up if the fractional part is .5 or greater.
	`sin(a)`	Sine.
	`sqrt(x)`	Square root.
	`tan(a)`	Tangent.
Discussion	The `Number` object also has some properties that are useful for mathematical operations.	
Example	`x = Math.cos(theta)` `y = Math.sin(theta)`	
See Also	`isNaN()`, `Number`	

max( )

Version 1.0

Method of the Math object

Returns the greater of two numbers.

Syntax   `Math.max(num1, num2)`

            num1, num2   Any numeric values or expressions.

Discussion   Note that "greater" means more positive: for example, `max(-1, -2)` returns -1.

Example   `larger = Math.max(a, b)`

See Also   `ceil()`, `floor()`, `Math`, `min()`

MAX_VALUE

Version 1.1   Read-only

Property of the Number object

Returns the largest number that can be represented in JavaScript.

Syntax   `Number.MAX_VALUE`

Discussion   This property's value is approximately 1.79E308. Any operation that attempts to compute a value greater than `MAX_VALUE` or less than negative `MAX_VALUE` returns `Number.POSITIVE_INFINITY` or `Number.NEGATIVE_INFINITY`

See Also   `MIN_VALUE`

menubar

Version 1.2   Signed scripts

Property of the window object

Specifies the state of the browser window's menu bar.

Syntax
: For the current window:
```
menubar
self.menubar
window.menubar
```
For other windows:
```
windowObj.menubar
```

windowObj   An expression denoting a `window` object.

Properties
: `visible`   A Boolean property indicating whether the menu bar is visible or not.

Discussion
: The menu bar is the strip at the top of a window containing pull-down menus such as File and Edit. You can use this object's single property, `visible`, to find out if the personal toolbar is displayed or to change its status.
  Note that you can only modify this property in a signed script.

Example
: This statement hides the menu bar in a window named `windowOne`:
```
windowOne.menubar.visible = false
```

See Also
: `locationbar, personalbar, scrollbars, statusbar, toolbar, window`

META_MASK

Version 1.2   Read-only

Property of the Event object

Returns a mask for checking if the Meta key was pressed during an event.

Syntax
: `Event.META_MASK`

Discussion
: This property is a bit mask for testing the `event.modifiers` property to find out if the Meta key was pressed when the event occurred.

Example   The following statements could be used in an event handler:

```
if (myEvent.modifiers & Event.META_MASK) {
    ...    // the Meta- key was pressed
}
else
    ...    // Meta- was not pressed
```

See Also   ALT_MASK, CONTROL_MASK, SHIFT_MASK, Event

method

Version 1.0   External

Property of the Form external object

Specifies how information from a form is sent to a server.

Syntax   *formObj*.method

formObj   document.*formName* or other expression denoting a Form object.

Discussion   This property is a string that initially reflects the METHOD attribute of an HTML <FORM> tag. The value should be either "get" or "post". Scripts can modify the value at any time.

Example   document.myForm.method = "post"

See Also   Form, submit( )

MimeType

Version 1.1   Read-only   External

External object

Provides information about a MIME data type that the browser supports.

Syntax   navigator.mimeTypes[*index*]

index   A string specifying a MIME type (see Discussion), or a number specifying a position in the array.

Properties	`description`	A string containing text that describes the MIME type.
	`enabledPlugin`	Reference to the Plugin object that supports this MIME type, or `null` if no plug-in is installed.
	`suffixes`	A string containing all filename suffixes (extensions) that the browser will recognize as containing data of this type. If there is more than one suffix, they are separated by commas and spaces.
	`type`	The standard name of the MIME type.

Discussion: Navigator typically recognizes over 100 MIME types for text, graphics, audio, video, and other types of data. The `navigator.mimeTypes` array contains one MimeType object for each supported type. Scripts can reference these array elements by either a numeric index or by a string index specifying the `type` of the desired object (see Examples).

Examples: For a typical Navigator installation, the statements:

```
t0 = navigator.mimeTypes[0].type
d0 = navigator.mimeTypes[0].description
s0 = navigator.mimeTypes[0].type
```

set the variables to `"audio/x-liveaudio"`, `"Streaming Audio Metafiles"`, and `"lam"`.

You can also use the MIME type (`type` property) as the array index; for example:

```
s1 = navigator.mimeTypes["audio/x-midi"].suffixes
```

sets the variable to `"mid, midi"`.

See Also: `mimeTypes`, Plugin, `plugins`

mimeTypes

Version 1.1   Read-only

Property of the `navigator` object

Provides information about MIME data types that the browser supports.

Syntax: `navigator.mimeTypes`

Properties/Methods: Being an array, `mimeTypes` has all the properties and methods of any `Array` object. However, since it is read-only, some methods such as `reverse()` cannot be used on it.

Discussion	Each element of this array is a MimeType object that describes one MIME data type that the browser supports.

Example	`document.write("The ", navigator.mimeTypes[0].type,`
	`" MIME type is for ",`
	`navigator.mimeTypes[0].description, " data.")`

See Also	MimeType

min( )

Version 1.0

Method of the `Math` object

Returns the lesser of two numbers.

Syntax	`Math.min(num1, num2)`
	num1, num2 Any numeric values or expressions.
Discussion	Note that "lesser" means more negative: for example, `min(-1, -2)` returns -2.
Example	`smaller = Math.min(a, b)`
See Also	`ceil( )`, `floor( )`, `Math`, `max( )`

MIN_VALUE

Version 1.1   Read-only

Property of the `Number` object.

Returns the smallest number that can be represented in JavaScript.

Syntax	`Number.MIN_VALUE`
Discussion	This property's value is approximately 2.22E-308. Note that "smallest" means closest to zero, not most negative. Any operation that attempts to compute a value smaller than `MIN_VALUE` will return zero.
See Also	`MAX_VALUE`

modifiers

Version 1.2　Special scope

Property of the event object

Returns a binary value specifying modifier keys that the user pressed when an event occurred.

Syntax　*eventObj*.modifiers

eventObj　　event, or an expression denoting a copy of event, such as a function argument passed to an event handler.

Discussion　This property's value contains individual bits that indicate whether the Shift, Ctrl, Alt, or Meta keys were pressed by the user at the time when an event occurred. This property is available for events triggered by the mouse, as well as the keyboard, allowing scripts to detect operations such as Shift+click.

To find out whether a specific key was pressed, use a logical AND of modifiers with one of the mask values Event.ALT_MASK, Event.CONTROL_MASK, Event.META_MASK, or Event.SHIFT_MASK. (See the following Examples.)

Note that the event object has limited scope: it can only be referenced in event handlers (see Chapter 7).

Examples　To find out if the Shift key was pressed:

```
if (ev.modifiers & Event.SHIFT_MASK) {
     ...    // pressed
}
else
     ...    // not pressed
```

To find out if both Shift and Ctrl were pressed:

```
if ((ev.modifiers & Event.SHIFT_MASK)
   && (ev.modifiers & Event.CONTROL_MASK)) {
     ...    // pressed
}
else
     ...    // not pressed
```

To find out if either Shift or Alt was pressed:

```
if (ev.modifiers
    & (Event.SHIFT_MASK | Event.ALT_MASK)) {
      ...     // pressed
}
else
      ...     // not pressed
```

Note that most of the preceding operations use the bitwise operators | and &, rather than the Boolean || and &&.

(These examples assume that the variable ev is an event object or a copy of one.)

See Also   event, Event

MOUSEDOWN

Version 1.2   Read-only

Property of the Event object

Returns a mask for capturing mouse events.

Syntax   Event.MOUSEDOWN

Discussion   This property is used to control event capturing (see Chapter 7). When the event is captured, the value of the which property of the event object will contain 1 for the left mouse button, or 3 for the right button. The modifiers property will contain the state of the Shift, Ctrl, Alt, and Meta keys.

JavaScript generates a mouse-down event when the user presses a mouse button. Note that some conditions create more than one event. For example, when the user clicks a mouse button, JavaScript will generate mouse-down, click, and mouse-up events, in that order.

Example   To enable capturing of mouse-down events (as well as click):

```
myWindow.captureEvents (Event.MOUSEDOWN | Event.CLICK)
```

See Also   captureEvents(), releaseEvents(), event, Event

MOUSEMOVE

Version 1.2   Read-only

Property of the Event object

Returns a mask for capturing mouse events.

Syntax   `Event.MOUSEMOVE`

Discussion   This property is used to control event capturing (see Chapter 7). When the event is captured, the value of the properties such as `pageX` and `pageY` will indicate the new location of the mouse cursor. The `modifiers` property will contain the state of the Shift, Ctrl, Alt, and Meta keys.

JavaScript generates a mousemove event when the user moves the mouse.

Example   To enable capturing of mouse-move events (as well as click):

`myWindow.captureEvents (Event.MOUSEMOVE | Event.CLICK)`

See Also   `captureEvents(), releaseEvents(), event, Event`

MOUSEOUT

Version 1.2   Read-only

Property of the Event object

Returns a mask for capturing mouse events.

Syntax   `Event.MOUSEOUT`

Discussion   This property is used to control event capturing (see Chapter 7). When the event is captured, the value of the properties such as `pageX` and `pageY` will indicate the new location of the mouse cursor. The `modifiers` property will contain the state of the Shift, Ctrl, Alt, and Meta keys.

JavaScript generates a mouse-out event for an object when the user moves the mouse cursor away from the object's region of the screen.

Example   To enable capturing of mouse-out events (as well as mouse-over):

`myWindow.captureEvents (Event.MOUSEOVER | Event.MOUSEOUT)`

See Also   `captureEvents(), releaseEvents(), event, Event`

MOUSEOVER

Version 1.2   Read-only

Property of the Event object

Returns a mask for capturing mouse events.

Syntax Event.MOUSEOVER

Discussion This property is used to control event capturing (see Chapter 7). When the event is captured, the value of the properties such as `pageX` and `pageY` will indicate the new location of the mouse cursor. The `modifiers` property will contain the state of the Shift, Ctrl, Alt, and Meta keys.

JavaScript generates a mouse-over event for an object when the user moves the mouse cursor onto the object's region of the screen.

Example To enable capturing of mouse-over events (as well as mouse-out):

myWindow.captureEvents (Event.MOUSEOVER | Event.MOUSEOUT)

See Also captureEvents(), releaseEvents(), event, Event

MOUSEUP

Version 1.2   Read-only

Property of the Event object

Returns a mask for capturing mouse events.

Syntax Event.MOUSEUP

Discussion This property is used to control event capturing (see Chapter 7). When the event is captured, the value of the `which` property of the `event` object will contain 1 for the left mouse button, or 3 for the right button. The `modifiers` property will contain the state of the Shift, Ctrl, Alt, and Meta keys.

JavaScript generates a mouse-up event when the user releases a mouse button. Note that some conditions create more than one event. For example, when the user clicks a mouse button, JavaScript will generate mouse-down, mouse-up, and click events, in that order.

| Example | To enable capturing of mouse-up events (as well as click):
| | `myWindow.captureEvents (Event.MOUSEUP | Event.CLICK)`
| See Also | `captureEvents()`, `releaseEvents()`, `event`, `Event`

MOVE

Version 1.2   Read-only

Property of the Event object

Returns a mask for capturing window movement events.

| Syntax | `Event.MOVE`
| Discussion | This property is used to control event capturing (see Chapter 7). When the event is captured, the value of the `screenX` and `screenY` properties will indicate the new location of the window.
| | JavaScript generates a window-move event when the user moves a window on the screen. Frames may also capture this event.
| Example | To enable capturing of window-move events (as well as resize):
| | `myWindow.captureEvents (Event.MOVE | Event.RESIZE)`
| See Also | `captureEvents()`, `releaseEvents()`, `event`, `Event`

moveAbove( )

Version 1.2

Method of the Layer object

Moves a layer to a position in the z-order immediately above another layer.

| Syntax | `layerObj.moveAbove(target)`
| | `layerObj` — `document.layers.layerName`, or other expression denoting a Layer object.
| | `target` — Layer object above which to move.

Discussion   The z-order controls which layer is "above" another when two layers overlap. This method moves a layer to a z-order position that is immediately above the *target* layer. After the operation, the moved layer will be a sibling of the *target*; if necessary, its `parentLayer` property will be changed. The `zIndex` property of the moved layer will be set to the same value as the *target*.

Example   `document.layers.layer1.moveAbove(document.layers.layer2)`

See Also   above, below, moveBelow( )

moveBelow( )

Version 1.2

Method of the Layer object

Moves a layer to a position in the z-order immediately below another layer.

Syntax   *layerObj*.moveBelow(*target*)

layerObj   `document.layers.`*layerName*, or other expression denoting a Layer object.

target   Layer object below which to move.

Discussion   The z-order controls which layer is "above" another when two layers overlap. This method moves a layer to a z-order position that is immediately below the *target* layer. After the operation, the moved layer will be a sibling of the *target*; if necessary, its `parentLayer` property will be changed. The `zIndex` property of the moved layer will be set to the same value as the *target*.

Example   `document.layers.layer1.moveBelow(document.layers.layer2)`

See Also   above, below, moveAbove( )

moveBy( )

Version 1.2   Signed scripts

Method of the Layer and window objects

Moves a window or layer by specified amounts.

Syntax
: For the current window:
```
moveBy(horiz, vert)
self.moveBy(horiz, vert)
window.moveBy(horiz, vert)
```

   For other windows and layers:
```
obj.moveBy(horiz, vert)
```

obj	An expression denoting a window or Layer object.
horiz	Number of pixels to move horizontally.
vert	Number of pixels to move vertically.

Discussion
: This method provides relative movement of a window or layer; that is, you specify the distance to move, rather than the destination. Positive arguments specify movement to the right or downward; negative values specify movement to the left or upward.

   To move a window to a position that is off the user's screen, this method must be called from a signed script with the UniversalBrowserWrite privilege enabled.

Example
: To move a window 100 pixels left and 50 pixels down, use a statement such as:
```
window.moveBy(-100, 50)
```

See Also
: Layer, moveTo( ), moveToAbsolute( ), window

moveTo( )

Version 1.2   Signed scripts

Method of the Layer and window objects

Moves a window or layer to a specified position.

Syntax
: For the current window:
```
moveTo(x, y)
self.moveTo(x, y)
window.moveTo(x, y)
```

For other windows and layers:

obj.moveTo(*x*, *y*)

obj	An expression denoting a window or Layer object.
x	Horizontal position in pixels.
y	Vertical position in pixels.

Discussion This method moves a window or layer so that its upper left corner is at the specified position. For a window, the position is relative to the computer's screen. For a layer, the position is relative to the parent layer, if any, or to the enclosing window or frame.

To move a window to a position that is off the user's screen, this method must be called from a signed script with the UniversalBrowserWrite privilege enabled.

Example To move a window to a position 100 pixels from the left side of the screen, and 50 pixels down from the top of the screen, use a statement such as:

window.moveTo(100, 50)

See Also Layer, moveBy( ), moveToAbsolute( ), window

moveToAbsolute( )

Version 1.2

Method of the Layer object

Moves a layer to a specified position within the enclosing window or frame.

Syntax *layerObj*.moveToAbsolute(*x*, *y*)

layerObj	document.layers.*layerName*, or other expression denoting a Layer object.
x	Horizontal position in pixels.
y	Vertical position in pixels.

Discussion This method moves a layer so that its upper left corner is at the specified position relative to the enclosing window or frame. If the layer has parent layers, their positions have no effect on this method's action.

Examples To move a layer to a position 100 pixels from the left side of the window or frame, and 50 pixels down from the top, use a statement such as:

window.moveToAbslute(100, 50)

See Also Layer, moveBy( ), moveTo( ), window

multiline, $*

Version 1.2

Property of the RegExp constructor

Specifies whether matching operations can operate in multi-line mode.

Syntax `RegExp.multiline`

Discussion This is a Boolean property. If it is `true`, operations that use regular expressions will operate in a way that helps perform matches in strings that contain Newline characters. Specifically, the symbol ^ in patterns will match the point just after a Newline, as well as its normal function of matching the beginning of the string. Similarly, the symbol $ will match the point just before a Newline, as well as the end of the string.

JavaScript automatically sets this property to `true` when calling an event handler for a text area form element. (It also sets `RegExp.input` to a copy of the text from the element.)

The symbol $* is an abbreviation for `multiline`.

Note that this is a property of the `RegExp` constructor, not of objects created by new `RegExp()`. That means that it is shared by all scripts running in the same window or frame. If you have several scripts that use regular expressions in one window, they may affect each other's results.

Example `RegExp.multiline = true`

See Also `exec()`, `input`, `match()`, `RegExp`, `replace()`, `search()`, `split()`, `test()`

name

Version 1.0 Read-only External

Property of the Anchor, Button, Checkbox, FileUpload, Form, Frame, Hidden, Image, Layer, Password, Plugin, Radio, Reset, Select, Submit, Text, Textarea and `window` objects

Reflects the name assigned to an object.

Syntax   `obj.name`

`obj`   An object of one of the types previously listed.

Discussion   This property returns a string containing the name of an object. In most cases, this name can be used to reference the object (see the following example). The source of the name depends on the object type:

- For Anchor, Button, Checkbox, FileUpload, Form, Frame, Hidden, Password, Radio, Reset, Select, Submit, Text, and Textarea objects, `name` reflects the `NAME` attribute of the HTML tag that created the object. It is read-only for these objects.
- For `Image` objects, if they are created by reflection of HTML tags, `name` reflects the `NAME` attribute of the HTML tag that created the object. If they are created by using `new Image()`, `name` is `null`. In either case, the value is read-only.
- For `Layer` objects, if they are created by reflection of HTML tags, `name` reflects the `NAME` attribute of the HTML tag that created the object and is read-only. For objects created by using `new Layer()`, `name` is initially undefined, but you can assign a value to it.
- For `window` objects, the `name` is assigned a value by the `open()` method when the window is created. For the browser's initial window, `name` is initially the empty string. In either case, you can assign other values.
- For Plugin objects, the name is determined by the plug-in application itself and is read-only.

Version 1.1
Version 1.2   This property was added to the FileUpload, Form, Image, and Plugin objects in JavaScript 1.1, and to the `Layer` object in JavaScript 1.2.

Examples   For a form defined by HTML such as:

```
<FORM NAME="userData">
    ...
    <INPUT TYPE="text" NAME="tbox">
    ...
</FORM>
```

The contents of the text box can be read by a statement such as:

```
userText = document.userData.tbox.value
```

since the name of a form can be used as a property of the enclosing document, and the name of a text box can be used as a property of the Form.

NaN

Version 1.1   Read-only

Property of the Number constructor

Returns a special value indicating "Not a Number."

Syntax   `Number.NaN`

Discussion   JavaScript returns NaN if a script performs some arithmetic operation that cannot yield a numeric value, such as computing the square root of a negative number. When NaN is compared to any numeric value, the result is always "not equal." To find out if an object contains NaN, use the isNaN() built-in function.

Note that NaN is a property of the Number constructor; that is, a property of Number itself, not of objects created by new Number().

Example   A function that searches a string for a ZIP code (5 consecutive digits) could return NaN if no zip code is found, by using statements such as:

```
function zipCode(str) {
   zipstr = str.match(/\d{5}/)
   if (zipstr == null)
      return Number.NaN
   else
      return Number(zipstr[0])
}
```

See Also   `MAX_VALUE, MIN_VALUE, NEGATIVE_INFINITY, POSITIVE_INFINITY`

navigator

Version 1.0   Read-only

Built-in object

Provides information about the browser.

Syntax   `navigator`

Properties

`appCodeName`	Returns the internal or "code name" of the browser.
`appName`	Returns the "official" name of the browser.
`appVersion`	Returns version, platform, and language/country information about the browser.
`language`	Returns a string identifying the browser's language.
`mimeTypes`	An array of MimeType objects that identify all the MIME data types that the browser supports.
`platform`	Returns a string identifying the browser's intended platform.
`plugins`	An array of Plugin objects that identify all plug-ins installed in the browser.
`userAgent`	Returns a string identifying the browser, which is sent to servers as part of HTTP data requests.

Methods

`javaEnabled()`	Returns `true` if the browser is able to run Java applets.
`preference()`	Reads and sets various preferences, equivalent to settings in Navigator's Preferences dialog.
`taintEnabled()`	Returns `true` if data tainting is enabled.

Discussion
Version 1.1
Version 1.2

The `mimeTypes` and `plugins` properties and the `javaEnabled()` and `taintEnabled` methods were added in JavaScript 1.1.

The `preference()` method was added in JavaScript 1.2.

Example
```
if (! navigator.javaEnabled())
    alert("Sorry, this browser cannot run a Java applet.")
```

See Also   MimeType, Plugin

NEGATIVE_INFINITY

Version 1.1　Read-only

Property of the Number object

Returns a special numeric value representing negative infinity.

Syntax　　Number.NEGATIVE_INFINITY

Discussion　This value behaves like infinity in arithmetic operations. A value multiplied by NEGATIVE_INFINITY returns NEGATIVE_INFINITY; a value divided by NEGATIVE_INFINITY returns zero. Converting it to a string returns "-Infinity".
　　The most negative value allowed in JavaScript is negative Number.MAX_VALUE (approximately -1.79E+308). Any operation that attempts to compute a result less than that will return NEGATIVE_INFINITY.

Example
```
if (result == Number.NEGATIVE_INFINITY)
    alert("Number too low!")
```

See Also　MAX_VALUE, MIN_VALUE, Math, NaN, POSITIVE_INFINITY, Number

netscape

Version 1.0

Property of the Packages object

Provides a number of objects and properties for use by scripts.

Syntax　　Packages.netscape
　　　　　netscape

Discussion　This package provides objects such as netscape.security, which is used by signed scripts to enable privileges. For more information, see Chapter 8.

See Also　java, Packages, sun

new

Version 1.0

Operator used in expressions

This operator is used to create a new object using a constructor function. For details, see Chapters 3 and 5.

next

Version 1.1   Read-only   Tainted   Signed scripts

Property of the `history` object

Returns the URL that the browser visited after the current one.

Syntax   `history.next`

Discussion   The `history` object is an array that keeps a record of URLs that the browser visits. The user can move backward through the array by pressing the browser's Back button, or when scripts call `history.back()` or `history.go()` with a negative argument. If the browser is positioned at the "front" of the history list (most recent element of the array), `next` returns the empty string.

Version 1.1
Version 1.2
In JavaScript 1.1, `next` can only be used when data tainting is enabled.
In JavaScript 1.2, `next` can only be used in a signed script with the `"UniversalBrowserRead"` privilege enabled.

Example   To create a link that works like the browser's Forward button, use HTML with a JavaScript URL such as:

`<A HREF="javascript:history.next">Go forward</A>`

See Also   `back()`, `forward()`, `go()`

Number

Version 1.1

Object type (constructor)

Creates a new Number object, or converts a value to a number.

Syntax   `Number(value)`

value   Any object or expression.

Properties

`MAX_VALUE`	The largest value that a number can have: approximately 1.79E+308. Any operations that attempt to exceed this value will return one of the "infinite" values described below.
`MIN_VALUE`	The smallest value that a number can have ("smallest" meaning closest to zero, not most negative): approximately 2.22E-308. Any operations that attempt to produce a result smaller than this will return 0.
`NaN`	A special value representing a non-numeric result, such as the square root of a negative number. NaN stands for "not a number." Arithmetic operations with this value always return zero. Comparisons to it always return "not equal," so to test for this value, scripts must use the built-in `isNaN()` function.
`NEGATIVE_INFINITY`	A special value that acts like negative infinity in numeric operations. Dividing by it always returns 0, adding to it always returns negative infinity, comparing to it always returns "greater," and so forth.
`POSITIVE_INFINITY`	A special value that acts like infinity in numeric operations. Dividing by it always returns 0, adding to it always returns infinity, comparing to it always returns "less," and so forth.

Discussion   Although numbers can be created by the new Number() constructor, JavaScript automatically creates numbers in response to assignment statements, so that

n = new Number(4)

is equivalent to

n = 4

In fact, Number() was not available in JavaScript 1.0, so all numbers had to be created by assignments.

Used without new, Number() is a type-conversion function that returns the numeric equivalent of its argument, or Number.NaN if the argument cannot be converted (see Examples). When converting strings, Number() interprets its argument as a decimal integer or floating-point number; it cannot convert strings containing hexadecimal or octal literals.

Examples   The expression:

Number("12")

returns 12.

Number("012")

also returns 12; since Number() cannot recognize octal values, it ignores the leading zero.

Number("0x12")

returns Number.NaN, since Number() cannot recognize hexadecimal values.

See Also   isNaN()

onabort

Version 1.1

Event handler of the Image object

Specifies statements to execute when the loading of an image is aborted.

Syntax *imageObj*.onabort

imageObj   document.*imageName*, or other expression denoting an Image object.

event Properties The following properties will be present in the event object passed to the onabort handler:

target   The object to which the event was originally sent, in case it has been captured.

type   Always contains "abort" for this event handler.

Discussion An abort event occurs when the user does something that stops an image from loading. The user may click the Stop button, click on a link in the document, load another document by selecting from the history list, and so forth.

A handler for this event may be assigned to the onabort property of an Image object, or specified by the ONABORT attribute of an HTML <IMG> tag (see Examples).

Examples To run the doNotGo() function if an image does not load, use a statement such as:

```
document.images[0].onabort = doNotGo
```

Note that there are no parentheses after doNotGo; this is a reference to the function, not a call.

Or, using HTML:

```
<IMG SRC="bell.gif" WIDTH=144 HEIGHT=119 ONABORT="doNotGo(event)">
```

See Also event, Image, onerror, onload

onblur

Version 1.0

Event handler of the Button, Checkbox, FileUpload, Frame, Layer, Password, Radio, Reset, Select, Submit, Text, Textarea, and `window` objects

Specifies statements to execute when an object loses focus.

Syntax `obj.onblur`

obj   An object of one of the previous types.

event Properties The following properties will be present in the `event` object passed to the `onblur` handler:

`target`   The object to which the event was originally sent, in case it has been captured.

`type`   Always contains `"blur"` for this event handler.

Discussion A blur event occurs when screen focus moves from one element, window, or frame to another. This may be caused by the `blur()` method, or by a user action such as clicking on another part of the screen, or using the Tab key to move around. The `onchange` event handler has a similar function for certain form elements, but it is called only when the text in the element has been changed.

A handler for this event may be assigned to the `onblur` property of an object, or specified by the ONBLUR attribute of an HTML tag (see Examples). For windows, the handler may placed in the <BODY> or <FRAMESET> tag (note, however, that the <FRAMESET> handler doesn't work on some operating systems—in particular, MS Windows). A document in a frame may assign its own handler; this overrides a handler in an enclosing <FRAMESET> tag. (A handler cannot be placed in a <FRAME> tag.)

You should be careful how you use `onblur`, as it can sometimes cause problems. For instance, an `onblur` handler on a form element will execute if the user switches to another application for a moment, which may not be what you want to happen. Also, handlers that generate alert boxes or otherwise modify the display may create an infinite loop of blur events.

Version 1.1 Originally, `onblur` was used only by the Select, Text, and Textarea objects. It was added to the Button, Checkbox, FileUpload, Frame, Password, Radio, Reset, Submit, and `window` objects in Version 1.1.

Version 1.2 This handler was added for the Layer object in JavaScript 1.2.

Examples
To run the `suddenMove()` function if the focus moves away from the second frame in the `frames` array:

```
frames[1].onblur = suddenMove
```

Note that there are no parentheses after `suddenMove`; this is a reference to the function, not a call.

To call `testAge()` when focus moves away from a text box:

```
<INPUT TYPE="text" NAME="ageBox" ONBLUR="testAge(event)">
```

See Also
event, Button, Checkbox, FileUpload, Frame, onchange, onfocus, Password, Radio, Reset, Select, Submit, Text, Textarea, Frame, window

onchange

Version 1.0

Event handler of the FileUpload, Select, Text, and Textarea objects

Specifies statements to execute when a form element loses focus after the contents of the element have changed.

Syntax
obj.onchange

obj An object of one of the types listed previously.

event Properties
The following properties will be present in the event object passed to the onchange handler:

target The object to which the event was originally sent, in case it has been captured.

type Always contains "change" for this event handler.

Discussion
A change event occurs when screen focus moves away from a form element after the user has changed its state. The movement away from the form element may be caused by the `blur()` method, or be due to a user action such as clicking on another form element, or using the Tab or Enter key to move around. The onblur event handler has a similar function for these and other form elements, but it is triggered even if the text in the form element has not been changed.

A handler for this event may be assigned to the onchange property of an object, or specified by the ONCHANGE attribute of an HTML tag.

Version 1.1

The onchange event handler was added to the FileUpload object in Version 1.1.

Examples
: To run the `testAge()` function after the user has changed the text of the `ageBox` form element:

```
forms[3].ageBox.onchange = testAge
```

Note that there are no parentheses after `testAge`; this is a reference to the function, not a call.
Or, using HTML:

```
<INPUT TYPE="text" NAME="ageBox" ONCHANGE="testAge(event)">
```

See Also
: event, FileUpload, onblur, onfocus, Select, Text, and Textarea

onclick

Version 1.0

Event handler of the document, Button, Checkbox, Link, Radio, Reset, and Submit objects

Specifies statements to execute when a form element is clicked.

Syntax
: `obj.onclick`

    obj   An object of one of the types listed previously.

event Properties
: The following properties will be present in the event object passed to the onclick handler:

target	The object to which the event was originally sent, in case it has been captured.
type	Always contains "click" for this event handler.
layerX	The mouse pointer's horizontal position in relation to the layer.
layerY	The mouse pointer's vertical position in relation to the layer.
pageX	The mouse pointer's horizontal position in relation to the document.
pageY	The mouse pointer's vertical position in relation to the document.
screenX	The mouse pointer's horizontal position in relation to the computer screen.
screenY	The mouse pointer's vertical position in relation to the computer screen.
which	1 for a left-mouse click, 3 for a right-mouse click.
modifiers	A bit mask specifying modifier keys held down when the event occurred.

Discussion	A click event occurs when the user clicks (presses and releases the mouse button) on an object. Also, these events can be forced by calling the `click()` method.

Mouse button operations can create several types of events. For example, a single mouse click by the user can result in mouse-down, mouse-up, and click events, in that order. The click event always occurs *after* both the mouse-down and mouse-up events.

The `onclick` handler can determine which mouse button was pressed by checking the `which` property of the `event` object, which will return 1 for the left button or 3 for the right. Other properties of `event` indicate the X and Y coordinates of the mouse cursor when the event occurred.

If the `onclick` handler returns `false`, it cancels any subsequent action for the event, such as loading a new document if the user clicked on a link. Note that the `onclick` handler itself will not be executed if the preceding `onmousedown` or `onmouseup` handler returned `false`.

A handler for this event may be assigned to the `onclick` property of an object, or specified by the ONCLICK attribute of an HTML tag. (To specify a handler for a `document` object, place it in the <BODY> tag.) |
| **Version 1.1** | The ability to return `false`, cancelling the action associated with the event, was added in JavaScript 1.1. |
| **Version 1.2** | This event handler was added to the `document` object in JavaScript 1.2. |
| Examples | To run the `clicked()` function if the user clicks on the third element in the form:

`document.forms[3].elements[2].onclick = clicked`

Note that there are no parentheses after `clicked`; this is a reference to the function, not a call.

To open a confirm dialog box when the user clicks on a link:

`<A HREF="adult2.htm" ONCLICK="return confirm('Remember, you must be 18 to view this page!')">The Naughty Bits</A>`

The handler returns `false` if the user clicks Cancel in the confirm dialog box, so the page would not load. |
| See Also | Button, Checkbox, document, event, Link, ondblclick, onfocus, Radio, Reset, Submit |

ondblclick

Version 1.2

Event handler of the Button, Checkbox, document, FileUpload, Hidden, Link, Password, Radio, Reset, Select, and Submit objects

Specifies statements to execute when the user double-clicks an object.

Syntax *obj*.ondblclick

obj An object of one of the types listed previously.

event Properties The following properties will be present in the event object passed to the ondblclick handler:

type	Always contains "dblclick" for this event.
target	The object to which the event was originally sent, in case it has been captured.
layerX	The mouse pointer's horizontal position in relation to the layer.
layerY	The mouse pointer's vertical position in relation to the layer.
pageX	The mouse pointer's horizontal position in relation to the document.
pageY	The mouse pointer's vertical position in relation to the document.
screenX	The mouse pointer's horizontal position in relation to the computer screen.
screenY	The mouse pointer's vertical position in relation to the computer screen.
which	1 for a left-mouse click, 3 for a right-mouse click.
modifiers	A bit mask specifying modifier keys held down when the event occurred.

Discussion A double-click event is one in which the user double-clicks on the object. Programming a handler for this event requires awareness of other related events that may occur first.

Mouse button operations can create several types of events. For example, a single mouse click by the user can result in mouse-down, mouse-up, and click events, causing three event handlers to be called in that order. A double-click by the user can result in as many as six events: mouse-down, mouse-up, double-click, another mouse-up, and finally two click events. The click events can be suppressed by having the onmousedown handler return false.

The `ondblclick` handler can determine which mouse button was pressed by checking the `which` property of the `event` object, which will return 1 for the left button or 3 for the right. Other properties of `event` indicate the X and Y coordinates of the mouse cursor when the event occurred.

Note that `ondblclick` does not function on Macintosh browsers.

A handler for this event may be assigned to the `ondblclick` property of an object, or specified by the `ONDBLCLICK` attribute of an HTML tag. (To specify a handler for a `document` object, place it in the `<BODY>` tag.)

Examples To call the `clickOne( )` function if the user double-clicks on the document:

```
document.ondblclick = clickOne
```

Note that there are no parentheses after `clickOne`; this is a reference to the function, not a call.

To run the `linkClick( )` function if the user double-clicks on a link:

```
<A HREF="nowhere1.htm" ONDBLCLICK="linkClick()">
```

See Also document, event, Link

ondragdrop

Version 1.2   Signed Scripts

Event handler of the `window` object

Specifies statements to execute when the user drags and drops a file onto the browser window.

Syntax For the current window:

```
ondragdrop
self.ondragdrop
window.ondragdrop
```

For other windows:

windowObj.ondragdrop

windowObj   An expression denoting a `window` object.

event Properties The following properties will be present in the `event` object passed to the `ondragdrop` handler:

type	Always contains `"dragdrop"` for this event.
target	The object to which the event was originally sent, in case it has been captured.
data	An array of strings containing the URLs of the dropped objects.

Discussion   A drag-drop event occurs when the user drags a file onto the browser window and releases the mouse button. The browser's default action for these events is to attempt to load that file (unless it's at an FTP site, in which case it asks the user if it should upload the file to the site). If `ondragdrop` returns `true`, the browser handles the file in this manner.

The `event.data` property will return an array of strings containing the URLs of the dropped files. Note that this property can only be read by a signed script with the `"UniversalBrowserRead"` privilege enabled (see Chapter 8).

A handler for this event may be assigned to the `onclick` property of a `window` object, or specified by the `ONCLICK` attribute of an HTML `<BODY>` tag.

Examples   To create a function that reads the dropped filenames, use statements such as:

```
function dd(ev) {
   for (i = 0; i < ev.data.length; i++)
      doSomethingWith(ev.data[i])
}
window.ondrapdrop = dd
```

Note that in the last statement there are no parentheses after `dd`; this is a reference to the function, not a call.

See Also   `event`, `window`

onerror

Version 1.1

Event handler of the Frame, Image, and window objects

Specifies statements to execute when an error occurs while loading a document or image.

Syntax   *obj*.onerror

obj   A `window` or `Image` object.

event Properties   The following properties will be present in the `event` object passed to the `onerror` handler for an `Image` object:

target   The object to which the event was originally sent, in case it has been captured.

type   Always contains `"error"` for this event handler.

Note that `onerror` handlers for Frame and `window` objects receive different data, as desribed below.

Discussion For `Image` objects, this event is generated when a problem is encountered while loading an image file. For Frame and `window` objects, this event is generated when a JavaScript syntax or runtime error is encountered while loading a web page with scripts. Errors in other windows, or other browser error conditions such as clicking on a link to a non-existent document, will not trigger the `onerror` handler.

For Frame and `window` objects, the `onerror` handler does *not* receive an argument containing an `event` object. Instead it is passed three arguments which are:

- A string message describing the error.
- A string containing the URL of the document that caused the error.
- A number indicating the line in the document where the error was detected. Note that if the document is completely loaded, the line number will indicate the end of the file, even if the error was caused by a script located somewhere else.

An example of a function to handle this follows.

You can set `onerror` to `null` to suppress JavaScript error messages. You can assign a handler for this event to the `onerror` property of a Frame, `window`, or `Image` object, or specified by the `ONERROR` attribute of an HTML `<BODY>` or `<IMG>` tag.

Examples To suppress all JavaScript error reporting:

```
window.onerror = null
```

A simple error-handling function can use statements such as:

```
function reportErr(txt, url, lno) {
  msgWin.document.write("Error: ", txt,
    " occurred in document: ", url,
    " at line ", lno, ".<BR>")
  return true
}
```

(This assumes that `msgWin` is another window that is already open.) The function returns `true` to stop JavaScript's usual error-message box from appearing.

To enable this function, use the statement:

```
window.onerror = reportErr
```

Note that there are no parentheses after `reportErr`; this is a reference to the function, not a call.

To handle an error for an image, use HTML such as:

```
<IMG NAME="Lighthouse" SRC="light.gif" ALIGN="left" BORDER="2"
    ONERROR="loadErr(event)">
```

The function `loadErr()` receives an `event` object as an argument.

See Also `event`, `onabort`, `Image`, `window`

onfocus

Version 1.0

Event handler of the Button, Checkbox, FileUpload, Frame, Password, Radio, Reset, Select, Submit, Text, Textarea, and `window` objects

Specifies statements to execute when an object receives focus.

Syntax *obj*.onfocus

obj   An object of one of the types listed previously.

event Properties The following properties will be present in the `event` object passed to the `onfocus` handler:

target   The object to which the event was originally sent, in case it has been captured.

type   Always contains `"focus"` for this event handler.

Discussion A focus event occurs when screen focus moves onto a form element, window, or frame. This may be caused by the `focus()` method, or by a user action such as clicking with the mouse, or using the Tab key to move around.

A handler for this event may be assigned to the `onfocus` property of an object, or specified by the `ONFOCUS` attribute of an HTML tag. For windows and frames, the handler may placed in the `<BODY>` tag. For frames, a handler may be placed in a `<FRAMESET>` tag (note, however, that this doesn't work on some operating systems—in particular, MS Windows). A handler in a frame's `<BODY>` tag overrides a handler in a `<FRAMESET>` tag. (A handler cannot be placed in the `<FRAME>` tag.)

You should be careful how you use `onfocus`, as it can sometimes cause problems. For instance, an `onfocus` handler that generates an alert box may create an infinite loop if focus returns to the object when you exit from the alert.

Version 1.1	Originally, `onfocus` was used only by the Select, Text, and Textarea objects. It was added to the Button, Checkbox, FileUpload, Frame, Password, Radio, Reset, Submit, and `window` objects in Version 1.1.

Examples	To run the `inComing()` function when the focus moves to a frame:
	
	`frames[1].onfocus = inComing`
	
	Note that there are no parentheses after `inComing`; this is a reference to the function, not a call.
	To call `runTotal()` when focus moves to the `total` text box:
	
	`<INPUT TYPE="text" NAME="total" ONFOCUS="runTotal(this.form)">`

See Also	`event`, Button, Checkbox, FileUpload, Frame, `onchange`, `onfocus`, Password, Radio, Reset, Select, Submit, Text, Textarea, Frame, `window`

onkeydown

Version 1.2

Event handler of the document, Image, Link, Text, and Textarea objects

Specifies statements to execute when the user presses a key on the keyboard.

Syntax	*obj*.onkeydown	
	obj	An object of one of the types listed previously.
event Properties	The following properties will be present in the `event` object passed to the onkeydown handler:	
	target	The object to which the event was originally sent, in case it has been captured.
	type	Always contains `"keydown"` for this event handler.
	layerX	The mouse pointer's horizontal position in relation to the layer at the time of the event.
	layerY	The mouse pointer's vertical position in relation to the layer at the time of the event.
	pageX	The mouse pointer's horizontal position in relation to the document at the time of the event.

pageY	The mouse pointer's vertical position in relation to the document at the time of the event.
screenX	The mouse pointer's horizontal position in relation to the computer screen at the time of the event.
screenY	The mouse pointer's vertical position in relation to the computer screen at the time of the event.
which	The ASCII value of the key pressed.
modifiers	A bit mask specifying modifier keys held down when the event occurred.

Discussion When the user presses a key, up to three types of events may be generated: key-down, key-press, and key-up, in that order. `onkeydown` is the first event handler called. If `onkeydown` returns `false`, the key-press event is canceled (but the key-up event will still occur). Note that if the key-press event is canceled for a text box or text area, the character that the user typed will not be passed on to the element.

The value of the character that the user typed is available in the `event.which` property. The states of the modifier keys (Shift, Ctrl, Alt, and Meta) are available in the `event.modifiers` property.

A handler for this event may be assigned to the `onkeydown` property of an object, or specified by the `ONKEYDOWN` attribute of an HTML tag. (To specify a handler for a `document` object, place it in the `<BODY>` tag.)

Examples To intercept characters that the user types into a text box, and have them appear somewhere else, use statements such as:

```
function reKey(ev) {
   moveChar(ev.which)
   return false
}
document.myForm.magicTextBox.onkeydown = reKey
```

Since the function returns `false`, the characters will not appear in the text box. Note that in the last statement, there are no parentheses after `reKey`; this is a reference to the function, not a call.

The same function could also be assigned to a text area by HTML such as:

```
<TEXTAREA COLS="40" ROWS="2" ONKEYDOWN="reKey(event)">
Type your first name in here.
</TEXTAREA>
```

See Also document, event, Image, Link, onkeypress, onkeyup, Textarea

onkeypress

Version 1.2

Event handler of the document, Image, Link, Text, and Textarea objects

Specifies statements to execute when the user presses or holds down a key on the keyboard.

Syntax *obj*.onkeypress

　　　　　obj　　　　　An object of one of the types listed previously.

event Properties The following properties will be present in the event object passed to the onkeypress handler:

　　target　　　　　The object to which the event was originally sent, in case it has been captured.
　　type　　　　　　Always contains "keypress" for this event handler.
　　layerX　　　　　The mouse pointer's horizontal position in relation to the layer at the time of the event.
　　layerY　　　　　The mouse pointer's vertical position in relation to the layer at the time of the event.
　　pageX　　　　　The mouse pointer's horizontal position in relation to the document at the time of the event.
　　pageY　　　　　The mouse pointer's vertical position in relation to the document at the time of the event.
　　screenX　　　　The mouse pointer's horizontal position in relation to the computer screen at the time of the event.
　　screenY　　　　The mouse pointer's vertical position in relation to the computer screen at the time of the event.
　　which　　　　　The ASCII value of the key pressed.
　　modifiers　　　A bit mask specifying modifier keys held down when the event occurred.

Discussion When the user presses a key, up to three types of events may be generated: key-down, key-press, and key-up, in that order. The key-press event, which calls the onkeypress handler, will only occur if the onkeydown handler does not return false.

The value of the character that the user typed is available in the event.which property. The states of the modifier keys (Shift, Ctrl, Alt, and Meta) are available in the event.modifiers property.

If the user holds a key down, repeated key-press events will occur. The minimum hold time and repetition rate depend on the platform.

If the onkeypress handler returns false, further processing of the event is canceled. In this case, if the event was caused by the user typing into a text box or text area, the character that the user typed will not be passed on to the element.

A handler for this event may be assigned to the onkeypress property of an object, or specified by the ONKEYPRESS attribute of an HTML tag. (To specify a handler for a document object, place it in the <BODY> tag.)

Examples To monitor characters that the user types into a text box, and collect them in a string, use statements such as:

```
function spy(ev) {
   userBuffer += String.fromCharCode(ev.which)
   return true
}
document.myForm.monitoredBox.onkeypress = spy
```

Since the function returns true, the characters will appear in the text box.

Note that in the last statement, there are no parentheses after spy; this is a reference to the function, not a call.

The same function could also be assigned to a text area by HTML such as:

```
<TEXTAREA COLS="40" ROWS="2" ONKEYPRESS="spy(event)">
Type your first name in here.
</TEXTAREA>
```

See Also document, event, Image, Link, onkeydown, onkeyup, Text, Textarea

onkeyup

Version 1.2

Event handler of the document, Image, Link, Text, and Textarea objects

Specifies statements to execute when the user releases a key on the keyboard.

Syntax *obj*.onkeyup

obj   An object of one of the types listed previously.

event Properties The following properties will be present in the event object passed to the onkeyup handler:

target	The object to which the event was originally sent, in case it has been captured.
type	Always contains "keyup" for this event handler.
layerX	The mouse pointer's horizontal position in relation to the layer at the time of the event.
layerY	The mouse pointer's vertical position in relation to the layer at the time of the event.

	pageX	The mouse pointer's horizontal position in relation to the document at the time of the event.
	pageY	The mouse pointer's vertical position in relation to the document at the time of the event.
	screenX	The mouse pointer's horizontal position in relation to the computer screen at the time of the event.
	screenY	The mouse pointer's vertical position in relation to the computer screen at the time of the event.
	which	The ASCII value of the key pressed.
	modifiers	A bit mask specifying modifier keys held down when the event occurred.

Discussion When the user presses a key, up to three types of events may be generated: key-down, key-press, and key-up, in that order. So the key-up event, which calls the onkeyup handler, is always last.

The value of the character that the user typed is available in the event.which property. The states of the modifier keys (Shift, Ctrl, Alt, and Meta) are available in the event.modifiers property.

A handler for this event may be assigned to the onkeyup property of an object, or specified by the ONKEYUP attribute of an HTML tag. (To specify a handler for a document object, place it in the <BODY> tag.)

Examples To record the exact time when the user releases a key, use statements such as:

```
function keyRel(ev) {
   reltime = new Date()
}
```

```
document.myForm.monitoredBox.onkeypress = keyRel
```

The Date object will contain the current time and date when the handler is executed.

Note that in the last statement, there are no parentheses after keyRel; this is a reference to the function, not a call.

The same function could also be assigned to a text area by HTML such as:

```
<TEXTAREA COLS="40" ROWS="2" ONKEYPRESS="keyRel(event)">
Type your first name in here.
</TEXTAREA>
```

See Also document, event, Image, Link, onkeydown, onkeypress, Text, Textarea

onload

Version 1.0

Event handler of the Frame, Image, Layer, and window objects

Specifies statements to execute when the browser loads an image or document.

Syntax
: *obj*.onload
: *obj* The Frame, Image, or window object.

event Properties
: The following properties will be present in the event object passed to the onload handler:
: target The object to which the event was originally sent, in case it has been captured.
: type Always contains "load" for this event handler.

Discussion
: For window objects, a load event occurs when the browser has finished loading a document or image into a window. When you are using multiple onload handlers for a document with frames, the handler in a child frame will be triggered before the handler in the parent; a frameset is not considered to have finished loading until all the documents in the frames have finished loading.

  For an Image object in a document, the event occurs when the enclosing document is first loaded if the src property of the <IMG> tag specifies a valid URL. Additional events occur any time a new image is loaded by modifying the object's src property.

  Also, if the Image object contains an animated GIF image, the onload event handler is called each time the image changes. Be very careful when using onload with such images, as rapid animation could produce a flood of events that causes your script to hang.

  For an Image object created using the new Image() constructor, the onload handler is never called.

  A handler for this event may be assigned to the onkeyup property of an object, or specified by the ONKEYUP attribute of an HTML <BODY>, <FRAMESET>, or <IMG> tag.

Version 1.1
: This handler was provided for Image objects in JavaScript 1.1.

Examples
: To run confirmEntry() when the document has finished loading:

  window.onload = confirmEntry

  Note that there are no parentheses after confirmEntry; this is a reference to the function, not a call.

Or, using HTML:

```
<BODY ONLOAD="confirmEntry(event)">
```

To display a message after an image has loaded:

```
<IMG SRC="tree.gif" ONLOAD="alert('Here is the image you requested')">
```

See Also event, Frame, Image, Layer onunload, window

onmousedown

Version 1.2

Event handler of the Button, document, and Link objects

Specifies statements to execute when the user presses a mouse button.

Syntax *obj*.onmousedown

obj   The Button, document, or Link object.

event Properties The following properties will be present in the event object passed to the onmousedown handler:

target	The object to which the event was originally sent, in case it has been captured.
type	Always contains "mousedown" for this event handler.
layerX	The mouse pointer's horizontal position in relation to the layer at the time of the event.
layerY	The mouse pointer's vertical position in relation to the layer at the time of the event.
pageX	The mouse pointer's horizontal position in relation to the document at the time of the event.
pageY	The mouse pointer's vertical position in relation to the document at the time of the event.
screenX	The mouse pointer's horizontal position in relation to the computer screen at the time of the event.
screenY	The mouse pointer's vertical position in relation to the computer screen at the time of the event.
which	1 for the left mouse button, 3 for the right mouse button.
modifiers	A bit mask specifying modifier keys held down when the event occurred.

Discussion Mouse button operations can create several types of events. For example, a single mouse click by the user can result in mouse-down, mouse-up, and click events, in that order. The mouse-down event always occurs first (see the following Example).

The `onmousedown` handler can determine which mouse button was pressed by checking the `which` property of the `event` object, which will return 1 for the left button or 3 for the right. Other properties of `event` indicate the X and Y coordinates of the mouse cursor when the event occurred.

If the `onmousedown` handler returns `false`, it prevents a click event from being generated. It also cancels any subsequent action for the event, such as loading a new document if the user clicked on a link.

A handler for this event may be assigned to the `onmousedown` property of an object, or specified by the `ONMOUSEDOWN` attribute of an HTML tag. (To specify a handler for a `document` object, place it in the `<BODY>` tag.)

Examples The relations between mouse button events can be seen with a link defined by HTML such as:

```
<A NAME="link1" HREF="javascript:msg('Link followed')"
 ONCLICK="msg('click')"
 ONDBLCLICK="msg('double')"
 ONMOUSEUP="msg('up')"
 ONMOUSEDOWN="msg('down')"
> Click here </A>
```

(This example assumes that msg( ) is a function that displays the text in another window.) Clicking once on the link results in messages "down, up, click, Link followed." Double-clicking the link results in "down, up, double, up, click, click, Link followed." If the `onmousedown` handler is changed to:

```
ONMOUSEDOWN="msg('down'); return false"
```

then a single click produces "down, up," and a double-click produces "down, up, double, up."

Normally, right-button clicks cause Navigator to pop up a small menu. To override this and provide a custom right-button handler, use statements such as:

```
function checkButt(ev) {
   if (ev.which == 3) {
      alert("Right click.")
      return false
   }
}

document.onmousedown = checkButt
```

Note that in the last statement, there are no parentheses after `checkButt`; this is a reference to a function, not a call.

See Also Button, `event`, `document`, Link, `onmousemove`, `onmouseout`, `onmouseover`, `onmouseup`

onmousemove

Version 1.2

Event handler for captured events

Specifies statements to execute when the user moves the mouse pointer.

Syntax   *obj*.onmousedown

obj   The object for which the event has been captured.

event Properties   The following properties will be present in the **event** object passed to the onmousemove handler:

target	The object to which the event was originally sent, in case it has been captured.
type	Always contains "mousemove" for this event handler.
layerX	The mouse pointer's horizontal position in relation to the layer at the time of the event.
layerY	The mouse pointer's vertical position in relation to the layer at the time of the event.
pageX	The mouse pointer's horizontal position in relation to the document at the time of the event.
pageY	The mouse pointer's vertical position in relation to the document at the time of the event.
screenX	The mouse pointer's horizontal position in relation to the computer screen at the time of the event.
screenY	The mouse pointer's vertical position in relation to the computer screen at the time of the event.

Discussion   Mouse movements are not normally passed to objects. A **window**, **document**, or **Layer** object can call captureEvents() to have these events passed to an onmousemove event handler. The X and Y coordinates of the mouse location are available to the handler as properties of the **event** object.

Use some caution when writing handlers for these events, since a single mouse movement by the user can generate a flood of events.

Examples   To cause a layer to follow the mouse cursor, you can create a handler and enable event capturing with statements such as:

```
function trackMouse(ev) {
  myLayer.pageX = ev.pageX
  myLayer.pageY = ev.pageY
}

document.captureEvents(Event.MOUSEMOVE)
document.onmousemove = trackMouse
```

Note that in the last statement, there are no parentheses after `trackMouse`; this is a reference to the function, not a call.

See Also `captureEvents()`, event, Event, onmouseout, onmouseover

onmouseout

Version 1.1

Event handler of the Area, Image, Layer, and Link objects

Specifies statements to execute when the user moves the mouse pointer off an object.

Syntax *obj*.onmouseout

obj   An Area, Image, Layer, or Link object.

event Properties   The following properties will be present in the event object passed to the onmouseout handler:

target	The object to which the event was originally sent, in case it has been captured.
type	Always contains "mouseout" for this event handler.
layerX	The mouse pointer's horizontal position in relation to the layer at the time of the event.
layerY	The mouse pointer's vertical position in relation to the layer at the time of the event.
pageX	The mouse pointer's horizontal position in relation to the document at the time of the event.
pageY	The mouse pointer's vertical position in relation to the document at the time of the event.
screenX	The mouse pointer's horizontal position in relation to the computer screen at the time of the event.
screenY	The mouse pointer's vertical position in relation to the computer screen at the time of the event.

Discussion   The mouse-over and mouse-out events allow a script to determine when the mouse cursor moves into and out of the region on the screen where an object is displayed. The onmouseout handler is called when the user moves the cursor away from an object.

For Area and Link objects, the onmouseout handler is not called unless the href property specifies a URL. To prevent this URL from having undesired side effects, you can use the do-nothing URL, javascript:void(0).

In order to use this event handler to write to the window status bar by modifying the `status` or `defaultStatus` properties, the handler must return `true`.

A handler for this event may be assigned to the `onmouseout` property of an object, or specified by the `ONMOUSEOUT` attribute of an HTML tag.

Version 1.2 This handler was provided for `Layer` objects in JavaScript 1.2.

Examples

To create an image that changes appearance when the cursor moves over it, uses statements such as:

```
document.images[0].onmouseover
    = new Function ("this.src = 'image2.gif'")
document.images[0].onmouseout
    = new Function ("this.src = 'image1.gif'")
```

where `image1.gif` is the default appearance, and `image2.gif` is the variation that is displayed when the mouse cursor moves over the image.

In HTML, the technique is a bit more complex, because the `<IMG>` tag does not have `ONMOUSEOVER` and `ONMOUSEOUT` attributes. To work around this, enclose the image in a link, using HTML such as:

```
<A HREF="someURL.html"
 ONMOUSEOVER="myPic.src = 'image2.gif'"
 ONMOUSEOUT="myPic.src = 'image1.gif'"
>
<IMG SRC="image1.gif" NAME="myPic" WIDTH=100 HEIGHT=100 >
</A>
```

See Also

Area, event, Image, Layer, Link, onmousedown, onmousemove, onmouseover, onmouseup

onmouseover

Version 1.0

Event handler of the Area, Image, and Link objects

Specifies statements to execute when the user moves the mouse pointer onto an object.

Syntax

obj.onmouseover

obj   An Area, Image, Layer, or Link object.

event Properties	The following properties will be present in the event object passed to the onmouseover handler:	
	target	The object to which the event was originally sent, in case it has been captured.
	type	Always contains "mouseover" for this event handler.
	layerX	The mouse pointer's horizontal position in relation to the layer at the time of the event.
	layerY	The mouse pointer's vertical position in relation to the layer at the time of the event.
	pageX	The mouse pointer's horizontal position in relation to the document at the time of the event.
	pageY	The mouse pointer's vertical position in relation to the document at the time of the event.
	screenX	The mouse pointer's horizontal position in relation to the computer screen at the time of the event.
	screenY	The mouse pointer's vertical position in relation to the computer screen at the time of the event.

Discussion The mouse-over and mouse-out events allow a script to determine when the mouse cursor moves into and out of the region on the screen where an object is displayed. The onmouseover handler is called when the user moves the cursor onto an object.

For Area and Link objects, the onmouseover handler is not called unless the href property specifies a URL. To prevent this URL from having undesired side effects, you can use the do-nothing URL, javascript:void(0).

In order to use this event handler to write to the window status bar by modifying the status or defaultStatus properties, the handler must return true.

A handler for this event may be assigned to the onmouseover property of an object, or specified by the ONMOUSEOVER attribute of an HTML tag.

Version 1.1 This handler was provided for Area objects in JavaScript 1.1.
Version 1.2 This handler was provided for Layer objects in JavaScript 1.2.

Examples To create an image that changes appearance when the cursor moves over it, uses statements such as:

```
document.images[0].onmouseover
   = new Function ("this.src = 'image2.gif'")
document.images[0].onmouseout
   = new Function ("this.src = 'image1.gif'")
```

where image1.gif is the normal appearance, and image2.gif is the variation that is displayed when the mouse cursor moves over the image.

In HTML, the technique is a bit more complex, because the `<IMG>` tag does not have `ONMOUSEOVER` and `ONMOUSEOUT` attributes. To work around this, enclose the image in a link, using HTML such as:

```
<A HREF="someURL.html"
 ONMOUSEOVER="myPic.src = 'image2.gif'"
 ONMOUSEOUT="myPic.src = 'image1.gif'"
>
<IMG SRC="image1.gif" NAME="myPic" WIDTH=100 HEIGHT=100 >
</A>
```

See Also Area, event, Image, Layer, Link, onmousedown, onmousemove, onmouseout, onmouseup

onmouseup

Version 1.2

Event handler of the Button, document, and Link objects

Specifies statements to execute when the user releases a mouse button.

Syntax *obj*.onmouseup

obj The Button, document, or Link object.

event Properties The following properties will be present in the event object passed to the onmouseup handler:

target	The object to which the event was originally sent, in case it has been captured.
type	Always contains `"mouseup"` for this event handler.
layerX	The mouse pointer's horizontal position in relation to the layer at the time of the event.
layerY	The mouse pointer's vertical position in relation to the layer at the time of the event.
pageX	The mouse pointer's horizontal position in relation to the document at the time of the event.
pageY	The mouse pointer's vertical position in relation to the document at the time of the event.

screenX	The mouse pointer's horizontal position in relation to the computer screen at the time of the event.
screenY	The mouse pointer's vertical position in relation to the computer screen at the time of the event.
which	1 for the left mouse button, 3 for the right mouse button.
modifiers	A bit mask specifying modifier keys held down when the event occurred.

Discussion Mouse button operations can create several types of events. For example, a single mouse click by the user can result in mouse-down, mouse-up, and click events, in that order. The mouse-up event always occurs when the user releases the mouse button.

The onmouseup handler can determine which mouse button was released by checking the which property of the event object, which will return 1 for the left button or 3 for the right. Other properties of event indicate the X and Y coordinates of the mouse cursor when the event occurred.

If the onmouseup handler returns false, it prevents a click event from being generated. It also cancels any subsequent action for the event, such as loading a new document if the user clicked on a link.

A handler for this event may be assigned to the onmouseup property of an object, or specified by the ONMOUSEUP attribute of an HTML tag. (To specify a handler for a document object, place it in the <BODY> tag.)

Examples To call clickButt() when the user releases the mouse button after clicking on a button:

```
document.forms[0].Butt1.onmouseup = clickButt
```

Note that there are no parentheses after clickButt; this is a reference to the function, not a call.

To add a confirmation box to a link, so that the link is activated only if the user clicks OK:

```
<A HREF="http://somewhere.html"
 ONMOUSEUP="return confirm('Are you sure?')">
Go somewhere</A>
```

See Also Button, event, document, Link, onmousedown, onmousemove, onmouseout, onmouseover

onmove

Version 1.2

Event handler of the window and Frame objects

Specifies statements to execute when the user moves a window or frame.

Syntax *obj*.onmove

obj A window or Frame object.

event Properties The following properties will be present in the event object passed to the onmove handler:

target The object to which the event was originally sent, in case it has been captured.
type Always contains "move" for this event handler.
screenX The mouse pointer's horizontal position in relation to the computer screen at the time of the event.
screenY The mouse pointer's vertical position in relation to the computer screen at the time of the event.

Discussion A handler for this event may be assigned to the onmove property of an object, or specified by the ONMOVE attribute of an HTML <BODY> or <FRAMESET> tag. A document in a frame may assign its own handler; this will be called before the handler in an enclosing <FRAMESET> tag. (A handler cannot be placed in a <FRAME> tag.)

Examples To check whether the window has been moved to a position where part of it is off the screen, use statements such as:

```
function checkWin() {
   if ((window.screenX + window.outerWidth > screen.width)
   || (window.screenY + window.outerHeight > screen.height)
   || (window.screenX < 0)
   || (window.screenY < 0))
     alert ("You might miss something!")
}

window.onmove = checkWin
```

Note that in the last statement, there are no parentheses after checkWin; this is a reference to the function, not a call.

To enable the handler using HTML:

```
<BODY ONMOVE="checkWin()">
```

See Also Frame, onresize, window

onreset

Version 1.1

Event handler of the Form object

Specifies statements to execute when the form is reset (cleared).

Syntax   *formObj*.onreset

     formObj   document.*formName*, or other expression denoting a Form object.

event Properties   The following properties will be present in the event object passed to the onreset handler:

     target   The object to which the event was originally sent, in case it has been captured.

     type   Always contains "reset" for this event handler.

Discussion   A reset event occurs when the user clicks on the form's Reset button, or when a script calls the reset() method.

A handler for this event may be assigned to the onreset property of a Form object, or specified by the ONRESET attribute of an HTML <FORM> tag.

Examples   If a web page contains two forms, the onreset handler of one can be used to reset the other with statements such as:

```
function clearForm2() {
   document.otherForm.reset()
}
```

`document.myForm.onreset = clearForm2`

Note that in the last statement, there are no parentheses after clearForm2; this is a reference to the function, not a call.

Use this technique with caution: If two forms call each other's onreset handlers, an infinite loop will result.

The handler could also be assigned by HTML such as:

`<FORM NAME="myForm" ONRESET="clearForm2()"`

See Also   Form, reset(), Reset, onsubmit

onresize

Version 1.2

Event handler of the window and Frame objects

Specifies statements to execute when the user changes the size of a window or frame.

Syntax *obj*.onmove

obj   A window or Frame object.

event Properties The following properties will be present in the event object passed to the onresize handler:

target   The object to which the event was originally sent, in case it has been captured.
type   Always contains "resize" for this event handler.
width   The width of the window or frame, in pixels.
height   The height of the window or frame, in pixels.

Discussion A handler for this event may be assigned to the onresize property of a window object, or specified by the ONRESIZE attribute of an HTML <BODY> or <FRAMESET> tag. A document in a frame may assign its own handler; this will be called after the handler in an enclosing <FRAMESET> tag. (A handler cannot be placed in a <FRAME> tag.)

Examples To check whether the window has been resized to a point where part of it is off the screen, use statements such as:

```
function checkWin() {
   if ((window.screenX + window.outerWidth > screen.width)
    || (window.screenY + window.outerHeight > screen.height)
    || (window.screenX < 0)
    || (window.screenY < 0))
      alert ("You might miss something!")
}

window.onresize = checkWin
```

Note that in the last statement, there are no parentheses after checkWin; this is a reference to the function, not a call.
To enable the handler using HTML:

```
<BODY ONRESIZE="checkWin()">
```

See Also Frame, onmove, window

onselect

Version 1.0

Event handler of the Text and Textarea objects

Specifies statements to execute when the user selects text in a text box or text area of a form.

Preliminary

Note that this event handler is announced by Netscape, but not fully implemented in some versions of Navigator. The information presented here is preliminary.

Syntax   `obj.onselect`

`obj`   A Text or Textarea object.

event Properties   The following properties will be present in the `event` object passed to the `onselect` handler:

`target`   The object to which the event was originally sent, in case it has been captured.

`type`   Always contains `"select"` for this event handler.

Discussion   This handler is called when the user selects (highlights) some text in a text box or text area by using the mouse and/or cursor movement keys.

See Also   `event, onfocus, onblur, onchange`

onsubmit

Version 1.1

Event handler of the Form object

Specifies statements to execute when the browser attempts to submit a form to the server.

Syntax   `formObj.onsubmit`

`formObj`   `document.formName`, or other expression denoting a Form object.

event Properties   The following properties will be present in the `event` object passed to the `onsubmit` handler:

`target`   The object to which the event was originally sent, in case it has been captured.

`type`   Always contains `"submit"` for this event handler.

Discussion This handler is called when the user clicks on a form's Submit button. If the `onsubmit` handler returns `false`, the form will not be submitted. If the handler returns anything else, or does not return any value, the browser submits the form to the server.

A handler for this event may be assigned to the `onsubmit` property of a Form object, or specified by the `ONSUBMIT` attribute of an HTML `<FORM>` tag.

Examples To add a confirmation dialog to a form, use statements such as:

```
function checkSub() {
   return(confirm("Are you sure all the blanks
      are filled in?"))
}

document.myForm.onsubmit = checkSub
```

Note that in the last statement, there are no parentheses after `checkSub`; this is a reference to the function, not a call.

Or, using HTML:

```
<FORM ONSUBMIT="checkSub()">
```

See Also Form, onreset, submit(), Submit

onunload

Version 1.0

Event handler of the Frame and `window` object

Specifies statements to execute when a document is unloaded.

Syntax `obj.onunload`

  `obj`   A Frame or `window` object.

event Properties The following properties will be present in the `event` object passed to the `onunload` handler:

  target   The object to which the event was originally sent, in case it has been captured.
  type   Always contains `"unload"` for this event handler.

Discussion   An unload event occurs when a document is removed from a browser window or frame. The user may click a link, select an entry from the history list or bookmarks, enter a URL into the Location bar, and so on, or a new document may be loaded by a script.

A handler for this event may be assigned to the `onunload` property of a `window` object, or specified by the ONUNLOAD attribute of an HTML <BODY> or <FRAMESET> tag. Note that an `onunload` handler in a frame will never be called; it may be included for portability, in case some user loads the document into a window rather than a frame.

Examples   To run Bye( ) when the document is unloaded:

```
window.onunload = Bye
```

Note that there are no parentheses after Bye; this is a reference to the function, not a call.

Or, using HTML:

```
<BODY ONUNLOAD="Bye(event)">
```

See Also   event, Frame, onload, window

open( )

DOCUMENT

Version 1.0   Version 1.1

Method of the document object
(See also open( ) as a method of the `window` object.)

Opens a data stream to write to a document.

Syntax   *docObject*.open(*mimeType*, rep)

docObject	document for the current document, or an expression denoting a document in any window.
mimeType	Optional string argument. If present, specifies the type of document to create (see Discussion).
rep	Optional string argument. If present and equal to "replace", the new document is opened without modifying the window's history list (see Discussion).

Discussion   This method opens a `document`'s data stream, clears any existing content, and allows a script to write to the document with the write( ) and writeln( ) methods, or erase it with the clear( ) method. To end the data stream and make sure all text is displayed, use close( ) after all writing is completed.

The *mimeType* argument, if present, specifies the MIME data type to be written; if you omit the *mimeType*, "text/html" is assumed. The built-in MIME types are:

text/html	ASCII text with HTML formatting.
text/plain	Plain ASCII text with end-of-line characters to delimit displayed lines. HTML formatting is not rendered; instead, the tags are displayed in the document.
image/gif	A GIF image file.
image/jpeg	A JPEG image file.
image/x-bitmap	An XBM image file.

If you specify another *mimeType*, the browser will assume you want to open the appropriate plug-in or viewer: For instance, specifying "application/x-director" would load the Macromedia Shockwave plug-in, if installed. If you specify a *mimeType* for which no plug-in is installed, the browser displays the Unknown File Type dialog box, which prompts the user to save, cancel, or specify the program to use as a viewer.

The replace parameter provides a way to ensure that the user cannot use the Back button, since this might unintentionally change or erase the display. If the window is initially blank, and will be loaded by write(), opening the document stream with document.open(*mimeType*, "replace") will make the new document the first document in the history list. Without "replace" the blank window would be the first entry in the history list, and the new document would be the second entry.

Version 1.1

open() was changed to clear any existing document content, starting in JavaScript 1.1.

The "replace" argument was added in JavaScript 1.1.

Examples

To open a document stream, write text to the document, and close the stream, use statements such as:

```
Win1.document.open()
Win1.document.write("Some guy hit my fender the ",
   "other day, and I said unto him, \"Be fruitful, ",
   " and multiply.\" But not in those words.<P>",
   " Woody Allen")
Win1.document.close()
```

To open a document stream and ensure that the new document will be in the same position in the history list:

```
Win1.document.open("text/html", "replace")
```

See Also close(), document, write(), writeln()

open( )

WINDOW

Version 1.0   Signed scripts

Method of the window object.
(See also open( ) as a method of the document object.)

Creates a new browser window and returns a new window object.

Syntax   wVar = winObj.open(URL, windowName, features)

wVar	Variable to hold the new window object.
winObj	Optional name of an existing window: self, window, parent, top, or any expression denoting a window object.
URL	A string specifying the URL of a document to load into the new window, or the empty string to create a blank window.
windowName	A string specifying an HTML name for the window, to be used by the TARGET attribute of a <FORM> or <A> tag to direct output to the window.
features	A string specifying options that define how the window appears and functions (see the following).

Window Features   Window features are specified by substrings of the features argument, separated by commas; do *not* leave a space between features, as all characters after a space are ignored. Some features can be enabled by simply naming them, or by specifying a value of "1" or "yes". Omitting a feature, or specifying a value of "0" or "no", disables the feature (do not use "true" or "false" for feature values). For example, any of "toolbar", "toolbar=1", or "toolbar=yes" causes a toolbar to be included in the new window.

Some features specify browser dimensions in pixels; their values are numeric. The exact size on users' screens will depend on their computers' hardware and software.

"directories"	Includes the directory buttons bar, also called the personal toolbar, in the window. (Some browsers do not support this feature.)
"location"	Includes the location or URL bar in the window.
"menubar"	Includes the menu bar in the window.
"resizable"	Allows the user to resize the window. If this feature is disabled, the window size will be fixed.
"scrollbars"	Includes scroll bars in the window. (The scroll bars will only appear in the window if necessary; if the contents of the window are all visible without scrolling, the scroll bars will not appear until additional content is written.)
"status"	Includes the status bar in the window.

`"titlebar"`	Prevents the window from having a title bar if the value is `"0"` or `"no"`. Title bars are included by default.
`"toolbar"`	Includes the toolbar in the window.
`"width"`	Specifies the width of the viewing area of the window, in pixels—the part in which documents are displayed. (This item was replaced by `"innerWidth"` in JavaScript 1.2, but `"width"` is still supported for compatibility with older browsers.)
`"height"`	Specifies the height of the viewing area of the window, in pixels. (This item was replaced by `"innerHeight"` in JavaScript 1.2, but `"height"` is still supported for compatibility with older browsers.)

Version 1.2 The following window features were added in JavaScript 1.2.

`"alwaysLowered"`	Causes the window to move "below" all other windows on the screen, even when it is active.
`"alwaysRaised"`	Causes the window to always appear "on top of" all other windows, even when some other window is active. (The exact function of this feature depends on the operating system. On a Macintosh, the window will remain above other browser windows, but may not be above windows in other applications.)
`"dependent"`	Creates a new window that isn't a child of the current window (by setting the value to `"0"` or `"no"`).
`"hotkeys"`	Disables most hotkeys if the window has no menu bar (does not affect the Exit and Security hotkeys).
`"z-lock"`	Specifies that the window does not rise above other windows when activated.
`"innerHeight"`	Specifies the height of the window's viewing area, in pixels.
`"innerWidth"`	Specifies the width of the window's viewing area, in pixels.
`"outerWidth"`	Specifies the width of the entire window, including borders, toolbar, etc. This feature takes precedence over `"innerWidth"`; if you set both, `"innerWidth"` will be ignored.
`"outerHeight"`	Specifies the height of the entire window, including borders, toolbar, and so forth. This feature takes precedence over `"innerHeight"`; if you set both, `"innerHeight"` will be ignored.
`"screenX"`	Specifies the distance in pixels from the left edge of your computer screen to the left edge of the window.
`"screenY"`	Specifies the distance in pixels from the top of your computer screen to the top of the window.

Discussion   This method creates a new browser window. You can load a particular document in that window with the *URL* argument. If you intend to create a document by writing to the window, specify the empty string for *URL*.

When using open( ) in the event handler of an HTML tag, you must specify *winObj*.open( ). In other cases, you can simply use open( ). (Using open( ) in an event handler calls document.open( ).)

If you omit *all* window feature names, JavaScript assumes you want them all. So if you want none of these features, simply name one like this:

toolbar=no.

Note that some window features can only be used in signed scripts (see Chapter 8). alwaysRaised, alwaysLowered, titlebar=no, and z-lock can only be used in signed scripts. Also, only a signed script can create a window that is smaller than 100 x 100 pixels, or that is not visible because its position is beyond the boundaries of the screen. All these actions can only be performed by a script with the "UniversalBrowserWrite" privilege.

Examples   To open a window with nothing but the location bar included:

window.open("someFile.htm", "Window1", "location")

To open a window with a variety of window features set:

window.open("window3.htm", "Window1",
    "resizable,outerHeight=450,outerWidth=450,scrollbars")

To open a window without a document, and then write to it:

Win2 = window.open("", "win2",
    "scrollbars,width=350,height=230")
var sText = "This is some text.<P>"
Win2.document.write("<H2>Secondary window</H2><HR><P>",
    sText)

See Also   close( ), window

opener

Version 1.1

Property of the window object

Specifies the name of the calling window when a window is opened using `open()`.

Syntax For the current window:

```
opener
self.opener
window.opener
```

For other windows:

windowObj.opener

windowObj   An expression denoting a `window` object.

Discussion When a window is opened, this property initially returns the `window` object that created it by calling `window.open()`. This allows a window to read and modify its opener (see Examples). Scripts can modify this property; for instance, it can be set to `null` in order to ensure that the new window can no longer reference its opener.

Examples A button that closes the window that opened the current window:

```
<INPUT TYPE="button" VALUE="Close this window"
  ONCLICK="window.opener.close()">
```

To change the background color of the document in the opener window:

```
window.opener.document.bgColor = 'red'
```

See Also `close()`, `open()`, `window`

Option

Version 1.1

Object type (constructor)

Creates an option for a select box in an HTML form.

Syntax
To construct a new object:

obj = new Option(*text, value, defaultSelected, selected*)

obj	Variable or object to which the new Option is assigned.
text	Optional string specifying a value for the object's text property.
value	Optional string specifying a value for the object's value property.
defaultSelected	Optional Boolean value for the object's defaultSelected property.
selected	Optional Boolean value for the object's selected property.

For external objects:

formObj.selectName.options[*optNum*]
formObj.elements[*index*].options[*optNum*]

formObj	document.*formName* or other expression denoting a Form object.
selectName	Name assigned by the NAME attribute of the HTML <SELECT> tag.
optNum	Number specifying the position of the object in the Select object's options array.
index	Number or string specifying the position of a Select object in the form's elements array.

Properties

defaultSelected	A Boolean value that specifies whether the option is initially selected (when the document is loaded, or after the form is reset). This property reflects the SELECTED attribute of the HTML <OPTION> tag.
index	The position of the option in the Select object's options array.
selected	A Boolean value that specifies whether the option is currently selected.
text	A string specifying text that appears when the option is displayed in the select box. This property reflects the text that appears after the HTML <OPTION> tag.
value	A string specifying the value sent to the server when the option is selected and the form submitted. This property reflects the VALUE attribute of the HTML <OPTION> tag.

Discussion   When Navigator loads a web page, it creates `Option` objects corresponding to all `<OPTION>` tags in the document. These tags are always enclosed by the `<SELECT>` and `</SELECT>` tags, which cause Navigator to create a Select object. You can reference `Option` objects as elements of a Select object's `options` array.

Also, you can use the `new Option()` constructor to create an `Option` object, and then add it to an existing Select object. Scripts can modify the `options` array by adding elements (`Option` objects), deleting them, or changing their properties. To delete an element from the `options` array, set it to `null`. Note that deleting elements compresses the array: Each option after the deleted one is assigned a new index (`options[5]` may become `options[4]`, for instance).

On some older browsers, after adding or deleting `Option` objects in a Select object, you must refresh the document by calling `window.history.go(0)`. Note that when you do this, variable values will be lost, so you may need to save them in cookies or form elements.

Examples   To create a new option, then place the new object into a selection list, use statements such as:

```
newChoice = new Option("Hamburger", "hb", false, true)
foodChoice.options[3] = newChoice
```

To change the text of the fourth entry (`options[3]`) in a selection list, use a statement such as.

```
document.myform.choice.options[4].text = newText
```

See Also   options, Select

options

Version 1.0   Read-only   External

Property of the Select external object

Reflects the options of a select box in a form.

Syntax   *formObj.selectName*.options
formObj.elements[*index*].options

formObj	`document.`*formName* or other expression denoting a Form object.
selectName	Name assigned by the `NAME` attribute of the HTML `<SELECT>` tag.
index	Number or string specifying the position of a Select object in the form's `elements` array.

Properties	`length`	The number of options in the selection box (the Select object).
	`selectedIndex`	The index number of the option that has been selected in the selection box. If more than one option is selected, this property returns the index of the first (lowest-numbered) one.

Discussion Each element of the `options` array is an `Option` object representing one of the options in a select box.

Version 1.1 The `type` property, the ability to modify the `text` property, the `Option()` constructor, and the ability to add and delete options were added in JavaScript 1.1.

Example To read the text of the currently selected option, use statements such as:

```
var current = document.myForm.mySelect.selectedIndex
var userChoice = document.myForm.mySelect.options[current].text
```

See Also `Option`, `Select`

outerHeight

Version 1.2   Signed scripts

Property of the `window` object

Specifies the height, in pixels, of the browser window.

Syntax For the current window:

```
outerHeight
self.outerHeight
window.outerHeight
```

For other windows:

```
windowObj.outerHeight
```

windowObj   An expression denoting a `window` object.

Discussion This property specifies the height of the entire browser window, including the menu bar, toolbars, status bar, and borders.

To set a value less than 100 pixels, this property must be used within a signed script with the `"UniversalBrowserWrite"` privilege (see Chapter 8).

Example `window.outerHeight = 480`

See Also `innerHeight`, `outerWidth`, `window`

outerWidth

Version 1.2   Signed scripts

Property of the window object

Specifies the width, in pixels, of the browser window.

Syntax   For the current window:

```
outerWidth
self.outerWidth
window.outerWidth
```

For other windows:

windowObj.outerWidth

windowObj   An expression denoting a window object.

Discussion   This property specifies the width of the entire browser window, including the scrollbar and borders.

To set a value less than 100 pixels, this property must be used within a signed script with the "UniversalBrowserWrite" privilege (see Chapter 8).

Example   `window.outerWidth = 800`

See Also   innerWidth, outerHeight, window

Packages

Version 1.1 Read-only

Built-in object

Provides access to Java packages.

Syntax
: `Packages`

Properties
: `java` — A package providing access to Java.
: `netscape` — A package providing access to Navigator resources such as plug-ins and security features.
: `sun` — A package providing debugging tools.

Discussion
: This object serves as a "holder" for Java packages installed in the browser. For details, see Chapter 8.

paddingBottom

Version 1.2

Property of style sheet objects

Specifies the distance between text or images and an HTML element's bottom border.

Syntax
: `styleObj.paddingBottom`
: `styleObj` — Style sheet object: a property of a `classes`, `ids`, or `tags` object.

Discussion
: JavaScript style sheets can be used to create boxes around text or images, using `borderTopWidth`, `borderRightWidth`, `borderBottomWidth`, `borderLeftWidth`, and `borderWidths()`. The `paddingBottom` property can be used to define how close the bottom border is to the text or image. It applies to block-level elements, and is not inherited.

This property may be set to:

- An absolute measurement, such as `"12pt"`.
- A measurement relative to the current font size, such as `"1.5em"`.
- A pixel measurement, such as `"18px"`.
- A percentage of the parent element's width, such as `"15%"`.

Note that for `paddingBottom` assignments to take effect, they must occur before the browser writes the styled text to the document. An assignment to `tags.body.paddingBottom` must be done within the `<HEAD>` ... `</HEAD>` section of the HTML.

Example This style sheet creates a class that puts borders around text or an image, and an ID that uses `paddingBottom` to define the distance between the text or image and the bottom border:

```
<STYLE TYPE="text/javascript">
    classes.box.all.borderTopWidth = "1em"
    classes.box.all.borderRightWidth = "6pt"
    classes.box.all.borderBottomWidth = "12px"
    classes.box.all.borderLeftWidth = "5%"
    classes.box.all.borderStyle = "3D"

    ids.padded.paddingBottom = "12pt"
</STYLE>
```

See Also `borderTopWidth`, `borderRightWidth`, `borderBottomWidth`, `borderLeftWidth`, `borderWidths()`, `classes`, `ids`, `paddingLeft`, `paddingRight`, `paddings()`, `paddingTop`, `tags`

paddingLeft

Version 1.2

Property of style sheet objects

Specifies the distance between text or images and an HTML element's left border.

Syntax *styleObj*.paddingLeft

   styleObj   Style sheet object: a property of a `classes`, `ids`, or `tags` object.

Discussion JavaScript style sheets can be used to create boxes around text or images, using `borderTopWidth`, `borderRightWidth`, `borderBottomWidth`, `borderLeftWidth`, and `borderWidths()`. The `paddingLeft` property can be used to define how close the left border is to the text or image. It applies to block-level elements, and is not inherited.

This property may be set to:
- An absolute measurement, such as "12pt".
- A measurement relative to the font size, such as "1.5em".
- A pixel measurement, such as "18px".
- A percentage of the parent element's width, such as "15%".

Note that for `paddingLeft` assignments to take effect, they must occur before the browser writes the styled text to the document. An assignment to `tags.body.paddingLeft` must be done within the `<HEAD>`...`</HEAD>` section of the HTML.

Example This style sheet creates a class that puts borders around text or an image, and an ID that uses `paddingLeft` to define the distance between the text or image and the left border:

```
<STYLE TYPE="text/javascript">
  classes.box.all.borderTopWidth = "1em"
  classes.box.all.borderRightWidth = "6pt"
  classes.box.all.borderBottomWidth = "12px"
  classes.box.all.borderLeftWidth = "5%"
  classes.box.all.borderStyle = "3D"

  ids.padded.paddingLeft = "12pt"
</STYLE>
```

See Also borderTopWidth, borderRightWidth, borderBottomWidth, borderLeftWidth, borderWidths(), classes, ids, paddingBottom, paddingRight, paddings(), paddingTop, tags

paddingRight

Version 1.2

Property of style sheet objects

Specifies the distance between text or images and an HTML element's right border.

Syntax *styleObj*.paddingRight

styleObj   Style sheet object: a property of a `classes`, `ids`, or `tags` object.

Discussion JavaScript style sheets can be used to create boxes around text or images, using `borderTopWidth`, `borderRightWidth`, `borderBottomWidth`, `borderLeftWidth`, and `borderWidths()`. The `paddingRight` property can be used to define how close the right border is to the text or image. It applies to block-level elements, and is not inherited.

This property may be set to:

- An absolute measurement, such as "12pt".
- A measurement relative to the font size, such as "1.5em".
- A pixel measurement, such as "18px".
- A percentage of the parent element's width, such as "15%".

Note that for `paddingRight` assignments to take effect, they must occur before the browser writes the styled text to the document. An assignment to `tags.body.paddingRight` must be done within the <HEAD> ... </HEAD> section of the HTML.

Example This style sheet creates a class that puts borders around text or an image, and an ID that uses `paddingRight` to define the distance between the text or image and the right border:

```
<STYLE TYPE="text/javascript">
    classes.box.all.borderTopWidth = "1em"
    classes.box.all.borderRightWidth = "6pt"
    classes.box.all.borderBottomWidth = "12px"
    classes.box.all.borderLeftWidth = "5%"
    classes.box.all.borderStyle = "3D"

    ids.padded.paddingRight = "12pt"
</STYLE>
```

See Also `borderTopWidth`, `borderRightWidth`, `borderBottomWidth`, `borderLeftWidth`, `borderWidths()`, `classes`, `ids`, `paddingBottom`, `paddingLeft`, `paddings()`, `paddingTop`, `tags`

paddings( )

Version 1.2

Method of style sheet objects

Specifies the distances between text or images and the borders around an HTML element.

paddings( )

Syntax *styleObj*.paddings(*topValue*, *rightValue*, *bottomValue*, *leftValue*)

styleObj — Style sheet object: a property of a classes, ids, or tags object.

topValue, rightValue, bottomValue, leftValue, — String or numeric values specifying the distances between the content and each border.

Discussion JavaScript style sheets can be used to create boxes around text or images, using borderTopWidth, borderRightWidth, borderBottomWidth, borderLeftWidth, and borderWidths( ). The paddingBottom, paddingLeft, paddingRight, and paddingTop properties can be used to set the distances from the content to the individual borders, or the paddings( ) method can be used to define all four distances at once. This method applies to block-level elements. It is not inherited.

Each argument value may be:

- An absolute measurement, such as "12pt".
- A measurement relative to the font size, such as "1.5em".
- A pixel measurement, such as "18px".
- A percentage of the parent element's width, such as "15%".
- A numeric value, which will be multiplied by the parent element's value to determine the property's actual value.

Note that for calls to paddings( ) to take effect, they must occur before the browser writes the styled text to the document. A call to tags.body.paddings(tags.body.paddings( ) must be done within the <HEAD> ... </HEAD> section of the HTML.

Example The following creates a style-sheet class that puts borders around text or an image, and a style-sheet ID that uses paddings( ) to define the distance between the text or image and the borders:

```
<STYLE TYPE="text/javascript">
   classes.box.all.borderTopWidth = "1em"
   classes.box.all.borderRightWidth = "6pt"
   classes.box.all.borderBottomWidth = "12px"
   classes.box.all.borderLeftWidth = "5%"
   classes.box.all.borderStyle = "3D"

   ids.padded.paddings("2em", "4em", "2em", "4em")
</STYLE>
```

See Also borderTopWidth, borderRightWidth, borderBottomWidth, borderLeftWidth, borderWidths( ), classes, ids, paddingBottom, paddingLeft, paddingRight, paddingTop, tags

paddingTop

Version 1.2

Property of style sheet objects

Specifies the distance between text or images and an HTML element's top border.

Syntax *styleObj*.paddingTop

styleObj   Style sheet object: a property of a `classes`, `ids`, or `tags` object.

Discussion JavaScript style sheets can be used to create boxes around text or images, using `borderTopWidth`, `borderRightWidth`, `borderBottomWidth`, `borderLeftWidth`, and `borderWidths()`. The `paddingTop` property can be used to define how close the top border is to the text or image. It applies to block-level elements, and is not inherited.

This property may be set to:

- An absolute measurement, such as `"12pt"`.
- A measurement relative to the font size, such as `"1.5em"`.
- A pixel measurement, such as `"18px"`.
- A percentage of the parent element's width, such as `"15%"`.
- A numeric value, which will be multiplied by the parent element's value to determine the property's actual value.

Note that for `paddingTop` assignments to take effect, they must occur before the browser writes the styled text to the document. An assignment to `tags.body.paddingTop` must be done within the `<HEAD>` ...`</HEAD>` section of the HTML.

Example This style sheet creates a class that puts borders around text or an image, and an ID that uses `paddingTop` to define the distance between the text or image and the top border:

```
<STYLE TYPE="text/javascript">
   classes.box.all.borderTopWidth = "1em"
   classes.box.all.borderRightWidth = "6pt"
   classes.box.all.borderBottomWidth = "12px"
   classes.box.all.borderLeftWidth = 2
   classes.box.all.borderStyle = "3D"

   ids.padded.paddingTop = "12pt"
</STYLE>
```

See Also   borderTopWidth, borderRightWidth, borderBottomWidth, borderLeftWidth, borderWidths(), classes, ids, paddingBottom, paddingLeft, paddingRight, paddings(), tags

pageX

EVENT

Version 1.2   Special scope

Property of the event object
(see also pageX as a property of the Layer object)

Returns the horizontal position, in pixels, measured from the left side of the page, where an event occurred.

Syntax   *eventObj*.pageX

eventObj   event, or an expression denoting a copy of event, such as a function argument passed to an event handler.

Discussion   This property returns a position relative to the page in which the event occurred. If the event occurred in a layer, the position is stored in the layerX property.

The event object has limited scope: it can only be referenced in event handlers.

Example   To determine the position where a mouse event occurred, use an event handler with statements such as:

```
function mouseClick(ev) {
   ...
   horiz = ev.pageX
   vert = ev.pageY
   ...
}
```

(This example assumes that the function is called with an event object passed to the ev argument.)

See Also   event, layerX, pageY, screenX

pageX

LAYER

Version 1.2

Property of the Layer object
(see also pageX as a property of the event object)

Specifies the distance, in pixels, from the left edge of the page to the left edge of the layer.

Syntax   `layerObj.pageX`
  `layerObj`   `document.layers.layerName,` or an expression denoting a Layer object.

Discussion   You can modify this property to change the position of the layer in relation to the document containing the layer. This works similarly to `left`, except that `left` positions the layer in relation to the parent layer.

Examples   This button moves the layer so that the left edge of the layer is 10 pixels to the right of the left edge of the document.

```
<INPUT TYPE="button" VALUE=" Left " onclick="layers.layer1.pageX = 10">
```

This button moves the layer so that the left edge of the layer is 10 pixels to the *left* of the left edge of the document.

```
<INPUT TYPE="button" VALUE=" Left "
   onclick="layers.layer1.pageX = -10">
```

See Also   `Layer, left, pageY, top`

pageXOffset

Version 1.2   Read-only

Property of the window object

Specifies the horizontal position, in pixels, of the left side of the document in relation to the left side of the browser's content area.

Syntax   For the current window

`pageXoffset`
`self.pageXoffset`
`window.pageXoffset`

For other windows:

windowObj.pageXoffset

windowObj   An expression denoting a `window` object

Discussion This property indicates where the left side of the document is in relation to the left side of the browser's content area. Zero means that the left side of the document is placed against the left side of the content area; other values indicate that the document has been scrolled horizontally.

You can use this property in conjunction with `scrollTo( )` or `scrollBy( )`, which are used to position the document.

Example To find the position of the current document, and place the value in variable `horizPos`:

`horizPos = parent.pageXOffset`

See Also `pageYOffset, scrollBy( ), scrollTo( ), window`

pageY

EVENT

Version 1.2 Special scope

Property of the event object
(see also pageY as a property of the Layer object)

Returns the vertical position, in pixels, measured from the top of the page, where an event occurred.

Syntax *eventObj*.pageX

eventObj   `event`, or an expression denoting a copy of `event`, such as a function argument passed to an event handler.

Discussion This property returns a position relative to the page in which the event occurred. If the event occurred in a layer, the position is stored in the `layerY` property.

The `event` object has limited scope: it can only be referenced in event handlers.

Example To determine the position where a mouse event occurred, use an event handler with statements such as:

```
function mouseClick(ev) {
   ...
   horiz = ev.pageX
   vert = ev.pageY
   ...
}
```

(This example assumes that the function is called with an *event* object passed to the *ev* argument.)

See Also   event, layerY, pageX, screenY

pageY

LAYER

Version 1.2

Property of the Layer object
(see also pageY as a property of the event object)

Specifies the distance, in pixels, from the top edge of the page to the top edge of the layer.

Syntax   *layerObj*.pageY

layerObj   document.layers.*layerName*, or an expression denoting a Layer object.

Discussion   You can modify this property to change the position of the layer in relation to the document containing the layer. This works similarly to *top*, except that *top* positions the layer in relation to the parent layer.

Examples   This button moves the layer so that the top edge of the layer is 10 pixels from the top of the document.

```
<INPUT TYPE="button" VALUE=" Left " onclick="layers.layer1.pageY = 10">
```

This button moves the layer so that the top edge of the layer is 10 pixels *above* the top edge of the document.

```
<INPUT TYPE="button" VALUE=" Left " onclick="layers.layer1.pageY = -10">
```

See Also   Layer, left, pageX, top

pageYOffset

Version 1.2   Read-only

Property of the `window` object

Specifies the vertical position, in pixels, of the top of the document in relation to the top of the browser's content area.

Syntax
: For the current window

    ```
    pageYoffset
    self.pageYoffset
    window.pageYoffset
    ```

    For other windows:

    windowObj.pageXoffset

    windowObj   An expression denoting a `window` object

Discussion
: This property indicates where the top of the document is in relation to the top of the browser's content area. Zero means that the top of the document is placed against the top of the content area; other values indicate that the document has been scrolled vertically.

    You can use this property in conjunction with `scrollTo( )` or `scrollBy( )`, which are used to position the document.

Example
: To find the position of the top of the current document, and place the value in variable `pos`:
  ```
  pos = parent.pageYOffset
  ```

See Also
: `pageXOffset, scrollBy( ), scrollTo( ), window`

parent

Version 1.0   Read-only

Property of the `window` object and Frame external object

Returns the window or frame that contains the current frame.

Syntax
: For the current window or frame:

```
parent
self.parent
window.parent
```
For other windows or frames:

windowObj.parent

windowObj   An expression denoting a `window` or Frame object.

Event Handlers   Since parent returns a reference to a `window` or Frame object, it has all the properties, methods, and event handlers of that window or Frame.

Discussion   This property refers to the frameset window of a frame, that is, the window or frame containing the current frame. `parent` may be used in a child frame to refer to a sibling frame as `parent.`*frameName* or `parent.frames[`*index*`]`. To refer to the grandparent, or the window if the frame is inside a child frame, use `parent.parent`.

For scripts running in a window, `parent` is equivalent to `window` or `self`. This allows scripts to run in either a window or a frame without changes.

Example   To call function `new1()` in a sibling frame named `frame1`:

`parent.frame1.new1()`

See Also   Frame, `top`, `window`

parentLayer

Version 1.2   Read-only

Property of the Layer object

Returns the layer of which the current layer is a child, or the containing window if this is not a child layer.

Syntax   *layerObj*.parentLayer

layerObj   `document.layers.`*layerName*, or an expression denoting a Layer object.

Discussion   This property returns the name of the layer containing this one, or, if the Layer object has no parent layer, the window containing the layer. You cannot use this property to modify the order of the layers, as it is read-only. To modify the ordering of layers, use the `zIndex` property, or the `moveAbove()` or `moveBelow()` methods.

Example   The statements below check to see whether the layer named smallLayer is the parent of the current layer, and call a function according to the result:

```
if(bigLayer.parentLayer.name == "smallLayer") {
   moveLeft()
}
else {
   moveRight()
}
```

See Also   above, moveAbove( ), moveBelow( ), siblingAbove, zIndex, Layer

parse( )

Version 1.0

Method of the Date constructor

Returns the specified date and time as a number of milliseconds from January 1, 1970, 00:00:00 GMT in local time.

Syntax   Date.parse(*string*)

string   A string specifying a date and time.

Discussion   This method parses a date string and returns the date in the form of the number of milliseconds since January 1, 1970, 00:00:00 GMT, in local time. parse( ) may be used to set dates from string values, in conjunction with setTime( ).

The parse( ) method accepts the IETF standard date syntax: "*wkday, nn mth yyyy hr:mm:sc* GMT"; for instance, "Sat, 30 Aug 1997 15:23:12 GMT". The method can understand U.S. time-zone abbreviations, or a time-zone offset. For instance, "Sat, 30 Aug 1997 15:23:12 GMT+0730", (meaning, seven hours 30 minutes west of the Greenwich meridian). You can omit time zone information to use the local time.

Note that parse( ) is a method of the Date constructor, not of Date objects you create with new Date( ). In other words, you must always write Date.parse( ), not myDateObj.parse( ).

Example
```
var testDate
   = Date.parse("Sat, 30 Aug 1997 15:23:12 GMT+0730")
```

See Also   Date, UTC( )

parseFloat( )

Version 1.0

Built-in function

Parses a string argument and returns a floating point number.

Syntax   `parseFloat(string)`

string   A string containing the value representing a number.

Discussion   `parseFloat()` accepts decimal points and exponents, and returns a floating point number. If `parseFloat()` encounters an invalid character, it returns the value parsed up to that point, ignoring the rest of the string.

If unable to parse a floating point number, `parseFloat()` returns NaN or 0 (depending on the browser version).

Version 1.1

Most JavaScript 1.0 browsers are incapable of returning NaN. Only Solaris and Irix versions of Netscape Navigator 2 (JavaScript 1.0) can return NaN; all others return 0 in its place. However, all versions of Netscape Navigator 3 (JavaScript 1.1) and later are able to return NaN. The `isNaN()` function can be used to check whether the value returned is NaN.

Examples   To parse a value in a text field (`txtNum`) and place the returned value into another text field (`txtFloat`):

```
function GetFloat(form) {
form.txtFloat.value = parseFloat(form.txtNum.value)
}
```

The following example returns NaN, because A is not a number (the number being parsed must be decimal):

`parseFloat("A")`

The following returns 1.72:

`parseFloat("172e-2")`

See Also   `isNaN()`, `parseInt()`

parseInt( )

Version 1.0

Built-in function

Parses a string argument and returns an integer.

Syntax parseInt(*string* [,*radix*])

string   A string representing a number.
radix   The radix (base) of the number in the string. This value may be 2 (binary), 8 (octal), 10 (decimal), or 16 (hexadecimal). The radix value may be omitted or set to 0, to allow JavaScript to determine the radix (see the following Discussion).

Discussion If *radix* is omitted or zero, JavaScript looks at the string and determines the base of the number in the string, using these rules:

- If the string begins with "0x", the radix is 16 (hexadecimal).
- If the string begins with "0", the radix is eight (octal).
- If the string begins with another value, the radix is 10 (decimal).
- If the first character cannot be converted to a number, parseInt( ) will return NaN or 0 (depending on the browser version).

If parseInt( ) encounters a character that cannot be a numeral in the specified radix, it returns the value parsed up to that point, ignoring the rest of the string.

Version 1.1 Most JavaScript 1.0 browsers are incapable of returning NaN. Only Solaris and Irix versions of Netscape Navigator 2 (JavaScript 1.0) can return NaN; all others return 0 in its place. However, all versions of Netscape Navigator 3 (JavaScript 1.1) and later are able to return NaN. The isNaN( ) function can be used to check whether the value returned is NaN.

Examples To parse a value in a text field (txtNum), using hexadecimal, and place the returned value into another text field (txtInteger):

```
function GetInteger(form) {
form.txtInteger.value = parseInt(form.txtNum.value, 16)
}
```

This example returns 35, because 23 in hexadecimal (2 * 16 + 3) is 35 in decimal (3 * 10 + 5):

```
parseInt("23&", 16)
```

See Also isNaN( ), parseFloat( )

Password

Version 1.0   External

External object

Reflects a password input field in an HTML form.

Syntax	*formObj.passwordName*	
	formObj.elements[*index*]	
	formObj	document.*formName* or other expression denoting a Form object.
	passwordName	String value representing a name assigned by the NAME attribute of the HTML <INPUT> tag.
	index	Number or string specifying an element of the form's elements array.
Properties	defaultValue	String that reflects the initial contents of the text area: the VALUE attribute.
	form	The form that contains this Password object.
	name	A string containing the name assigned by the NAME attribute of the HTML <INPUT> tag.
	type	A string specifying the type of input field; this always contains "password" for Password objects.
	value	String specifying the current contents of the password box.
Methods	blur()	Removes focus from the password box.
	focus()	Sets focus on the password box.
	select()	Selects (highlights) the text in the password box.
Event Handlers	onBlur, onFocus	
Discussion		A password field looks just like a text box, but when the user types something into it, asterisks are displayed in place of the typed text. This is done in order to conceal the typed value from anyone looking over the user's shoulder.

When Navigator loads a web page, it creates Password objects corresponding to all <INPUT> tags that use the TYPE="PASSWORD" attribute. You can reference these objects as properties of a Form object, or as elements of the form's elements array.

Version 1.1   The type property was added in JavaScript 1.1.

Example
: The contents of a password box can be read by a statement such as:

```
userPsw = document.myForm.passText.value
```

where `passText` is a password box in the form named `myForm`.

See Also
: Form, Text

pathname

AREA, LINK

Version 1.0 Read-only External

Property of the Area and Link external objects
(see also `pathname` property of the `location` object)

Reflects the pathname portion of a URL.

Syntax
: *docObject*.links[*index*].pathname
  docObject   document for the current document, or an expression denoting any `document` object.
  index   Number or string specifying an element of the `links` array.

Discussion
: This property reflects the pathname portion of the URL, that is, everything from the end of the `hostname` up to and including the filename.

  Version 1.1 In JavaScript 1.0, this property is only available for Link objects. It was added to Area objects in JavaScript 1.1.

Example
: For a link created by HTML such as:

```
<A HREF="http://www.netscape.com/dir1/dir2/index.htm">
    Click here for more info</A>
```

the statement:

```
var path = document.links[0].pathname
```

sets the variable `path` to `"/dir/dir/index.htm"`. (The reference to `links[0]` assumes that this is the first link in the document.)

See Also
: Area, `hash`, `host`, `hostname`, `href`, Link, `links`, `port`, `protocol`, `search`

pathname

LOCATION

Version 1.0　Tainted

Property of the `location` object
(see also `pathname` property of the Area and Link external objects)

Specifies the pathname information of a URL.

Syntax
: `locationObj.pathname`

  `locationObj`　　`location` for the current window, or an expression denoting a `location` object in any window.

Discussion
: This property reflects the pathname portion of the URL of the document displayed in the browser, that is, everything from the end of the `hostname` up to and including the filename. When working with a file on your local hard drive, the `pathname` includes /, the hard disk letter, and |. For instance, rather than `directory1/directory2/old.htm`, the `pathname` would be, for instance, `/e|directory1/directory2/old.htm`.

  Modifying `pathname` causes the window to be reloaded using the new URL. Note, however, that it is considered safer to set the `href` property to ensure that the entire URL is correctly updated.

  If setting the `pathname` property from the event handler attribute of an HTML tag, you must specify `window.location.pathname` instead of simply using `location.pathname`. There are actually two `location` properties; `window.location` and `document.location`. Calling `location` without specifying the object is the equivalent of `document.location`, so to use the `pathname` property you must specifically reference `window.location.pathname`. (Note that `document.location` is a synonym for `document.URL`.)

Example
: The following example sets the value of the `pathname` property, loading a new page:

  `window.location.pathname = "/directory1/subdirect/old.htm"`

See Also
: `hash`, `host`, `hostname`, `href`, `port`, `protocol`, `search`, `URL`, `location`

personalbar

Version 1.2 Signed scripts

Property of the `window` object

Specifies the state of the browser window's personal toolbar.

Syntax For the current window:

`personalbar`
`self.personalbar`
`window.personalbar`

For other windows:

`windowObj.personalbar`

`windowObj`   An expression denoting a `window` object.

Properties `visible`   A Boolean property indicating whether the personal toolbar is visible or not.

Discussion The personal toolbar, also sometimes called the directory bar, is a customizable toolbar introduced in Netscape Navigator 4. Buttons can be added to this bar by moving bookmarks into the Personal Toolbar folder in the Bookmarks window. You can use this object's single property, `visible`, to find out if the personal toolbar is displayed, or to change its status.

Note that you can only change this property in a signed script.

Example This statement hides the personal toolbar in a window named `windowOne`:

`windowOne.personalbar.visible = false`

See Also `locationbar, menubar, scrollbars, statusbar, toolbar, window`

PI

Version 1.0 Read-only

Property of the Math object

Returns the approximate value of π, 3.141592653589793.

- Syntax: `Math.PI`

- Example: `a = Math.PI`

- See Also: E, LN10, LN2, LOG10E, LOG2E, Math, SQRT1_2, SQRT2

pixelDepth

Version 1.2 Read-only

Property of the screen object

Specifies the number of bits per pixel in the current video mode of the computer on which the browser is running.

- Syntax: `screen.pixelDepth`

- Discussion: The `pixelDepth` value is related to the `colorDepth` value, as the number of colors that can be displayed on a video monitor is dependent on the number of bits used to create each pixel on the screen.

- Example: To display the screen's pixel depth:
  `document.write(screen.pixelDepth)`

- See Also: `availHeight`, `availWidth`, `height`, `width`, `colorDepth`, `screen`

platform

Version 1.2　Read-only

Property of the `navigator` object

Identifies the operating system for which the browser was compiled.

Syntax　`navigator.platform`

Discussion　The `platform` property contains a string indicating the operating system for which the browser was compiled. Possible values include `"Win32"`, `"Win16"`, `"Mac68k"`, `"MacPPC"`, and various UNIX types. This is not necessarily the same as the actual operating system in which the browser is running, though. For instance, a `Win16` browser may be running in Windows NT.

　　This property was intended for use with the JAR Installation Manager, a Netscape software product that supports automatic installation of new software on the user's computer.

Example　To display the operating system for which the browser was compiled:
`document.write(navigator.platform)`

See Also　`appCodeName, appName, appVersion, language, userAgent, navigator`

Plugin

Version 1.1　External

External object

A plug-in program installed in the browser.

Syntax　`navigator.plugins[index]`

　　index　　A number specifying a position in the `plugins` array, or a string specifying the name of a plug-in (the `name` property).

Properties
- `name`　　The plug-in's name.
- `description`　　A description of the plug-in.
- `filename`　　The path and filename of the plug-in program.
- `length`　　The number of MIME data types that the plug-in can handle.
- `[index]`　　Array elements that return MIME types that the plug-in supports (see Discussion).

Discussion
: A plug-in is a software module that extends the browser's capabilities by allowing it to display or manipulate a file format that the basic browser is not capable of working with. Navigator has a Plugin object for each plug-in installed in the browser. You can reference these objects as elements of the `navigator.plugins` array.

Besides its named properties, a Plugin object has array elements that indicate the MIME types handled by the plug-in. Each element within this array is a MimeType object. The Plugin object's properties are read-only; you cannot modify them in order to "install" a plug-in.

There is some confusion about the term "plug-in." A plug-in is *not* a file embedded into the Web document with the `<EMBED>` tag, although many people use the term to refer to these files. Embedded files are reflected by Embed objects in a document's `embeds` array. A plug-in is a program, installed in the browser, used to handle the embedded files.

Examples
: To write a list of plug-ins installed on the browser to the web page:

```
for (i=0; i < navigator.plugins.length; i++) {
   document.write("<B>", i, ": ",
   navigator.plugins[i].name, ":</B><BR>",
   navigator.plugins[i].filename, "<BR>",
   navigator.plugins[i].description, "<BR>",
   navigator.plugins[i].length, "<P>")
}
```

To create a variable containing the path and filename of the LiveAudio plug-in file:

```
var liveFile = navigator.plugins["LiveAudio"].filename
```

See Also
: Embed, embeds, enabledPlugin, MimeType, mimeTypes, navigator, plugins

plugins

Version 1.1   Read-only

Property of the `navigator` object

Reflects all plug-ins in the browser.

Syntax
: `navigator.plugins`

Properties
: `length` — The number of Plugin objects (the number of plug-ins installed in the browser).

Methods	`refresh()`	Refreshes the `plugins` array, making newly installed plug-ins available to the browser, and (optionally) reloading the document.
Discussion		Each element of the `plugins` array is a Plugin object reflecting one plug-in that is installed in the browser. See the Plugin object for more information.
Example		To display the number of plug-ins installed on the browser: `document.write(navigator.plugins.length)`
See Also		Embed, `embeds`, `enabledPlugin`, MimeType, `mimeTypes`, `navigator`, Plugin

port

AREA, LINK

Version 1.0   External

Property of the Area and Link external objects
(see also `port` property of the `location` object)

Specifies the port number of a URL, if any.

Syntax	`docObject.links[index].port`	
	docObject	`document` for the current document, or an expression denoting any `document` object.
	index	Number or string specifying an element of the `links` array.
Discussion		The port portion of the URL specifies the port used by the server for communication with the World Wide Web. The `port` property is a substring of the `href` property. Also, the `port` property and the `hostname` properties are substrings of the `host` property. Most URLs do not specify the port; the default port, if none is specified, is 80. However, if the port is not specified the `port` property will be empty.
Version 1.1		In JavaScript 1.0, this property is only available for Link objects. It was added to Area objects in JavaScript 1.1.

Example		For a link created by HTML such as:
		`<A HREF="http://www.bigserver.com:70/shopping/index.htm">`
		`To the shop...</A>`

the statement:

```
var shopPort = document.links[0].port
```

will set the variable shopPort to 70. (The reference to links[0] assumes that this is the first link in the document.)

See Also Area, hash, host, hostname, href, Link, links, pathname, protocol, search

port

LOCATION

Version 1.0   Tainted

Property of the location object
(see also port property of the Area and Link external objects)

Specifies the port number of a URL, if any.

Syntax *locationObj*.port

locationObj   location for the current window, or an expression denoting a location object in any window.

Discussion The port portion of the URL specifies the port used by the server for communication with the World Wide Web. The port property is a substring of the href property. Also, the port property and the hostname properties are substrings of the host property.

Most URLs do not specify the port; the default port, if none is specified, is 80. However, if the port is not specified the port property will be empty.

Modifying port causes the window to be reloaded using the new URL. Note, however, that it is considered safer to set the href property, to ensure that the entire URL is correctly updated.

If setting the port property from the event handler attribute of an HTML tag, you must specify window.location.port instead of simply using location.port. There are actually two location properties; window.location and document.location. Calling location without specifying the object is the equivalent of document.location, so to use the port property you must specifically call window.location.port. (Note that document.location is a synonym for document.URL.)

Example The following example sets the value of the port property, loading a new page:

```
window.location.port = "70"
```

See Also hash, host, hostname, href, pathname, protocol, search, URL, location

POSITIVE_INFINITY

Version 1.1   Read-only

Property of the Number object

Returns a special numeric value representing infinity.

Syntax   `Number.POSITIVE_INFINITY`

Discussion   This value behaves like infinity in arithmetic operations. A value multiplied by `Number.POSITIVE_INFINITY` is infinity; a value divided by `Number.POSITIVE_INFINITY` is zero. Converting it to a string returns `"Infinity"`.

POSITIVE_INFINITY may be used to check to see whether a value is above the maximum allowed value in JavaScript (`Number.MAX_VALUE`, approximately 1.79E+308). All numeric values above that maximum value are represented as `POSITIVE_INFINITY`.

Example   To check to see whether a value stored in `nMax` is above the maximum allowed value in JavaScript, and to call the `over()` function if it is:

```
if (nMax == Number.POSITIVE_INFINITY)
   over()
else
   under()
```

See Also   `MAX_VALUE, MIN_VALUE, Math, NaN, NEGATIVE_INFINITY, Number`

pow( )

Version 1.0

Method of the Math object

Returns a number raised to a power (base^{exponent}).

Syntax   `Math.pow(base, exponent)`
    base   The base. Any numeric value or expression.
    exponent   The exponent. Any numeric value or expression.

Example The statement:

var n = Math.pow(8,3)

sets n to 512 (8 to the power of 3).

See Also exp( ), log( ), Math

preference( )

Version 1.2 Signed scripts

Method of the `navigator` object

Reads and sets browser user preferences.

Syntax To read a preference setting:

navigator.preference(*pref*)

To set a preference:

navigator.preference(*pref*, *setting*)

pref   A string specifying the preference being read or set.
setting The value to assign to the preference.

Use the preferences( ) method to set the following preferences:

Browser Preference	JavaScript Preference Name	Value
Automatically load image	"general.always_load_images"	true or false
Enable Java	"security.enable_java"	true or false
Enable JavaScript	"javascript.enabled"	true or false
Enable style sheets	"browser.enable_style_sheets"	true or false
Enable autoinstall	"autoupdate.enabled"	true or false
Accept all cookies	"network.cookie.cookieBehavior"	0
Accept only cookies that are returned to originating server		1
Disable cookies		2
Warn before accepting cookie	"network.cookie.warnAboutCookies"	true or false

Note that more preferences will be added to this list soon.

Discussion   This method reads and sets user preferences, which are normally displayed and changed using the browser's Preferences dialog box. This method can only be used in a signed script that has the "`UniversalPreferencesRead`" or "`UniversalPreferencesWrite`" privilege.

Example   To set the browser's preferences to enable style sheets:

```
navigator.preferences("browser.enable_style_sheets", true)
```

See Also   `navigator`

previous

Version 1.1   Read-only   Tainted

Property of the `history` object

Returns the URL of the previous document displayed (the previous entry in the history list).

Syntax   `history.previous`

Discussion   This property returns the URL of the page that would be displayed if the user clicked the browser's Back button. This property is empty unless data tainting has been enabled on the user's computer (see Chapter 8). However, note that you can move through the history list, whether tainting is enabled or not, using `go( )`, and `forward( )`.

Version 1.2   In JavaScript 1.2, this property returns empty unless it is referenced from a signed script.

Example   To check to see if the URL of the last page displayed contains "`acme.com`":

```
if (history.previous.indexOf("acme.com") != -1) {
   history.go(-1)
}
```

See Also   `back( )`, `current`, `forward( )`, `history`, `next`, `reload( )`, `replace( )`

print( )

Version 1.2

Method of the `window` object and Frame external object

Prints the document in the window or frame, equivalent to the user clicking the browser's Print button.

Syntax For the current window:
```
print( )
self.print( )
window.print( )
```
For other windows:
```
windowObj.print( )
```
windowObj   An expression denoting a `window` object.

Example To print the document in the window named `windowTwo`:
```
windowTwo.print( )
```

See Also `stop( )`, `window`

prompt( )

Version 1.0

Method of the `window` object

Displays a prompt dialog box, and returns a value types by the user.

Syntax `prompt(message, default)`

message   A string specifying the message that will appear in the dialog box.

default   A string specifying the default text that will appear in the dialog's text box.

Discussion The prompt dialog box contains a message, a text box in which the user can type something, an OK button, and a Cancel button. If you do not specify a *default* input text, the word `undefined` appears in the text box. To display a blank text box, specify the empty string for *default*, as in `prompt(message, "")`.

When a prompt box is displayed, the processing of the script is halted until the user clicks on one of the buttons. If the user clicks the OK button, `prompt( )` returns a string containing the contents of the text box. If the user clicks the Cancel button, `prompt( )` returns `null`.

To create a customized prompt dialog box, you can open a new window using `window.open( )`; this method allows you to specify the window title and other features that `prompt()` cannot control.

Example To display the prompt dialog box in the following illustration, and store the result in a variable:

```
userReply = prompt("Please enter your user name.",
    "anonymous")
```

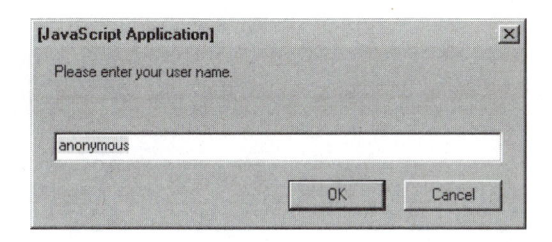

See Also `alert( )`, `confirm( )`, `window`

protocol

AREA, LINK

Version 1.0   Read-only   External

Property of the Area and Link external objects
(see also `protocol` property of the `location` object)

Reflects the protocol portion of an URL, from the beginning of the URL up to and including the colon (`http:`, `ftp:`, `gopher:`, and so forth).

Syntax *docObject*.links[*index*].protocol

docObject   `document` for the current document, or an expression denoting any `document` object.

index   Number or string specifying an element of the `links` array.

Discussion In JavaScript 1.0, this property is only available for Link objects. It was added
Version 1.1 to Area objects in JavaScript 1.1.

Example For a link created by HTML such as:

```
<A HREF="gopher://bigserver.com/">Visit our gopher server</A>
```

the statement:

```
var thisProto = document.links[0].protocol
```

sets the variable `thisProto` to `"gopher:"`. (The reference to `links[0]` assumes that this is the first link in the document.)

See Also Area, hash, host, hostname, href, Link, links, pathname, port, search

protocol

LOCATION

Version 1.0   Tainted

Property of the `location` object
(see also `protocol` property of the Area and Link external objects)

Specifies the protocol portion of an URL, from the beginning of the URL up to and including the colon (`http:`, `ftp:`, `gopher:`, and so forth).

Syntax *locationObj*.protocol

locationObj   `location` for the current window, or an expression denoting a `location` object in any window.

Discussion This property reflects the protocol portion of the URL of the document displayed in the specified window. The `protocol` property is a substring of the `href` property.

   Modifying `protocol` causes the window to be reloaded using the new URL. Note, however, that it is considered safer to set the `href` property, to ensure that the entire URL is correctly updated.

   If setting the `protocol` property from the event handler attribute of an HTML tag, you must specify `window.location.protocol` instead of simply using `location.protocol`. There are actually two `location` properties: `window.location` and `document.location`. Calling `location` without specifying the object is the equivalent of `document.location`, so to use the `protocol` property you must specifically call `window.location.protocol`. (Note that `document.location` is a synonym for `document.URL`.)

Example The following example sets the value of the `protocol` property, loading a new page:

```
window.location.protocol = "gopher:"
```

See Also hash, host, hostname, href, pathname, port, search, URL, location

prototype

Version 1.1

Property of all objects constructed with new

Adds new properties and methods to existing objects.

Syntax *obj*.prototype.*newProp* = *value*

    obj   Any constructed object.
    newProp   Name of the new property or method.
    value   Default value of the new property.

Discussion This property allows you to create new properties for any objects that are created by calling a constructor with the new operator. This includes built-in objects like strings and arrays, as well as any new object types that you create. When you create a new property, it is added to all existing objects of that type, as well as any objects that you create afterwards. To create a method, make the new property's `value` a reference to a function (see Example).

Example To create a String property called `language` for use in a multilingual web page, use statements such as:

```
String.prototype.language = "English"
```

To create a String method called `last` that returns the last character in a string, use statements such as:

```
function lc() {
   return this.charAt(this.length - 1)
}
```

```
String.prototype.last = lc
```

Note that there are no parentheses after `lc` in the preceding statement; this is a reference to the function, not a call.

See Also constructor

Radio

Version 1.0   External

Property of the Form external object

Reflects a set of radio (option) buttons in a form.

Syntax	*formObj*.*radioName*[*buttonNum*] *formObj*["*radioName*"][*buttonNum*] *formObj*.elements[*index*]	
	formObj	document.*formName*, or an expression denoting a Form object in any document.
	radioName	Name specified in the NAME attribute of the HTML <INPUT> tag.
	index	Number specifying the position of the button in the form.
	buttonNum	Number specifying one button of a set.
Properties	checked	A Boolean value specifying the state of the button, checked or unchecked.
	defaultChecked	Reflects the CHECKED attribute of the <INPUT> tag; returns true if the attribute is initially checked.
	form	Returns the Form object that contains the button.
	length	The number of individual buttons within the radio-button set.
	name	Reflects the name specified in the NAME attribute of the HTML <INPUT> tag.
	type	Reflects the value specified in the TYPE attribute of the HTML <INPUT> tag. This is always "radio" for Radio objects.
	value	Reflects the value specified in the VALUE attribute of the HTML <INPUT> tag, which is passed to a server if the button is checked when the form is submitted.
Methods	blur()	Removes focus from the button.
	click()	Simulates a mouse click on the button.
	focus()	Sets focus on the button.
Event Handlers	onblur, onclick, onfocus	

Discussion   When Navigator loads a web page, it creates Radio objects corresponding to all HTML <INPUT> tags with the TYPE="radio" attribute. Buttons with the same NAME attribute are assembled into an array. You can reference these objects as elements of the array, or as elements of the form's elements array.

Version 1.1   The type property, onblur and onfocus event handlers, and blur and focus methods were added in Version 1.1.

Example   For a set of radio buttons defined by HTML:

```
<FORM NAME="myForm">
    ...
    <INPUT TYPE="radio" NAME="myRadio" VALUE="N" CHECKED>
    North <BR>
    <INPUT TYPE="radio" NAME="myRadio" VALUE="C">
    Central <BR>
    <INPUT TYPE="radio" NAME="myRadio" VALUE="S">
    South <BR>
    ...
</FORM>
```

the expression document.myForm.myRadio[0].checked will return true immediately after the document is loaded, since the CHECKED attribute is specified for the first button. If the user clicks the "South" button, myRadio[0].checked will become false, and myRadio[2].checked will become true.

See Also   elements, Form

random( )

Version 1.0

Method of the Math object

Returns a pseudo-random number.

Syntax   Math.random( )

Discussion   This method returns a number between zero and one. The value is based on the computer's time-of-day clock.

Version 1.1   This method only worked on the UNIX versions of Navigator in JavaScript 1.0; in JavaScript 1.1 it works in all the Navigator browsers.

Example   var randomNumber = Math.random( )

See Also   Math

referrer

Version 1.0　Read-only　Tainted

Property of the document object

Returns the URL of the document in which the user clicked on a link to load the current document.

Syntax　*docObject*.referrer

　　　　　docObject　　document for the current document, or an expression denoting a document in any window.

Discussion　This property will return the empty string if the user did not reach the current page by clicking a link: for instance, if the document was loaded from a bookmark, or by typing the URL into the Location text box. It will also be empty if the server does not provide environment variable information.

Example　This example shows HTML that names the page from which the visitor has arrived at a site:

```
The URL of the document you are seeking has changed. Please inform the
    owner of the document you've just come from
<SCRIPT LANGUAGE="JAVASCRIPT">
<!--
document.write(" (" + document.referrer + ")")
// -->
</SCRIPT>
 that this link has changed.
```

See Also　document, history

refresh( )

Version 1.1

Method of the plugins array

Makes newly installed plug-ins available, and may also reload documents containing plug-ins.

Syntax　navigator.plugins.refresh(*reload*)

　　　　　reload　　　　Optional argument. If included and true, causes Navigator to reload all open documents containing HTML <EMBED> tags.

Discussion	When the user installs a plug-in, the plug-in cannot be used until the browser has been closed and reopened, or until the refresh() method is used. This method will refresh the plugins array, making the newly installed plug-in available. If the *reload* argument is true, Navigator also reloads all open documents that contain <EMBED> tags.

Example	This function refreshes the plugins array, and reloads the documents containing <EMBED> tags.
	
	``
	function reloadPlugs() {
	   navigator.plugins.refresh(true)
	}
	``

See Also	plugins, reload( ), replace( )

RegExp

Version 1.2

Object type (constructor)

Creates a new regular expression object; also provides properties that control matches and return results.

Syntax	v = new RegExp(*pattern, modifiers*)	
	v	Variable or object to which the new RegExp is assigned.
	pattern	String specifying a regular expression pattern.
	modifiers	String containing i and/or g modifiers.
Properties	global	Returns true if the g modifier was used to specify a global match. This property is read-only.
	ignoreCase	Returns true if the i modifier was used to specify a case-insensitive match. This property is read-only.
	LastIndex	Used to control global matches with the exec( ) and test( ) methods.
	name	A numeric value that specifies the position at which to start the next match, that is, the next character after the point where the last match stopped.
	source	Returns a string containing the pattern. This property is read-only.

Methods	compile(*pattern*, *mods*)	Converts a `RegExp` object to a compiled form for faster execution.
	exec(*str*)	Searches for a match in a specified string, and provides several types of result information.
	test(*str*)	Searches for a match in a specified string, and returns `true` if one is found. This method does not provide as much information as `exec()`, but it executes more quickly.
	(*str*)	The "null method," equivalent to `exec(str)`. (See Discussion.)
Properties	$1, $2, ... $9	Returns the first nine values that were memorized as specified by parentheses in the pattern. The properties are read-only.
	input, $_	Specifies the string to be searched. The `exec()` and `test()` methods use this value if they are called without an argument.
	lastMatch, $&	Returns the last characters matched. This property is read-only.
	lastParen, $+	Returns the last memorized value, if any. This property is read-only.
	leftContext, $`	Returns characters from the start of the searched string to just before the start of the last match. Note the ` (accent grave) character, not apostrophe. This property is read-only.
	multiline, $*	If true, allows searches to continue past line break characters in strings.
	rightContext, $'	Returns characters from just after the last match to the end of the string. This property is read-only.
Discussion		Regular expressions are a powerful tool for manipulating text. A regular expression, also called a pattern, is a sequence of characters that defines a string or set of strings that can be searched for and replaced (see Examples).

Like strings and numbers, `RegExp` objects can be created without explicitly calling `RegExp()`. For example:

`var myExp = /fred/i`

is largely equivalent to:

`var myExp = new RegExp("fred", "i")`

but there are some differences. The first form compiles the expression, so that matches can be executed more quickly. The second way provides more flexibility, since its arguments are strings whose values can be created or changed while the script is executing. Patterns created by `new RegExp()` can be compiled later by the `compile()` method.

There are some syntactic differences in the two ways of writing the expression. When calling `RegExp()`, the / characters are not used to enclose the pattern. Also, since the characters inside the argument are subject to the usual rules for strings, you may need to add \ characters, avoid line breaks, and so forth, to ensure that the desired string value is passed to `RegExp()`.

JavaScript provides a "null method" that is an abbreviation for `exec()`. For example, if the variable `re` is a `RegExp` object and `str` is a string, then `re(str)` is equivalent to `re.exec(str)`.

Note that the `RegExp` constructor has some properties of its own; that is, they are properties of `RegExp` itself, not of objects created by new `RegExp()`. These properties provide status and control that apply to all `RegExp()` constructed objects of all scripts running in a single window or frame. This means that if several scripts that use these properties are running in one window, they may affect each others' results.

JavaScript's syntax for regular expressions is based on the Perl language. For more details on regular expressions, see Chapter 3.

Examples To create a regular expression that matches the name Fred:

```
pat = new RegExp("Fred")
```

To create a regular expression that matches the name Fred in any combination of uppercase and lowercase letters:

```
pat = new RegExp("fred", "i")
```

To create a regular expression that matches one or more digits:

```
pat = new RegExp("\\d+")
```

(Note the extra \ character needed because the argument is a string literal.)

To create a regular expression that matches a telephone number consisting of groups of 3, 3, and 4 digits, with a single dash between groups:

```
pat = /\d{3}-\d{3}-\d{4}/
```

The preceding statement creates a compiled expression, but is otherwise equivalent to:

```
pat = new RegExp("\\d{3}-\\d{3}-\\d{4}")
```

releaseEvents( )

Version 1.2

Method of the document, Layer, and window objects

Terminates capturing of the specified type(s) of events.

Syntax `obj.releaseEvents(mask)`

`obj`   Reference to a `window`, `document`, `Frame`, or `Layer` object.
`mask`   Bit mask that specifies events.

Discussion This method releases events that have previously been set for capturing using `captureEvents( )`. The mask value must be a bitwise OR of some of the values which are available as properties of the `Event` object:

Event.ABORT	Event.KEYDOWN	Event.MOUSEUP
Event.BLUR	Event.KEYPRESS	Event.MOVE
Event.CHANGE	Event.KEYUP	Event.RESET
Event.CLICK	Event.LOAD	Event.RESIZE
Event.DBLCLICK	Event.MOUSEDOWN	Event.SELECT
Event.DRAGDROP	Event.MOUSEMOVE	Event.SUBMIT
Event.ERROR	Event.MOUSEOUT	Event.UNLOAD
Event.FOCUS	Event.MOUSEOVER	

If a window is the original target of an event, it will continue to receive the event even after releasing it.

Example To release the `CLICK`, `DBLCLICK`, and `DRAGDROP` events for a window, use a statement such as:

`myWindow.releaseEvents(Event.CLICK | Event.DBLCLICK | Event.DRAGDROP)`

See Also `captureEvents( )`, `enableExternalCapture( )`, `Event`, `handleEvent( )`, `routeEvent( )`

reload( )

Version 1.1

Method of the `location` object

Reloads the current document in the browser window.

Syntax   `location.reload(newCopy)`

   newCopy   Optional argument. If included and `true`, the browser retrieves the document from the server using an unconditional HTTP GET command. This ensures that the document is copied from the server. (See the following.)

Discussion   This method reloads the document specified by `location.href`.

   The `reload( )` method carries out the same reload operation that would be carried out if the user clicked the browser's Reload button. This is controlled, to some degree, by the browser's Preferences settings for its cache. If the preference is set to anything but Every Time, when the user clicks the Reload button a conditional GET request is sent to the server. This means that the page may be reloaded from the cache rather than the server; the page is only sent from the server if its last-modified time is later than that of the page stored in the cache. (There is, however, a little-known technique for forcing Netscape Navigator to use an unconditional GET request, forcing a reload from the server regardless of the document dates: the user must hold the Shift key when clicking the Reload button.)

   You can make `reload( )` operate in either manner. Use `location.reload( )` to make a conditional GET request, or `location.reload(true)` to make an unconditional GET request (the same as pressing Shift while clicking Reload).

   Note that when using this method from within an event handler, you must write `window.location.reload( )`.

   Documents may also be reloaded using the `refresh( )` method of the `plugins` array.

Example   Clicking on the following button sends an unconditional GET request to the server, forcing a reload of the current document:

```
<INPUT TYPE="button" VALUE="Reload from the server"
   ONCLICK="window.location.reload(true)">
```

See Also   `go( )`, `location`, `refresh( )`, `replace( )`, `window`

replace( )

LOCATION

Version 1.1

Method of the `location` object
(see also `replace` as a method of `String`)

Loads the specified document into the browser, replacing the current history list entry.

Syntax `location.replace(url)`

url String value specifying the URL of the document to load into the browser.

Discussion Note that the effect of this method is different from loading a page into the browser by clicking a link or entering a URL into the Location bar. The `replace( )` method replaces the current history list entry with the specified URL, so the user will be unable to use the history list to return to the page that called `replace( )`. To load a page into the browser *without* replacing the history list entry, use `go( )`.

When using `replace( )` in an event handler, you must use `window.location.replace(url)`. If you don't, JavaScript will assume you are referring to `document.location`, which is a synonym for `document.URL`.

This method is a JavaScript 1.1 method, so it won't work in Netscape Navigator 2. However, you can emulate the method in Navigator 2 by entering the following at the top of a web page:

```
if (location.replace == null)
    location.replace = location.assign
```

Example Clicking on the following button loads `newpage.htm` into the browser, replacing the current history entry:

```
<INPUT TYPE="button" VALUE="Replace Current Document"
    ONCLICK="window.location.replace('newpage.htm')">
```

See Also `go( )`, `location`, `reload( )`, `window`

replace( )

STRING

Version 1.2

Method of the String object
(see also replace as a method of location)

Replaces a specified substring with another.

Syntax   *stringObj*.replace(*regexp*, *newText*)

    stringObj   String object or expression.
    regexp   A regular expression specifying the substring(s) to be replaced.
    newText   String object or expression specifying the replacement text.

Discussion   This method returns a string containing a copy of the original string in which one or more substrings that match the regular expression have been replaced with the specified new value. Note that the original string is not modified.

If the regular expression includes the g (global) modifier, all matching substrings will be replaced; without it, only the first match will be replaced. If the regular expression includes the i (case-insensitive) modifier, uppercase and lowercase letters will be considered equivalent.

Example   For a string defined by:

```
var s = "abBbc"
```

the statement:

```
result = s.replace(/b/, "X")
```

sets result to aXBbc (replacing the first occurrence of b).

```
result = s.replace(/b/g, "X")
```

sets result to aXBXc (replacing both occurrences of b).

```
result = s.replace(/b/gi, "X")
```

sets result to aXXXc (replacing all occurrences of b and B).

See Also   RegExp, slice( ), split( )

reset( )

Version 1.1   External

Method of the Form external object

Resets an HTML form.

Syntax   *formObj*.reset( )

formObj   document.*formName*, or other expression denoting a Form object in any document.

Discussion   The reset( ) method simulates a click on a Reset button in a form. That is, it resets all the values in the form to their defaults. reset( ) can be used even if no Reset button is present in the form.

Example   If the standard HTML Reset button seems too plain, you can create a "graphic button" by placing an image in a link that calls reset( ) such as:

```
<A HREF="javascript:document.myForm.reset()">
<IMG SRC="eraser.gif"></A>
```

See Also   onreset, Reset, submit( )

Reset

Version 1.0   Read-only   External

Property of the Form external object

Reflects a Reset button in a form.

Syntax   *formObj*.*resetName*
formObj.elements[*index*].item

formObj   document.*formName*, or other expression denoting a Form object.
resetName   Name specified in the NAME attribute of the HTML <INPUT> tag.
index   Number specifying the position of the Reset button in the form.

Properties	form	Returns the Form object that contains the Reset button.
	name	Reflects the name specified in the NAME attribute of the HTML <INPUT> tag.
	type	Reflects the value specified in the TYPE attribute of the HTML <INPUT> tag. This is always "reset" for Reset objects.
	value	Reflects the value specified in the VALUE attribute of the HTML <INPUT> tag. This is the Reset button's label that appears on the screen.
Methods	blur()	Removes focus from the button.
	click()	Simulates a mouse click on the button.
	focus()	Sets focus on the button.
Event Handlers	onblur, onclick, onfocus	

Discussion   Reset buttons are created by the HTML <INPUT> tag with the TYPE="reset" attribute. When Navigator loads a web page, it creates Reset objects corresponding to all Reset buttons in the document. You can reference these objects as properties of a Form object or as elements of a form's elements array.

The effect of a Reset button cannot be canceled by defining an onclick event handler; once the user has clicked on the button, the reset will be carried out and cannot be stopped.

Version 1.1

The type property, onblur and onfocus event handlers, and blur and focus methods were added in Version 1.1.

Example   document.myForm.reset()

See Also   elements, Form, reset

RESET

Version 1.2 Read-only

Property of the Event object

Returns a mask for capturing form reset events.

Syntax   Event.RESET

Discussion   This property is used to capture and release reset events, which occur when a form is reset (cleared). For more details on event handling, see Chapter 7.

Example To enable capturing of reset events (as well as submit):
`myWindow.captureEvents (Event.RESET | Event.SUBMIT)`

See Also `captureEvents()`, `event`, `Event`, `onreset`, `releaseEvents()`

RESIZE

Version 1.2   Read-only

property of the Event object

Returns a mask for capturing resize events.

Syntax `Event.RESIZE`

Discussion This property is used to control event capturing (see Chapter 7).

Example To enable capturing of resize events:
`myWindow.captureEvents(Event.RESIZE)`

See Also `captureEvents()`, `releaseEvents()`, `Event`

resizeBy( )

Version 1.2   Signed scripts

Method of the window and Layer object

Resizes a window or layer by moving the bottom right corner.

Syntax `windowObj.resizeBy(horiz, vert)`

`windowObj`	A window or Layer object.
`horiz`	The number of pixels by which to resize the window or layer horizontally.
`vert`	The number of pixels by which to resize the window or layer vertically.

Discussion   After resizing a window, the document contents are redrawn to fit the new size. After resizing a layer, the document contents are not redrawn; the layer may be clipped. The `Layer` object's `clip.bottom` and `clip.right` properties are modified.

To make a window smaller than 100 pixels by 100 pixels, you must use a signed script.

Example   To increase `windowOne`'s size by 100 pixels horizontally and 200 vertically:

`windowOne.resizeBy(100, 200)`

To increase `windowOne`'s size by 100 pixels horizontally and reduce it by 200 vertically:

`windowOne.resizeBy(100, -200)`

See Also   `clip`, `Layer`, `resizeTo()`, `window`

resizeTo( )

Version 1.2   Signed scripts

Method of the `window` or `Layer` object

Resizes a window or layer to the specified dimensions.

Syntax   *windowObj*.resizeBy(*width*, *height*)

windowObj   A `window` or `Layer` object.
width   The new width of the window or layer, in pixels.
height   The new height of the window or layer, in pixels.

Discussion   After resizing a window, the document contents are redrawn to fit the new size. After resizing a layer, the document contents are not redrawn; the layer may be clipped. The `Layer` object's `clip.bottom` and `clip.right` properties are modified.

To make a window smaller than 100 pixels by 100 pixels, you must use a signed script.

Example   To change `windowOne`'s size to 550 pixels wide by 300 high:

`windowOne.resizeBy(550, 300)`

See Also   `clip`, `Layer`, `resizeBy()`, `window`

return

Version 1.0

Keyword used in statements

This keyword is used to exit from a function and to return a value to the caller. For more details, see "Returning Values" in Chapter 4.

reverse( )

Version 1.1

Method of the Array object

Reverses the elements in an Array object.

Syntax *arrayObj*.reverse( )

arrayObj   Name of an array, or expression denoting an Array object.

Discussion   This method moves the first entry of an array to the last position and vice versa. Note that unlike most JavaScript methods, reverse( ) actually modifies the specified array; it does not return a copy.

Example   bigList.reverse( )

See Also   Array, join( ), sort( )

right

Version 1.2

Property of the clip object

Specifies the right clipping limit of a layer.

Syntax *layerObj*.clip.right

layerObj   document.*layerName*, or other expression denoting a Layer object.

Discussion   This property specifies the right clipping limit for a layer, in pixels. It is initially equal to the width of the layer. Decreasing its value causes columns of pixels at the right side of the layer to become invisible, allowing the lower layers or the enclosing document to be seen.

Example   To cause the right 64 columns of pixels in a layer to be clipped, use a statement such as:

```
document.layers.myLayer.clip.right -= 64
```

See Also   `bottom`, `height`, `left`, `top`, `width` (properties of `clip`); `Layer`

rightContext, $'

Version 1.2   Read-only

A property of the RegExp constructor

Returns the portion of a string after the most recent match.

Syntax   `RegExp.rightContext`

Discussion   This property's value is set when a regular expression match is performed by the `exec()`, `match()`, `replace()` (of `String`), or `test()` methods. `rightContext` returns a string containing characters from the string that was searched, from the point immediately after the match to the end of the string.

The symbol `$'` is an abbreviation for `rightContext`.

Note that this is a property of the `RegExp` constructor, not of objects created by new `RegExp()`. That means that it is shared by all scripts running in the same window or frame. If you have several scripts in one window that use regular expressions, they may affect each other's results.

Example   After executing statements such as:

```
str = "Smith,John"
pat = /,/
pat.exec(str)
```

`RegExp.rightContext` will return `"John"`.

See Also   `$1, $2 ... $9`, `leftContext`, `lastMatch`, `lastParen`, `RegExp`

round( )

Version 1.0

Method of the Math object

Returns the value rounded to the nearest integer.

Syntax
: `Math.round(value)`

    value   Numeric value or expression to be rounded.

Discussion
: The value is rounded to the nearest integer: if the value's fractional part is .5 or greater, it is rounded to the next higher integer. If the fractional part is less that .5, it is rounded to the next lower integer.

    Note that "lower" in this case means closer to zero. For instance, `Math.round(3.4)` returns 3, and `Math.round(-3.4)` returns -3.

    You can force rounding to the next greater (more positive) integer using `ceil()`, or to the next lower (more negative) integer using `floor()`.

Examples
: The statement:

    `alert(Math.round(15.49999))`

    displays 15 in an alert box, while:

    `alert(Math.round(15.50001))`

    displays 16.

See Also
: `floor()`, `ceil()`, `Math`

routeEvent( )

Version 1.2   Special scope

Method of the window, document, and Layer objects

Passes a captured event to any other event handlers that may receive it, and returns a value returned by the next handler.

Syntax   *obj*.routeEvent(*event*)

obj   Reference to a window, document, Frame, or Layer object.
event   An event object, or a copy of one.

Discussion   After an event is captured, this method can be used to pass it to other event handlers to which it would have been passed if capturing were not in effect. The event may then be passed to another handler that has enabled capturing for it, or to its original target.

routeEvent( ) returns whatever value is returned by the event handler to which the event is passed.

Note that the event object has limited scope: it can only be referenced in event handlers (see Chapter 7).

Example   An event handler that allows other handlers to receive an event may use a structure such as:

```
function myHandler(ev) {
    ...                         // process the event here
    rv = routeEvent(ev)         // pass it to other handlers
    return (rv)                 // return what they return
}
```

(This example assumes that the argument ev is an event object, or a copy of one.)

See Also   captureEvent( ), enableExternalCapture( ), event, handleEvent( ), releaseEvents( )

screen

Version 1.2 Read-only

Built-in object

Returns information about the display screen.

Syntax `screen`

symbol	Description
`availHeight`	The height of the screen, in pixels, not counting any permanent or semi-permanent features such as a taskbar.
`availWidth`	The width of the screen, in pixels, not counting any permanent or semi-permanent features such as a taskbar.
`colorDepth`	The maximum number of colors that can be displayed, based on hardware and/or operating system limits.
`height`	The height of the complete screen, in pixels.
`pixelDepth`	The number of bits per pixel in the display device.
`width`	The width of the complete screen, in pixels.

Properties (above)

Example This statement opens a new window whose height is almost equal to the entire screen and whose width is equal to half the screen:

```
ww = window.open("", "w1",
      "height=" + (screen.height - 40)
      + ",width=" + (screen.width / 2) )
```

screenX

S

Version 1.2 Special scope

Property of the event object

Returns the horizontal position, in pixels, measured from the left side of the display screen, where an event occurred.

Syntax *eventObj*`.screenX`

eventObj	`event`, or an expression denoting a copy of `event`, such as a function argument passed to an event handler.

Discussion Note that if the user can move browser windows around on the screen, the value of `screenX` may vary in a way that a script cannot predict. So this property should be used with care. The `pageX` or `layerX` properties may be more convenient, since they are measured from points within Navigator windows.

The `event` object has limited scope: it can only be referenced in event handlers.

Example To determine the screen location where an event occurred, use an event handler with statements such as:

```
function mouseClick(ev) {
    ...
    horiz = ev.screenX
    vert = ev.screenY
    ...
}
```

This example assumes that the function is called with an `event` object passed to the `ev` argument.

See Also event, layerX, pageX, screenY

screenY

Version 1.2 Special scope

Property of the event object

Returns the vertical position, in pixels, measured from the left side of the display screen, where an event occurred.

Syntax *eventObj*.screenY

  eventObj   event, or an expression denoting a copy of event, such as a function argument passed to an event handler.

Discussion Note that if the user can move browser windows around on the screen, the value of `screenY` may vary in a way that a script cannot predict. So this property should be used with care. The `pageY` or `layerY` properties may be more convenient, since they are measured from points within Navigator windows.

The `event` object has limited scope: it can only be referenced in event handlers.

| Example | To determine the screen location where an event occurred, use an event handler with statements such as:

```
function mouseClick(ev) {
    ...
    horiz = ev.screenX
    vert = ev.screenY
    ...
}
```

This example assumes that the function is called with an `event` object passed to the `ev` argument.

| See Also | event, layerY, pageY, screenX

scroll( )

Version 1.1

Method of the window object

Moves the document within the browser window to a specific position.

| Syntax | For the current window:

```
scroll(horizontalCoord, verticalCoord)
self.scroll(horizontalCoord, verticalCoord)
window.scroll(horizontalCoord, verticalCoord)
```

For other windows:

```
windowObj.scroll(horizontalCoord, verticalCoord)
```

windowObj	An expression denoting a `window` object.
horizontalCoord	The number of pixels to measure from the left side of the document; this point will be moved to the left border of the browser's display area.
verticalCoord	The number of pixels to measure from the top of the document; this point will be moved to the top of the browser's display area.

| Discussion | The specified position will be placed at the top-left corner of the browser's display area. The document is measured in pixels from the top left corner (point 0,0).

The `scroll( )` method is an earlier version of the JavaScript 1.2 `scrollTo( )` method. The `scroll( )` method remains for backward compatibility.

Example	This statement moves the document in the current window such that the point 1000 pixels down and 100 pixels to the right is placed in the top left corner of the browser's display area.

`self.scroll(100,1000)`

See Also	`scrollto( )`, `scrollBy( )`, `window`

scrollbars

Version 1.2   Signed scripts

Property of the `window` object

Specifies the state of the browser window's scrollbars.

Syntax	For the current window:

```
scrollbars
self.scrollbars
window.scrollbars
```

   For other windows:

`windowObj.scrollbars`

	windowObj	An expression denoting a `window` object.
Properties	`visible`	A Boolean property indicating whether the scroll bars are visible.
Discussion	Scroll bars are the bars at the bottom and right sides of a window that are used to scroll through the document. You can use this object's single property, `visible`, to find out whether the scroll bars are displayed or to change their status. If `visible` is true, the scroll bars are displayed.	
	Note that you can only use this property in a signed script with the `"UniversalBrowserRead"` or `"UniversalBrowserWrite"` privileges.	
Example	This statement hides the scrollbars in a window named `windowOne`:	

`windowOne.scrollbars.visible = 0`

See Also	`locationbar, menubar, personalbar, statusbar, toolbar, window`

scrollBy( )

Version 1.2

Method of the window object

Moves the document within the browser window.

Syntax   For the current window:
```
scrollBy(horizontal, vertical)
self.scrollBy(horizontal, vertical)
window.scrollBy(horizontal, vertical)
```
    For other windows:
```
windowObj.scrollBy(horizontal, vertical)
```
windowObj	An expression denoting a window object.
horizontal	The number of pixels to move the document horizontally.
vertical	The number of pixels to move the document vertically.

Discussion   This method is a "relative" scroll, as opposed to the "absolute" scrolling provided by scrollTo( ). The arguments specify the amount of movement, not the destination.

Example   This statement moves the document in the current window 50 pixels to the right, and 100 pixels down.
```
self.scrollBy(50,100)
```

See Also   scrollTo( ) window

scrollTo( )

Version 1.2

Method of the window object

Moves the document within the browser window to a specific position.

Syntax   For the current window:
```
scrollTo(horizontalCoord, verticalCoord)
self.scrollTo(horizontalCoord, verticalCoord)
window.scrollTo(horizontalCoord, verticalCoord)
```

For other windows:

`windowObj.scrollTo(horizontalCoord, verticalCoord)`

`windowObj`	An expression denoting a `window` object.
`horizontalCoord`	The number of pixels to measure from the left side of the document; this point will be moved to the left border of the browser's display area.
`verticalCoord`	The number of pixels to measure from the top of the document; this point will be moved to the top of the browser's display area.

Discussion The specified position will be placed at the top-left corner of the browser's display area. The document is measured in pixels, from the top left corner (point 0,0).

Example This statement moves the document in the current window such that the point 1000 pixels down and 100 pixels to the right is placed in the top left corner of the browser's display area.

`self.scrollBy(100,1000)`

See Also `scroll()`, `scrollTo()`, `window`

search

AREA, LINK

Version 1.0   Read-only   External

Property of the Area and Link external objects
(see also search property of the location object)

Reflects the query portion of a URL.

Syntax `docObject.links[index].search`

`docObject`	document for the current document, or an expression denoting any `document` object.
`index`	Number or string specifying an element of the `links` array.

Discussion This property reflects the query portion of the URL, if any. The query starts with a question mark (?) and continues to the end of the URL.

Version 1.1 In JavaScript 1.0, this property is only available for Link objects. It was added to Area objects in JavaScript 1.1.

Example For a link created by HTML such as:

```
<A HREF="http://searchEngine.com?name=Fred&ID=09876">
Request info for Fred 09876
</A>
```

the statement:

```
var lq = document.links[0].search
```

will set the variable lq to "?name=Fred&ID=09876". (The reference to links[0] assumes that this is the first link in the document.)

See Also Area, Link, links

search

LOCATION

Version 1.0 Tainted

Property of the location object
(see also search property of the Area and Link external objects)

Specifies the query information of a URL.

Syntax *locationObj*.search

locationObj location for the current window, or an expression denoting a location object in any window.

Discussion Modifying search causes the window to be reloaded using the new URL. Note, however, that it is considered safer to set the href property to ensure that the entire URL is correctly updated.

Queries are used in http:// URLs to request specific information. For instance:

```
http://guide-p.infoseek.com/Title/
    ?qt=iceland+hiking&col=WW&sv=N1&Search.x=45&Search.y=9
```

This is a query at the "infoseek" search site. In this case, the search property would contain everything from the ? to the end of the URL:

?qt=iceland+hiking&col=WW&sv=N1&Search.x=45&Search.y=9.

The query contains variable and value pairs, each pair separated by an ampersand.

If setting the search property using an event handler, you must specify window.location.search instead of simply using location.search. There are actually two location properties; window.location and document.location. Calling location without specifying the object is the equivalent of calling document.location, so to use the search property you must specifically call window.location.search. (Note that document.location is a synonym for document.URL.)

Example The following example sets the value of the search property, carrying out a search and loading a new page:

```
window.location.search =
    "?qt=ben+jerry&col=WW&sv=N1&Search.x=45&Search.y=9"
```

See Also hash, host, hostname, href, pathname, port, protocol, URL, location, links

search( )

Version 1.2

Method of the String object

Searches for a match to a regular expression in a specified string and returns the position of the first matching substring, or -1 if no match was found.

Syntax *stringObj*.search(*regexp*)

stringObj   String object or expression to be searched.
regexp   Regular expression to match.

Discussion This method is used to determine whether a string matches a particular regular expression. You may also use the RegExp methods test( ) and exec( ), or the String object's match( ) method, which provide different results.

Example The following function can look for a regular expression pat in the data provided by a form. The value returned by search( ) is placed into the result variable and then copied back to the form.

```
function matchIt(form) {
    txt = form.data.value
    pat = /is/
    result = txt.search(pat)
    form.results.value = result
}
```

See Also exec( ), match( ) test( ), RegExp, String

Select

Version 1.0   External

External object

Reflects a select box in an HTML form.

| Syntax | `docObject.formName.selectName` |
| | `docObject.formName.elements[index]` |

	docObject	`document` for the current document, or an expression denoting a `document` object in any window.
	formName	Name of a form assigned by the `NAME` attribute of the HTML `<FORM>` tag.
	selectName	Name of a select box assigned by the `NAME` attribute of the HTML `<SELECT>` tag.
	index	Number or string specifying an element of the `elements` array.

Properties	`form`	The form in which this select box is located.
	`length`	Number of options (length of the `options` array).
	`name`	Reflects the name assigned by the `NAME` attribute of the HTML `<SELECT>` tag.
	`options`	Array of `Option` objects reflecting the options in the select box.
	`selectedIndex`	Number of the currently selected option, or the first of several selected options, or -1 if none are selected.
	`type`	String containing `"select-multiple"` if multiple selections are allowed, and `"select"` otherwise.

Methods	`blur()`	Removes focus from the select box.
	`focus()`	Sets focus on the select box.

Event Handlers   `onblur`, `onchange`, `onfocus`

Discussion   When Navigator loads a web page, it creates Select objects corresponding to all select boxes in the document. You can reference these objects as elements of the form. Each Select object contains one or more `Option` objects corresponding to all options in the select box.

Version 1.1   Starting with JavaScript 1.1, scripts can add or remove options in a select box at any time. To add an option, create a new `Option` object with the `Option()` constructor function; to delete an option, set it to `null` (see Examples).

Examples   To find out what option is currently selected, use a statement such as:

```
choice = document.myForm.mySelect.selected
```

To add new options to a select box, use statements such as:

```
newOpt = new Option(label, value, defaultSel, sel)
l = document.myForm.mySelect.length
document.myForm.mySelect.options[l++] = newOpt
```

To remove an option, use a statement such as:

```
document.myForm.mySelect.options[n] = null
```

See Also   Form, Option

select( )

Version 1.0

Method of the Password, Text, and Textarea external objects

Selects (highlights) the text in a form input element.

Syntax   *docObject.formName.boxName*.select( )
docObject.formName.elements[*index*].select( )

docObject	document for the current document, or an expression denoting a document in any window.
formName	Name of a form assigned by the NAME attribute of the HTML <FORM> tag.
boxName	Name of a text box, password box, or text area, as assigned by the NAME attribute of the HTML <INPUT> or <TEXTAREA> tag.
index	Number or string specifying an element of the elements array.

Discussion   Selecting text helps the user to modify it, since any keypresses by the user will apply to that text. Selected text is highlighted on the screen, so the user can see that it is selected.

You may need to use the select( ) method in conjunction with the focus( ) method focus( ) will move the cursor to the box |:, then select( ) will select the text within the box. Used alone, select( ) will not work unless the focus is not already on the box.

Example
: These statements set focus on an element named `passOne`, in a form named `form1`, and then select the text within that box:

```
document.form1.passOne.focus()
document.form1.passOne.select()
```

See Also
: `blur()`, `focus()`, `elements`, `Password`, `Text`, `Textarea`

SELECT

Version 1.2   Read-only

Property of the Event object

Returns a mask for capturing select events.

Syntax
: `Event.SELECT`

Discussion
: This property is used to capture and release select events, which occur when the user selects text in a text box or text area of a form. For more details on event handling, see Chapter 7.

Example
: To enable capturing of select events (as well as change):

```
myWindow.captureEvents (Event.SELECT | Event.CHANGE)
```

See Also
: `captureEvents()`, `event`, `Event`, `onselect`, `releaseEvents()`

selected

Version 1.0   Tainted

Property of the Option object

Specifies whether an option in a selection box is selected; `true` if the option is selected, `false` if it is not.

Syntax
: `selectName.options[index].selected`
  `objectName.selected`

selectObj	`document.`*formName*`.`*selectName* or other expression denoting a Select object.
index	The index number of an option in the `options` array.
objectName	The name of an `Option` object created using `new Object()`.

Discussion   You can change the selection of objects in select boxes by changing an option's `selected` value; the display of the selection list changes immediately.

Selection boxes allow multiple options to be selected if the `<SELECT>` tag includes the `MULTIPLE` attribute. In this case, the `selected` property allows you to select or unselect any option in the list, without modifying the other options.

There is also a `selectedIndex` property, but this is mostly used for cases in which the `MULTIPLE` attribute is not present. If you select an option using `selectedIndex`, you automatically unselect all other options; and if more than one option is selected, `selectedIndex` only returns the first one.

Example   To cause an option to be selected, use a statement such as:

```
SelectList1.options[4].selected = true
```

Note that item 4 is actually the fifth item in the list, as the array starts with item 0.

See Also   `defaultSelected, index, selectedIndex, elements, options, Option, Select`

selectedIndex

Version 1.0   Tainted

A property of the Select object and the `options` array

Specifies which option in a selection box is selected.

Syntax   *selectObj*.selectedIndex
selectObj.options.selectedIndex

selectObj   `document.`*formName*`.`*selectName* or other expression denoting a Select object.

Discussion   This property returns -1 if none of the options in the list have been selected; otherwise, it returns an integer indicating which option has been selected, starting at 0 for the first option.

The selection list is updated immediately when you modify `selectedIndex`.

Selection boxes allow multiple options to be selected if the `<SELECT>` tag includes the `MULTIPLE` attribute. The `selectedIndex` property is mainly intended for select boxes without the `MULTIPLE` attribute. When you select an option, you will automatically deselect any other selected options. If multiple options are selected, this property returns the first (lowest-numbered) one.

There is also a `selected` property; this is mostly used for cases in which the `MULTIPLE` attribute is present, as it allows you to modify individual options without affecting others in the list.

Example To select an option, use a statement such as:

```
SelectList1.options.SelectedIndex = 4
```

Note that item 4 is actually the fifth item in the list, as the array starts with item 0.

See Also `defaultSelected`, `index`, `selected`, `elements`, `options`, `Select`

self

Version 1.0   Read-only

A property of the Frame and `window` objects

A way to refer to the current window or frame.

Syntax `self`

Discussion `self` is used to reference the current `window` or Frame object, and is synonymous with `window`.

Note, however, that it's usually unnecessary to use the `self` property, as the current window or frame is assumed if no window or frame is specified. Thus `document.write("comment")` is the same as `self.document.write("comment")`. However, you might need to use the `self` property to clarify a reference to the current window or frame when there is another object of the same name as the property or method you are using.

Example To read the URL of the document displayed in the current window, you can use a statement such as:

```
var sURL = self.location
```

Without the reference to `self`, the statement might not work correctly if there is an object named `location` in your script.

See Also `window`, Frame

setDate( )

Version 1.0

Method of the Date object

Sets the day of the month stored in a Date object.

Syntax dateObj.setDate(day)

    dateObj   Date object or expression.
    day   An integer value from one to 31 representing the day of the month.

Example To set the day of the month in a Date object to the 13th, use a statement such as:

importantDate.setDate(13)

See Also getDate( ), setHours( ), setMinutes( ), setMonth( ), setSeconds( ), setTime( ), setYear( ), Date

setHours( )

Version 1.0

Method of the Date object

Sets the hour of the day stored in a Date object.

Syntax dateObj.setHours(hours)

    dateObj   Date object or expression.
    hours   An integer from 0 to 23 representing the hour of the day.

Discussion Note that the hour is set according to "military" time, that is, using a 24 hour clock, with 0 representing midnight and 12 representing noon.

Example To set the hour in a Date object to 23 (11:00 PM), use a statement such as:

importantDate.setHours(23)

See Also getHours( ), setDate( ), setMinutes( ), setMonth( ), setSeconds( ), setTime( ), setYear( ) Date

setInterval( )

Version 1.2

Method of the Frame and `window` objects

Causes a script to be executed repeatedly at a specified time interval.

Syntax `ID = setInterval(function, msec, arg1, ... argn)`

`ID`	An identifier that can be used by the `clearInterval()` method to stop the script from repeating.
`function`	A string containing a JavaScript expression or function.
`msec`	A numeric value specifying the interval, in milliseconds, after which the script is run.
`arg1, ... argn`	Optional arguments to be passed to the function.

Discussion This method provides a way to execute a script repeatedly. The script repeats until the frame or window holding the script is closed, or until the `clearInterval()` method is used.

Note that the function or expression must be a string value.

If you wish to run a script once after a specified interval, use the `setTimeout()` method.

Example To have a function named `blink()` run every five seconds, use a statement such as:

```
blinkID = setInterval("blink()", 5000)
```

The value returned in `blinkID` can be used by `clearInterval()` to stop the function from repeating.

See Also `clearInterval()`, `setTimeout()`

setMinutes( )

Version 1.0

Method of the `Date` object

Sets the minutes after the hour stored in a `Date` object.

Syntax `dateObj.setMinutes(minutes)`

`dateObj`	Date object or expression.
`minutes`	An integer from 0 to 59 representing the minute of the hour.

Example To set the minute in a Date object to :03, use a statement such as:

importantDate.setMinutes(3)

See Also getMinutes( ), setDate( ), setHours( ), setMonth( ), setSeconds( ), setTime( ), setYear( ), Date

setMonth( )

Version 1.0

Method of the Date object

Sets the month stored in a Date object.

Syntax *dateObjectName*.setMonth(*month*)
dateObj   Date object or expression.
month   An integer from 0 to 11 representing the month.

Discussion The numbers are numbered from 0 (January) to 11 (December).

Example To set the month in a Date object to May, use a statement such as:

importantDate.setMonth(4)

Note that although May is the 5th month, the value 4 is used here, since month values start at zero.

See Also getMonth( ), setDate( ), setHours( ), setMinutes( ), setSeconds( ), setTime( ), setYear( ), Date

setSeconds( )

Version 1.0

Method of the Date object

Sets the seconds after the minute stored in a Date object.

Syntax *dateObj*.setSeconds(*seconds*)
dateObj   Date object or expression.
seconds   An integer from 0 to 59 representing the seconds past the minute.

Example
: To set the second in a Date object to :45, use a statement such as:

```
importantDate.setSeconds(45)
```

See Also
: getSeconds(), setDate(), setHours(), setMinutes(), setMonth(), setTime(), setYear(), Date

setTime( )

Version 1.0

Method of the Date object

Sets the time and date stored in a Date object.

Syntax
: `dateObj.setTime(time)`

  dateObj Date object or expression.
  time An integer, or a property of an existing object, representing the number of milliseconds since January 1, 1970, 00:00:00 GMT (universal time).

Discussion
: This is typically used to synchronize one object's date and time with another, in conjunction with the getTime( ) method.

Example
: This statement copies the date and time held by the Date object named importantDate to the Date object named anotherDate.

```
anotherDate.setTime(importantDate.getTime())
```

See Also
: getTime(), setDate(), setHours(), setMinutes(), setMonth(), setSeconds(), setYear(), Date

setTimeout( )

Version 1.2

Method of the Frame and window objects

Causes a script to be executed after a specified time delay.

Syntax
: `ID = setTimeout(function, msec, arg1, ... argn)`

  ID An identifier that can be used by the clearTimeout( ) method to stop the script from executing.

function	A string containing a JavaScript expression or function.
msec	A numeric value specifying the delay time, in milliseconds, after which the script is run.
arg1, ... argn	Optional arguments to be passed to the function.

Discussion This method provides a way to execute a script after a specified delay. The script only runs once; it will not repeat. If you wish to repeat a script, use the setInterval() method (JavaScript 1.2).

The setTimeout() method does not pause the script in which it is called. It schedules the specified future event, and the script that called setTimeout() continues immediately.

Example To schedule a function (LetsMove()) to run five seconds after a web page has loaded, write an HTML event handler such as:

```
<BODY onload="move = setTimeout('LetsMove()', 5000)">
```

The value returned in move can be used by clearTimeout() to stop the method from executing.

See Also clearTimeout(), setInterval()

setYear( )

Version 1.0

Method of the Date object

Sets the year stored in a Date object.

Syntax *dateObj*.setYear(*year*)

dateObj	Date object or expression.
year	An integer value representing the year.

Discussion If the specified *year* is out of the range that Date objects can accept, zero is used.

Note that getYear() truncates years from 1900 to 1999 to the lower two digits; thus getYear() may not return the value specified by setYear(), even though the internal form of the date is correct.

Example To set the year in a Date object, use a statement such as:

```
importantDate.setYear(1999)
```

See Also getYear(), setDate(), setHours(), setMinutes(), setMonth(), setSeconds(), setTime(), Date

SHIFT-MASK

Version 1.2   Read-only

Property of the Event object

Returns a mask for checking if the Shift key was pressed during an event.

Syntax   `Event.SHIFT_MASK`

Discussion   This property is a bit mask for testing the `event.modifiers` property to find out if the Shift key was pressed when the event occurred.

Example   The following statements could be used in an event handler.

```
if (myEvent.modifiers & Event.SHIFT_MASK) {
    ...     // the Shift key was pressed
}
else
    ...     // Shift was not pressed
```

See Also   `ALT_MASK, CONTROL_MASK, META_MASK, Event`

siblingAbove

Version 1.2   Read-only

Property of the Layer object

Returns the sibling layer immediately above the specified layer in the z-order.

Syntax   `layerObj.siblingAbove`

layerObj   `document.layers.layerName`, or an expression denoting a Layer object.

Event Handlers   Since `siblingAbove` returns a reference to a `Layer` object, it has all the properties, methods, and event handlers of the referenced layer.

Discussion   This property returns the sibling layer that is immediately above the specified one in the z-index order. The z-index order is used to position layers, and is initially set by the Z-INDEX attribute of the <LAYER> tag. A low number indicates a low position in the order; in an area where two layers overlap, the one with the higher z-index is displayed.

If the Layer object has no sibling layer above it in the z-index order, the property returns null. Note that this property only applies to siblings; the above property can be used to access parent and child layers.

This is a read-only property. To modify the z-index ordering of layers, use the zIndex property, or the moveAbove() or moveBelow() methods.

Example
The following statements check to see whether the layer named smallLayer is positioned immediately above the current layer, and call a function according to the result:

```
if(bigLayer.siblingAbove.name == "smallLayer") {
  moveLeft()
}
else {
  moveRight()
}
```

See Also
above, below, Layer, moveAbove(), moveBelow(), siblingBelow, zIndex

siblingBelow

Version 1.2　Read-only

Property of the Layer object

Returns the sibling layer immediately below the specified layer in the z-order.

Syntax
layerObj.siblingBelow

layerObj　　　document.layers.*layerName*, or an expression denoting a Layer object.

Properties
Since siblingBelow returns a reference to a Layer object, it has all the properties, methods, and event handlers of the referenced layer.

Discussion
This property returns the sibling layer that is immediately below the current one in the z-index order. The z-index order is used to position layers, and is initially set by the Z-INDEX attribute of the <LAYER> tag. A low number indicates a low position in the order; in an area where two layers overlap, the one with the higher z-index is displayed.

If the Layer object has no sibling layer below it in the z-index order, the property returns null. Note that this property only applies to siblings; the below property can be used to access parent and child layers.

This is a read-only property. To modify the z-index ordering of layers, use the zIndex property, or the moveAbove() or moveBelow() methods.

Example The following statements check to see whether the layer named `smallLayer` is positioned immediately below the current layer, and call a function according to the result:

```
if(bigLayer.siblingBelow.name == "smallLayer") {
   moveLeft()
}
else {
   moveRight()
}
```

See Also `above`, `below`, `Layer`, `moveAbove()`, `moveBelow()`, `siblingAbove`, `zIndex`

sin( )

Version 1.0

Method of the Math object

Returns the sine of a number.

Syntax `Math.sin(number)`
number   A number representing the size of an angle in radians.

Discussion `sin` returns a number between -1 and 1.

Example `y = Math.sin(theta)`

See Also `acos()`, `asin()`, `atan()`, `atan2()`, `cos()`, `tan()`, `Math`

slice( )

ARRAY

Version 1.2

Method of the Array object
(See also `slice()` as a method of the String object)

Copies part of an `Array` object and creates a new array containing that information.

slice( )

Syntax `newArray = arrayObj.slice(begin, end)`

newarray	The name of the new `Array` object being created by copying from *arrayObj*.
ArrayObj	Array object from which the information is being copied.
begin	Number specifying the first element to copy.
end	Optional number that specifies the last element to copy (see Discussion). If omitted, copying continues to the end of the array.

Discussion Note that array indexes are zero-based. So, for instance, if you specify `arrayName.slice(9)` you will begin copying at the tenth element.

The *end* argument, if present, may be positive or negative:

- If positive, it specifies the (index + 1) of the last element to copy.
- If negative, it specifies how many elements at the end of the array *not* to copy.
- If it is not specified, `slice` copies to the end of the array.

Since the new array is a copy, the original array remains unchanged, and adding new elements to either array does not affect the other. However, JavaScript copies objects by reference; so if any of the copied elements are objects, modifying their values in either array will affect the other. Strings, numbers, and other primitive values are copied by value, not by reference; so modifying a string or number in one array will not affect the other.

Example After executing these statements:

```
var myArray = new Array("A", "B", "C", "D", "E", "F", "G")

a01 = myArray.slice(0, 1)
a03 = myArray.slice(0, 3)
a3 = myArray.slice(3)
a2m1 = myArray.slice(2, -1)
a2m2 = myArray.slice(2, -2)
```

a01 contains a single element with value "A".
a03 contains three elements "A", "B", and "C".
a3 contains four elements "D", "E", "F", and "G".
a2m1 contains four elements "C", "D", "E", and "F".
a2m2 contains three elements "C", "D", and "E".

See Also `concat( )`, `join( )`, Array

slice( )

STRING

Version 1.2

Method of the String object
(See also slice( ) as a method of the Array object)

Copies part of a string and returns a new string containing the copied text.

Syntax
newString = *stringObj*.slice(*begin*, *end*)

newString	The new string being created by copying text from the *stringObj* string.
stringObj	The string from which the text is copied.
begin	Number specifying the first character to copy.
end	Optional number that specifies the last character to copy (see Discussion). If omitted, copying continues to the end of the string.

Discussion
Note that string indexes are zero-based. So, for instance, if you specify *stringName*.slice(9) you will begin copying at the tenth character.

The *end* argument, if present, may be positive or negative:

- If positive, it specifies the (index + 1) of the last character to copy.
- If negative, it specifies how many character at the end of the string *not* to copy.
- If it is not specified, slice copies to the end of the string.

Since the new string is a copy, the original string remains unchanged.

Example
After executing these statements:

```
var myString = "ABCDEFG"

s01 = myString.slice(0, 1)
s03 = myString.slice(0, 3)
s3 = myString.slice(3)
s2m1 = myString.slice(2, -1)
s2m2 = myString.slice(2, -2)
```

s01 contains "A".
s03 contains "ABC".
s3 contains "DEFG".
s2m1 contains "CDEF".
s2m2 contains "CDE".

See Also
concat( ), split( ), substr( ), substring( ), String

small( )

Version 1.0

Method of the String object

Returns a string containing HTML code to format the string in small characters.

Syntax *stringObj*.small()

   stringObj   String object or expression to be formatted in small characters.

Discussion This method returns a string consisting of HTML code. The code includes the HTML <SMALL> and </SMALL> tags so that, if the returned string is written to a document using the `write` or `writeln` properties, it will appear in a smaller size.

Example The statement:

document.write("And now for the ", "fine print.".small())

will write to the web page:

> And now for the fine print.

See Also big( ), blink( ), bold( ), fixed( ), fontcolor( ), fontsize( ), italics( ), split( ), strike( ), sub( ), sup( ), String

sort( )

Version 1.1

Method of the Array object

Sorts elements of an Array object according to a specified function or in dictionary order.

Syntax *arrayObj*.sort(*function*)

   arrayObj   Name of the array or expression denoting an Array object.
   sortFunction An optional function used to define the sort order. (Do not put parentheses after the function name.)

Discussion   If you don't specify a function to define the sort order, the elements are sorted "lexicographically," that is, according to dictionary order, not numerical order (see Examples). The elements are converted to strings to determine their correct order.

To sort the array in another way, you can define the order by creating a function that compares two elements and returns a value specifying which is greater. Specifically, the function should accept two arguments and return a numeric value that is:

- Less than zero if the first argument is "less" than the second by whatever criterion you choose.
- Zero if the two arguments are "equal."
- Greater than zero if the first argument is "greater" than the second.

Note that the *function* argument must be a reference, not an actual call to the function. Generally, you just write the name of the function, without any arguments or parentheses.

One common use of a comparing function is to sort the array by numerical, rather than lexicographic, order. This requires the function to convert the arguments to numbers and then compare them, but a simple shortcut is to perform the conversion and comparison by simply subtracting the values, as in:

```
function compareNumbers(a, b) {
   return a - b
}
```

Sorting by a user-specified function can also be useful if you need to modify the lexicographic order, perhaps to make uppercase and lowercase letters equivalent or if the array contains user-defined objects that must be compared by examining certain properties.

JavaScript uses a *stable* sort: if two elements *a* and *b* have equal value, and *a* is at a lower-numbered position than *b* before the sort, it will still be at a lower-numbered position after the sort.

Version 1.2   While `sort()` works for all JavaScript 1.2 browsers, it does not function for all browsers in earlier versions of JavaScript. In JavaScript 1.1, `sort()` converts undefined array elements to `null`. In JavaScript 1.2, `sort()` does not change the value of undefined elements, and it sorts them to the high end of the array.

Examples For an array such as:

```
var myArray = new Array("10", "2", "2001", "1", "9")
```

the statement:

```
myArray.sort()
```

results in the elements being placed in lexicographic order:

`"1" "10" "2" "2001" "9"`

Sorting it with the preceding numerical comparison function shown:

```
myArray.sort(compareNumbers)
```

results in numerical ordering:

`"1" "2" "9" "10" "2001"`

See Also `join()`, `reverse()`, `Array`

source

Version 1.2

Property of the RegExp object

Returns a copy of the text of the regular expression.

Syntax *reObj*.source

reObj   Regular expression object constructed by `new RegExp()`.

Discussion This property returns a string containing the text of the regular expression. The beginning and ending slashes, and any modifiers specified after the ending slash, are not included in the string.

Example For the regular expression variable declared by:

```
var rex = /(\w+)@\w+.com/
```

the expression `rex.source` returns the string `"(\w+)@\w+.com"`.

See Also `RegExp`

split( )

Version 1.1

Method of the String object

Converts a string object into an array of substrings.

Syntax `arrayObj = stringObj.split(separator, limit)`

  `arrayObj`   Name of an object to accept the resulting array.
  `stringObj`   A string value or expression.
  `separator`   An optional string or regular expression that specifies the boundary between substrings. If the separator is omitted, `split()` will return an array with a single element containing the entire string.
  `limit`   An optional numeric value that specifies a limit on the number of Array elements that may be returned.

Discussion The `split()` method returns an array formed by scanning a string and finding substrings divided by the specified separator. The original string remains unchanged. Characters corresponding to the separator are removed, not copied to any array elements. If a limit value is specified, the length of the returned array will not exceed the limit; if the string contains more than this number of substrings, the additional ones will not be returned.

Version 1.2 A number of important changes were added in JavaScript 1.2. The use of a regular expression as a separator, and the limit argument, are not supported in Version 1.1.

Also in JavaScript 1.2, if you use the `LANGUAGE="JavaScript1.2"` attribute in the `<SCRIPT>` tag, then a separator string containing a single space (`" "`) allows `sort()` to regard any group of spaces, tabs, line feeds, and carriage returns as a single separator.

Example The string:

```
var s = "A,-B,,-CD"
```

can be divided in the following ways:

  `s.split(",")`   returns four elements: "A" "-B" (empty string) "-CD"
  `s.split("-B")`   returns two elements: "A," ",,-CD"
  `s.split(/-[A-Z]/)`   returns three elements: "A," "," " D"

See Also `charAt()`, `indexOf()`, `lastIndexOf()`, `Array`, `String`

sqrt( )

Version 1.0

Method of the Math object

Returns the square root of a number.

Syntax Math.sqrt(*number*)

number A positive numeric value or expression.

Discussion If the number is a negative number, Math.sqrt() returns -NaN or 0, depending on the JavaScript version and operating system.

Version 1.1 Starting with JavaScript 1.1, NaN works in all of the Netscape Navigator versions; in JavaScript 1.0, NaN could only be returned on the UNIX browsers.

Example SquareRoot = Math.sqrt(bigNumber)

See Also SQRT1_2, SQRT2, Math

SQRT1_2

Version 1.0   Read-only

Property of the Math object

Returns the square root of one-half; one over the square root of two; one-half the square root of two (0.7071067811865476...).

Syntax Math.SQRT1_2

Example document.write(Math.SQRT1_2)

See Also E, LN2, LN10, LOG2E, LOG2E, PI, SQRT2, Math

SQRT2

Version 1.0   Read-only

Property of the Math object

Returns the square root of 2 (1.4142135623730951...).

Syntax   `Math.SQRT2`

Example   `document.write(Math.SQRT2)`

See Also   E, LN2, LN10, LOG2E, LOG2E, PI, SQRT1_2 , Math

src

IMAGE

Version 1.1

Property of the Image object
(See also src as a property of the Layer object)

Specifies the URL of the image file.

Syntax   `documentObj.imageName.src`
`documentObj.images[index].src`

- `documentObj` — document for the current document, or an expression denoting any document object.
- `imageName` — The name of the Image object, as specified by the HTML SRC attribute.
- `index` — A numeric value specifying an element in the images array, or a string value specifying the name of the Image object.

Discussion   When Navigator loads a web page, it creates Image objects whose src property is initially set by the SRC attribute of the <IMG> tags. Scripts can modify this property at any time to load another image. The effect is immediate; if another image, such as the LOWSRC image, is loading when you set the src property, loading is aborted and the specified src image is loaded. The image loaded by src will be scaled to fit the size of the original image if necessary.

An Image object can also be created using the new Image() constructor; in this case, of course, there is no SRC attribute. You must set the src property in order to load an image.

Example
The following example displays an animated eye that blinks when the mouse cursor moves over it. The script creates three Image objects, and loads a .GIF file into each object by modifying the src properties. The function blink() rapidly copies each image to the eye object, which is created by an <IMG> tag.

```
var eye1 = new Image()
eye1.src = "eye-open.gif"

var eye2 = new Image()
eye2.src = "eye-half.gif"

var eye3 = new Image()
eye3.src = "eye-clos.gif"

function blink() {
   document.eye.src = eye2.src
   setTimeout("document.eye.src = eye3.src", 100)
   setTimeout("document.eye.src = eye2.src", 200)
   setTimeout("document.eye.src = eye1.src", 300)
}
<A HREF="javascript:void(null)" onmouseover="blink()">
<IMG name="eye" src="eye-open.gif"> </A>
```

See Also   complete, lowsrc, Image, images

src
LAYER

Version 1.2

Property of the Layer object
(See also src as a property of the Image object)

Specifies the URL of the document in the layer.

Syntax   *documentObj.layerName*.src
         documentObj.layers[*index*].src

documentObj	document for the current document, or an expression denoting any document object.
layerName	The name of the Layer object, as specified by the HTML SRC attribute.
index	A numeric value specifying an element in the layers array, or a string value specifying the name of the Layer object.

Discussion | When Navigator loads a web page, it creates `Layer` objects whose `src` property is initially set by the SRC attribute of the <LAYER> tags. Scripts can modify this property at any time to load another document.

A `Layer` object can also be created using the `new Layer()` constructor; in this case, of course, there is no SRC attribute. You can set the `src` property in order to load an image.

Example | The following example creates a button that the user can click to display a different document (`scoreprev.htm`) in the layer named `scoresLayer`.

```
<FORM>
Click here to see last week's scores:<P>
<INPUT TYPE="button" VALUE="Last Week's Scores"
   ONCLICK="scoresLayer.src ='scoreprev.htm'">
</FORM>
```

See Also | `bgColor`, `name`, `Layer`, `layers`

status

Version 1.0   Tainted

Property of the `window` object

A temporary message displayed in the browser's status bar.

Syntax | *windowObj*.status

windowObj — Any valid way of referring to a window, a window name, `self`, `window`, `top`, `parent`, or an expression denoting any `window` object.

Discussion | This property is often used to display a temporary message in the status bar when the user points at a link. To do this, the `onmouseover` event handler is used; the event handler must return `true` for this to function.

Note that there's also a `defaultStatus` property; use this to display a message in the status bar that will remain until changed. The status message is only temporary, displayed during the event. For instance, if you set up a button to set status, the message is only displayed as long as the mouse pointer is over the button.

Example In the following example, the message "Click here to see more information" appears in the status bar.

```
<A HREF="next.htm" onmouseover="self.status='Click here to see more
    information'; return true">More Info.</A>
```

Note the `return true` statement, which is required at the end of an `onmouseover` event handler to set `status`.

See Also defaultStatus, window, statusbar

statusbar

Version 1.2   Signed scripts

Property of the window object

Specifies the state of the browser window's status bar: the bar at the bottom of the window that displays status messages.

Syntax For the current window:

statusbar
self.statusbar
window.statusbar

For other windows:

windowObj.statusbar

windowObj   An expression denoting a `window` object.

Properties visible   A Boolean property indicating whether the status bar is visible.

Discussion You can use this object's single property, `visible`, to find out whether the status bar is displayed or to change its status. If `visible` is true, the status bar is displayed.

Note that you can only use this property in a signed script with the "UniversalBrowserRead" or "UniversalBrowserWrite" privileges.

Example To hide a window's status bar, use a statement such as:

windowOne.statusbar.visible = 0

See Also locationbar, menubar, personalbar, scrollbars, toolbar, window

stop( )

Version 1.2

Method of the `window` object

Stops the current download, equivalent to the user clicking Navigator's Stop button or pressing the Esc key.

Syntax
: `windowObj.stop( )`

  `windowObj`   Any valid way of referring to a window, a window name, `self`, `window`, `top`, `parent`, or an expression denoting any `window` object.

Example
: `windowTwo.stop( )`

See Also
: `window`

strike( )

Version 1.0

Method of the `String` object

Returns a string containing HTML code to format the string in over-struck characters.

Syntax
: `stringObj.strike( )`

  `stringObj`   String object or expression to be formatted.

Discussion
: This method returns a string consisting of HTML code. The code includes the HTML `<STRIKE>` and `</STRIKE>` tags so that, if the returned string is written to a document using the `write` or `writeln` methods, it will appear in a strike-through font.

Example   The statement:

```
document.write("Please remove the following: ", "this text.".strike())
```

will write to the web page:

> Please remove the following: ~~this text.~~

See Also   big(), blink(), bold(), fixed(), fontcolor(), fontsize(), italics(), small(), sub(), sup(), String

String

Version 1.0

Object type (constructor)

Creates a new String object, or converts a value to a string.

Syntax   `var = new String(value)`
    var   Variable or object to which the new object is assigned.
    value   Initial value for the object.

Properties   `length`   Returns the number of characters in the string.

Methods
`anchor()`	Returns a string with HTML tags to format the string as an anchor.
`big()`	Returns a string with HTML tags to format the string as large characters.
`blink()`	Returns a string with HTML tags to format the string as blinking characters.
`bold()`	Returns a string with HTML tags to format the string as bold characters.
`charAt(index)`	Returns string containing a single character from the specified position.
`charCodeAt(index)`	Returns a numeric value representing a single character from the specified position.

concat(*str*)	Returns a string containing two strings concatenated.
fixed()	Returns a string with HTML tags to format the string as fixed-width characters.
fontcolor()	Returns a string with HTML tags to format the string in the specified color.
fontsize()	Returns a string with HTML tags to format the string in the specified size.
String.fromCharCode (*num1*, *num2*, ...)	Returns a string constructed by converting the specified numeric values to characters. Note that this is a method of String itself, not of objects constructed by it.
indexOf(*target*, *start*)	Searches a string, and returns a number indicating the first position (or the first position past a specified starting point) at which the target string is found.
italics()	Returns a string with HTML tags to format the string as italicized characters.
lastIndexOf (*target*, *start*)	Searches a string in reverse order (from the last character to the first), and returns a number indicating the "first" (going backwards) position (or the first position past a specified starting point) at which the target string is found.
link(*URL*)	Returns a string formatted as a hypertext link.
match(*regexp*)	Searches a string for matches to the specified regular expression; returns several types of results.
replace(*regexp*, *newStr*)	Searches a string for matches to the specified regular expression, and returns a string in which the matches are replaced with the specified substitute.
search(*regexp*)	Searches for a match to the specified regular expression, and returns the position of the first matching substring, or -1 if no match was found.
slice(*begin*, *end*)	Returns a string containing a copy of a specified section of a larger string.
small()	Returns a string with HTML tags to format the string as small characters.
split(*separator*, *limit*)	Returns an array containing substrings found by dividing a string at each occurrence of the specified separator, up to a specified maximum number.
strike()	Returns a string with HTML tags to format the string as over-struck characters.
sub()	Returns a string with HTML tags to format the string as subscript characters.

substr(*begin, length*)	Returns a string containing a copy of a specified section of a larger string.
substring(*from, to*)	Returns a string containing a copy of a specified section of a larger string.
sup()	Returns a string with HTML tags to format the string as superscript characters.
toLowerCase()	Returns a string with all uppercase letters converted to lowercase.
toUpperCase()	Returns a string with all lowercase letters converted to uppercase.

Discussion Although strings can be created by the String() constructor, JavaScript automatically creates strings in response to assignment statements, so that

```
s = new String("Hello")
```

is equivalent to

```
s = "Hello"
```

In fact, the String() constructor was not available in JavaScript 1.0, so all strings had to be created by assignments.

Used without new, String() is a type-conversion function that returns the string equivalent of its argument (see Example).

JavaScript strings are *immutable*: once created, they cannot be modified. To modify a string variable, you must actually do some operation that creates a copy with the desired changes and then assign the new string to the variable.

Note that some early versions of Navigator had problems handling strings longer than 255 characters. Additional version dependencies are listed subsequently.

Version 1.1 JavaScript 1.1 added String() as a constructor and type-conversion function, the split() method, and the ability to pass strings between scripts in different windows.

Version 1.2 JavaScript 1.2 added the charCodeAt(), concat(), fromCharCode(), match(), replace(), search(), slice(), and substr() methods; added new features to split(); and changed the behavior of substring().

Example To create strings:

```
string1 = "supercalifragilistic"
string2 = new String("expialidocious")
longString = string1.concat(string2)
```

To convert a numeric value to a string:

```
str = String(someNumber)
```

sub( )

Version 1.0

Method of the String object

Returns a string containing HTML code to format the string in subscript characters.

Syntax *stringObj*.sub( )

stringObj String object or expression to be formatted in subscript characters.

Discussion This method returns a string consisting of HTML code. The code includes the HTML _{and} tags so that, if the returned string is written to a document using the write or writeln properties, it will appear in a subscript font.

Example The statement

document.write("Our new company name!: CMI", "3".sub())

will write to the web page:

> Our new company name!: CMI₃

See Also big( ), blink( ), bold( ), fixed( ), fontcolor( ), fontsize( ), italics( ), small( ), strike( ), sup( ), String

submit( )

Version 1.0

Method of the Form external object

Submits a form, equivalent to the user clicking a Submit button.

Syntax *formObj*.submit( )

formObj document.*formName*, or an expression denoting a Form object in any document.

Discussion   The manner in which the form is submitted is specified by the form's `method` and `action` properties, which reflect the METHOD and ACTION attributes of the HTML <FORM> tag.

For security reasons, `submit()` does not work if the `action` property specifies an URL that begins with `news:`, `snews`, or `mailto:`. The form submission may work correctly if the user clicks the Submit button.

Example   To submit a form, use a statement such as:

```
document.OrderForm.submit()
```

You can also use `submit()` by specifying an index number in the `forms` array:

```
document.forms[1].submit()
```

See Also   `action`, `method`, `target`, `reset()`, `forms`, `onsubmit`, `Form`, `Submit`

Submit

Version 1.0 External

Property of the Form external object

Reflects a submit button in an HTML form.

Syntax   *formObj.submitName*
formObj["*submitName*"]
formObj.elements[*index*]

formObj	`document.`*formName*, or an expression denoting a Form object in any document.
submitName	Name specified in the NAME attribute of the HTML <INPUT> tag.
index	Number specifying the position of the Submit button in the form.

Properties

`form`	The Form object that contains this object.
`name`	Reflects the NAME attribute of the HTML <INPUT> tag.
`type`	Reflects the TYPE attribute of the HTML <INPUT> tag (this is always "submit" for Submit objects).
`value`	A string specifying the text that appears in the button on the screen.

Methods	`blur()`	Removes focus from the Submit button.
	`click()`	Simulates a mouse click on the button.
	`focus()`	Sets focus on the Submit button.
Event Handlers	`onblur, onclick, onfocus`	

Discussion When Navigator loads a web page, it creates Submit objects corresponding to all submit buttons in the document. You can reference these objects as properties of the form, or as elements in the form's `elements` array.

Version 1.1   The `type` property, `blur()` and `focus()` methods, and `onBlur` and `onFocus` event handlers were added in JavaScript 1.1.

Example To change the text label on a submit button, use a statement such as:

`document.myForm.mySumit.value = "Click here to send"`

See Also Form, `submit()`

SUBMIT

Version 1.2   Read-only

Property of the Event object

Returns a mask for capturing form submit events.

Syntax `Event.SUBMIT`

Discussion This property is used to capture and release submit events, which occur when the user submits a form. For more details on event handling, see Chapter 7.

Example To enable capturing of submit events (as well as reset):

`myWindow.captureEvents (Event.SUBMIT | Event.RESET)`

See Also `captureEvents()`, event, Event, onsubmit, `releaseEvents()`

substr( )

Version 1.2

Method of the String object

Returns a substring of a specified position and length.

Syntax   `newString = stringObj.substr(begin, length)`

newString   The new string being created by copying text from the *stringObj* string.
stringObj   The string from which the text is copied.
begin   Number specifying the first character to copy.
length   Optional number that specifies the length of the substring. If omitted, the substring continues to the end of the string. If zero or negative, `substr()` returns an empty string.

Discussion   Note that string indexes are zero-based. So, for instance, if you specify *stringName*.`substr(9)` you will begin copying at the tenth character.
Since the new string is a copy, the original string remains unchanged.

Example   The statements:

```
s = "something"
t = s.substr(4, 4)
```

set the variable t to "thin".

See Also   `slice()` (method of String), String, `substring()`

substring( )

Version 1.0   Version 1.2

Method of the String object

Returns a specified substring of a string.

Syntax   `newString = stringObj.substring(N1, N2)`

newString   The new string being created by copying text from the *stringObj* string.
stringObj   The string from which the text is copied.
N1   Number specifying the first character to copy (see Discussion).
N2   Optional number that specifies the last character to copy (see Discussion).

Discussion

Note that string indexes are zero-based. So, for instance, if you specify `stringName.substring(9)` you will begin copying at the tenth character. Since the new string is a copy, the original string remains unchanged.

The behavior of `substring()` is controlled by the indexes *N1* and *N2* in the following ways:

- If *N1* is less than zero, `substring()` uses zero instead of the actual value.
- If *N2* is greater than `stringObj.length`, `substring()` uses `stringObj.length` instead of the actual value.
- If *N2* is omitted, `substring()` returns characters from *N1* to the end of the string.
- If *N1* is less than *N2*, `substring()` returns characters *N1* to (*N2* - 1).
- If *N1* and *N2* are equal, `substring()` returns an empty string.
- If *N1* is greater than *N2*, their functions are reversed; that is, `substring()` returns characters from *N2* to (*N1* - 1), except in JavaScript 1.2 scripts (see the following).

Version 1.2

In JavaScript 1.2, if the `<SCRIPT>` tag includes the `NAME="Javascript1.2"` attribute, and then if *N1* is greater than *N2*, `substring()` generates an "Out of Memory" error.

Example

The statements:

```
s = "JavaScript"
t = s.substring(0, 3)
```

will set t to contain "Java".

See Also

`slice()` (method of String), String, `substr()`

suffixes

Version 1.1   Read-only

Property of the MimeType object

Returns a string listing file name suffixes (also called extensions) that Navigator recognizes as data for a MIME type.

Syntax   `navigator.mimeTypes[index].suffixes`

index   A string identifying a MIME type, such as `"text/plain"` or `"audio/midi"`.

Discussion   Suffixes are short strings, usually three or four characters, that identify the type of data in a file. Each MimeType object's suffixes property lists any suffixes known to contain data of that type.

Example   On a typical Windows 95 installation, these statements

```
document.write("Text: ", navigator.mimeTypes["text/plain"].suffixes,
   "<BR>")
document.write("HTML: ", navigator.mimeTypes["text/html"].suffixes,
   "<BR>")
```

will display:

```
Text: txt, text, htm
HTML: html, htm
```

See Also   MimeType, mimeTypes

sun

Version 1.0

Java package

This package provides debugging tools. For more details, consult Java documentation. For a description of JavaScript's interface to Java, see Chapter 8.

sup( )

Version 1.0

Method of the String object

Returns a string containing HTML code to format the string in superscript characters.

Syntax   *stringObj*.sup( )

stringObj   String object or expression to be formatted as a superscript.

Discussion This method returns a string consisting of HTML code. The code includes the HTML ^{and} tags so that, if it is written to a document using the write() or writeln() methods, it will appear in a superscript font.

Example The statement:

document.write("Our new company name!: ABC", "4".sup())

will write to the web page:

> Our new company name!: ABC[4]

See Also big(), blink(), bold(), fixed(), fontcolor(), fontsize(), italics(), small(), strike(), sub(), String

switch

Version 1.2

Keyword used in statements

This keyword is used to create multi-way branch structures. For details, see Chapter 4.

tags

Version 1.2 External

Property of the document object

Specifies style sheet properties for HTML tags.

Syntax   *docObject*.tags.*tagName*

     docObject   `document` for the current document, or an expression denoting a document in any window.

     tagName   Name of an HTML tag.

Properties   `tags` may have a property corresponding to each HTML tag for which style properties are assigned. The name of each property is the same as the tag, such as H1, P, and so forth. Note that, unlike most JavaScript identifiers, uppercase and lowercase are equivalent for these property names; that is, `document.tags.H1` is equivalent to `document.tags.h1`.

Each property of `tags` will itself have properties, which specify the actual styles applied to the tag. The available properties are summarized next:

Font Properties	`fontFamily`	Font name: actual or generic.
	`fontSize`	Number or keyword specifying text size.
	`fontStyle`	Keyword specifying italics and/or small capitals.
	`fontWeight`	Number or keyword specifying text "boldness."
Text Properties	`lineHeight`	Number or expression specifying line spacing.
	`textAlign`	Keyword specifying horizontal position of text.
	`textDecoration`	Keyword specifying underline, overline, overstrike, or blink.
	`textIndent`	Number or expression specifying indentation for the first line of a paragraph.
	`textTransform`	Keyword specifying capitalization.
	`verticalAlign`	Keyword specifying vertical position of text.
Block-level Properties	`align`	Keyword specifying horizontal position (floating) of HTML object.
	`borderBottomWidth,` `borderLeftWidth,` `borderRightWidth,` `borderTopWidth`	Number specifying the width of the border.
	`borderColor`	Keyword specifying color of border.
	`borderStyle`	Keyword specifying style of border.

	`clear`	Keyword specifying whether floating objects may be positioned alongside this object.
	`height`	Number or keyword specifying the height of the HTML object.
	`marginBottom,` `marginLeft,` `marginRight,` `marginTop`	Number or expression specifying the spacing between HTML objects.
	`paddingBottom,` `paddingLeft,` `paddingRight,` `paddingTop`	Number or expression specifying the spacing between HTML object content and border.
	`width`	Number, expression, or keyword specifying the width of the HTML object.
Color & Background Properties	`color`	String specifying text color.
	`backgroundImage`	String specifying URL of image file.
	`backgroundColor`	String specifying background color.
Classification Properties	`display`	Keyword specifying how object is displayed.
	`listStyleType`	Keyword specifying how objects are marked or numbered.
	`whiteSpace`	Keyword specifying handling of white space characters.

Methods Note that `tags` itself has no methods. These methods are actually used on the properties of `tags`, that is, the specific styles associated with an HTML tag.

`borderWidths()`	Sets the four border width properties for the style.
`margins()`	Sets the four margin properties for the style.
`paddings()`	Sets the four padding width properties for the style.

Discussion This property serves as a "holder" for any style sheet properties that have been assigned to HTML tags in the document. It may be used in scripts or in style sheets. When it is used in style sheets, you can write `tags` instead of `document.tags`, since all style sheet statements are evaluated in the context of `document`.

To apply a style sheet property to all HTML tags, assign it to `document.tags.body` (see second Example).

Note that for `tags` property assignments to take effect, they must occur before the browser writes the styled text to the web page. Assignments to properties of `tags.body` must be done within the `<HEAD>` ... `</HEAD>` section of the HTML.

Examples To cause all <H3> headings to be italicized:

document.tags.H3.fontStyle = "italic"

To cause all text to be blue:

document.tags.body.color = "blue"

See Also classes, ids

taint( )

Version 1.1

Built-in function

Adds data tainting to a script or object.

Syntax taint(*obj*)

obj   Optional name or expression denoting a property, variable, function, or object to taint. If omitted, will taint the script itself.

Discussion Starting with Version 2.02, Navigator restricted scripts from (passing private information—such as session histories and directory structures—to different servers. In Navigator 3, though, a feature called data tainting was introduced. When tainting is enabled, if a script attempts to transfer tainted data, Navigator opens a dialog box notifying the user of the transfer, and allowing the user to cancel it if desired.

Some objects and properties are tainted by default, but you can add tainting to data or scripts that are normally untainted using taint( ). You can also remove tainting with untaint( ).

taint( ) does not modify the item being tainted. It returns a tainted copy of the value, or, in the case of an object, a tainted reference to the value.

Version 1.2 Data tainting has been superseded by a new security system, object signing, added to JavaScript 1.2. For more information on tainting and security, see Chapter 8.

Example To taint the src property of a Layer object, which is not normally tainted, use a statement such as:

layer1.src = taint(layer1.src)

See Also domain, taintEnabled( ), untaint( )

taintEnabled( )

Version 1.1

Method of the `navigator` object

Returns `true` if data tainting has been enabled.

Syntax `navigator.taintEnabled()`

Discussion Starting with Version 2.02, Navigator restricted scripts from passing private information—such as session histories and directory structures—to different servers. In Navigator 3, though, a feature called data tainting was introduced. When tainting is enabled, if a script attempts to transfer tainted data, Navigator opens a dialog box notifying the user of the transfer, and allowing the user to cancel it if desired.

Data tainting is disabled by default; it can be enabled by the user with the `NS_ENABLE_TAINT` environment variable. taintEnabled( ) returns `true` if tainting is enabled, `false` otherwise.

Data tainting has been superseded by a new security system, object signing, added to JavaScript 1.2. For more information on tainting and security, see Chapter 8.

Example
```
if (navigator.taintEnabled()) {
    x = taint(x)
```

See Also `domain` property, `taint()`, `untaint()` functions

tan( )

Method of the `Math` object

Returns the tangent of a number.

Syntax `Math.tan(number)`

number   A number representing the size of an angle in radians.

Example `t = Math.tan(theta)`

See Also `acos()`, `asin()`, `atan()`, `atan2()`, `cos()`, `sin()`, `Math`

target

AREA, LINK

Version 1.0 External

Property of the Area and Link external objects
(see also target as a property of the event and Form objects)

Specifies the name of a window to display the results when a link is followed.

Syntax   *docObject.formName*.links[*index*].target
    docObject   document for the current document, or an expression denoting a document in any window.
    index   Number specifying an Area or Link object in the document's links array.

Discussion   Normally, when the user clicks a link in a browser window, the web page or other results are displayed in the same window. This property allows a link's result to be displayed in a different window. If the specified window is not already open, Navigator will open it automatically.

This property's value is initially set to the TARGET attribute in the HTML <A> or <AREA> tag. Scripts may modify this value at any time. Note that the value is not the name of a JavaScript variable; it is the value of the window's name property, which is specified in the open( ) method if the window is already open.

Version 1.1   This property was added to Area objects in JavaScript 1.1.

Example   document.links[0].target = "anotherWin"

See Also   Area, Link, links, window

target

EVENT

Version 1.2 Special scope

Property of the event object
(see also target as a property of the Area, Form, and Link objects)

Returns the object to which an event was directed.

Syntax   *eventObj*.target
    eventObj   event, or an expression denoting a copy of event, such as a function argument passed to an event handler.

Properties   Since this property returns a reference to an object, it has the same properties, methods, and event handlers as the referenced object.

Discussion   This property is useful when one handler function serves several objects, since it allows the event handler to identify the object to which the event was passed. When event capturing is in effect, this property specifies what object would have handled the event if capturing was not in effect.
  Note that the `event` object has limited scope: it can only be referenced in event handlers (see Chapter 7).

Example   An event handler can determine the type of object at which an event occurred by a statement such as:

```
alert("The event occurred at a " + ev.target.type + "object.")
```

This example assumes that the variable `ev` is an event object, or a copy of one.

See Also   `captureEvents()`, `event`

target

FORM

Version 1.0   External

Property of the Form external object
(see also `target` as a property of the Area, event, and Link objects)

Specifies the name of a window for results of a form submission.

Syntax   *docObject.formName*.target
    docObject.forms[*index*].target

  docObject   document for the current document, or an expression denoting a document in any window.
  formName   Name of a form, as specified by the `NAME` attribute of the HTML `<FORM>` tag.
  index   Number specifying a Form object in the document's `forms` array.

Discussion   When a browser submits a form, the destination server may return a response, which is normally displayed in the same window from which the form was sent. This property is used to specify an alternate window or frame for the response. If the specified window is not already open, Navigator will open it automatically.

This property's value is initially set to the TARGET attribute in the HTML <FORM> tag. Scripts may modify this value at any time. Note that the value is not the name of a JavaScript variable; it is the value of the window's name property, which was specified in the open( ) method if the window is already open.

Example   `document.myForm.target = "resultWin"`

See Also   Form, window

test( )

Version 1.2

Method of the RegExp object

Searches for a match to a regular expression in a specified string, and returns `true` if a match is found.

Syntax   `regexp.test(string)`

    `regexp`   The regular expression being used for the search.
    `string`   Optional string variable or expression to be searched. If omitted, `exec( )` searches `RegExp.input`.

Discussion   This method is used to determine whether a string matches a particular pattern. You can also use the `RegExp` method `exec( )`, or the `String` object's `match( )` method, which provide more information, although they do not execute as quickly.

Example   To test whether a form element contains a string of digits, use a statement such as:

```
if(! /^[0-9]+$/.test(document.myForm.txt.value)) {
   alert("Invalid number entered.")
}
```

See Also   `exec( )`, `match( ) search( )`, RegExp, String

Text

Version 1.0   External

External object

Reflects a text box in an HTML form.

Syntax   *formObj.boxName*

*formObj.*elements[*index*]

formObj	document.*formName* or other expression denoting a Form object.
boxName	String value representing a name assigned by the NAME attribute of the HTML <TEXT> tag.
index	Number or string specifying an element of the form's elements array.

Properties

defaultValue	Reflects the VALUE attribute of the HTML <TEXT> tag: the initial text in the box when the web page is loaded.
form	Returns the form that contains this text box.
name	Reflects NAME attribute of the HTML <TEXT> tag.
type	Reflects the TYPE attribute of the HTML <INPUT> tag (this is always "text" for Text objects).
value	A string specifying the text that appears in the box on the screen.

Methods

blur()	Removes focus from the text box.
focus()	Sets focus on the text box.
select()	Selects (highlights) the text in the box.

Event Handlers   onblur, onchange, onfocus, onselect

Whenever one of these event handlers is called, the text in the element is copied to RegExp.input.

Discussion   When Navigator loads a web page, it creates Text objects corresponding to all text boxes in the document. You can reference these objects as elements of the form's elements array.

Version 1.1   The type property was added in JavaScript 1.1.

Example   For a text box declared by HTML such as:

<INPUT TYPE="text" NAME="address">

The text in the box can be read by a statement such as:

userAddress = document.myForm.address.value

See Also   Form

text

Version 1.0   Tainted

Property of the `Option` object

Specifies the text displayed in one option of a select box in a form.

Syntax   *selectObj*.options[*index*].text
selectName.text

selectObj   document.*formName*.*selectName*, or an expression denoting an option of a select box in any document.
index   Number specifying the position of the Submit button in the form.
selectName   Name or expression denoting an `Option` object created by `new Option()`.

Discussion   This property specifies the text that is displayed in the corresponding line of the selection list on the screen. The value is initially set to the text following the HTML `<OPTION>` tag. Scripts can modify the value at any time, and the change will be immediately displayed on the screen.

Version 1.1 Before JavaScript 1.1, changes to the property did not result in updating the screen.

Example   For a select box created by HTML such as:

```
<SELECT NAME="mySelect" SIZE="4" MULTIPLE>
 <OPTION VALUE="A" SELECTED> Individual
 <OPTION VALUE="B"> Student
 <OPTION VALUE="C"> Family
 <OPTION VALUE="D"> Corporation
</SELECT>
```

The text of an option can be changed by a statement such as:

`document.myForm.mySelect.options[0].text="(Default)"`

See Also   Form, `Option`, Select

textAlign

Version 1.2

Property of style sheet objects

Specifies the horizontal alignment of text.

Syntax   *styleObj*.textAlign

styleObj   Style sheet object: a property of a `classes`, `ids`, or `tags` object.

Discussion   This property controls the alignment of text within the HTML object. The value may be one of the following:

`"center"`	Text lines are centered.
`"justify"`	Text lines are flush at the left and right margins.
`"left"`	Text lines are flush left (ragged right).
`"right"`	Text lines are flush right (ragged left).

This property applies to all block-level elements and is inherited. Its initial value depends on the browser.

Note that for `textAlign` assignments to take effect, they must occur before the browser writes the styled text to the document. An assignment to `tags.body.textAlign` must be done within the <HEAD> ... </HEAD> section of the HTML.

Example   To cause all <H2> headings to be centered:

```
document.tags.H2.textAlign = "center"
```

See Also   `align`, `classes`, `ids`, `tags`, `verticalAlign`

Textarea

Version 1.0   External

External object

Reflects a text area input field in an HTML form.

Textarea

Syntax	`formObj.textName`	
	`formObj.elements[index]`	
	`formObj`	`document.formName` or other expression denoting a Form object.
	`textName`	String value representing a name assigned by the `NAME` attribute of the HTML `<TEXTAREA>` tag.
	`index`	Number or string specifying an element of the form's `elements` array.
Properties	`defaultValue`	String that reflects the initial contents of the text area: the text between the HTML `<TEXTAREA>` and `</TEXTAREA>` tags.
	`form`	The form that contains this text area.
	`name`	A string containing the name assigned by the `NAME` attribute of the HTML `<TEXTAREA>` tag.
	`type`	A String specifying the type of input field; this always contains `"textarea"` for Textarea objects.
	`value`	String specifying the current contents of the text area.
Methods	`blur()`	Removes focus from the text area.
	`focus()`	Sets focus on the text area.
	`select()`	Selects (highlights) the text in the area.
Event Handlers	`onblur`, `onchange`, `onfocus`, `onkeydown`, `onkeypress`, `onkeyup`, `onselect`	
	Whenever one of these event handlers is called, the text in the element is copied to `RegExp.input`.	

Discussion

When Navigator loads a web page, it creates Textarea objects corresponding to all HTML `<TEXTAREA> ... </TEXTAREA>` tags in the document. You can reference these objects as properties of a Form object, or as elements of the form's `elements` array.

Version 1.1
Version 1.2

The `type` property was added in JavaScript 1.1.

The `onkeydown`, `onkeypress`, and `onkeyup` event handlers were added in JavaScript 1.2.

Example

The contents of a text area can be read by a statement such as:

`userText = document.myForm.bigText.value`

where `bigText` is a text area in the form named `myForm`.

See Also   Form, Text

textDecoration

Version 1.2   External

Property of style sheet objects

Specifies underlining, overlining, strike-through, or blinking text.

Syntax
: `styleObj.textDecoration`

  styleObj   Style sheet object: a property of a `classes`, `ids`, or `tags` object.

Discussion
: This property controls the appearance of text within the HTML object. The value may be one of the following:

`"blink"`	Text blinks.
`"line-through"`	Text is overstruck (~~like this~~).
`"none"`	Text has no decoration.
`"overline"`	Text is displayed with a line over it.
`"underline"`	Text is displayed with a line under it.

  This property applies to all HTML objects. Its initial value is `"none"`.

  Note that for `textDecoration` assignments to take effect, they must occur before the browser opens the document. For this reason, the assignments should be done within the `<HEAD>` ... `</HEAD>` section of the HTML.

Example
: To cause all `<H2>` headings to be underlined:

  `document.tags.H2.textDecoration = "underline"`

See Also
: `classes`, `ids`, `tags`

textTransform

Version 1.2   External

Property of style sheet objects

Specifies the capitalization of text.

Syntax
: `styleObj.textTransform`

  styleObj   Style sheet object: a property of a `classes`, `ids`, or `tags` object.

Discussion This property controls the appearance of text within the HTML object. The value may be one of the following:

"capitalize"	Display the first letter of each word in uppercase.
"lowercase"	Display all text in lowercase.
"none"	Text has no explicit capitalization.
"uppercase"	Display all text in uppercase.

This property applies to all HTML elements. Its initial value is "none".

Note that for textTransform assignments to take effect, they must occur before the browser writes the styled text to the document. An assignment to tags.body.textTransform must be done within the <HEAD> ... </HEAD> section of the HTML.

Example To cause all <H2> headings to be displayed in all capital letters:

```
document.tags.H2.textTransform = "uppercase"
```

See Also classes, fontStyle, ids, tags

this

Version 1.0   Read-only   Special scope

Built-in object

What it does.

Syntax this

Discussion The value of this depends on where it is used. Its main uses are in constructor functions and in event handlers attached to HTML tags. In constructor functions, it refers to the object being created for example:

```
function person(first, last, yrs) {
   this.firstName = first
   this.lastName = last
   this.age = yrs
}
```

This function can create a new person object when used with the new operator, as in:

```
var Mary = new person("Mary", "Jones", 34)
```

For more details on objects and constructors, see Chapter 5.

In event handlers of HTML tags, `this` refers to the object that reflects the HTML tag. It is commonly used in forms, as in:

```
<FORM NAME="ageForm">
  Enter your age:
  <INPUT TYPE="text" NAME="age">
  <INPUT TYPE="button" NAME="pushMe" VALUE="Check it"
    ONCLICK="checkAge(this.form.age.value)">
</FORM>
```

`this` is used in the button's `ONCLICK` handler, where its value is the button itself; that is, the Button object `document.ageForm.pushMe`. `this.form` is a reference to the enclosing Form object, `document.ageForm`. (The `form` property is available for all form element objects.)

See Also constructor, form, Form

title

Version 1.0 Read-only Tainted

Property of the document object

Returns a string containing a document's title.

Syntax   *docObject*.title

docObject   document for the current document, or an expression denoting a document in any window.

Discussion A document's title is the text between the `<TITLE></TITLE>` tags. `title` will return `null` if there is no document title.

Example `document.write("Welcome to the " + document.title + " page.")`

See Also URL, document

toGMTString( )

Version 1.0

Method of the Date object

Returns a string containing a date and time in universal time (GMT).

Syntax   *dateObj*.toGMTString( )
dateObj   Date object or expression.

Discussion   This method converts the time and date in a `Date` object to a string, using universal time (also called GMT or UTC) and adjusting for the local time zone. The exact appearance of the string depends on the platform.

Example   To write the current time and date in both local and universal formats, use a statement such as:

```
rightNow = new Date( )
document.write("It is now ", rightNow, " local, or ",
    rightNow.toGMTString( ), ".<BR>")
```

See Also   Date, toLocaleString( )

toLocaleString( )

Version 1.0

Method of the Date object

Returns a string containing a date and time in local time.

Syntax   *dateObj*.toLocaleString( )
dateObj   Date object or expression.

Discussion   This method converts the time and date in a `Date` object to a string, using the local time zone. The exact appearance of the string depends on the platform.

Example
```
rightNow = new Date( )
document.write("It is now ", rightNow.toLocaleString( ), ".")
```

See Also   Date, toGMTString( )

toLowerCase( )

Version 1.0

Method of the `String` object

Returns a string converted to lowercase text.

Syntax   *stringName*.toLowerCase( )

stringName   Any string object or expression.

Discussion   toLowerCase( ) returns a copy of the specified string with all uppercase letters converted to lowercase.

Example   To convert a user's text input to lowercase, use statements such as:

```
var rawText = document.myForm.myText.value
var lowerC = rawText.toLowerCase()
```

See Also   toUpperCase( ), String

toolbar

Version 1.2   Signed scripts

Property of the `window` object

Specifies the state of the browser window's toolbar.

Syntax   For the current window:

```
toolbar
self.toolbar
window.toolbar
```

For other windows:

```
windowObj.toolbar
```

windowObj   An expression denoting a `window` object.

Properties	`visible`	A Boolean property that specifies whether the toolbar is visible or not.

Discussion The toolbar is the bar at the top of a window that contains buttons such as Back, Forward, Home, Print, and so forth. `toolbar` has a single property, `visible`, that specifies whether the toolbar is displayed.

Note that you can only use this property in a signed script with the `"UniversalBrowserRead"` or `"UniversalBrowserWrite"` privileges.

Example This statement hides the toolbar in a window named `windowOne`:

`windowOne.toolbar.visible = 0`

See Also `locationbar, menubar, personalbar, scrollbars, statusbar, window`

top

CLIP

Version 1.2 External

Property of the `clip` object
(see also `top` as a property of Layer and `window`)

Specifies the upper clipping limit of a layer.

Syntax `layerObj.clip.top`

`layerObj`   `document.layerName`, or other expression denoting a Layer object.

Discussion This property specifies the upper clipping limit for a layer, in pixels. It is initially zero. Increasing its value causes rows of pixels at the top of the layer to become invisible, allowing the lower layers or the enclosing document to be seen.

Example To cause the upper 64 rows of pixels in a layer to be clipped, use a statement such as:

`document.layers.myLayer.clip.top = 64`

See Also `bottom, height, left, right, width` (properties of `clip`) Layer

top
LAYER

Version 1.2   External

Property of the Layer object
(see also top as a property of clip and window)

Specifies the vertical position of the top of the layer.

Syntax   `layerObj.top`

`layerObj`   `document.layerName`, or other expression denoting a Layer object.

Discussion   This property controls the vertical position of the layer. It specifies the distance in pixels, from the top of the layer to the top of the parent layer (if any) or the window. Scripts can modify this value at any time, and the position of the layer on the screen will be immediately updated.

Example   To place a layer 100 pixels down and 200 pixels right from the top left corner of a window, use statements such as:

```
document.layers.layer1.top = 100
document.layers.layer1.left = 200
```

See Also   Layer, left

top
WINDOW

Version 1.0   External

Property of the window object and Frame external object
(see also top as a property of clip and Layer)

Returns the "topmost" or "outermost" window, the one that contains all frames and framesets enclosing the script.

Syntax   `top`

Properties   Since top returns a reference to a window object, it has all the properties, methods, and event handlers of that window.

Discussion: When a script runs in a frame, references to `window` will return the Frame object, rather than the actual browser window. A script in a frame can often reference the enclosing window with `parent`, but sometimes frames are nested two or more levels deep, in which case `parent` will return another frame. `top` always returns the window, not a frame or sub-frame, in which the script is executing.

Example: To modify the browser window's status bar message from within a sub-frame, use a statement such as:

```
top.status = "Here is a message from a sub-sub-frame."
```

See Also: Frame, `parent`, `window`

toString( )

Version 1.0

Method of all objects

Returns a string representing the value of an object.

Syntax: *obj*.toString(*radix*)

obj   Any object.
radix   An optional argument specifying a radix for converting numeric values to strings.

Discussion: Besides being used in scripts, `toString( )` is called automatically in certain cases, such as for type conversion and the `document.write( )` method. All built-in objects have a `toString( )`; for user-defined objects, you may create your own. If `toString( )` is called for a user-defined object that has no method assigned, and the object does not have a value that can be converted to a string, the returned value will be the string "[object *type*]" where *type* is the object type or the name of its constructor function.

For more information on object constructors and methods, see Chapter 5.

Version 1.1   Starting with JavaScript 1.1, the optional *radix* argument may be specified for converting numeric values (see Example).

Example: To convert a number to a string in hexadecimal, use a statement such as:

```
hexValue = "0x" + someNumber.toString(16)
```

See Also: String

toUpperCase( )

Version 1.0

Method of the `String` object

Returns a string converted to uppercase text.

Syntax   *stringName*.toUpperCase( )
          stringName   Any string object or expression.

Discussion   toUpperCase( ) returns a copy of the specified string with all lowercase letters converted to uppercase.

Example   To convert a user's text input to uppercase, use statements such as:

```
var rawText = document.myForm.myText.value
var upperC = rawText.toLowerCase( )
```

See Also   toUpperCase( ), String

type

EVENT

Version 1.2   Read-only   Special scope

Property of the event object
(see also `type` as a property of form element and MimeType objects)

Returns a string identifying the type of event.

Syntax   *eventObj*.type
          eventObj   event, or an expression denoting a copy of event, such as a function argument passed to an event handler.

Discussion   This property returns a string such as `"click"` or `"mouseover"` that identifies the type of event. Possible values are:

"abort"	"keydown"	"mouseup"
"blur"	"keypress"	"move"
"click"	"keyup"	"reset"
"change"	"load"	"resize"
"dblclick"	"mousedown"	"select"
"dragdrop"	"mousemove"	"submit"
"error"	"mouseout"	"unload"
"focus"	"mouseover"	

The **event** object has limited scope: it can only be referenced in event handlers.

Example A function that handles several different types of events can select different operations with a structure such as:

```
switch(ev.type) {
  case "click":
    ...              // handle click event
    break

  case "dblclick":
    ...              // handle double click event
    break

// etc.

}
```

(This example assumes that ev is an **event** object, or a copy of one.)

See Also event

type

FORM ELEMENTS

Version 1.1   Read-only   External

Property of Button, Checkbox, FileUpload, Hidden, Password, Radio, Reset, Select, Submit, Text, and Textarea objects
(see also type as a property of the event and MimeType objects)

Returns a string identifying the type of a form element.

Syntax	*formObj.elementName*.type *formObj*["*elementName*"].type *formObj*.elements[*index*].type
	formObj document.*formName*, or an expression denoting a Form object in any document. *elementName* Name specified in the NAME attribute of the HTML <INPUT> tag. *index* Number specifying a position in the form's elements array.
Discussion	This property identifies the type of form element. The value reflects the TYPE attribute of the HTML <INPUT> tag, and is one of the following:

Object	Value
Button	"button"
Check box	"checkbox"
FileUpload	"file"
Hidden	"hidden"
Password	"password"
Radio	"radio"
Reset	"reset"
Select (without MULTIPLE attribute)	"select-one"
Select (with MULTIPLE attribute)	"select-multiple"
Submit	"submit"
Text	"text"
Textarea	"textarea"

Example   A function that is passed several different types of elements can select different operations with a structure such as:

```
function doInput(element) {
   switch(element.type) {
      case "checkbox":
         ...              // handle checkbox
         break

      case "radio":
         ...              // handle radio button
         break

   // etc.

   }
}
```

See Also   elements, Form

type

MIMETYPE

Version 1.2　Read-only　Special scope

Property of the MimeType object
(see also type as a property of the event object and form element objects)

What it does.

Syntax
: `navigator.mimeTypes[index].type`

    index　　　A number or string identifying an element or property of the `mimeTypes` object.

Discussion
: This property returns a string that specifies the data type associated with the MimeType object.

Example
: For a typical installation of Navigator 4.01 on a Windows 95 platform, the statement:

    `type0 = navigator.mimeTypes[0].type`

    will set the variable `type0` to `"audio/x-liveaudio"`.

See Also
: MimeType, mimeTypes

typeof

OPERATOR

See Chapter 3.

unescape( )

Version 1.0

Built-in function

Returns a string in which numeric equivalents of special characters are converted to their original character forms.

Syntax unescape(*string*)

string   Any String object or expression.

Discussion This function searches a string for occurrences of the substring %*xx*, where *xx* is a hexadecimal code representing a character. It returns a string in which these substrings have been replaced by the actual characters that they represent.

This function is the opposite of escape( ). These two functions may be useful to prevent special characters, such as quotation marks or white space, from interfering with normal handling of the string.

Example The statement:

s = escape("You%20%26%20me")

returns the string "You & me".

See Also escape( )

UNLOAD

Version 1.2 Read-only

Property of the Event object

Returns a mask for capturing unload events.

Syntax Event.UNLOAD

Discussion This property is used to capture and release unload events, which occur when a document is unloaded due to some user action that loads a new document. For more details on event handling, see Chapter 7.

Example	To enable capturing of unload events (as well as load): `myWindow.captureEvents (Event.LOAD | Event.UNLOAD)`
See Also	`captureEvents()`, `event`, `Event`, `onunload`, `releaseEvents()`

untaint( )

Version 1.1

Built-in function

Removes data tainting from a script or object.

Syntax	`untaint(obj)`
	obj Optional name or expression denoting a tainted property, variable, function, or object. If omitted, untaint the script itself.
Discussion	Starting with Version 2.02, Navigator restricted scripts from passing private information—such as session histories and directory structures—to different servers. In Navigator 3, though, a feature called data tainting was introduced. When tainting is enabled, if a script attempts to transfer tainted data, Navigator opens a dialog box notifying the user of the transfer and allowing the user to cancel it if desired. Some objects and properties are tainted by default. `untaint()` removes tainting from them, as well as from objects that were tainted using the `taint()` function. Once untainted, the data can be sent to other servers without confirmation from the user. Note, however, that a script can only untaint data that originated in that script. `untaint()` does not modify the item being tainted. It returns an untainted copy of the value, or, in the case of an object, an untainted reference to the value.

Version 1.2

Data tainting has been superseded by a new security system, object signing, added to JavaScript 1.2. For more information on tainting and security, see Chapter 8.

Examples	To taint the `src` property of a `Layer` object, which is not normally tainted, use a statement such as:
	
	`layer1.src = taint(layer1.src)`
	
	To untaint a value retrieved from a different window, use a statement such as:
	
	`cleanData = untaint(otherWindow.variable)`

See Also	`domain`, `taint()`, `taintEnabled()`

URL

Version 1.0   Read-only   Tainted

Property of the document object

The complete URL of the document currently displayed in the window.

Syntax   document.URL

Discussion   When the document is first loaded, this property is equivalent to window.location.href. However, window.location.href may be changed by redirection. document.URL does not change and may not be modified by scripts. If you wish to display a new document, modify window.location or one of its properties, or use history.go().

There is also a document.location property which is equivalent to document.URL. Its use is questionable, since Netscape has already announced that it will be removed in a future release. However document.location is present in some other browsers that do not support document.URL.

Example   To include the URL of the document in a Confirm dialog box:

answer = confirm("You have arrived at this Web page: " + document.URL + ". Click OK to continue, or Cancel to return to the previous page")

See Also   go( ), location (properties of document and window), document, window

userAgent

Version 1.0   Read-only

Property of the navigator object

Returns a string containing the user-agent information for the browser.

Syntax   navigator.userAgent

Discussion   This property identifies the type of browser in which the document has been loaded. It is sent to the web server as part of HTTP data transfers.

Example   document.write("Your browser is:
<B>", navigator.userAgent + "</B>
 Please upgrade to the latest version.")

This will write the following to the window (depending on the browser version, of course):

> Your browser is:
> **Mozilla/4.01 [en] (Win95; I)**
> Please upgrade to the latest version.

See Also   `appCodeName, appName, appVersion, navigator`

UTC( )

Version 1.0

Method of the `Date` constructor

Returns the specified date and time as a number of milliseconds from January 1, 1970, 00:00:00 in universal time (UTC or GMT).

Syntax   `Date.UTC(year, month, day, hrs, min, sec)`

`year`	A year. Values from 0 to 99 are assumed to represent years from 1900 to 1999. Other values represent the actual year.
`month`	A month from zero to 11.
`day`	A day of the month from 1 to 31.
`hrs`	Optional hour from zero to 23.
`min`	Optional minute from zero to 59.
`sec`	Optional second from zero to 59.

Discussion   This method accepts values representing a local date and time and returns a single numeric value. This is the same format used by `getTime( )` and `setTime( )`.

Note that `UTC( )` is a method of the `Date` constructor, not of `Date` objects you create with `new Date( )`. In other words, you must always write `Date.UTC( )`, not `myDateObj.UTC( )`.

Example   To convert a set of time and date numbers to a single value, use a statement such as:

`timeValue = Date.UTC(yr, mo, dy, hr, min, sec)`

This single statement is equivalent to:

`t = new Date(yr, mo, dy, hr, min, sec)`
`timeValue = t.getTime( )`

See Also   `getTime( ), parse( ), setTime( ), Date`

value

Version 1.0   External   Tainted

Property of the Button, Checkbox, FileUpload, Hidden, `Option`, Password, Radio, Reset, Submit, Text, and Textarea objects

Specifies the value in a form input element.

Syntax   *formobj.elementName*.value
formobj["*elementName*"].value
formobj.elements[*index*].value

formObj	document.*formName* or other expression denoting a Form object.
elementName	Name assigned by the NAME attribute of an HTML tag.
index	Number or string specifying an element of the form's elements array.

Discussion   This property returns a string that specifies the value contained in or selected by a form element. The meaning of the "value" depends on the type of element, described as follows.

Button, Reset, Submit   For these button-type objects, value specifies the text that appears on the button. It is initially set by the VALUE attribute of the HTML <INPUT> tag. Scripts can modify value, and the new text will appear on the screen, although the button will not be resized to fit it.

Checkbox, Option, Radio   For these selector-type objects, value is not displayed on the screen, but is sent to the server if the form is submitted while the object is checked or selected. It is initially set by the VALUE attribute of the HTML <INPUT> tag. Scripts can modify the value.

Version 1.1   This property was added to Option objects in JavaScript 1.1.

FileUpload   For these objects, value is the complete pathname of the file selected by the user. This property is read-only.

Version 1.1   This property was added to FileUpload objects in JavaScript 1.1.

Hidden   For these objects, value is not displayed on the screen, but is sent to the server when the form is submitted. It is initially set by the VALUE attribute of the HTML <INPUT> tag. Scripts can modify the value.

Text, Textarea	For these objects, value is the text displayed in the element. Users can modify it interactively. Scripts can modify `value`, and the new text will appear on the screen.
Example	To create a text box with an initial value, use HTML such as:

```
<INPUT TYPE="text" NAME="countryBox" VALUE="USA">
```

To read the current contents of the box, use a statement such as:

```
userCountry = document.myForm.countryBox.value
```

See Also   Form

valueOf( )

Version 1.1

Method of all objects

Returns the primitive value of an object.

Syntax	`obj.valueOf( )`
	`obj` Any object.
Discussion	Although it is rarely used in scripts, `valueOf( )` is called automatically when a primitive value is needed, such as in evaluating expressions. Some built-in objects have a `valueOf( )`; for example, `Date` objects have a `valueOf( )` method that returns a string containing the date and time specified by the object. For user-defined objects, you may create your own method. If an object has no method assigned, `valueOf( )` returns a reference to the object itself. For more information on object constructors and methods, see Chapter 5.

var

Keyword used in statements

This keyword is used to declare variables. For details, see Chapter 2.

verticalAlign

Version 1.2   External

Property of style sheet objects

Specifies the vertical positioning of text.

Preliminary   *Note that this property is announced by Netscape, but not fully implemented in Navigator as of version 4.01. The information presented here is preliminary.*

Syntax   `styleObj.verticalAlign`

`styleObj`   Style sheet object: a property of a `classes`, `ids`, or `tags` object.

Discussion   This property controls the alignment of text within the HTML object. The value may be one of the following keywords:

`"baseline"`	Aligns the baseline of the element (or the bottom, if the element doesn't have a baseline) with the baseline of the parent.
`"sub"`	Positions the element as a subscript.
`"super"`	Positions the element as a superscript.
`"top"`	Aligns the top of the element with the highest element on the line.
`"text-top"`	Aligns the top of the element with the top of the parent element's font.
`"middle"`	Aligns the vertical midpoint of the element (typically an image) with the baseline plus half the x-height of the parent.
`"bottom"`	Aligns the bottom of the element with the lowest element on the line.
`"text-bottom"`	Aligns the bottom of the element with the bottom of the parent element's font.

The value may also be a percentage of the element's `lineHeight` value, expressed as a string with a percent sign such as `"10%"`.

This property applies to all HTML objects. Its initial value is `"baseline"`.

Note that for `verticalAlign` assignments to take effect, they must occur before the browser writes the styled text to the document. An assignment to `tags.body.verticalAlign` must be done within the `<HEAD>` ... `</HEAD>` section of the HTML.

For more information on style sheets, see Chapter 6.

See Also   `align`, `classes`, `ids`, `tags`, `textalign`

visible

Version 1.2   Signed scripts

Property of the `locationbar`, `menubar`, `personalbar`, `scrollbars`, `statusbar`, and `toolbar` objects.

Indicates whether the screen component is visible; a Boolean value (1, 0, `true`, `false`).

Syntax
For the current window:

objectName.visible
self.*objectName*.visible
window.*objectName*.visible

For other windows:

windowObj.*objectName*.visible

windowObj	An expression denoting a `window` object.
objectName	`locationbar`, `menubar`, `personalbar`, `scrollbars`, `statusbar`, or `toolbar`.

Discussion
This property can be used to display or remove a window's location bar, menu bar, personal bar, scroll bars, status bar, or toolbar. It can only be modified in a signed script with the `"UniversalBrowserRead"` or `"UniversalBrowserWrite"` privileges.

Example
To remove the location bar from a window, use a statement such as:

window1.locationbar.visible = false

See Also
`locationbar`, `menubar`, `personalbar`, `scrollbars`, `statusbar`, `toolbar` objects

visibility

Version 1.2   External

Property of the Layer object

Specifies whether the layer is displayed on the screen.

Syntax
layerObj.visibility

layerObj	`document`.*layerName*, or other expression denoting a Layer object.

Discussion	This property is a string whose value may be one of the following: `show` — to make the layer visible. `hide` — to make the layer invisible. `inherit` — to display the layer if its parent layer (or, if there is no parent, the enclosing window or frame) is visible.
Example	To hide a layer, use a statement such as: `document.myLayer.visibility = "hide"`
See Also	`Layer`, `visible`

vlinkColor

Version 1.0

Property of the document object

Specifies the color in which visited links are displayed.

Syntax	`docObject.vlinkColor` `docObject` — `document` for the current window's document, or an expression denoting a document object.
Discussion	This property may be set to a string of six hexadecimal digits, with an optional leading pound sign (#) character, in the form *rrggbb*, where *rr* specifies red, *gg* specifies green, and *bb* specifies blue. `vlinkColor` may also be set to one of the color names listed in Appendix C. The returned value is always in hexadecimal with a leading #. This property is initially set to the color specified by the `VLINK` attribute, if any, of the HTML `<BODY>` tag.

Examples	`document.vlinkColor = "00ff00"` // no red
	                                  // max. green
	                                  // no blue
	
	`parent.document.vlinkColor = "#8000ff"` // 50% red
	                                           // no green
	                                           // max. blue
	
	`otherWindow.document.vlinkColor`
	`    = "cornsilk"` // Netscape keyword

See Also	`alinkColor`, `bgColor`, `fgColor`, `linkColor`, `document`

void

Operator used in expressions

This operator prevents an expression from returning a value. For details, see Chapter 3.

vspace

Version 1.1 Read-only

Property of the `Image` object

Returns the distance, in pixels, between the top and bottom edges of an image and the surrounding text.

Syntax
: *imageObj*.vspace

  imageObj   document.*imageName*, or other expression denoting an Image object.

Discussion
: If the image object was created using the Image( ) constructor, then vspace is 0. Otherwise vspace is the value set by the VSPACE attribute of the <IMG> tag.

Example
: To write the vspace value to the page, use a statement such as:

  ```
  document.write("The first image is ", document.images[0].vspace "
      pixels from the text.")
  ```

See Also
: border, height, hspace, width, Image

which

Version 1.2   Read-only

Property of the event object

Returns a number identifying the key or mouse button that was pressed to generate an event.

Syntax *eventObj*.which

eventObj   event, or an expression denoting a copy of event, such as a function argument passed to an event handler.

Discussion For keyboard events, this property returns a number representing the character code in the ISO Latin-1 character set. For mouse events, this property returns 1 for the left button or 3 for the right button. The modifiers property indicates whether the Shift, Ctrl, or Alt keys were pressed when the event occurred.

Note that the event object has limited scope: it can only be referenced in event handlers (see Chapter 7).

Example To convert a character code from a keyboard event into a string, use a statement such as:

```
typedChar = String.fromCharCode(event.which)
```

See Also event, modifiers

while

Keyword used in statements

This keyword is used to create loop structures. For details, see Chapter 4.

whiteSpace

Version 1.2　External

Property of style sheet objects

Specifies the handling of white space characters in text.

Syntax　`styleObj.whiteSpace`

　　　　　`styleObj`　　　Style sheet object: a property of a `classes`, `ids`, or `tags` object.

Discussion　This property controls the way white space characters (space, tab, Newline, and so forth) are displayed. The value may be one of the following:

　　`"normal"`　　A series of white space characters is treated as a single one, and lines of text are filled to the available width, regardless of where Newline characters are placed.

　　`"pre"`　　White space characters are interpreted literally. This is equivalent to using the HTML `<PRE>` ... `</PRE>` tags. It is useful for text such as computer source code and sample printouts.

　This property applies to all block-level objects. Its initial value is `"normal"`.

　Note that for `whiteSpace` assignments to take effect, they must occur before the browser writes the styled text to the document. An assignment to `tags.body.whiteSpace` must be done within the `<HEAD>` ... `</HEAD>` section of the HTML.

Example　To create a style named `printout` that causes text to be displayed as pre-formatted, use a statement such as:

`document.ids.printout.whitespace = "pre"`

See Also　`classes`, `ids`, `tags`

width

CLIP

Version 1.2 External

Property of the `clip` object
(see also `width` as a property of the event, Image, screen, and style sheet objects)

Specifies the clipping width of a layer.

Syntax   *layerObj*.clip.width

layerObj   `document.`*layerName*, or other expression denoting a Layer object.

Discussion   This property returns the clipping width for a layer, in pixels: the difference between the current values of `clip.left` and `clip.right`. Modifying this property actually changes the value of `clip.right` to produce the desired new width.

Example   To reduce the currently visible part of a layer by removing 40 pixels at the right side, use a statement such as:

`document.layers.myLayer.clip.width -= 40`

See Also   `bottom`, `left`, `height`, `right`, `top` (properties of `clip`), Layer

width

EVENT

Version 1.2 Read-only

Property of the event object
(see also width as a property of the `clip`, Image, screen, and style sheet objects)

Returns the width, in pixels, of a window or frame after it is resized by the user.

Syntax   *eventObj*.width

eventObj   event, or an expression denoting a copy of event, such as a function argument passed to an event handler.

Discussion	Note that the **event** object has limited scope: it can only be referenced in event handlers (see Chapter 7).

Example	`if (ev.type == "resize") {`
	`    newWidth = ev.width`
	`    newHeight = ev.height`
	`}`
	
	(This example assumes that the variable **ev** is an event object, or a copy of one.)

See Also	**event**, **height**

width

IMAGE

Version 1.1   Read-only

Property of the **Image** object
(see also width as a property of the **clip**, **event**, **screen**, and **style sheet** objects)

Returns the width of an image, in pixels.

Syntax	*imageObj*.width
	imageObj **document.***imageName*, or other expression denoting an **Image** object.
Discussion	For images in web pages, this property reflects the **WIDTH** attribute of the `<IMG>` tag. For **Image** objects created using the **new Image()** constructor, this property returns the actual width of the image stored in the object.
Example	The following example will write an image's width to the page: `document.write("This image is " + document.Image1.width " pixels wide.")`
See Also	**border**, **height**, **hspace**, **vspace** properties, **Image** object

width

SCREEN

Version 1.2 Read-only

Property of the screen object
(see also width as a property of the `clip`, event, Image, and style sheet objects)

The width of the screen on which the browser is displayed, measured in pixels.

Syntax `screen.width`

Example The following example places the pixel width value into a numeric variable named `nScreenWidth`. For instance, if the screen is using the 800 x 600 video resolution, `nScreenWidth` will contain 800.

`nScreenWidth = screen.width`

See Also `availHeight, availWidth, height, properties, screen` object

width

STYLE SHEET OBJECTS

Version 1.2

Property of style sheet objects
(see also `width` as a property of the `clip`, event, Image, and `screen` objects)

Specifies the width of HTML elements.

Syntax `styleObj.width`

  `styleObj`   Style sheet object: a property of a `classes`, `ids`, or `tags` object.

Discussion This property controls the width of HTML elements. The value may be one of the following:
- An absolute measurement such as `"12pt"`.
- A measurement relative to the current font size such as `"1.5em"`.
- A pixel measurement such as `"18px"`.

- A percentage of the parent element's width such as "25%".
- The keyword "auto".

This property applies to all block-level elements, as well as to replaced elements such as images, and is not inherited. Its initial value is "auto".

Note that for width assignments to take effect, they must occur before the browser writes the styled text to the document. An assignment to tags.body.width must be done within the <HEAD> ... </HEAD> section of the HTML.

See Also   classes, height, ids, tags

window

Version 1.0

Built-in object

An object representing the browser window.

Syntax   For the current window:

self
window

(nothing)—the current window is a default context (see Discussion).
  For other windows:

windowObj

windowObj   An expression denoting a window object.

Properties

Version 1.1
closed	Specifies whether a window has closed.
defaultStatus	The default status bar message.
document	The currently displayed document.
frames	An array listing the window's Frame objects in the order in which they appear in the document.
history	The window's history list.

Version 1.2
innerHeight	The height of the window's internal document area, in pixels.

Version 1.2
innerWidth	The width of the window's internal document area, in pixels.
length	The number of frames in the window.
location	The full (absolute) URL of the document displayed by the window. (Don't confuse this with document.location.)

Version 1.2		`locationbar`	State of the window's location bar. This is an object in its own right.
Version 1.2		`menubar`	State of the window's menu bar. This is an object in its own right.
		`name`	The name assigned to the window when opened.
Version 1.1		`opener`	Reference to the window in which a script used `window.open` to open the current window.
Version 1.2		`outerHeight`	The height of the entire window, including borders, toolbar, and so forth.
Version 1.2		`outerWidth`	The width of the entire window, including borders, toolbar, and so forth.
Version 1.2		`pageXOffset`	The current horizontal position of the page displayed in the window.
Version 1.2		`pageYOffset`	The current vertical position of the page displayed in the window.
		`parent`	Reference to the current window; included for compatibility with frames.
Version 1.2		`personalbar`	State of the window's "personal" toolbar (the new customizable button bar in Navigator 4).
		`self`	A synonym for the current window or frame.
Version 1.2		`scrollbars`	State of the window's scrollbars.
		`status`	A message in the status bar.
Version 1.2		`statusbar`	State of the window's statusbar.
Version 1.2		`toolbar`	State of the window's toolbar.
		`top`	Reference to the actual browser window, not a frame or sub-frame, in which the script is executing.
		`window`	A synonym for the current window or frame; equivalent to `self`.
Methods		`alert(message)`	Displays an Alert message box.
Version 1.1		`blur()`	Removes focus from the window.
Version 1.2		`captureEvents(bitmask)`	Captures all events of the specified type(s).
Version 1.2		`clearInterval(ID)`	Cancels a repeating script that was started by `setInterval()`.
		`clearTimeout(ID)`	Cancels a delayed script that was started by `setTimeout()`.
Version 1.1		`close()`	Closes the window. Starting with JavaScript 1.1, if you use this method to close a window other than one opened by JavaScript using the `open` method, the user sees a confirmation box, and the window is not closed unless the user confirms the close. It *will* close the window *without* confirmation if there's only one open window, though.
		`confirm(message)`	Displays a Confirm message box, and returns `true` if the user clicks OK, or `false` if the user clicks Cancel.

	Method	Description
	`disableExternalCapture()`	Disables external event capturing set by the `enableExternalCapture()` method.
	`enableExternalCapture()`	Allows a window with frames to capture events in pages loaded from different servers.
Version 1.2	`find(string, matchCase, backward)`	Searches the web page for the specified text; can optionally open the Search dialog box to allow the user to control the search. Returns `true` if the search succeeds.
Version 1.1	`focus()`	Sets focus to the window.
Version 1.2	`home()`	Displays the browser's home page, as specified in the browser's Preferences dialog.
Version 1.2	`moveBy(horiz, vert)`	Moves the window by the specified number of pixels horizontally and vertically.
Version 1.2	`moveTo(horiz, vert)`	Moves the top-left corner of the window to the specified position on the screen.
	`open(URL, name, features)`	Opens a new window.
Version 1.2	`print()`	Prints the contents of the window (equivalent to clicking the browser's Print button).
	`prompt(message, default)`	Opens a Prompt dialog box, and returns text typed by the user, or `null` if the user clicked the Cancel button.
Version 1.2	`releaseEvents(bitmask)`	Disables capturing for the specified type(s) of event(s).
Version 1.2	`resizeBy(horiz, vert)`	Resizes the window by moving the bottom-right corner the specified amount.
Version 1.2	`resizeTo(width, height)`	Resizes the window to the specified height and width.
Version 1.2	`routeEvent()`	Passes a captured event along the event hierarchy.
Version 1.1	`scroll(horiz, vert)`	Scrolls the document in the window to a particular position.
Version 1.2	`scrollBy(horiz, vert)`	Scrolls the document in the window by the specified number of pixels.
Version 1.2	`scrollTo(horiz, vert)`	Scrolls the document in the window to the specified position. Added to JavaScript 1.2, this method replaces `scroll()`.
Version 1.2	`setInterval(function, time, arg, arg, ...)`	Causes a script to be repeatedly executed at a specified time interval.
	`setTimeout(function, time)`	Causes a script to be executed after a specified time delay.
Version 1.2	`stop()`	Stops the download (equivalent to clicking the browser's Stop button).

Event Handlers

Version 1.1	`onblur`
Version 1.2	`ondragdrop`
Version 1.1	`onerror`
Version 1.1	`onfocus`
	`onload`
Version 1.2	`onmove`
Version 1.2	`onresize`
	`onunload`

Event handlers are defined in the `<BODY>` or `<FRAMESET>` tag. (The `onblur` and `onfocus` handlers don't work correctly in some platforms if placed in `<FRAMESET>`.)

Discussion

This may be regarded as a "top-level" object, of which every object is a property unless explicitly assigned to some other object. For instance, when a script declares a variable named `foo`, it is equivalent to creating a property `window.foo`. Similarly, to call the `window.print()` method, you can simply write a call to `print()`. (This does not apply to statements in the event handler attributes of HTML objects; for them, the top-level object is `document`.)

Note that Frame objects function like `window` objects in most respects. When a script runs in a frame, references to `window` will actually return the Frame object.

The `self` and `window` properties are equivalent; either may be used to refer to the current window. (This means that `window` is actually a property of itself.) You can also refer to the current window using `top` (the top-most browser window that encloses all frames and sub-frames) and sometimes `parent` (the window or frame containing the current frameset).

To access other windows, they must be opened using the `open()` method, which returns a reference that can be stored in a variable (see Example). `open()` also assigns a window name that HTML elements can use to reference the window.

Examples

The following statement opens a window with the HTML name `Window1`, loads a document named `child.htm`, and sets several window features: the window will be resizable, the status bar will be visible, and the window will be 500 pixels x 575 pixels.

```
Win1 = open("child.htm", "Window1",
   "resize,status,height=400,width=575")
```

`open()` returns a reference to the newly opened window in the variable `Win1`. To manage the window, use statements such as:

```
Win1.document.write("This is a new window.")
Win1.resizeTo(320, 480)
```

See Also `document`, `Frame`

with

Keyword used in statements

This keyword is used to simplify complex references to objects. For details, see Chapter 4.

write( )

Version 1.0

Method of the document object

Writes the specified values to a document in a window.

Syntax *docObject*.write(*expression1*, *expression2*, ...)

docObject document for the current document, or an expression denoting a document object in any window.
expression Any literal, variable, object, or expression.

Discussion If you use the write method within <SCRIPT>...</SCRIPT> tags, the output is written to the current web page at the point where the script occurs, unless you use open first.

If you use the write method in an event handler, a new document is automatically opened, even if you don't use the open method. This will erase the window's current contents.

It's a good idea to always use document.close( ) after document.write( ); otherwise the text, or part of the text, may not be written to the window.

Arguments of write may be of any type, but they are converted to strings (by the toString( ) method) before being written to the document.

When HTML code is written, some characters may have to be escaped or it may not be written correctly. This is particularly true when writing comments; the HTML parser will ignore comments written directly as a write parameter. For instance, this won't work:

window2.document.write("<!--This is a comment-->")

Add the backslash (\) symbol to escape the characters:

window2.document.write("\<!--This is a comment--\>)

Version 1.1 In JavaScript 1.1, the user can print or save the output from write using the File menu commands.

Examples
To write strings (including HTML tags), a number, and a variable (`time`) to the current window, use a statement such as:

```
document.write("<P>Please turn up at the meeting on the 15th at ",
   time, ". Reference: ", 5436547)
```

To write an expression to another window:

```
window2.document.write(lastName + ", " + firstName)
```

To write one of two values, depending on the result of a conditional expression:

```
window2.document.write((sButton == "A") ? "A" : "B")
```

See Also
document, writeln()

writeln( )

Version 1.0

Method of the document object

Writes the specified values to a document in a window; equivalent to write, except that the values are followed by a Newline character.

Syntax
`docObject.writeln(expression1, expression2, ...)`
docObject   `document` for the current document, or an expression denoting a `document` object in any window.
expression   Any literal, variable, object, or expression.

Discussion
The only difference between `writeln` and `write` is that `writeln` adds a newline character after the last value. Note that newlines are equivalent to spaces and other white space characters, except within the <PRE> ... </PRE> or <XMP> ... </XMP> tags.
See `write` for more information.

See Also
write(), document

x

ANCHOR

Version 1.0   Read-only   External

Property of the Anchor external object
(see also x as a property of the event object)

Returns the horizontal position of the anchor on the screen, in pixels.

Syntax   `docObject.anchors[index].x`

    `docObject`   document for the current document, or an expression denoting a document in any window.
    `index`   Position of the anchor in the `links` array.

Discussion   This property returns the distance from the anchor to the left side of the document.

Example   `linkX = document.anchors[3].x`

See Also   Anchor, Link, y (property of Anchor)

x

EVENT

Version 1.2   Read-only

Property of the event object
(see also x as a property of the Anchor object)

Returns the cursor's horizontal position in the layer in which an event occurred, or the width of a window or frame that has been resized.

This is provided for compatibility with early beta versions of Netscape Navigator 4. The official release has several types of horizontal and vertical measurements, and scripts should avoid using x.

See Also   `event`, `layerX`, `pageX`, `screenX`, `width`, `y` (property of `event`)

y

ANCHOR

Version 1.0 Read-only External

Property of the Anchor external object
(see also y as a property of the event object)

Returns the vertical position of the anchor on the screen, in pixels.

Syntax
    `docObject.anchors[index].y`
    `docObject`   document for the current document, or an expression denoting a document in any window.
    `index`   Position of the anchor in the `links` array.

Discussion   This property returns the distance from the anchor to the top of the document.

Example   `linkY = document.anchors[3].y`

See Also   Anchor, Link, x (property of Anchor)

y

EVENT

Version 1.2 Read-only

Property of the event object
(see also y as a property of the Anchor object)

Returns the cursor's vertical position in the layer in which an event occurred, or the height of a window or frame that has been resized.
    This is provided for compatibility with early beta versions of Netscape Navigator 4. The official release has several types of horizontal and vertical measurements, and scripts should avoid using y.

See Also   `event`, `height`, `layerY`, `pageY`, `screenY`, x (property of `event`)

zIndex

Version 1.2

Property of the Layer object

Returns the position of a layer in the z-order that determines whether any layer is "above" another.

Syntax *layerObj*.zIndex

layerObj   document.*layerName*, or other expression denoting any Layer object.

Discussion The z-order determines whether a layer is "above" another, that is, which one will be displayed in a region of the screen where two layers overlap. Higher numbers indicate "higher" (more visible) positions.

The zIndex property defines the position of a layer in relation to its sibling layers (that is, other child layers of the same parent layer). Child layers are always displayed above the parent.

The value of zIndex is initially set to the Z-INDEX attribute of the HTML <LAYER> tag. Scripts can modify the value at any time, and the screen display will be updated to reflect the new value. The Layer object has a number of properties and methods that help you to manage the z-order of layers.

Example document.layers.layer2.zIndex = 3

See Also above, below, Layer, moveAbove( ), moveBelow( ), siblingAbove, siblingBelow

Appendices

III

Appendix A
Reserved Words

The words listed below cannot be used when you are naming variables, functions, methods, or objects. Some of these words are not currently part of the JavaScript language, but are reserved by Netscape for future use. Also avoid using the names of built-in objects, functions, and methods, such as **Date**, **getDate**, **Math**, and **sqrt**. Whereas you can sometimes use such names, you may in some cases run into a conflict.

abstract	else	interface	synchronized
boolean	extends	long	this
Boolean	false	native	throw
break	final	new	throws
byte	finally	null	transient
case	float	package	true
catch	for	private	try
char	function	protected	typeof
class	goto	public	var
const	if	return	void
continue	implements	reset	while
default	import	short	with
delete	in	static	
do	instanceof	super	
double	int	switch	

Appendix B
Symbols

This appendix lists the symbols used by JavaScript. For more information on their use, see the introductory chapters.

+   Addition/concatenation operator; adds two numerical values together, joins two strings together.
*   Multiplication operator; multiplies two values together.
/   Division operator; divides one value by another.
%   Modulus operator; shows the remainder after dividing one number into another.
-     Subtraction operator; subtracts one value from another or changes a value to a negative value (unary negation).
++   Increment operator; increments a value (adds one to it).
--   Decrement operator; decrements a value (subtracts one from it).
!   Boolean NOT; tells you what value the variable *doesn't* contain. X = !Y would mean that if Y is true, X is set to false; and if Y is false, X is set to true.
&&   Boolean AND; X=Y && Z means that X is only true if Y *and* Z are both true. The actual returned value is the value of one of the operands; for details, see Chapter 3.
|| Boolean OR; X=Y || Z means that X is true if Y *or* Z (or both of them) are true. The actual returned value is the value of one of the operands; for details, see Chapter 3.
^   Bitwise Exclusive OR (XOR); X = Y ^ Z.
=   Assignment operator; assigns a value to the left operand.
&=   Bitwise AND assignment; the result is stored in the left operand.

^=	Bitwise Exclusive OR assignment; the result is stored in the left operand.
|=	Bitwise OR assignment; the result is stored in the left operand.
+=	Addition assignment; adds the operands together and modifies the operand on the left side.
-=	Subtraction assignment; subtracts the operand on the right from the one on the left and modifies the operand on the left.
*=	Multiplication assignment; multiplies the operands together, then modifies the operand on the left.
/=	Division assignment; divides the operand on the left by the one on the right, then modifies the one on the left.
%=	Modulus assignment; divides the operand on the left by the one on the right, then assigns the remainder to the operand on the left.
<	Conditional operator; less than.
<=	Conditional operator; less than or equal to.
>	Conditional operator; greater than.
>=	Conditional operator; greater than or equal to.
==	Conditional operator; equal to. Works slightly differently in JavaScript 1.2 from the way it worked in JavaScript 1 and 1.1. See Chapter 3 for details.
!=	Conditional operator; not equal to. Works slightly differently in JavaScript 1.2 from the way it worked in JavaScript 1 and 1.1. See Chapter 3 for details.
?:	Shorthand if statement operator, or ternary operator (? is used in combination with :, as in variable = (condition) ? value1 : value2).
" "	Double-quotation marks; enclose string literals and instructions in event handlers.
' '	Single-quotation marks; enclose string literals and instructions in event handlers. Double and single quotes are equivalent; either one can enclose the other in a string literal.
;	Separates individual statements on a line.
.	Indicates an object property or method name, e.g., document.write.
,	Separates arguments in a function call; also has sequencing functions (see Chapters 3 and 4).
( )	Encloses parameters (arguments) after a function name and sets operator precedence.
[ ]	Encloses an index in an array element reference; also used to declare arrays (see Chapter 2).
{ }	Encloses blocks of script within statements, functions, and loops; also used to declare objects (see Chapter 5).
~	Bitwise complement (NOT).

<<=	Bitwise left shift assignment.
&	Bitwise logical AND.
<<	Bitwise left shift.
|	Bitwise logical OR.
>>	Bitwise right shift.
^	Bitwise logical XOR.
>>>	Bitwise zero-fill right shift.
>>=	Bitwise right shift assignment.
>>>=	Bitwise zero-fill right shift assignment.
<!-- //-->	HTML comment tags, used in JavaScripts to hide scripts from non-JavaScript browsers; everything between the symbols is ignored by non-JavaScript browsers.
//	JavaScript comment line; everything to the right of the symbol is assumed to be a comment and ignored.
/* */	JavaScript comment block; everything between the asterisks is assumed to be a comment and ignored.

Appendix C
Color Codes

You can specify colors in JavaScripts either by entering the hexadecimal representation of the color or by entering the color names. Colors are used by various properties and methods, as well as within some HTML tags (such as **<BODY BGCOLOR="bisque">** and **<FONT COLOR="seagreen">Text </font>**). The actual color displayed varies among browsers and, of course, also depends on the video mode, video card, and video monitor.

Listed below are the color names you can use. We've also shown each color's red, green, and blue hexadecimal values. To see what these colors actually look like, see our Color Chart Web page on the CD.

It's generally easier to use the color name. However, if you want to use the hexadecimal value, you simply enter the six hexadecimal digits together, preceded by a pound sign. For instance, to use aliceblue, you would enter **#F0F8FF**.

Color	Red	Green	Blue
aliceblue	F0	F8	FF
antiquewhite	FA	EB	D7
aqua	00	FF	FF
aquamarine	7F	FF	D4
azure	F0	FF	FF
beige	F5	F5	DC
bisque	FF	E4	C4
black	00	00	00

Color	Red	Green	Blue
blanchedalmond	FF	EB	CD
blue	00	00	FF
blueviolet	8A	2B	E2
brown	A5	2A	2A
burlywood	DE	B8	87
cadetblue	5F	9E	A0
chartreuse	7F	FF	00
chocolate	D2	69	1E
coral	FF	7F	50
cornflowerblue	64	95	ED
cornsilk	FF	F8	DC
crimson	DC	14	3C
cyan	00	FF	FF
darkblue	00	00	8B
darkcyan	00	8B	8B
darkgoldenrod	B8	86	0B
darkgray	A9	A9	A9
darkgreen	00	64	00
darkkhaki	BD	B7	6B
darkmagenta	8B	00	8B
darkolivegreen	55	6B	2F
darkorange	FF	8C	00
darkorchid	99	32	CC
darkred	8B	00	00
darksalmon	E9	96	7A
darkseagreen	8F	BC	8F
darkslateblue	48	3D	8B
darkslategray	2F	4F	4F
darkturquoise	00	CE	D1
darkviolet	94	00	D3
deeppink	FF	14	93
deepskyblue	00	BF	FF
dimgray	69	69	69
dodgerblue	1E	90	FF
firebrick	B2	22	22
floralwhite	FF	FA	F0
forestgreen	22	8B	22
fuchsia	FF	00	FF
gainsboro	DC	DC	DC
ghostwhite	F8	F8	FF

Appendix C: Color Codes

Color	Red	Green	Blue
gold	FF	D7	00
goldenrod	DA	A5	20
gray	80	80	80
green	00	80	00
greenyellow	AD	FF	2F
honeydew	F0	FF	F0
hotpink	FF	69	B4
indianred	CD	5C	5C
indigo	4B	00	82
ivory	FF	FF	F0
khaki	F0	E6	8C
lavender	E6	E6	FA
lavenderblush	FF	F0	F5
lawngreen	7C	FC	00
lemonchiffon	FF	FA	CD
lightblue	AD	D8	E6
lightcoral	F0	80	80
lightcyan	E0	FF	FF
lightgoldenrodyellow	FA	FA	D2
lightgreen	90	EE	90
lightgrey	D3	D3	D3
lightpink	FF	B6	C1
lightsalmon	FF	A0	7A
lightseagreen	20	B2	AA
lightskyblue	87	CE	FA
lightslategray	77	88	99
lightsteelblue	B0	C4	DE
lightyellow	FF	FF	E0
lime	00	FF	00
limegreen	32	CD	32
linen	FA	F0	E6
magenta	FF	00	FF
maroon	80	00	00
mediumaquamarine	66	CD	AA
mediumblue	00	00	CD
mediumorchid	BA	55	D3
mediumpurple	93	70	DB
mediumseagreen	3C	B3	71
mediumslateblue	7B	68	EE
mediumspringgreen	00	FA	9A

Color	Red	Green	Blue
mediumturquoise	48	D1	CC
mediumvioletred	C7	15	85
midnightblue	19	19	70
mintcream	F5	FF	FA
mistyrose	FF	E4	E1
moccasin	FF	E4	B5
navajowhite	FF	DE	AD
navy	00	00	80
oldlace	FD	F5	E6
olive	80	80	00
olivedrab	6B	8E	23
orange	FF	A5	00
orangered	FF	45	00
orchid	DA	70	D6
palegoldenrod	EE	E8	AA
palegreen	98	FB	98
paleturquoise	AF	EE	EE
palevioletred	DB	70	93
papayawhip	FF	EF	D5
peachpuff	FF	DA	B9
peru	CD	85	3F
pink	FF	C0	CB
plum	DD	A0	DD
powderblue	B0	E0	E6
purple	80	00	80
red	FF	00	00
rosybrown	BC	8F	8F
royalblue	41	69	E1
saddlebrown	8B	45	13
salmon	FA	80	72
sandybrown	F4	A4	60
seagreen	2E	8B	57
seashell	FF	F5	EE
sienna	A0	52	2D
silver	C0	C0	C0
skyblue	87	CE	EB
slateblue	6A	5A	CD
slategray	70	80	90
snow	FF	FA	FA
springgreen	00	FF	7F

Color	Red	Green	Blue
steelblue	46	82	B4
tan	D2	B4	8C
teal	00	80	80
thistle	D8	BF	D8
tomato	FF	63	47
turquoise	40	E0	D0
violet	EE	82	EE
wheat	F5	DE	B3
white	FF	FF	FF
whitesmoke	F5	F5	F5
yellow	FF	FF	00
yellowgreen	9A	CD	32

Appendix D
The ISO ISO 8859-1 Latin 1 Character Set

The following table shows the entity codes that you can use in your HTML documents to represent characters in the ISO ISO 8859-1 Latin 1 character set. For instance, in order to create the Yen character (¥), you would enter ¥ into the HTML source code. Note that some characters have alternatives. For instance, in order to create the pound-sterling symbol (£), you can use either £ or £. Several of these "alternatives" were designed in order to allow HTML authors to "escape" various characters that are used in HTML tags (the <, >, &, and " characters). This alternative enables an author to display one of these special characters on the face of the web page, rather than use the character for an HTML tag.

Note also that the entity codes &130; to &159; won't work in many browsers, as these were not part of HTML 2. However, they should all work in JavaScript-compatible browsers (with the exception of &153;, as noted in the table).

Entity Code	Character	Description	Alternative
&#00; - &#08;		Unused	
&#09;		Horizontal tab	
&#10;		Line feed	
&#11; - 		Unused	
&#13;		Carriage return	
&#14; - &#31;		Unused	
&#32;		Space	
&#33;	!	Exclamation mark	
&#34;	"	Quotation mark	&quot;
&#35;	#	Number sign	
&#36;	$	Dollar sign	
&#37;	%	Percent sign	
&#38;	&	Ampersand	&amp;
&#39;	'	Apostrophe	
&#40;	(	Left parenthesis	
&#41;	)	Right parenthesis	
&#42;	*	Asterisk	
&#43;	+	Plus sign	
&#44;	,	Comma	
&#45;	-	Hyphen	
&#46;	.	Period	
&#47;	/	Solidus - slash	
&#48;	0	Digit, 0	
&#49;	1	Digit, 1	
&#50;	2	Digit, 2	
&#51;	3	Digit, 3	
&#52;	4	Digit, 4	
&#53;	5	Digit, 5	
&#54;	6	Digit, 6	
&#55;	7	Digit, 7	
&#56;	8	Digit, 8	
&#57;	9	Digit, 9	
&#58;	:	Colon	
&#59;	;	Semicolon	
&#60;	<	Less than	&lt;
&#61;	=	Equals sign	
&#62;	>	Greater than	&gt;
&#63;	?	Question mark	
&#64;	@	"At" sign	
&#65;	A	Letter A	

Appendix D: The ISO ISO 8859-1 Latin 1 Character Set

Entity Code	Character	Description	Alternative
&#66;	B	Letter B	
&#67;	C	Letter C	
&#68;	D	Letter D	
&#69;	E	Letter E	
&#70;	F	Letter F	
&#71;	G	Letter G	
&#72;	H	Letter H	
&#73;	I	Letter I	
&#74;	J	Letter J	
&#75;	K	Letter K	
&#76;	L	Letter L	
&#77;	M	Letter M	
&#78;	N	Letter N	
&#79;	O	Letter O	
&#80;	P	Letter P	
&#81;	Q	Letter Q	
&#82;	R	Letter R	
&#83;	S	Letter S	
&#84;	T	Letter T	
&#85;	U	Letter U	
&#86;	V	Letter V	
&#87;	W	Letter W	
&#88;	X	Letter X	
&#89;	Y	Letter Y	
&#90;	Z	Letter Z	
&#91;	[	Left square bracket	
&#92;	\	Reverse solidus - backslash	
&#93;	]	Right square bracket	
&#94;	^	Caret	
&#95;	_	Horizontal bar - underline	
&#96;	`	Grave accent - back apostrophe	
&#97;	a	Letter a	
&#98;	b	Letter b	
&#99;	c	Letter c	
&#100;	d	Letter d	
&#101;	e	Letter e	
&#102;	f	Letter f	
&#103;	g	Letter g	
&#104;	h	Letter h	
&#105;	i	Letter i	

Entity Code	Character	Description	Alternative
&#106;	j	Letter j	
&#107;	k	Letter k	
&#108;	l	Letter l	
&#109;	m	Letter m	
&#110;	n	Letter n	
&#111;	o	Letter o	
&#112;	p	Letter p	
&#113;	q	Letter q	
&#114;	r	Letter r	
&#115;	s	Letter s	
&#116;	t	Letter t	
&#117;	u	Letter u	
&#118;	v	Letter v	
&#119;	w	Letter w	
&#120;	x	Letter x	
&#121;	y	Letter y	
&#122;	z	Letter z	
&#123;	{	Left "curly" brace	
|	|	Vertical bar	
&#125;	}	Right "curly" brace	
&#126;	~	Tilde	
&#127; - 		Unused	
&#130;	‚	Single low-9 quotation mark	&#8218;
&#131;	ƒ	Latin small letter f with hook	&#402;
&#132;	„	Double low-9 quotation mark	&#8222;
&#133;	…	Horizontal ellipsis	&#8230;
&#134;	†	Dagger	&#8224;
&#135;	‡	Double dagger	&#8225;
&#136;	ˆ	Modifier letter circumflex accent	&#710;
&#137;	‰	Per mille sign	&#8240;
&#138;	Š	Latin capital letter S with caron	&#352;
&#139;	‹	Single left-pointing angle quotation mark	&#8249;
&#140;	Œ	Latin capital dipthong OE, ligature	&#338;
&#145;	'	Left single "curly" quotation mark	&#8216;
&#146;	'	Right single "curly" quotation mark	&#8217;
&#147;	"	Left double "curly" quotation mark	&#8220;
&#148;	"	Right double "curly" quotation mark	&#8221;
&#149;	•	Bullet	&#8226;
&#150;	–	En dash	&#8212;
&#151;	—	Em dash	&#8211;

Appendix D: The ISO ISO 8859-1 Latin 1 Character Set

Entity Code	Character	Description	Alternative
&#152;	˜	Small tilde	&#732;
&#153;	™	Trademark sign	™ and ™

(Note, use ™ as &153; and ™ currently do not work in Netscape Navigator 4.)

Entity Code	Character	Description	Alternative
&#154;	š	Latin small letter s with caron	&#353;
&#155;	›	Single right-pointing angle quotation mark	&#8250;
&#156;	œ	Latin small dipthong OE, ligature	&#339;
&#159;	Ÿ	Latin capital letter Y with diaeresis	&#376;
		Nonbreaking space	
&#161;	¡	Inverted exclamation	&iexcl;
&#162;	¢	Cent sign	&cent;
&#163;	£	Pound sterling	&pound;
&#164;	¤	General currency sign	&curren;
&#165;	¥	Yen sign	&yen;
&#166;	¦	Broken vertical bar	&brvbar;
&#167;	§	Section sign	&sect;
&#168;	¨	Umlaut - diaeresis	&uml;
&#169;	©	Copyright	&copy;
&#170;	ª	Feminine ordinal	&ordf;
&#171;	«	Left angle quote, guillemotleft	&laquo;
&#172;	¬	Not sign	&not;
&#173;	–	Soft hyphen	&shy;

(Note, use ­ rather than ­ to ensure compatibility with largest number of browsers.)

Entity Code	Character	Description	Alternative
&#174;	®	Registered trademark	&reg;
&#175;	¯	Macron accent	&macr;
&#176;	°	Degree sign	&deg;
&#177;	±	Plus or minus	&plusmn;
&#178;	²	Superscript two	&sup2;
&#179;	³	Superscript three	&sup3;
&#180;	´	Acute accent	&acute;
&#181;	µ	Greek "mu," micro- sign	&micro;
&#182;	¶	Paragraph sign	&para;
&#183;	·	Middle dot	&middot;
&#184;	¸	Cedilla	&cedil;
&#185;	¹	Superscript one	&sup1;
&#186;	º	Masculine ordinal	&ordm;
&#187;	»	Right angle quote, guillemotright	&raquo;
&#188;	¼	Fraction, one-fourth	&frac14;
&#189;	½	Fraction, one-half	&frac12;

Entity Code	Character	Description	Alternative
&#190;	¾	Fraction, three-fourths	&frac34;
&#191;	¿	Inverted question mark	&iquest;
&#192;	À	Capital A, grave accent	&Agrave;
&#193;	Á	Capital A, acute accent	&Aacute;
&#194;	Â	Capital A, circumflex accent	&Acirc;
&#195;	Ã	Capital A, tilde	&Atilde;
&#196;	Ä	Capital A, diaeresis or umlaut mark	&Auml;
&#197;	Å	Capital A, ring	&Aring;
&#198;	Æ	Capital AE dipthong, ligature	&AElig;
&#199;	Ç	Capital C, cedilla	&Ccedil;
&#200;	È	Capital E, grave accent	&Egrave;
&#201;	É	Capital E, acute accent	&Eacute;
&#202;	Ê	Capital E, circumflex accent	&Ecirc;
&#203;	Ë	Capital E, diaeresis or umlaut mark	&Euml;
&#204;	Ì	Capital I, grave accent	&Igrave;
&#205;	Í	Capital I, acute accent	&Iacute;
&#206;	Î	Capital I, circumflex accent	&Icirc;
&#207;	Ï	Capital I, diaeresis or umlaut mark	&Iuml;
&#208;	Ð	Capital Eth, Icelandic	&ETH;
&#209;	Ñ	Capital N, tilde	&Ntilde;
&#210;	Ò	Capital O, grave accent	&Ograve;
&#211;	Ó	Capital O, acute accent	&Oacute;
&#212;	Ô	Capital O, circumflex accent	&Ocirc;
&#213;	Õ	Capital O, tilde accent	&Otilde;
&#214;	Ö	Capital O, diaeresis or umlaut mark	&Ouml;
&#215;	x	Multiply sign	&times;
&#216;	Ø	Capital O, slash	&Oslash;
&#217;	Ù	Capital U, grave accent	&Ugrave;
&#218;	Ú	Capital U, acute accent	&Uacute;
&#219;	Û	Capital U, circumflex accent	&Ucirc;
&#220;	Ü	Capital U, diaeresis or umlaut mark	&Uuml;
&#221;	Ý	Capital Y, acute accent	&Yacute;
&#222;	Þ	Capital THORN, Icelandic	&THORN;
&#223;	ß	Small sharp s, German, sz ligature	&szlig;
&#224;	à	Small a, grave accent	&agrave;
&#225;	á	Small a, acute accent	&aacute;
&#226;	â	Small a, circumflex accent	&acirc;
&#227;	ã	Small a, tilde accent	&atilde;
&#228;	ä	Small a, diaeresis or umlaut mark	&auml;
&#229;	å	Small a, ring	&aring;

Appendix D: The ISO ISO 8859-1 Latin 1 Character Set

Entity Code	Character	Description	Alternative
&#230;	æ	Small ae dipthong, ligature	&aelig;
&#231;	ç	Small c, cedilla	&ccedil;
&#232;	è	Small e, grave accent	&egrave;
&#233;	é	Small e, acute accent	&eacute;
&#234;	ê	Small e, circumflex accent	&ecirc;
&#235;	ë	Small e, diaeresis or umlaut mark	&euml;
&#236;	ì	Small i, grave accent	&igrave;
&#237;	í	Small i, acute accent	&iacute;
&#238;	î	Small i, circumflex accent	&icirc;
&#239;	ï	Small i, diaeresis or umlaut mark	&iuml;
&#240;		Small eth, Icelandic	&eth;
&#241;	ñ	Small n, tilde	&ntilde;
&#242;	ò	Small o, grave accent	&ograve;
&#243;	ó	Small o, acute accent	&oacute;
&#244;	ô	Small o, circumflex accent	&ocirc;
&#245;	õ	Small o, tilde	&otilde;
&#246;	ö	Small o, diaeresis or umlaut mark	&ouml;
&#247;	÷	Division sign	&divide;
&#248;	ø	Small o, slash	&oslash;
&#249;	ù	Small u, grave accent	&ugrave;
&#250;	ú	Small u, acute accent	&uacute;
&#251;	û	Small u, circumflex accent	&ucirc;
&#252;	ü	Small u, diaeresis or umlaut mark	&uuml;
&#253;	ý	Small y, acute accent	&yacute;
&#254;	þ	Small thorn, Icelandic	&thorn;
&#255;	ÿ	Small y, diaeresis or umlaut mark	&yuml;

Appendix E
Finding More JavaScript Information

This appendix lists a variety of sources of JavaScript information. Note that you can find a web page containing these links on the CD bundled with this book.

General Reference Materials

You can find a variety of reference materials directly related to JavaScript, most of which are produced by Netscape Communications.

Netscape's JavaScript Authoring Guide

There are various versions of the Netscape JavaScript Authoring Guide available:

Netscape 2 Version

http://www.netscape.com/eng/mozilla/2.0/handbook/javascript/

http://home.netscape.com/eng/mozilla/Gold/handbook/javascript/

Netscape 3 Version

http://home.netscape.com/eng/mozilla/3.0/handbook/javascript/

Netscape 4 Version

Once the Authoring Guide for Netscape 4 is completed, it will probably be located here:

http://home.netscape.com/eng/mozilla/4.0/handbook/javascript/

What's New in JavaScript 1.2 for Navigator 4.0

http://developer.netscape.com/library/documentation/communicator/jsguide/js1_2.htm

You can also download the documentation from Netscape to your hard disk, though it's not always up to date. Try http://developer.netscape.com/library/documentation/ or directly at http://developer.netscape.com/library/documentation/jshtm.zip.

You can also find the Netscape documentation in a variety of other formats, though again, it is not always completely up to date.

JavaScript Authoring Guide in WinHelp Format

http://www.jchelp.com/javahelp/javahelp.htm

This site has the Netscape documents placed into a Windows Help file.

Other Reference Materials

The following two locations also contain useful related information:

JavaScript 1.1 Specification in a PostScript File

http://home.netscape.com/eng/javascript/

DevEdge Documentation Library

http://developer.netscape.com/library/documentation/

Links to lots of useful documentation.

Introductions & Tutorials

A variety of sites contain tutorials and courses that teach JavaScript's basic principles:

The Official Netscape JavaScript 1.2 Book Web Site

http://www.netscapepress.com/support/javascript1.2/

This site is associated with *The Official Netscape JavaScript 1.2 Book*, by Peter Kent and John Kent, also from Netscape Press. It contains 220 JavaScript examples, including an Area Code application and a Telephone Book application.

Introduction to JavaScript by Stefan Koch (was known as "Voodoo")

http://rummelplatz.uni-mannheim.de/~skoch/js/script.htm

This site contains good tutorials, plus background information and useful links. It's also mirrored at the U.S. and New Zealand sites listed below as well as at various other sites in other languages.

http://www.webconn.com/java/javascript/intro/

http://www.cit.ac.nz/smac/javascr/

The JavaScript FAQ

http://www.freqgrafx.com/411/jsfaq.html

Frequently asked questions about JavaScript. This FAQ is a work in progress by Andy Augustine. Useful information on JavaScript bugs, too.

Information on Specific Features

The following web pages provide information about specific features of JavaScript.

Security & Encryption

Netscape Object Signing

http://developer.netscape.com./library/documentation/signedobj/
    overview.html

http://home.netscape.com/assist/security/objectsign/datasheet.html

Documents about the new object-signing technology being introduced to JavaScript 1.2.

Netscape Security Solutions

http://home.netscape.com/assist/security/

More leads to information about Netscape security, including object signing and related subjects.

Signed Scripts

http://developer.netscape.com/library/documentation/communicator/
    jsguide/js1_2.htm

Using the JAR Packager

http://developer.netscape.com/library/documentation/signedobj/usejar/
    index.html

Information about creating digital signatures, certificates, and Java Archive (JAR) files.

JAR Packager

http://developer.netscape.com/software/signedobj/jarpack.html

You can download the JAR Packager from this site.

Netscape Developer Support Library, Security Information

http://developer.netscape.com./library/documentation/
    doclist.html#security

Links to a variety of security-related articles.

Using RSA Public Key Cryptography for Internet Security

http://home.netscape.com/newsref/ref/rsa.html

An overview of the use of public-key cryptography, the security system used for signing objects and scripts.

Style Sheets & Layers

JavaScript-Based Style Sheets

http://developer.netscape.com/library/documentation/

http://developer.netscape.com/library/documentation/communicator/
    stylesheets/jssindex.htm

Creating Multiple Layers of Content

http://developer.netscape.com/library/documentation/communicator/
    layers/index.htm

Other Features

Codestock on JavaScript 1.2 Enhancements

http:// developer.netscape.com/library/documentation/communicator/
    codestock.html

Information about the new JavaScript 1.2 features from a developer's conference.

Visual JavaScript

http://developer.netscape.com/members/doc/gold/doc/visual_javascript/

The new Visual JavaScript provides tools to help you create scripts quickly and efficiently. This web page is currently only available to Netscape DevEdge members.

Persistent Client State HTTP Cookies Preliminary Specifications

`http://www.netscape.com/newsref/std/cookie_spec.html`

Background information about working with cookies.

Web Interactivity–JavaScript, CGI Facilitates Dynamic Web Pages

`http://www.ostrabo.uddevalla.se/dis/javascript/man874p.html`

Information about using JavaScript with CGI.

Developer News & Bulletins

The following sources provide regular information about JavaScript in the form of newsletters and bulletins. Also see the list of "Discussion Groups" if you want to keep up with the latest developments.

DevEdge Online

`http://developer.netscape.com/`

Netscape's developer's support site has links to lots of useful information, directly and indirectly related to JavaScript. Some areas of this site are free, some are open only to registered DevEdge members.

Netscape DevEdge ONE News Subscription

`http://developer.netscape.com/subscription_reg.html`

Subscribe to a free newsletter related to Netscape development topics.

JavaScript Libraries

Here are a few JavaScript libraries from which you can borrow scripts:

JavaScript 411

`http://www.freqgrafx.com/411/`

The JavaScript Library at the JavaScript Index

`http://www.sapphire.co.uk/javascript/lib/`

JavaScript: Simple Little Things to Add to Your Pages

`http://tanega.com/java/java.html`

The JavaScript Archive

`http://planetx.bloomu.edu/~mpscho/jsarchive/`

JavaScript Applets
http://www.oz.net/~alden/javascript/jsintro.html

Timothy's JavaScript Page
http://www.essex1.com/people/timothy/
http://www.sapphire.co.uk/javascript/collections.html
More libraries are listed at the **JavaScript Index**

Resource Sites

These are currently some of the best JavaScript link sites:

Gamelan JavaScript List
http://www.gamelan.com/pages/Gamelan.related.javascript.html
Lots of JavaScript stuff. Gamelan has a Java list, too.

The JavaScript Index
http://www.sapphire.co.uk/javascript/
Links to many JavaScript samples and resources.

Yahoo's JavaScript Category
http://www.yahoo.com/Computers_and_Internet/Programming_Languages/JavaScript/
Not as much stuff as the first two sites listed, but pretty good nonetheless.

Here are other JavaScript sites worth checking. Not so many links, but often good examples, tutorials, and so on:

Netscape's JavaScript Introduction Page
http://www.netscape.com/comprod/products/navigator/version_2.0/script/
An introductory promotional page for JavaScript, with links to the authoring guide and resources page.

Netscape's JavaScript Resources Page
http://www.netscape.com/comprod/products/navigator/version_2.0/script/script_info/
A small list of links to example JavaScripts and JavaScript resources.

Unofficial JavaScript Resource Center
http://www.ce.net/users/ryan/java/
Useful samples, loads of links.

LiveSoftware's JavaScript Resource Center
`http://jrc.livesoftware.com/`
JavaScript examples, two newsgroups, and a chat room.

JavaScript 411
`http://www.freqgrafx.com/411/`
Very useful site. It has a snippets library (take bits of JavaScript code for your web pages), the JavaScript FAQ, and tutorials.

TeamJava's Home Page
`http://www.teamjava.com/`
Java and JavaScript consultants, plus lots of links to JavaScript stuff.

Eric's JavaScript Page
`http://www.pass.wayne.edu/~eric/javascript/`
A small JavaScript links page.

Discussion Groups

The JavaScript Mailing List
There is an unofficial repository of information in the form of a mailing list for people interested in JavaScript. For more information about the list or to view old messages, point your web browser to http://www.obscure.org/javascript/.

To join, send e-mail to **majordomo@obscure.org** with this in the body of the message: **subscribe javascript**.

To get a digest—a single message each day containing all the list's messages pasted together—send e-mail to **majordomo@obscure.org** with the following in the body of the message: **subscribe javascript-digest**.

Java Message Exchange
`http://porthos.phoenixat.com/~warreng/WWWBoard/wwwboard.html`
A Web-based discussion group.

Netscape's JavaScript Newsgroup
`snews://secnews.netscape.com/netscape.devs-javascript`
This newsgroup is on the secnews.netscape.com secure news server. You can enter the above URL into Netscape Navigator's Location bar and press Enter to access this newsgroup. (For more information on this newsgroup, and the following, see http://developer.netscape.com/index.html.)

Netscape's LiveWire Newsgroup
Netscape also has a LiveWire newsgroup; again, only for the developers. snews://secnews.netscape.com/netscape.devs-livewire

comp.lang.javascript Newsgroup
This newsgroup is available at many local news servers.

LiveSoftware's JavaScript Newsgroups
JavaScript Development Group: news://news.livesoftware.com/livesoftware.javascript.developer
JavaScript Examples Group: news://news.livesoftware.com/livesoftware.javascript.examples
Go to the LiveSoftware news server (news.livesoftware.com) to participate in these newsgroups. In Netscape, for instance, just type the full URL—news://news.livesoftware.com/livesoftware.javascript.examples, for instance—into the Location box and press Enter to open the Newsgroup window, connect to the server, and open the newsgroup. For more information, go to the LiveSoftware site: http://jrc.livesoftware.com/

Internet Relay Chat
You may find a #javascript channel on Internet Relay Chat.

For more information about JavaScript chat groups, newsgroups, and mailing lists, see the JavaScript Index: http://www.sapphire.co.uk/javascript/.

And you can also search for the word **javascript** at the major search engines to find yet more sources of information.

Appendix F
About the Companion CD-ROM

The Companion CD-ROM included with your copy of *Official Netscape JavaScript 1.2 Programmer's Reference* contains a hypertext version of the book and two files created by the author, a color chart, and links from Appendix E, "Finding More JavaScript Information."

To View the CD-ROM

Please open the README.HTM file in your favorite browser. You will see a small menu offering several links.

Technical Support

Technical support is available for installation-related problems only. The technical support office is open from 8:00 A.M. to 6:00 P.M. Monday through Friday and can be reached via the following methods:

- Phone: (919) 544-9404 extension 81
- Faxback Answer System: (919) 544-9404 extension 85
- E-mail: help@vmedia.com
- FAX: (919) 544-9472
- World Wide Web: **http://www.vmedia.com/support**
- America Online: keyword *Ventana*

Limits of Liability & Disclaimer of Warranty

The authors and publisher of this book have used their best efforts in preparing the CD-ROM and the programs contained in it. These efforts include the development, research, and testing of the theories and programs to determine their effectiveness. The authors and publisher make no warranty of any kind expressed or implied, with regard to these programs or the documentation contained in this book.

The authors and publisher shall not be liable in the event of incidental or consequential damages in connection with, or arising out of, the furnishing, performance, or use of the programs, associated instructions, and/or claims of productivity gains.

Some of the software on this CD-ROM is shareware; there may be additional charges (owed to the software authors/makers) incurred for their registration and continued use. See individual program's README or VREADME.TXT files for more information.

Index

A

absolute units 56
accessing JavaScript, from Java applets 77
alert() 61
altering order of operators 24
animation 59
applets. *See* Java applets
arguments, function 38
arguments object 14
arithmetic 18
Array indexes 14, 15
Array object 14
arrays 14–16
    with string indexes 15–16
    syntax for creating 15
assignment 19–20
audio files 52

B

backslash (\) character 11, 26
binary operators 17
bit masks, properties for testing
    event.modifiers property 72 (table)
bit-shifting operators 20
bitwise operators 20
block-level properties 58
block structuring 32
Boolean operators 21
Boolean values 12
brace ([]) characters 32
branching 12
break statement 36
bright style class 55
browsers
    compatibility of with JavaScript 6–7
    without JavaScript, supporting 6
built-in objects 14, 45

C

Call by value 38
caller properties object 14
case sensitivity 3, 5
certificate authorities (CAs) 79
characters. *See also* symbols
    backslash (\) 11
    brace ([]) 32
    dot (.) 44
    double equal sign (==) 32
    entity codes for ISO
        ISO 8859-1 Latin 1 character set 469, 470–475 (table)
    equal sign (=) 19
    inserting into strings 18
    operator 21
    operators for numeric values 18
    parentheses () 17, 24
    semicolon (;) 31
    special symbols in patterns 26
    square brackets ([]) 14
    underscore (_) 13
child frames 53
child layers 54
classes, style 55–56
classes object 57
classification properties 58
client-side maps 60
: operator 32
color 5, 59
color & background properties 58
commas 23, 31
comments 4–5
comparison for equality 22
comparison operators 21–22
compatibility of browsers with JavaScript 6–7
concatenating strings 22
conditional expressions 22, 32
confirm() 62
constructors 44, 45
continue statement 37
conversion rules, for passing Java data to scripts 77
converting values 25
cookie property 73–74
cookies 73–74
copies of attribute values. *See* reflections
curly brackets 32

D

data tainting 78–79
data types 9–16
decimal integers 9
declarations 9–16
    function 37–38
delete operator 23
deleting objects 46
delimiters 4–5
dialogs 61–63
digital signatures 79
document layers 52
document objects
    cookie property for 73–74
    properties 52
documents 52–53
    writing to 53
dot (.) character 44
double equal sign (==) character 32
do...while loop 34

E

empty strings, creating 11
em units 56
entity codes for ISO
   ISO 8859-1 Latin character set 469, 470–475 (table)
equality, in JavaScript 1.2 22
equal sign (=) character 19
event capturing 70–71
    values for 71–72 (table)
event handlers 3, 69
    assigning 39
event handling 67–72
Event object 71–72
event object 14, 69–70
events, types of 67, 68–69 (table)
exiting from a loop 36
export function 82
expressions 17–29
    assignment 19
    conditional 22
    evaluation of 17
    regular 25–29, 29
external objects 76
    types 45–46
ex units 56

F

files
    including in web pages 52
    placing scripts in separate 4
find() 62
floating point numbers 10
flushing text buffers 53

font properties 57
for...in loop 35–36
for loop 34–35
form elements 65, 66 (table)
Form objects 63
forms 63–66
    creating in web pages 52
    JavaScript in 65
frames 53
Function object 38
functions 37–39, 37–49

G

global objects 51
global operations 29
global variables 13
g modifier 29
graphics 59–60

H

helper applications 83
hexadecimal integers 9
HTML
    and JavaScript 2–3
    reflections 5–6
    tags 54–55

I

ids object 57
image map regions 52
image maps 60
Image object 59
images 52
import function 82
integers 9
ISO ISO 8859-1 Latin
   character set 469, 470–475 (table)

J

Java applets 52
    accessing from JavaScript 76–77
Java archive (JAR) files 79, 80
Java console 77–78
Java packages 77
JavaScript
    about 1
    accessing Java applets from 76–77
    equality in 22
    in forms 65
    supporting browsers without 6
    versions 6–7
    vs. Java 2

Index

L
layers 54
    document 52
length property 15
links 52
LiveConnect 76–78
local variables 13
logical operators 19, 20
loops 12, 34–37
loop variables 31

M
mathematical functions, methods for 18
Math object 10, 18
measurement units, in style sheets 56–57
methods 48–49
    about 43
    applying regular expressions to strings 29
    for mathematical functions 18
    of navigator object 76
    universal 49
multiple labels 33
multi-way branch 32–33

N
Navigator environment 75–83
Navigator objects 76–77
negative values 9
netscape packages 77
new operator 23
null value 12
Number object 10–11
numbers 9–11
    floating-point 10
numeric operations, special values for 10–11
numeric values, operators for 18

O
object properties
    assigning event handlers to 39
    tainted by default 78 (table)
objects 12, 14, 43–47
    about 43
    adding properties to 47
    built-in 45
    deleting 46
    document 54–55
    external 45–46
    Function 38, 39
    properties as 47
    RegExp 27–28
    style sheet, properties for 57–58
    tags 55
    that reflect form elements 65, 66 (table)
    window 51

object signing 79
octal integers 9
operand values 20
operator precedence 23
operators 17–29
    altering order of 24
    binary 17
    bit-shifting 20
    bitwise 20
    Boolean 21
    characters for 21
    : 32
    comparison 21–22
    delete 23
    logical 19
    new 23
    for numeric values 18
    + 22
    precedence of 24
    ? 32
    special 23–24
    typeof 23
    unary/binary, about 17
    void 23

P
Packages 77
parentheses () characters 17, 24
    in patterns 27
patterns 25
    declaring 27–28
    regular expression 13
    special symbols in 26
    symbols in for complex structures 26–27
percentages 56
picas 56
pixel units 57
plug-ins 83
+ operator 22
points 56
precedence, of operators 24
primitive values 12, 46
print() 61, 63
privileges 80–81, 81
    using without a signature 82
prompt() 62
properties 43–47
    about 43–47
    adding 47
    bit masks for testing event.modifiers property 71–72 (table)
    document object 54–55
    for event handling 68–69 (table)
    of navigator object 76
    as objects 47
    for style sheet objects 57–58
prototype property 47

Q

? operator   32

R

references   20, 46
reflections
   of attribute values   5–6
   HTML   5–6
RegExp object   27–28
regular expressions   13, 25–29, 29
relative units   56
reverse method   48

S

scripts
   contents of   4–6, 31
   for creating cookies   74
   in separate files   4
   signed   82
   syntax of   5
   writing signed   80
security   78–82
semicolon (;) character   31
separate files, scripts in   4
signatures   80
   using privileges without   82
signed scripts, writing   80
square brackets ([]) characters   14
statements   31–37
   with   40
   assignment   20
   break   36
   continue   37
   format of   5
   return   39
   special purpose   40
   var   40
string indexes, arrays with   15–16
String object   11
strings   11
   concatenating   22
style classes   55–56
style properties
   definitions   56–57
   for style sheet objects   57–58
style sheets   54–58
   measurement units in   56–57
switch statement   32–33
symbols. *See also* characters
   for complex structures   26–27
   list of those used by JavaScript   459–461
syntax
   conditional execution   32
   for creating arrays   15
   for regular expressions   25
   of scripts   5

T

tags object   57
   referencing   55
tainting, data   78–79
targets   80
text
   appearance of   54–58
   style properties for   56–57
text buffers, flushing   53
text properties   57
this object   14
type conversion   25
   for passing JavaScript to applets   77
typeof operator   23

U

unary operators, about   17
undefined values   12
underscore (_) character   13
units of measurement, in style sheets   56–57
universal methods   49
URLs, placing JavaScript code in   3

V

values   12
   Boolean   12
   Call by   38
   converting   25
   for event capturing   71–72 (table)
   negative   9
   null   12
   numeric, characters operators for   18
   operand   20
   and references   46
   returning   39
   undefined   12
variables   13–14
   built-in   5–6
variable scope   13–14
variable types   14
var statement   40
video files   52
void operator   24

W

while loop   34
window object   51, 61
windows   51–52
   Java console   77–78
with statement   40
writing to a document   53